DECONSTRUCTING
AFRICAN THOUGHTS AND PRACTICE

Segun Ogungbemi

DECONSTRUCTING
African Thoughts and Practices

Copyright © 2022 by **Segun Ogungbemi**

PaperBack ISBN: 978-1-957809-32-8

Printed in the United States of America. All rights reserved solely by the author. This book or parts thereof may not be reproduced in any form, stored in a retrieval system, or transmitted in any form by any means—electronic, mechanical, photocopy.

Published by:

Cornerstone Publishing
A Division of Cornerstone Creativity Group LLC
Info@thecornerstonepublishers.com
www.thecornerstonepublishers.com

Author's Contact

To book the author to speak at your next event or to order bulk copies of this book, please, send email to:

seguno2013@gmail.com

FOREWORD

The long history of philosophical discourse in ancient times advanced universality as best practice though, some great thinkers of antiquity envisioned a geography of philosophical temper reserved for Europe and America to the exclusion of Africa. This temper served the racists interest of the likes of Georg Wilhelm Friedrich Hegel to whom Greece was the only reserved birthplace of philosophy. In contrast, there were scholars who treasured communication and collaboration between different traditions and cultures, given that intercultural interactions and encounters are a fact of human existence. This is the noble route taken by the revered Professor Segun Ogungbemi in this book. The overall assumption here is that, the world has become a global community with knowledge and wisdom not only displayed as a universal commodity, it is appropriated with cultural distinctions in manifest paradoxes. In Africa, this paradox manifests in the clash between cultural identity and cultural diversity. This is the setting that underscores the *raison d'être* of the book, ***Deconstructing African Thoughts and Practices***.

Instigated by the pangs of particularism and the vanguards of racism in western traditions, the book seeks a deconstruction of the essential ingredients of intercultural philosophy with a view to showing how a pluralistic approach that can be used by African philosophers to address the pressing issues in contemporary Africa. In this noble attempt, Professor Segun Ogungbemi argues, Africa and African culture and civilization have been exposed to the globalizing dynamics for mutual complementarity and enrichment. This according to him will not only enable African scholars to reflect and interpret other cultures but also appropriate what has enabled other cultures to excel and transform the African condition. It is thus not out of place to assume correctly that this book is an exercise in intercultural studies that calls for an intensive and qualified discourse on the part of all concerned. A thorough reading of the book avails a discourse that allows a healthy interrogation of all cultural philosophies from a cross-cultural point of view with fundamental similarities and illuminating differences between them.

In four parts of unequal number of chapters, the book interrogates specific ethical and moral values, issues in human relations, cultural and traditional practices, customs and social values, religious beliefs and practices. In part One the book raises ethical issues of environmental ethics resulting from exploitation and appropriation of Africa's natural and human resources with the resultant environmental challenges, poverty and insecurity that have made living in harmony and peace almost impossible with nature and man. Part Two interrogates the governance structure of African politics and bemoans the poor leadership recruitment system that has thrown up *kakistocrats* (the unfit to rule) that have left Africa ravaged by poverty, sickness and a politically and culturally divided and insecure people. Part Three offers some critical insights into the inherent values of/in African religious beliefs, and raised fundamental questions particularly, about belief in Abrahamic God/religions in Nigeria and beyond. The book draws on African philosophical temper to question the assumptions of these religions traditions within the precinct of its pragmatic value. Drawing a comparative Study of Olodumare the Yoruba Supreme Being and Judeo-Christian God, the author argues that the obscurity, ambiguity and contradictions inherent in man's search for meaning has the capacity of undermining belief in a metaphysical reality outside human geographic space.

In part four, Professor Segun Ogungbemi addresses the Yoruba worldview in the context of identity, language and social relations as a rational basis for spirituality and survival. The author's reference to Yoruba population in Brazil, Cuba, Haiti, Caribbean Islands, United States of America, Britain, Benin Republic, Sierra-Leon, Liberia etc under a religio-cultural heritage and works of art in Western museums and galleries testifies to the significance of Yoruba ingenuity and contributions to ancient, modern and contemporary civilizations. In this philosophical journey, the author undertakes to resolve some existential quandaries about the meaning of life like curses and misfortunes, death, immortality and morality among others.

A careful reading of the book leaves no one in doubts as to the explosive, topical, controversial and indeed, thought-provoking dialogue that goes beyond and thinks through African cultural differences. To this end, the book brilliantly and excellently achieves the task a critical revision and alternative approaches to understanding African thoughts and practices in the most elucidating array of solutions aimed at decoding African verities ever attempted by many professional philosophers. In fact the devotion of separate chapters in this book on the Yoruba worldview linking the continental and diaspora Yoruba exemplify ingenuity and contribution to the development of intercultural dialogue. More so, the coverage of such subject areas as *Knowledge, Beliefs and Values* in chapter ten, novel issues like

The Challenges of Boko Haram in Multi-Religious Space in Chapter thirteen, *The Yoruba Narratives of Curses and Misfortunes* in Chapter seventeen and *Death, Immortality and Morality* in chapter eighteen makes the book a major contribution to knowledge in the study of intercultural philosophy.

It may not be exaggeration to say that the book, ***Deconstructing African Thoughts and Practices*** is an excellent book in African Studies in the 21st century. Bursting with intellectual energy and ambition, the book provides a good account of issues needing debate in our distressed African continent. In accessible language, Professor Ogungbemi articulates many of today's key moral, ethical, political and social issues with methodical and insightful analysis of topics in African Philosophy and practice.

In this book, Professor Segun Ogungbemi has not only succeeded in bringing together the various philosophical concepts on intercultural philosophy in a single volume, he has done so in a comprehensive, lucid, excellent crisp and, above all, readable way. The most admirable aspect of this book is its willingness to confront every important aspect of the African social triad; *politics, morality* and *security* in the most intelligent and comprehensive manner. A bald summary of this interesting and passionately argued book does insufficient justice to the subtlety of many of the detailed arguments it contains.

It is not in doubt that this book is a masterpiece in African Philosophy. The author's analysis herein deconstructs the most controversial areas in African cultural philosophy, i.e. ethics politics, intercultural relations and religions, and gives focus to the whole edifice of African philosophical studies. Here understood, the expository philosophical discourse in this book stands tall as one of the best commentary on African Ideas. As a persuasive critique of present day theory and practice of African philosophy and praxis, Professor Segun Ogungbemi has in this book offered a ripened fruit of sustained reflection on the synergy between philosophy and culture in Africa. The author has indeed upgraded the quality of scholarship that is found wanting in many contributions to contemporary philosophical studies on Africa.

Coming at propitious time as another bold attempt at effecting a diminution in the yawning-gap that exists in the availability of well- researched academic materials on Africa, the book is a valuable addition to the existing body of knowledge for readers interested in incisive introduction to a crucial debate across the blurred boundary of ancient and contemporary African philosophy and culture. Structured to fit into the universal body of knowledge accessible by all people from all worlds, the book is intended for those who seek wisdom about Africa and African affairs. All lovers of knowledge and wisdom who seek and promote total quality human person should make this book their companion.

Alloy S. Ihuah, PhD

Professor of Philosophy,

Benue State University,

Makurdi-Nigeria.

January 31, 2022

DEDICATION

To lovers of humanity and in loving memories of my youngest sister, Funmilayo Ogungbemi, my cousin and mentee Dr. Ola Alege, my former student and colleague, Professor Ade Ali, my friend and colleague, Professor David Tuesday Adamo, my dynamic colleague and confidant, Professor Olu Aboluwoye, my childhood friend, Hon. J. Molemodile, my former teacher and mentor, Chief Bolaji Iyekolo and my brother-in-law, Victor Arise whose tragic death in Houston shook us to our bone marrows.

CONTENTS

FOREWORD I
DEDICATION V
PREFACE VIII
ACKNOWLEDGEMENTS XI

Part One
LIVING IN HARMONY WITH NATURE

CHAPTER 1
The Role Of Africa In World Resources And Reserves 4

CHAPTER 2
Modern Science And Technology In Conflict With African Environmental Ethics 18

CHAPTER 3
The Conflict In The Niger-Delta And National Interest 30

Part Two
POLITICS, CUSTOMS AND SOCIAL VALUES

CHAPTER 4
Pan-Africanism And Nationalist Consciousness 46

CHAPTER 5
Poverty In Africa: Its Causes And Moral Solutions 62

CHAPTER 6
Traditional Customs And Values In Contemporary Political Behavior In Nigeria` 84

CHAPTER 7
Yoruba Nation: The Desire For Self-Determination 104

CHAPTER 8
Marriage For A Meaningful Existence 122

CHAPTER 9
African Women At The Receiving End 138

Part Three
PHILOSOPHY OF RELIGION

CHAPTER 10
Knowledge, Beliefs And Values 154

CHAPTER 11
Belief In God 170

CHAPTER 12
A Comparative Study Of Olodumare The Yoruba Supreme Being And Judeo-Christian God 184

CHAPTER 13
The Challenges Of Boko Haram Insurgency In A Multi-Religious Space 210

Part Four
TRADITION, CULTURE AND VALUES

CHAPTER 14
Traditional Religious System 228

CHAPTER 15
Esu The Phenomenon Of Existence 242

CHAPTER 16
A Philosophical Analysis Of Yemoja In A Cross Cultural Context 256

CHAPTER 17
The Yoruba Philosophical Narratives Of Curses And Misfortunes 276

CHAPTER 18
Death, Immortality And Morality 290

CHAPTER 19
Towards The Perfectibility Of Man And Its Challenge To Africa 306

PREFACE

Sometimes we tend to ignore a subtle advice to act on genuine academic concerns from our colleagues but consciously and unconsciously in our lonely moment or in our meditations the impulse becomes irresistible. This was a vivid experience I had when in 2017 Dr. Adeshina Afolayan now Professor of Philosophy in the Department of Philosophy University of Ibadan advised me to publish my articles in journals and chapters in books in some reputable local or international publishing companies. At that time, there was a publishing company in Germany that approached me on the same issue but it was not on my priority list. My first priority was to write my autobiography, which I actually started in 2016 and the second priority was to have departments of philosophy created at two newly established Federal Universities in Oye in Ekiti State and Lokoja in Kogi State in Nigeria respectively. Professor Kayode Soremekun was the Vice-Chancellor of Federal University of Oye (FUOYE) who was warmly receptive to the creation of Department of Philosophy. He spontaneously requested me to write a B.A. Philosophy degree program and work with the Director of Academic Programs, Professor Olusegun Olademiji. I was delighted with his response and I began to work on the program with assistance of several colleagues namely, Dr. Solomon A. Laleye, Dr. Sunday Layi Oladipupo, Professor Ade Ali and Professor Oladele Balogun. The effort resulted into the creation of the Department of Philosophy with enrolment of many students in 2021. I was not able to make much progress on that of Federal University Lokoja apart from a direct contact with the Vice-Chancellor, Professor Angela Freeman Miri who was interested in the program and she requested that I write a proposal, which I did and sent to her. She was not able to create Department of Philosophy before her term of office expired in February 2021. Before then, I had already relocated to Texas, USA in 2018. When a new Vice Chancellor, Professor Olayemi Akinwumi was subsequently appointed; he created Department of Philosophy in 2021.

About three months ago, I woke up from my slumber and procrastination with a renewed vigor to work on this book and my son; Segun Ogungbemi Jr. gave me a booster to expedite action on the project. I was searching for a befitting title for the book that will stimulate interest amongst scholars and intellectuals who are not necessarily in the discipline of philosophy but are generally moved by passion for its intellectual values, and those who are in the discipline of philosophy particularly, African Philosophy. The struggle to get a suitable and marketable strategy for the book gave birth to its title: *Deconstructing African Thoughts and Practices*. The book is essentially for the general public because it deals with various aspects of our humanity.

The book has four parts and each part has unequal number of chapters that address specific ethical and moral values, issues in human relations, cultural and traditional practices, customs and social values, religious beliefs and practices. Each topical issue in these chapters has been critically interrogated for clarity and understanding. There are six chapters that appear in this book that have not been published in any journals or as chapters in books. These are Chapter 5: "Poverty in Africa: Its Causes and Moral Solution". Chapter 6: "Traditional Customs and

Values to Contemporary Political Behavior in Nigeria" Chapter 7: "Yoruba Nation: A Political Response to Injustice". It was originally titled: "Oduduwa State: A Renaissance for Development" and submitted for publication in a book project to be edited by a colleague. I have withdrawn my contribution to the book project and included it in this book. Chapter 13: The Challenges of Boko Haram in Multi-Religious Space", Chapter 17: "The Yoruba Narratives of Curses and Misfortunes" and Chapter 18: "Death, Immortality and Morality". It was originally entitled, "The Yoruba Narratives of Forigbepe meaning, curses and misfortunes". The "word" Forigbepe is however interchangeably used in the body of the discourse. I have asterisked all the Chapters already published with minor but cogent adjustments and indicated where and when they have been published at the end of each chapter.

Part I raises ethical issues about the generosity of Africa to the rest of the world in terms of sharing her natural and human resources voluntarily or involuntarily but in return, the continent and her peoples have been disproportionately rewarded with environmental degradation, poverty and crises that have made living in harmony and peace impossible with nature. It further deals with why Homo sapiens have to coexist with nature for their own existential and corporate interests and failure to do so could trigger dangerous environmental consequences. Each chapter addresses specific environmental ethical concerns as it relates to people living in different geographical landscapes and spaces.

Part II is about what Africans have done to improve themselves since independence of their countries from colonial imperialists. It interrogates how Africans have governed themselves and provided basic infrastructural needs to their people now that their leaders are in the driver seats of the continent. How much of modernity/contemporary cutting-edge science and technology influenced their customs and social values? Are the people better off today or they are worse off?

Part III offers some philosophical insights to what values are inherent in African religious beliefs, and raised fundamental questions particularly, about belief in Abrahamic God/religions in Nigeria and by implication throughout the continent of Africa. Given the obscurity, ambiguity and contradictions in man's search for meaning in religion, is it not the case that religions or God they serve is a human invention rather than his metaphysical reality outside human geographical space? This may be provocative but that is the nature of philosophy to help us believe any religious propositions according to evidence.

Part IV addresses the Yoruba pungent for their traditional beliefs system no matter where they live and no matter their existential condition either at home or in diaspora. If there is any single ethnic group in Africa that preserves their cultural traditions, beliefs systems and practices in African history, there seems to be no other than the Yoruba in Nigeria. Wherever they went during trans-Atlantic slave trade behold; they did not abandon their Orisha, identity, language and social relations. It became a rational basis for their spirituality, survival and nostalgic yearning for their home in Africa. That is why we have a large population of them in Brazil, Cuba, Haiti, Caribbean Islands, United States of America, Britain, Benin Republic, Sierra-Leon, Liberia etc still worshiping, Ogun, Esu, Yemoja, Sango, Obatala amongst others. Here in Nigeria the religion has refused to be conquered and become extinct. Yoruba works of art, or Yoruba aesthetics are replete with concrete evidence in Western museums and galleries testifying to the significance of Yoruba ingenuity and contributions to ancient, modern/contemporary civilizations with academic, intellectual and amusement appeals to humanity. Given the trajectory and capacity of science and technology to ameliorate human suffering, the concept of human final destiny is philosophically interrogated with the attempt to advance knowledge of perfectibility of man in order to free him from diseases, fear of the unknown and death.

ACKNOWLEDGEMENTS

Writing this book would have been almost impossible without contributions of spirited scholars namely, Professors Adeshina Afolayan the prime mover of the idea of the book, Alloy Ihuah was kind enough to write the foreword of the book, Toyin Falola (TF), th*e Irunmole Iwe* for his useful suggestions, Benson Ohihon Igboin, and Dr. Sunday Layi Oladipupo who proofread the manuscript and Segun Ogungbemi Jr. for his generous support with provision of serene environment for me to write the book. I am indebted to Professors Oluwafemi Mimiko, Karim Bangura, J. Abiodun Balogun and his wife, Adetutu, Mom Marita Morgan, Asiwaju Jide Omokore and his wife, Angela, Chief Ezekiel Onaolapo Okeniyi and his wife, Elizabeth, Navy Commander (CDR) Victor Lofinmakin and his wife, Dolapo, Samuel Elijah Iyelolu and his wife, Toyin, Olusegun Victor Awo and his wife, Obiaderi who have shown interest in my research projects. And finally, I thank my wife, Olori Olayemi Ogungbemi and all my children and grandson, Yetunde, Temidayo, Tinuke and Segun III for their supportive hands of love always.

Part One

LIVING IN HARMONY WITH NATURE

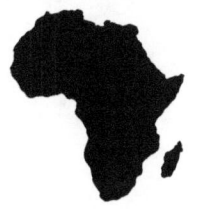

CHAPTER 1
The Role Of Africa In World Resources And Reserves

Introduction

We do not know for certain when the first human beings appeared on this planet earth. What is certain, however, is that they did not know all that the universe got in stock for them. It is through necessity that they became aware of the enormous natural resources at their disposal with attendant responsibilities if they were to survive and flourish. In other words, they had to apply their cognitive faculties to unearth and fashion the kind of knowledge, science and technology that could enhance their quality and luxury of life. The domineering force of the natural environment by man cannot be attributed to the first people who inhabited the earth. It is the exploitation of the natural resources by modern man and its effect on him and the rest of the habitats that warrant a new method of dealing with nature and its resources.

Generally speaking, the world resources and reserves that man depends on for survival are basically human and natural resources. Each of these resources can further be sub-divided into several components depending on the subject matter. For instance, human resources can be sub-divided into Rational Resources, Moral Resources, Scientific/Technological Resources, and Religious Resources etc. Similarly, Natural Resources can be sub-divided into Agricultural Resources, Mineral Resources, and Water Resources etc. Whichever way and manner these resources are discussed, the center of the subject matter is often, if not always, man and his environment. Man is always at the center of the discourse, because he is the "dramatist". This being so, my interest in this chapter is to present some philosophical and ethical arguments as a contribution to the ongoing debate on the role of Africa to world resources and reserves. I will begin with Africa's energy resources and develop what I have called a common-sense ethics, good governance and finally suggest an appropriate means to conserve the resources.

Energy Resources

Before I begin to discuss energy resources in Africa, I want to give a concise background of my interest on the issue. Sometime in July 1982, I went to do a research work at University of London. As I was walking around the institution, I missed my way. Instead of asking for a direction from someone, I felt I could trace my way to the institution. As I was using my sense of direction, I found a bookshop. As a student, one of the things that interested me was how and where to get bookstores where I could buy books that were relevant to my research work. But sometimes, one accidentally stumbles, on a material or materials that can cause a detour in one's thought. That was exactly what happened to me as I entered the bookshop and browsed through. As I continued to browse, I saw a small book titled *The Wealth of Nigeria* by G. Brian Stapleton. The first thought that came to my mind was that if I could get the wealth of Nigeria here in London, then there would be no need to go back to Dallas where I came from! Although I did not get the kind of wealth I thought I could get in the book, there was another form of wealth, which the author exposed me to: Nigeria's natural resources! Since that time, I have taken keen interest in Africa's natural resources.

Writing on African natural resources, Ali A. Mazuri gave a succinct insight as to the enormous natural resources in Africa. He writes:

> Estimates of Africa's resources are on the whole tentative. Not enough prospecting for resources under the ground has taken place, but it is already fair to say that Africa has 96 per cent of the non-communist world's diamonds, 60 per cent of its gold, 42 per cent of its cobalt, 34 per cent of its bauxite and 28 per cent of its uranium. Africa's iron reserves are probably twice those of the United States, and its reserves of chrome are the most important by far outside the Soviet Union (now Russia). The West interest in Africa's oil has also significantly increased, partly in proportion to the political uncertainties surrounding the Middle Eastern suppliers. Then there are Africa's water resources, with some of the greatest rivers of the world. Potentialities for building dams and generating hydro-

electric power have only just begun to be exploited. Solar energy for domestic and public purposes is still in its infancy. But it should be remembered that Africa is the most exposed of all the continents to the sun.[1]

There are, of course, other mineral and natural resources that are found in Africa that have been used. For instance, copper, gold, tantalite, cobalt, platinum etc are found in abundance in the continent.

The land, water, air and sun add to the aesthetic wealth of Africa. It is believed that Africa ranks among the world's largest agricultural potentials. It is appropriate to say that nature or providence has treated Africa as the most beloved continent in the world. Having said that, I am aware of some natural disasters in Africa that had claimed many lives namely, storms and floods. Generally, natural disasters had been in existence before human begins begun to occupy the universe. So one has to bear in mind that natural occurrences have to perform their functions and human beings should learn to co-exist with nature. The most pathetic of African condition as Mazuri observes is that despite the huge natural resources found in Africa, the truth of the matter is that the continent is one of the poorest in the world. A situation in which Africa that has most of the world known natural resources in the world and yet the poorest is an anomalous underdevelopment.[2] The question now is: What has Africa got in return for sharing her resources with the rest of the world, particularly from Western world and China?

If Africa is going to make any significant contributions to the preservation of natural resources particularly in the area of energy resources, the question we need to raise is which ones must she use and reserve? Some of the natural resources used for energy that will be discussed are coal, oil and gas, hydroelectric power and solar energy.

(i)   Coal

Coal is found in reasonable quantities and quality in Africa, particularly in South Africa, Nigeria, Ethiopia, Mozambique, Morocco, and Swaziland amongst other places. The demand for coal for domestic and industrial use in large quantities was as a result of industrial revolution in Europe. Pekka Kuusi explains, "The growth of industry during the 19th century was very dependent upon coal and cast iron. Coal was used in the manufacturing of both steam engines and cast iron and thus its production dominated the whole economic development of the 19th century."[3]

The use of coal for human economic development over the years has positive and negative effects. The positive aspect of coal as a source of energy made the industrial demand on the part of the Europeans to look beyond their immediate environments. Africa was infected with the European curiosity to meet the domestic and industrial need of coal. The exploration and exploitation of African coal contributed to the European expansion of their industries and market of their finished products. Africa that was once considered a dark continent became the path of light to European economy and development. It was this development that brought about western civilization to Africa with its correspondent burden. On the negative nature of the use of coal as a source of energy Kuusi writes:

> Man, overtaken by his self-regulating evaluation, has pulled coal … from the ground as a bee takes nectar from the flowers, and has thus made his life better, more varied and stronger. Nevertheless, it took 200 years after the inventing of the steam engine to ask the question, how long can this rate of energy exploitation go on?[4]

The question raised by Kuusi became necessary as a result of the negative impact of coal for domestic and industrial consumptions. In other words, the question was probably raised due to the awareness of the health hazards that the use of coal generated. Louis Pojman throws more light on this matter. He writes, "So we burn fossil fuels, especially coal, which unbeknownst to the public at large, is probably more dangerous than nuclear energy, causing more cancer, polluting the air with sulphur dioxide, and producing acid rain, which is destroying our rivers and lakes and killing trees."[5]

The lesson to be learnt from the negative impact of the use of coal for human social and economic development is that, no matter how good something is, if care is not taken, it is its side effects that will bring its joy and comfort to a halt. There is a proverb in Yoruba which says, *Okere to nje ogede to re di mo, ko mo pe nkan to dun ni yio pa oun*, meaning a squirrel that is eating bananas with amusement does not know that its enjoyment that will kill him. If modern man is consumed by his technology of luxury and comfort without appropriate measures of care of the environment, his case is like that of a squirrel who eats bananas with amusement and joy which in the end will lead to his demise. That is why the observation of Charles Hartshorne is relevant. "For it is now clear that not only does technological man expand at the expense of other forms of life but in principle he faces limits beyond which his own expansion is impossible or self-defeating. Did any philosopher foresee this outcome?"[6]

Of course today, it is not only philosophers who foresee the danger of expansion without appropriate measure to control human greed and its corollary effects on the environment. To Africans, the use of coal for economic reasons without adequate protection from its hazards portends a lot of risk, hence a need to make use of other natural energy resources that are not harmful to human existence. The coal can be reserved for those who have the technology to control its use in their countries or continents.

(ii)   Water for hydroelectric Power

Some of the abundant water resources that have been used in Africa to generate hydro-electric power are Kainji dam on River Niger, Shiroro gorge on Kaduna river, both in Nigeria, Volta river scheme in Ghana, the Inga dam and Inga-Shaba power line in the Democratic Republic of Congo, formerly Zaire among others have served their countries and neighbours. What are needed are the expansion of these water resources and the exploitation of new ones with the use of modern technology. If this is done it will go along way to make Africa self-energy sufficient. But more importantly, energy generated from water resources is more environmentally friendly in terms of pollution it generates than coal.

(iii)   Solar Energy

It is obvious that the geographical location of Africa has naturally endowed her with abundance of sunshine. Since necessity, they say, is the mother of invention, modern technological device that has been used in the industrial nations to exploit the solar system to generate power for domestic and industrial use will be beneficial to African States because Africa, if it lacks anything, certainly not the ray of light from the sun. This is one area that has thrown a challenge to African scientists and scholars and African leaders. If there is a political will on the part of African leaders and scientists with some form of partnership with the developed countries to tap this natural power supply for a general use in Africa, it will reduce drastically Africa's over dependence on oil, gas, coal, water etc for their domestic and industrial consumptions. And when this happens, there will be "left-overs" for reserves. I am aware that some African countries have begun to exploit the solar system for energy on a small scale. It is necessary to take a giant stride to achieve a more robust objective in the supply of electricity to majority of Africans in the rural and urban communities. In this regard, Nigeria, South Africa, Libya and Egypt should take the lead because of their human and economic resources.

This does not mean that these countries should limit their achievement of solar energy to themselves alone. What it means, is that they should take this role and make the supply of energy from solar power to the rest of Africa in the spirit of African brotherhood. There are some environmental issues that may arise from power generated from solar system because it is generally believed that there is no source of energy, which does not generate pollution. Hartshorne argues, "It is important to realize that all forms of power involve pollution. Electricity seems clean in our houses but the generating plants are not and never will be entirely so."[7]

The fear of Hartshorne is understandable but the level and amount of pollution generated from solar energy, it seems to me, cannot be compared to that of coal, oil and nuclear energy. If this is true, which I think it is, the ethical and moral question we need to ask is will the use of solar energy maximize the greatest good for the greatest number of Africans? Such a utilitarian approach should guide our yearning for energy resources from the sun.

(iv) Oil Mineral

There are several African countries where oil is produced in commercial quantity namely, Nigeria, Libya, Egypt, Gabon, Sudan, Angola etc. There are also some African countries that are potentially rich in oil mineral resources namely, Cameroun, Chad, Sao Tome and Principe etc. Oil is generally the economic gold mine of some countries in Africa that produce it in commercial quantities. For instance, Libya, Nigeria, Gabon etc are among the leading producers of oil in commercial quantities in Africa. The demand for oil for domestic and industrial use is high in industrial countries in the world, particularly, Europe, America, Japan and China. So the market demands for Africa's oil is generally in Western Europe and China. It is as if without adequate supply of crude oil to Western Europe and United States of America, the whole world will collapse. Mazuri writes, "The West's interest in Africa's oil has also significantly increased, partly in proportion to the political uncertainties surrounding the Middle Eastern suppliers. Had Nigeria joined the Arab oil embargo of the United States in 1973, the consequences for America would have been severe."[8]

This reminds me of my experience in the U.S. when I was a student at Southern Methodist University Dallas. I took a course in Ethics in the Fall semester, 1978 under Professor Joseph Allen. Being a Nigerian, and having come from Nigeria, he would want to know my moral position on the use of oil as a political and economic weapon on the U.S. if she would not support Nigeria against apartheid regime in South Africa. At that time, Nigeria was seen as a good ally of the United

States. My position then was diplomatic but down deep in my mind, I felt Nigeria should use oil power, if and only if, it could help to dismantle the illegal regime that had no respect for human dignity, equity and justice. Even then I felt that Nigeria should weigh her position by taking a rational and moral course so that in the end, she would not pay severely for her position. This was under Jimmy Carter. When Ronald Reagan became President of the United States of America in 1981 and Nigeria's former President Shehu Shagari was interviewed on the issue of using oil power against the U.S., he did not hesitate to state categorically that if there were need for Nigeria to pressure U.S. into action on South Africa, it would be done. Aaron Segal later reported that, "Washington prefers to believe, more so under Reagan than Carter, that Lagos is bluffing about the use of oil weapon while Lagos insists that it is not"?[9] At that time, Lagos was the seat of Government of Nigeria but now Abuja Federal Capital Territory. The event that followed under Reagan Administration proved that Lagos was indeed bluffing. President Reagan government decided to use its oil reserves to flood the market for Americans were buying it at a cheaper rate. Because US government did not import oil there was an oil glut and Nigeria crude oil, which was sold between $38.00 and $40.00 per barrel slumped to about $10.00. The Nigerian foreign policy then failed to take into cognizance of the overt support Nigeria gave Jimmy Carter on his bid for the second term against Reagan who was eyeing the position. Furthermore, the memory of 1973 of Arab oil embargo was still fresh in the mind of Americans and anyone who at that time threatened to use oil power against them would not be taken lightly. Political and social impulse of Nigerian policy at that time overrated its influence. It must be noted that Nigeria's economic revenue was basically from oil and the U.S. was the leading consumer of the product. To threaten a country like the US with oil power, to me, was to carry our foreign policy; on such matters too far.

The use of oil, the world over, has generated some serious concern. Kuusi explains:

> We do not yet know what the total reserve of fossil fuels under the ground is. Nevertheless, a sustainable energy cannot be founded upon rapid exploitation of fossil fuels. An annual increase of approximately 5% in the use of primary energy would in less than ten generations – by the year 2200-mean that primary energy use would be 40,000 times more than at present.[10]

Going by this estimate, it is plausible that the fear of Kuusi will be allayed if we are collectively more prudent in over desire for more industrial development that will provide Africans and the world over with more luxury and comfort. There is another dimension that makes the call more imperative: environmental pollution or environmental crisis that is the outcome of human use of oil as sources of energy for domestic and industrial use. It is for this reason that Africa must not contribute more to the energy crisis that is looming ahead.

Common-Sense Ethics and Good Governance

If Africa is going to make any useful contribution to the call for prudence in the use of energy resources and provide for the future, there is a need to apply common-sense ethics and good governance. The ethics of common sense has its root in human cognition. Humans, being rational cannot afford to ruin themselves because it is counter-intuitive to do so. Therefore a rational choice is to be concerned for one another.

There is also another dimension of man that acts contrary to this notion or moral concept: the irrational or emotional or better still psychological impulses that are enveloped in greed and selfishness. When there is no adequate control of human impulses or the drum major instinct of a corporate state, the competitive race for superiority sets in. And when that happens, the need for common sense has no moral warrant. Thomas Hobbes, a British Philosopher gave a proper picture of man in the state of nature in which common sense ethics is not applied. He described this state of nature as a time of war in which "every man is enemy to every man ... and which is worst of all, continual fear, and danger of violent death; and the life of man, solitary, poor, nasty, brutish, and short."[11] Although one may argue as John Locke, another British philosopher did that man in the state of nature is a complete gentleman, a decent human being. But looking at human behaviour particularly in recent times, the activities of the terrorists all over the world seem to support the view of Hobbes rather than that of Locke. The terrorist attack on the U.S. cities on September 11, 2001, is a manifestation of the brutal nature of man. In recent time such obnoxious event took place in London and it has not stopped. Killing of the innocent people by the terrorists in Africa and elsewhere is a demonstration of loss of moral conscience and common values. The primary objectives of ethics of common sense are live and let live. It takes into consideration human dependence on the environment for survival by applying a traditional African value of nature-relatedness. If man is to survive and co-exist with nature, the concept to nature-relatedness that Africans in the rural areas have been practicing teaches that one should not take from nature more than he needs.[12] The environmental crisis that industrial nations have caused is as a result of taking more from nature than they need. Kuusi seems to agree with this view. He argues, "Life should be ideal and bountiful, but, on the contrary, we feel insecurity in the midst of abundance. Developing science and renewing technology are seen as the requirements for the growth of production, but at the same time as threats to our very existence."[13]

Contemporary Africans have imbibed Western culture and values and have infected some of their rural areas, which also affected the way and manner the environment has been exploited with total disregard for traditional value of nature-relatedness.

From the ongoing, the ethics of common sense and the concept of nature-relatedness is very much the same coin although with different sides. Ethics of common sense, however, propels the impulses of man to reason within human cognition in order to behave to nature that sustains him. But the desire for wants and accumulation of wealth and power has exacerbated the degree of corruption and poor leadership that has characterized the state of affairs in modern Africa. George Saitoti writes, "In the African countries, however, the institutional arrangements adopted at independence failed to adequately constrain the state, allowing civil servants and politicians to abuse their mandates and engage in corruption, rent seeking and other forms of political opportunism."[14]

In some African countries even before independence, elementary form of corruption was in existence. For instance, in Nigeria, Stapleton writes:

> The simple statement that in assessing output only payment for goods or services rendered should be counted set difficult problems in Nigeria. Presents should certainly not be included, but what of a 'present' where the giver definitely expects some service in return: bribes, *kola* dashes, may be socially regarded as payment for services even if officially they are illegal; they should be counted. In some cases, however, regrettable it may be and despite what the laws say, the giving of such presents may be the only way of obtaining some necessary and useful service.[15]

One may be surprised to find the above statement of Stapleton at the developmental stage of Nigeria. But that seemed to be the developmental growth of corruption, which the law enforcement of the time should have dealt with. But unfortunately it was left to grow to a full-blown 'disease' that now defies a cure. Of course, corruption is found everywhere in the world, the difference is the method and degree. A nation that provides basic infrastructure, education, employment etc, for its people even if there are pockets of corruption which do not necessarily become a cog in the wheel of progress, it will in most cases not become a public outcry. Corruption becomes a public outcry when the public is suffering while the leaders live in luxury without any concern for those they lead or govern. In the spirit and vision of common-sense ethics, such a behavior commonly displayed by corrupt African leaders and politicians is not in consonance with African cultural values. The economic values that African states have derived from the sale of energy resources require prudent spending on education and basic infrastructure. It is through sound education, research and good governance that Africans can become 'masters' of their own resources and economy.

One is more encouraged by the collaborative effort of African leaders on the establishment of the New Partnership for Africa Development (NEPAD) that seeks "to reduce poverty, accelerate growth and to establish sustainable development in African in 21st century."[16] This approach that emanated from African leaders is a by-product of ethics of common sense. It is time for Africans and their leaders to go back to the basics of African moral values that enhance the spirit of brotherhood and self-respect. A situation in which African leaders go to small countries that are not as naturally endowed as their own to beg for aid does indeed dishonor African collective sense of respect and dignity. It has become a general practice of some African leaders to engage in taking foreign loans that are used on elephant projects from where they put a good percentage of the funds into their own local and foreign banks leaving their countries in perpetual debt burden.

Writing on corruption in Africa, one bears in mind that some foreign partners are involved in this ugly trade. So corruption is a two-way traffic. So those who accuse African leaders of corruption ought at the same time accuse their collaborators. If corruption should be dealt with, industrial nations where African monies are kept must have a moral will of common sense and return it to African countries where it was stashed away. Some foreign countries e.g. Switzerland, Luxembourg etc that have been cooperating with African countries to make sure that such stolen monies do not have a safe haven in their countries deserve commendation. And we hope Britain, the U.S. France and others will follow suit.

It must be noted here that the recent development by the Western world including the US to write off the debt burden of some African countries is a welcome development. I hope African leaders will learn a great lesson having seen the troubles they went through to get the debt relief. But in recent time, it seems Nigeria government has not. A moral self-reflection of common sense which warns that once beaten, twice shy ought to be embraced by African leaders in their pursuit of good governance. I want to agree with Allen that, "Genuine love for one's country on the part of a public official takes the form of faithfulness in regard to the responsibility of one's office on behalf of the citizenry."[17] The genuine love for Africans by their leaders and politicians demands a total commitment and dedication to service rather than self-love, which has characterized their political and social behavior.

Strategy for Energy Reserves

If Africa is going to contribute to the world energy reserves, it must be done in the spirit of collective responsibility with the rest of the world. It must be done with mutual understanding of the common sense ethics since it will lead to mutual benefits. But what method or strategy should be adopted in order to preserve our energy resources? As I have shown in this discourse the energy resources that Africa has in abundance i.e. coal, oil, water and sun among others, Africans have to rely heavily on solar energy, and waterpower for hydroelectric supply since the natural geographical location of African has bestowed on her regular supply of these natural resources. What is required is the technological know-how that industrial nations can contribute to enhance sustainable supply of the electricity. When this is done, Africa will then make her coal and oil more readily available for use in other parts of the world where they are mostly needed.

The rest of the world should apply the same common sense ethics in the use of energy in their countries as well. It will not be morally sound for Africa to be reserving energy while some countries will be using their resources for imperialist purposes. It has been shown that the states of the world namely, United States of America and Russia have been responsible for half "the total consumption of primary energy."[18] There is a need for some concession on the part of those nations that consume energy in such a high proportion. Considering the effect of pollution on humans and the environment at large, Hartshorne warns:

> A sticky aspect the environmental crisis is that although every increase in production tends to increase pollution and destruction of nature the present level of production leaves half of mankind poorly supplied.... Consequently, unless production increases a good deal, either the rich and moderately well-to-do will make severe material sacrifices, or the underprivileged will be even worse off than they are

now ... No matter how one calculates, the environmental prospects are grim. Centuries of loose thinking, flabby optimism, stupid or hypocritical social ethics or lack of ethics are catching up with us.[19]

Of course, Hartshorne is right in his observation and warning. It is therefore more compelling for the industrial nations to embrace a non-hypocritical ethics: ethics of common sense that seeks the welfare or the general well being of humankind.

Conclusion

It seems to me it is time to focus on how the rest of the world can cooperate with Africa to make it possible to achieve the goal of reserving energy resources. But in doing so, Mazuri's view will serve as the word of our elders:

> Let us sign a global treaty to help establish greater and social justice not only between men but also between societies. Thanks to the West's inventiveness, the clock of technology has indeed gone past the hour. It has ominous chimes of destruction. What is more it is an alarm clock, still ringing. 'Ladies and gentlemen, it is time to wake up'. In the new dawn the poor and the meek of Africa may not inherit the earth but hopefully they will finally inherit their own continent.[20]

It is hoped that the rest of the world will co-inherit Africa. With the current trend of events in which the universe has become a global village and consequently a world government will emerge so that the world natural resources will be equitably shared in terms of needs so as to have more left for reserves for the future.

There is bound to be some cynics and pessimists who will doubt the vision of a world government bearing in mind the unwillingness of the rich and the powerful to condescend to such an arrangement. For instance, Pojman notes that transnational corporations are the richest and powerful artificial persons. For instance, "Wal-Mart ($246 billion in revenues, 2003) General Motors, Exxon-Mobil, Royal Dutch Shell, ... these companies having enormous economic power have tremendous political potential. Exxon-Mobil has more ships than the British navy ... Halliburton and the companies have security forces in Iraq now, armies to defend their people and property."[21] Considering their military strength and political backing of their home country, do we think those who own these companies will subscribe to the reality of a world government that is not controlled by them? At best, in my view, they will probably agree in principle or simply consider it a utopian ideology. The events around the world e.g. terrorism (which has no human face), communication and better understanding of the global village plus the yearning for peace and the need for one another to co-exist will eventually, I think, lead to a change of attitude to those who hold to power and wealth because at the end of it all, it is to the interest of humanity. It becomes necessary for the rest of the world to cooperate with Africa to embrace the voice of reason, common sense ethics and nature-relatedness so as to preserve world energy resources and reserves. But the issue is: will the superpowers and leading global industrial countries, with their drum major instinct for power and domination; cooperate and use this principle of common sense, ethics/nature-relatedness and reject economic strategy of "Economic Hit Man[22]" of John Perkins?

Notes

1. Ali A. Mazrui, *The African Condition* (London: Heinemann, 1982), pp. 71-72.
2. Ibid; p. 72.
3. Pekka Kuusi, *This World of Ma*n (Oxford: Penguin Press, 1985), p. 151.
4. *Ibid;* p. 220.
5. Louis Pojman, *Environmental Ethics* (Boston: Jones and Bartlett Publishers, 1994), p. 1.
6. Charles Hartshorne, "The Environmental Results of Technology" in *Philosophy and Environmental Crisis* (ed) William T. Blackstone (Athens: University of Georgia Press, 1974), p. 11.
7. Ibid; p. 74.
8. Mazuri, *op. cit*, p. 71.
9. Aaron Segal,
10. Kuusi, *op. cit*, p. 220.
11. Hobbes, *Leviathan (*London: Collier Macmillan, 1978), p. 100.
12. See Segun Ogungbemi, "An African Perspective on the Environmental Crisis" in *Environmental Ethics: Reading in Theory and Practice* (Boston: Jones and Bartlett Publishers, 1994), pp. 203-209.
13. Kuusi, *op. cit*, p. 152.
14. George Saitoti, "Reflection in African Development", *Journal of Third World Studies* Vol. XX, No. 2 (Fall, 2003): p. 15.

15. G. Brain Stapleton, *The Wealth of Nigeria* (Ibadan: Oxford University Press, 1967), pp. 89-90.

16. The Punch, (Lagos) 26th July, 2005.

17. Joseph L. Allen, *Love and Conflict* (Nashville: Abingdon Press, 1989), p. 271.

18. Kuusi, *op. cit*, p. 220.

19. Hartshorne, *op. cit*, p. 76.

20. Mazuri, *op. cit*, p. 89.

21. Louis Pojman, "Big is Beautiful or the Case for World Government", Unpublished, 2005.

22. John Perkins, *The New Confessions of an Economic Hit Man* (Oakland: Berrett-Koehler Publishers, 2016), pp. 309-338.

* Segun Ogungbemi (2008) "The Role of Africa in World Resources and Reserves" *Journal of Philosophy and Development,* Department of Philosophy, Olabisi Onabanjo University, Ago-Iwoye, Ogun State, Nigeria, 10 (1&2) 133-149.

CHAPTER 2

Modern Science And Technology In Conflict With African Environmental Ethics

Introduction

There is no gain saying that modern science and technology has contributed to the development of Africa both positively and negatively to the extent that there is hardly anywhere in Africa where the two double barrel blessings are not being felt. Of course, Africa had developed her own science and technology before the advent of modern science and technology, which sought to ameliorate human sufferings and provide a slow pace development with cognizance that man and environment co-exist and insofar as man realized this fact and treated nature with caution there would be harmony and peace. But failure to recognize this fact man and nature will be in conflict and it is man that will be worse for it. It is this lack of understanding on the part of modern man of science and technology or the unwillingness on his part to recognize this fact that this chapter is concerned about. In other words, the conflict that arises between modern science, technology and African environmental ethics is the lack of understanding of how in Africa, environment is treated and the role of man in living with nature as man-nature relatedness. African environmental ethics has taught the African man over the ages not to take from nature more than he needs, and to be in harmony with nature he must do so with the traditional moral value of common sense ethics, if his life is to flourish. The exploration of oil in Africa and the exploitation of other essential minerals with the attendant pollution, deforestation that is causing environmental disasters in the continent and the global warming that the world is experiencing are as a result of modern man and his technological total disregard for African environmental ethical values. In all this, what should be done? What role should an African philosopher play? Is African traditional moral value of environment relevant to contemporary solution to environmental crisis? These and other issues have been discussed in this chapter. But first let me begin in a nutshell with man and the cosmos, the universe.

Man and the Universe

The natural world in which man is encapsulated is a jungle with constant catastrophic occurrences namely, earthquakes, volcano eruptions, storms, tornadoes, hurricanes, droughts, famine, diseases, death, and many others that threaten the existence of all the living things. The universe is always prone to environmental crises as a result of natural disasters. The cosmos or the universe is not a serene or a complete orderly environment. All the living things exist with the attendant exposure to dangers of varying degrees. It is a world of the survival of the fittest as explained by Charles Darwin. To survive in a universe of conflict of interests, man has to apply his faculty of reasoning to manipulate his environment for his survival but in doing so there is need for him to embrace some moral values and principles to enhance his survival. The unfolding knowledge of the environment to survive has made cutting edge science and technology a veritable tool to wage war against his vulnerability to nature. That is why science is construed as a field where "observations and measurements are made, theories are put forward and statements about the way of bringing about certain conditions, by means of experiments, are made."[1] And technology was originally considered as "craft, or at best as mere application of scientific findings."[2] But with modern development in science and technology the two fields of knowledge have become a means by which man exercises his faculty to control and dominate his natural estate. In traditional African society however, the idea of man dominating his natural world was not part of their understanding of the relationship between man and his environment. This knowledge pre-occupied their attitude to nature until their contact with the Europeans and Americans who had a different view on how the natural environment ought to be treated. Let me begin from the cradle of the world, Africa.

Science and Technology in a Traditional African Society

To begin with there is a need to clarify the notion of science and technology from the prevalent belief of African science, which bothers on magic and unverifiable metaphysical assumptions. By African traditional science and technology that existed before the arrival of the Europeans to Africa, I mean the observable and experimented knowledge applied scientifically and technologically to manufacture or produce hardware for domestic, aesthetic, agricultural, military, medical, and social needs of the people. May I say further that the difference between African science and technology and that of the western world then and now, it seems to me, is the degree or level of perfection and commercialization. Now the question is, if Africa had ever developed her own science and technology before the arrival of the Europeans, how come it did not make any enviable impact on the continent? Furthermore what has happened to African science and technology since the advent of the European form of science and technology? In other words, has African science and technology become obsolete and irrelevant to the needs of Africans and to the rest of the world or is it completely moribund? These are genuine questions that deserve concrete answers. Basically the areas that the development of traditional science and technology at that time concentrated largely on were agriculture, medicine, weaving otherwise known today as textile industry, iron smelting that is, iron and steel industry, hides and skin industry, among others. According to Samuel Johnson in his book, *The History of the Yoruba*s:

> Before the period of intercourse with Europeans, all articles made of iron and steel, from weapons of war to pins and needles were of home manufacture; ... *Workers in leather* were formerly their own tanners, each one learns to prepare whatever leather he wants to use; black, white, green, yellow, are the prevailing colours given to leather. Every worker is expected to know, and to be able to execute the various crafts performed with leather, e.g. saddlery, sheaths to swords and knives, leather ornaments on hats, waistbands for children, leather cushions, bolsters boots and shoes, sandals etc.[3]

In a similar vein J. Olubi Sodipo writes:

> There is evidence to show that up till about the end of the 15th century A.D., there was little difference in the material and technical circumstances of many African peoples and those of many European peoples. Thus, we are not surprised at the account that when the Portuguese travelers or adventurers landed at the banks of the River Congo towards the end of that century, they met a flourishing state whose material circumstances impressed them (the

Portuguese). The courtiers of King Ambas were dressed in robes of silk and broke, and King Nzinga an Nkuwa exchanged embassies with the King of Portugal on equal terms.[4]

Furthermore Adu Boahen writes on the advanced civilization of some African peoples:

> … the most remarkable thing about the Yoruba was the very high civilization that they developed. This is evident from the richness of their art. As far back as the fourteenth and fifteenth centuries, the Yoruba were producing works of art in bronze, ivory and wood. Most of these pieces which are coming to light now through archaeology have amazed scholars by their artistic beauty and naturalism, and are fetching fantastically high prices in the salesrooms in Europe and America.[5]

Boahen explains further that "… the Benin most certainly rose and attained an advanced stage of development about fifty years before any European ever set foot on Benin soil, and two hundred years before the commencement of the great European demand for slaves."[6]

The question that arises from the development of Africa through their own science and technology before the Europeans came to the continent is what impeded their advancement? The answer to this question is greed. Boahen writes "…though civil and inter-state wars were known in Africa before the coming of Europeans, … these wars became more and more demoralizing…as a recent African historian has pointed out; fighting was motivated by greed not by self-preservation nor imperial ambitions."[7]

Let me amplify what Boahen says by stating that it was not greed alone that collapsed the existing science and technology developed by the indigenous Africans before the intrusion of the Europeans to the continent but it played one of the major factors. It appeared as if the early development of African technology even though not as sophisticated as one could imagine compared to our modern understanding of science and technology it however got to a level in which the technology began to destroy the technologists- in this case the Africans. The use of arms and ammunition in warfare to capture their fellow men and women and used them as slaves became prevalent. So when the Europeans came with more superior firearms than the locally made tools it exacerbated the greed and ignorance of the warlords and made way for the escalation of wars among the tribal groups. Slavery became a quick way of enriching the strong and the advancement of traditional technology was abandoned. The traditional ethics of sanctity of life and common sense ethics of not taking from nature more than one needs that could enhance the quality of life was pushed to oblivion and the consequence of it was slavery, colonization and neo-colonization which have been a burden to the continent. The weapons used during the tribal warfare did not constitute a serious threat to the environment. As a matter of fact, there was no upsurge of population increase because of reduction in population as a result of slave trade. In other words, land, water, air were less polluted and the ozone layers were not depleted as a result of human activities.

Traditional science and technology is not completely moribund in most African societies because those who cannot afford the finished products of western technology still patronize the local products e.g. hoes and cutlasses mainly used by subsistent farmers, locally made guns, textiles of different kinds used for traditional occasions like weddings, funeral ceremonies, chieftaincy title celebrations, among others. The local manufacturing of these products does not constitute any serious threat to the environment. In other words, both the production and goods produced are environmentally friendly. And in the area of medicine or health delivery for example, traditional orthopedic method of taking care of broken bones is still relevant to the needs of the people because of the high cost of orthodox medicine which the poor masses cannot afford. The use of herbs, leaves, roots for the treatment of different ailments among Africans is very prevalent. It is not the case therefore that traditional science and technology has no bearing in contemporary African society. What has been said about the advancement of African peoples before their contacts with the western world is not to resurrect the glorious past of Africa but to show in brief that a giant continent like Africa was at no time devoid of knowledge of science and technology to ameliorate the sufferings of her diverse peoples. In other words, as Toyin Falola rightly noted, even though Africa had in the past made its contributions to human civilization "its intellectual significance should not be lost on us."[8] The truth of the matter is that no human race can cope with the exigencies of life without some form of science and technology however crude or refined and that of Africa cannot be treated in isolation.

Modern Science and Technology and Human Environment

A curious mind may ask what modern science and technology is and its significance to humankind? Given the nature of this discourse, modern science and technology is a field of study that is based on observation, experiment and practical demonstration of knowledge with the attendant objective to make our world a better living environment. It is in this regard that Robert K. Merton explains, "…in modern times, especially during the last three centuries, the centre of interest seems to have shifted to science and technology."[9] In support of this observation of Merton, Colin Chant and John Fauvel in their book, *Darwin to Einstein Historical Studies on Science and Belief* give credence to why the shift.

> Science touched the imagination by its tangible results…Over the course of Queen Victoria's reign, those tangible results multiplied rapidly and extensively. The average Englishman came to enjoy better food, soft clothing, and a warmer home. Although his landscape might have become less lovely and the air he breathed less pure, he could live longer and dwell in greater security from the vicissitudes of nature than any man before him.[10]

The view expressed above during the Victorian period accepted the fact that the new technology that had improved the life of the people also portends danger in terms of pollution inhaled then. It was probably mild at the time but today it is more deadly. Louis Pojman explains:

> Nuclear power could provide safe, inexpensive energy to the world, but instead it has been used to exterminate cities and threaten a global holocaust. Disasters like the nuclear plant steam explosion at Chernobyl in the former Soviet Union have spread harmful radiation over thousands of square of miles and cause public distrust of the nuclear power industry. Nuclear waste piles up with no solution in sight. But our modern way of life does require energy, lots of it. So we burn fossil fuels, especially coal, which, unbeknownst to the public at large, is probably more dangerous than nuclear energy, causing more cancer, polluting the air with sulphur dioxide, and producing acid rain, which is destroying our rivers and lakes and killing trees.[11]

It is not only in Europe, America and other developed countries that the search for energy has created environmental crisis. For instance in Africa, foreign energy corporations have been exploring for oil namely, Shell, Exxon Mobil, Arco, Chevron among others. For more than two decades, these foreign companies have engaged in oil and gas exploration for example, in Nigeria, and particularly in the Niger Delta region causing a lot of environmental hazards and subjecting the people in the area to all sorts of deplorable conditions. The basic agricultural and fishing industries that had been in existence before these companies began their oil exploitation of the area have been abandoned because of pollution that is hazardous not only to the land and water but also to the health of the inhabitants. The oil and gas flaring where these essential minerals are produced in Nigeria and other places in Africa like Gabon, Sudan, Angola etc, have multiplying effects on the ozone layers which have far reaching consequences on the climatic regions of the world. That is to say, the world at large also bears the burdens of the activities of the foreign companies that pollute human environment however remote where such activities take place. Let me say in brief that most of the oil companies that have caused environmental crisis in Nigeria have one way or the other got involved in the cleaning of the oil spillages in the Niger Delta region. The Federal government of Nigeria on its part set up Niger Delta Development Commission (NDDC) to execute development projects in the region. Akpoili Timothy notes, "the Commission has built roads, bridges, jetties, schools, clinics; provided portable drinking water and electricity, supported local fishing industries and trained youths in various vocations."[12] In the democratic government of President Umaru Yar'Adua, a Federal Ministry of Niger Delta was established to address, in a comprehensive manner, the problems of the region and to create peace to enhance the development needed. The issue now is whether the means of solving the region's problem are not coming too little and too late. That probably explains the incessant conflict in the region. It is not only the Niger Delta area of Nigeria that has witnessed a negative impact of the by-products of modern science and technology, there are toxic wastes dumped on the shores of African countries by the industrial countries knowing fully well that they are harmful to their fellow human beings. The heinous crime committed by the industrial countries that dumped the hazardous wastes on African shores has no moral justifications even though some African leaders accepted the practice in exchange for a foreign aid. The gruesomely negative effects of science and technology on the environment have become worrisome because of the premium we generally place on human as a being of existential values. This does not mean that science and technology is not beneficial to humankind.

In a contemporary African society, hardly can anyone deny the fact that science and technology of the time has not made some positive impact on the society. Generally speaking, it has improved human transportation, education, industries, communication and information dissemination, employment, security, population, agriculture, energy, health, longevity etc. It is true that the world as we know it today is better than some centuries ago. People talk about the world as a global village because of what science and technology has made it to be. But the truth of the matter is that a small fraction of the world population has the largest share of the apple pie of the technology. According to Charles Hartshorne:

> Technology, besides making it possible for larger numbers to enjoy the goods of life, makes it possible for an additional huge number to live at least marginally, and even marginal living is better than nothing. The will to live may be sustained by minimal satisfactions, but they are still satisfactions. In sum, technology has greatly enlarged three groups of people, those with minimal, mediocre, or optimal modes of living.[13]

If those with minimal and the mediocre as explained by Hartshorne share the benefits of technology equally with those of optimal mode of living, what will happen to human environment? This is a moral issue, which Oswaldo De Rivero further raised in his book, *The Myth of Development*, "… how could the 5 billion inhabitants of the underdeveloped world adopt the consumption patterns at present shared by only 1 billion inhabitants of the advanced capitalist societies, without causing a real environmental catastrophe?"[14] If the luxury enjoyed by the rich and the middle class in the world with a few crumbs left for the poor and yet the hazardous and the polluted environment are shared globally in the same proportion, it seems the moral justification is indefensible. What could encourage the advanced world to engage in massive exploitation of natural resources without a serious recourse to moral implications of their behavior is probably responsible for the dilemma the global world is currently facing. It appears the biblical teaching about the way the western man sees himself in relation to his natural habitat is in the sense that he is superior to it because God has made him to dominate and use everything on earth at his discretion. The Bible also teaches him that this world is not his home, it is a temporary abode. Man has an eternal home with bliss and eternal contentment. Therefore he can afford to make use of his environment on earth according to his whims and caprices. But the truth of the matter is that the reality in human existence seems to suggest that this universe is the ultimate home of man and whatever he does must be done consciously with this understanding, if his life is to flourish because nobody has gone to the world beyond and returned to give us a scientific and philosophical explanation of its reality. The traditional African has a different view of the relationship between man and the environment that makes him to exist relatively in harmony with nature as opposed to the western world of modern science and technology with a domineering attitude.

The Nature of African Traditional Environmental Ethics

In Africa, man is believed to coexist with nature. Man is not the center of the universe or to dominate nature but to use it to enhance his quality of life. He is made aware that any misuse or abuse of his environment could be detrimental to his existence. For instance, the current trauma of COVID-19 and its variants have caused million deaths and economic recession in the world. This reminds us of the traditional wisdom: the vulnerability of man in the prevalence of pervasive technology and its deadly consequences. It teaches man not to take more from nature than what he needs. By keeping to this environmental moral code of conduct towards the management of his natural and human resources it will serve his short and long term interests. This environmental principle is called ethics of nature-relatedness or ethics of care of nature. The main reason for man to keep to this moral principle perhaps is because already man's environment is polluted by natural catastrophes and if human activities are not controlled, that may make the universe inhabitable. But this ethics of care of nature must not be seen as absolute even though it may have a universal appeal and application. I am aware that this natural ethical code of conduct to nature raises some questions that will make its moral and epistemological justification warranted. For instance, how do we know how much we need considering human nature of greed and insatiable wants? Who judges whether we have taken more than we need from nature? And if we have taken less from the natural resources, is there any reward for it? What happens if one takes more than he needs from the natural resources? Are there penalties that will not aggravate the already polluted environment? To a traditional African intellectual, these questions are subjects of human conscience and the principle of common sense to answer. Both human conscience and the principle of common sense are guided by reason, experience and the will. The ethics of care of nature or nature-relatedness asserts that human natural resources do not need man for its existence and functions. As a matter of fact, it will not surprise us if these natural resources had rational capacity and they asked humans what kind of beings they are because of the ways and manners they have related and used the environment. The fact remains that humans cannot do without the natural resources but they can exist without us. By using the natural resources indiscriminately in the name of development we are invariably endangering our own existence. Put succinctly, the ethics of nature-relatedness is an ethics that encourages humans to have a cooperative attitude to nature and to coexist peacefully with it bearing in mind that it is from nature that they derive nurture, growth, survival and sustainability. It is an ethics that calls for caution and perhaps an alternative approach to the reckless application or use of modern science and technology in our time.[15] In other words, all forms of human activities that have contributed to environmental pollution, degradation, depletion of ozone layers, deforestation etc, are substantial evidences that modern science and technology has made man to take more from the natural resources than he needs and it is in conflict with the ethics of nature-relatedness and common sense.

Conclusion

So far, I have not provided an absolute moral rule by which we should treat our natural resources. This is because such moral rule does not exist. What I have done by giving an objective overview of how modern science and technology has added some positive values to human existence and at the same time pointed out the danger of not applying environmental ethical principle of nature-relatedness to the management of the natural resources at his disposal amounted to endangering our own existence. Let me illustrate what the man of science and technology has done to our world with a story my father told me sometime ago. He told me that if you feed a child everyday and one day you fail to feed him, the child will invariably remember that day more often than the rest of the days you have fed him. Of course, one may say that the child is an ingrate but the truth of the matter is that his confidence in the person who feeds him is being betrayed. Similarly, the truth of the matter is that although the world appreciates the development, luxury and comfort human technology has provided in a few decades, the negative by-products of technology that threaten human environment do indeed begin to erode our confidence in its application to human survival. Like the story I have narrated above, it is not the case that humans are ungrateful to what technology has made us to be in our time, but truly, if there is no ethical principle to guide the use and management of our natural resources, then the ecosystems on which human life depends for survival are at the risk of extinction. What should philosophers or environmental ethicists do? Walter H. O'Brian properly addresses the answer to this question, "We shall have to write a new ethic and reorient ourselves to a quite different world. A difficult task? Yes, and an imperative one. We really have no choice if man and nature are to thrive."[16] The idea of not taking more than one needs from nature, the belief in nature-relatedness and common sense ethics that have been part of African way of dealing with the environment is certainly a rational and appropriate moral approach. The role of philosophers or environmental ethicists is to provide moral principles or ethical theories that are practicable in nature. It is the responsibility of our political leaders to enact policies that will give directives of what modern scientists and technologists should follow.

Whatever policies our political leaders worldwide make to avert the environmental crisis created by modern science and technology, it seems imperative to recognize the ethics of nature-relatedness for its universal application.

Notes

1. Friedrich Rapp, "The Philosophy of Technology: A Review" *Interdisciplinary Science Review* vol.10.No.2 (1985):130.
2. Ibid.,1.
3. Samuel Johnson, *The History of the Yorubas* (1921); repr. Lagos: C.S.S. Bookshop, 1976), 120.
4. J. Olubi Sodipo, "Philosophy, Science, Technology and African Traditional Thought" in *Philosophy and Cultures*, ed. H. Odera Oruka and D.A.Masolo, (Nairobi: Bookwise Limited, 1983), 38.
5. Adu Boahen, *Topic in West African History*, (1966; repr. London: Longman, 1980), 91.
6. Ibid.,111.
7. Ibid., 112.
8. Toyin Falola, *Africa in World Politics*, (Akure: Environs Publishers, 2006), 5.
9. Robert K. Merton, *Science, Technology and Society in Seventeen Century England*, (Sussex: Harvester Press, 1978), 3.
10. Colin Chant and John Fauvel, *Darwin to Einstein Historical Studies on Science and Belief*, (Essex: Longman, 1980), 47.
11. Louis Pojman, "On Ethics and Environmental Concerns" in *Environmental Ethics: Reading in Theory and Application*, ed. Louis Pojman, (Boston: Jones and Bartlett Publishers, 1994), 1.
12. Akpoili Timothy, "Developing the Delta Region," *The Punch*, July 18, 2006, Opinion.
13. Charles Hartshorne, "The Environmental Results of Technology" in *Philosophy and Environmental Crisis*, ed. William T. Blackstone, (Athens: University of Georgia Press, 1980), 70.
14. Oswaldo De Rivero, *The Myth of Development*, (London: Zed Books, 2001), 8.

15. Cf, Segun Ogungbemi, "An African Perspective on the Environmental Crisis" in *Environmental Ethics: Reading in Theory and Application*, ed. Louis Pojman, 203-209.

16. Walter H. O'Brian, "Man, Nature, and the History of Philosophy" in *Philosophy and Environmental Crisis*, ed. William T. Blackstone, 89.

* Segun Ogungbemi (2015) "Modern Science and Technology in Conflict with African Environmental Ethics" in Readings in Philosophy: Problems and Issues, ed. S. Ade Ali and Emmanuel O. Akintona, (Lagos: Triumph Publishers, 258-269.

CHAPTER 3

The Conflict In The Niger-Delta And National Interest

Introduction

The Niger Delta region in Nigeria comprises of nine states namely, Delta, Bayelsa, Rivers, Akwa-Ibom, Cross River, Edo, Ondo, Abia and Imo. The region is naturally endowed with natural resources like other parts of the country, particularly crude oil and gas. Because the region has large deposits of oil and gas resources, which most parts of the country do not have; and more importantly the world market is in need of those resources, and of course, the country itself depends largely on them as well, it has made the region very important not only to Nigeria but also to the world economy. It has become very glaring that Nigerian economy is over dependent on those resources at the expense of exploration or exploitation and utilization of other resources, like agriculture and other minerals that are in abundance in other parts of the country. This has made Niger Delta ironically vulnerable to environmental degradation, pollution and gross underdevelopment. As a result of oil exploration, exploitation and gas flaring by oil and gas corporations like Shell BP, Exxon-Mobil, Total, Chevron, Esso among others, the inhabitants of the region and particularly, the elites and the leaders over the years felt that they have been unduly exploited and a need for justice to be applied to alleviate their problem which generally has not been adequately addressed by the Nigerian government, hence the conflict. Therefore, the crisis in the Niger Delta region in Nigeria is a conflict of interests that borders on some specifics of human nature, the environment, security and development that Nigerian government needs to address by embracing a moral and philosophical approach. But in doing so, the nation state must consider the general interest of the citizenry. I have therefore, discussed issues of vital importance that are related significantly to the crisis in the Niger Delta region and the nation state and proffer some moral and philosophical solutions. Before we consider the moral and philosophical aspects of this work, it is important to know in brief the nature of the natural environment and the Niger Delta region.

Natural Environment/ Niger Delta Region

Before the advent of man in the region it can be postulated that the habitats enjoyed the serenity of peace and its aesthetic natural appeal except perhaps occasional natural occurrences like storms, boisterous winds etc which on their own have added to natural wonder for any intelligent beings to appreciate and grapple with because of its metaphysical and empirical splendor. But that was not to continue eternally as the presence of man was going to change all that. It could be likened to the biblical story of the creation of the universe which when its creation was consummated with the making of man, the Creator was pleased with his artistic work and concluded that it was very good but he later regretted to have included man in the creation of the universe. Now let us see how the creation of the Niger Delta region in Nigeria encapsulates the creation of the Hebraic universe. The natural estate of man as far as he was concerned was and still is self-preservation and how to cope with the exigencies of life. The natural environment with which he was to co-exist provided a convoluted thought of his role in a polarity of existence plus his natural instinct of aggressiveness, egoism, adventurism, and pride. The first group of humans that populated what we know as Niger Delta region was basically living a rural agricultural life style with a complete ignorance of most of the things in the environment. Perhaps they were more concerned about how to feed and live; what we can call a minimal existence. They were probably living a philosophical life of eat, drink and be merry for tomorrow you die. Their knowledge of most of the natural resources at their disposal namely, oil and gas was like the allegory of the cave by Plato, the little ray of light had not shone for the people inside to see, hence its ignorance. People living in the Hebraic knowledge of the Universe did not even know that the group of people living in the Niger Delta existed neither the people of the region were aware of the existence of other human beings who could have courage to come and invade their region. The question is, were the ethnic groups, Edos, Itsekiris, Ijaws, Ibibios, Ogonis, Ilajes, Urhobos, Effiks, Isokos etc the original occupants of the region or they were mere invaders whose descendants today claim its ownership? By the virtue of their occupation as agrarians and fishermen and women who by natural accident of adventurism, in the course of farming and fishing, found the region conducive for their existence. Is it not true to say that before humans began the occupation of the region and generally the universe, the other living habitats were the original owners? The idea of ownership of land, water and mineral resources emanated from the inability of the other habitats to claim their ownership because of the level of their intelligence. It could also be the case that the biblical idea that Adam the first man created by the Hebraic Being entrusted the universe into his hand thereby making man the owner of all the natural resources which eventually became the basis for all human tribes to become owners of their environments. It could also be the case that the various ethnic groups of the Niger Delta area believe that the Creator of their universe made them the sole owners of whatever is in their region and they can be used for their well being. In other words, they have a moral claim and justification to use natural resources as they deem fit hence the beginning of their contribution to environmental deforestation, degradation and pollution. The belief that man has the sole authority to use whatever therein on earth as he likes with impunity because everything is under his control is not acceptable to the environmental ecologists who believe in animal rights.[1] As far as the environmental ecologists are concerned, it is nothing but human arrogance and a way to morally justify the injustices of man's treatment of animals and the environment. As far as they are concerned, man only coexists with nature and he has no moral rights to use his rational power and authority to violate the rights of other beings like animals. While the people of Niger Delta region might not subscribe to the ethics of the environmental ecologists, it does appear that they have their traditional environmental ethics of not taking more than they need from nature so that the gods would not be angry with them. By living according to the traditional ethical precepts of relating to nature with care, the environment was able to tolerate the level of their pollution, deforestation and degradation before the advent of modern science and technology with the attendant total disregard to the moral principle of traditional environmental life of the indigenes.

The genesis of oil exploration in Nigeria

The exploration of oil in Nigeria by Shell BP yielded some success in 1956 four years before her independence. At that time it was believed that the oil deposit in Nigeria particularly at Oloibiri now in Bayelsa State was of commercial quantity that was not expected to last long. As a matter of fact by 1957 according to G. Brian Stapleton (1967: 219) Nigeria exported one thousand metric tons of oil. The people in the Niger Delta region before then did not know that they were in the land "flowing with milk and honey" to use the Biblical metaphor to describe natural endowment of wealth. If the people had the premonition of the richness of the natural oil and gas deposited in a large quantity in their region and the knowledge of modern science and technology to do the exploration on their own, plus the vision that if they were to be part of Nigeria and would be denied the right to own their God given resources, as they currently experience in Nigeria, perhaps they would have opted not to be part of the country. The question is: why didn't the people in the Niger Delta area have knowledge of the natural resources of oil and gas before the advent of western science and technology? Richard Olaniyan (1982: 7) raised a fundamental question relating to the issue of African past and its environment, which is germane and relevant to Niger Delta region. "Why did the African culture fail to reach a level of technology comparable to that of Euro-America?" Olaniyan goes on to say that, "Without contact with the new ways and challenges coming from other societies where the new techniques had been evolved, it was impossible to effect any transformation in the traditional methods of solving problems posed by environmental constraints" (Olaniyan, 1982: 7). When some major western oil corporations, namely, Shell, Mobil, Exxon, Chevron etc discovered that the oil and gas found in the Niger Delta area is of large quantity and quality, they knew that Nigerian government would consider it a natural economic boom that could accelerate development throughout the country. Since a new way of doing things has been introduced through western science and technology in Nigeria specifically the oil and gas industry in the Niger Delta region: what are its impacts on the people, environment and the development of the region? Olaniyan observed that modern science and technology as good as it is, it nevertheless has its devastating effects on man and the environment.

He argues, "The traditional balance between man and nature has been complicated by the intrusion of a third factor into the equation, that is, science and technology. Although technology gives man greater control of his environment, its potential is double-edged: technology ill-applied, can as easily upset the delicate balance as it can, when carefully applied, lend itself to solving man's problems" (Olaniyan, 1982:9).

The environment of the areas where oil and gas activities take place became worse for it, that is, the traditional farming and fishing of the people in those areas suffer pollution, degradation and neglect. And the people are saying why this? The environment from where the oil and gas are produced would naturally wonder, if they had the capacity to reason, the kind of co-tenants human beings are. The natural aesthetic beauty of the land and water has been degraded and polluted. The peace that had been part of the inhabitants before modern technology was employed to exploit the oil and gas has turned to nightmare.

It is not the case that the Niger Delta area has not benefited from the advancement of the new technology in their area. The natural environment of their ancestors has witnessed new development that has turned some of the rural areas to urban or cosmopolitan cities namely, Port Harcourt, Yenagoa, Calaba, Warri, etc. The introduction of western technology gave rise to new form of life and institutions of higher learning, industries, and businesses with employment opportunities including tourism, which made some of the towns and cities the pride of Nigerians. Is the introduction of modern technology the cause of the insurrection in the region?

Crisis in the Niger Delta

When it comes to the root cause of conflict between the rulers and the ruled the observation of Kwame Nkrumah is instructive. "The nature and cause of the conflict between the ruling class and the exploited class is influenced by the development of productive forces, that is, changes in technology; the economic relations which these forces condition; and the ideologies that reflect the properties and the psychology of the people living in the society" (Nkrumah, 1978:74).

It is against this backdrop that the crisis in the Niger Delta can be adequately viewed. The agitations of the Niger Delta people for a redress of injustice done to them in terms of denial of infrastructure, pollutions of the environment by the industrial oil companies, etc is not a recent phenomenon. It has an historical background that dated to the time Isaac Adaka Boro and his armed group decided, according to Edwin Madunagu, "…to challenge the power and authority of the Nigerian State in the Niger Delta in January and February 1966…" (*The Guardian*, Thursday, June 25, 2009, 73). That struggle was not to last because of the military coup of January 15, 1966 and the subsequent Nigerian Civil War from 1967 to 1970. The struggle against the oil corporations particularly, Shell BP to clean up the oil spillages in Ogoniland was spearheaded by Ken Saro-Wiwa, a social critic and an environmentalist who was murdered together with eight Ogonis who were accused of killing four Ogonis leaders under the Abacha administration. Most people saw the gruesome killings of Ken Saro-Wiwa and his group under Abacha administration on November 10, 1995 as a violation of their human rights. The international community was infuriated by the way and manner Abacha ordered their execution most especially when the Commonwealth which Nigeria is a member appealed to Abacha to temper justice with mercy while holding its meeting in Auckland. (Ogungbemi, 2007:54-55). Some years after the death of Ken Saro-Wiwa and his group including Abacha who ordered their execution, Shell Corporation however, made a good gesture of compensation to the family of Ken Saro-Wiwa that was seen from the standpoint of moral conscience after the evil deed had been done. The intellectual and a nonviolent approach of Ken Saro-Wiwa and his group was seen by the different interest groups that later emerged as militants in the Niger Delta region as an unproductive method to get justice from the Federal government. The militants felt that a more robust, vibrant and militant approach was a better option. How did it all begin, one may ask? According to Simon Ekpe:

> Some said youths who were armed to help rig elections transformed into militants after they were abandoned by their sponsors. Others have also claimed that those who were armed to protect ships involved in oil theft later acquired enough money through the oil trade to arm themselves and ward off security agencies that might try to stop them. They too later became militants. (*The Punch*, Wednesday, August 12, 2009, 80)

It does appear that the root cause of the militants to choose a violent approach rather than the rule of law or a nonviolent approach to get moral and legal justice is basically greed and corruption. There is another group that can be classified as the elites that comprises of political and office holders, traditional rulers and elders in the Niger Delta region who appears as unseen hands supporting the militants but their demands for justice are truly genuine and reasonable. Some of their reasonable demands are: development of the area in terms of basic infrastructure and amenities, i.e., roads, water, housing, electricity, hospitals, employment for the youths, environmental protection of the land, air and water, security, resource control of the oil minerals and gas, creation of more states in the area etc. As far as the elite group is concerned, the above demands are sacrosanct that cannot be compromised, if there is going to be peace and harmony that will secure and protect the national interest in the region. Suffice to say however, that some other privileges and demands by the elite had been met by the Federal Government namely, establishment of a Ministry of Niger Delta Affairs, upgraded the Institute of Petroleum Technology to a Federal University of Petroleum University located at Effurun and of course, the monthly revenue allocation to their states which is based on derivation of 13%.

It is a fact that more than 85% of national oil revenues come from the region. In spite of what the Federal government has done the elite felt that their demands have not been adequately and properly placed on the front burner of the Federal Government policy therefore, the struggle to get justice became imperative hence their clandestine support of the militants. The ethical issue therefore is: should a militant approach be a moral course to be used against the state rather than a noble and just means? Should the state use force to repress the insurgent act of the militants bearing in mind that national interest and national security is the primary duty of the state? Which way ought the Federal Government of Nigeria take to bring peace to the area; and the whole nation at large, and to have more economic revenues from the region and retain the confidence of the oil corporations exploiting oil and gas in the region? In other words, what should government do to assuage the perceived injustices done to the Niger Delta region? Has government solution seen as coming too little and too late? What of the oil corporations exploiting oil in the region? Do they have confidence that the solution of government to the problems in the region will enable them to do their business with the assurance of security of both life and property? And how is Nigeria image being portrayed internationally bearing in mind of the importance of the country as one of the largest oil producing states particularly in Africa and the world in general? In short whatever happens to the oil region in Nigeria has its impact on the global economy. The world is a global village when it comes to economy, communications and information dissemination etc.

The dimension of violence in the region which characterized the activities of the militants and their sponsors inadvertently affected the economy of the state and painted an ugly picture of the former President Yar'Adua administration as weak and ineffective. It has portrayed the government as a toothless dog that cannot live up to its constitutional responsibility to the nation in terms of security of life and property. Of course, I believe no government that is worth its salt would fold its arms and allow such militants and their allies to carry on their lawless activities without being repelled. What has government done? There were two concrete approaches at the disposal of Federal Government to employ namely, dialogue and military force. The Yar'Adua administration undoubtedly used both methods. The dialogue approach which is civil in nature involved all the stakeholders in the region with a view to stopping the militants from their destructive devices of oil and gas installations and put an end to kidnappings and killings of innocent citizens and foreigners who work in the oil sector and to allow the Niger Delta Development Commission (NDDC) to continue its development of the region. When the method of dialogue did not dissuade the militants from their violent act against national interest the right thing the state ought to do according to Arnold Wolfers (1975:56-57) was to resort to force. "Firmness and even resort to force may under certain circumstances require less loss of life, less human suffering, less destruction of faith and principle than the most sincere attempt to eliminate the causes of hostility by concessions." It became expedient for the Federal Government to use a minimum force of action by setting up a Joint Military Task Force (JTF). The attendant result of government's Joint Military Task Force (JTF) to dislodge the militants in their various camps was not without causalities of innocent individuals on both sides although the casualties of the indigenes of the south-south region were considered greater particularly the people of the Gbaramatu kingdom. The impact of the use of force or the military might of the Federal Government and perhaps with the subtle diplomacy by the stakeholders in the region made the militants to have a rethink of their criminal activities against the state. The Yar'Adua administration came with a solution of amnesty for the militants who are willing to lay down their arms for peace. The duration set for the militants to turn in their ammunition for peace was from August 6 - October 1, 2009. There were expressions of doubt and criticisms of government against this course of action by social critics all over the country that the amnesty would not work. Besides, critics have argued why should government set aside fifty billion naira to rehabilitate repentant militants when the money could have been set aside for more domestic and infrastructural development of the area? But this skeptic and pessimist view has not deterred the government that believes in the positive action of the amnesty. Whether the amnesty worked or not, requires an in-depth study.. The relatively positive response from the militants so far to the offer of amnesty, the Yar'Adua administration feels convinced that the amnesty would work. Be that as it may, the acceptance of inadequate provision of infrastructure and the underdevelopment of the Niger Delta by President Yar'Adua that forms a part of the proclamation of the amnesty raises some moral questions. If the government was aware that the people of Niger Delta have not been given their moral and economic entitlements in terms of the development of the region, why did the Federal Government over the years have to wait until the militants raised arms against the state before giving them their dues considering the strategic importance of the region to the economy of the nation state? Were the previous governments so oblivious of their constitutional responsibility to the people in the Niger Delta? Normally, one would have considered the adage that says a stitch in time saves nine instructive and the government would have borrowed a leaf from it to avert the tragedies and economic wastes over the years in the region, which is the hallmark of a good state.

A Good State and Good Governance

A good state according to Plato is one that a philosopher king or queen who becomes a philosopher and governs by the precepts of reason and justice for the harmonious existence and peace of the citizenry governs it. (Plato, 1975).[2] The purpose of having a good state according to Aristotle is for one to achieve a supreme good of life which is a life of contemplation. It is a life of supreme happiness or satisfaction. To Aristotle it is a life of contemplation that brings happiness. (Bedau ed., 1971).[3] One derives supreme goodness from philosophy. In other words, philosophy invigorates the importance of human value. Aristotle is right, but human happiness cannot be divorced from material and social needs. Furthermore, according to (Thomas Hobbes, 1978),[4] the role of the state is to ensure that there is peace and security. And the state can do so even if it has to curtail some of the freedoms of individuals. However, there are others like John Locke, John Stuart Mill etc who believe that the major reasons why we have a state are to secure human liberty and property because all these contribute to the well-being of both individuals and the state (Locke, 1965 and Mill, 1962).[5] Within Africa, for example, Nkrumah and Obafemi Awolowo propounded a socialist political system that would provide the basic needs of their people which is a characteristic of a good state.[6] I am not unmindful of other African political theorists like Julius Nyerere, Daniel arap Moi, Kenneth Kaunda etc who have contributed to how African peoples could overcome poverty, diseases, and live a better life under the governance of good leadership.

Having given a brief synopsis of a good state, can we say that Nigeria is a good state? It may be difficult to answer positively or negatively depending on the side one is politically and economically considering the rebranding effort of the nation by the Yar'Adua administration. Or it depends on the experience or orientation one has of what is going on in the country. From our experience, the military have demonstrated at different times their displeasure over the ineptitudes of the leadership of this country by staging coups (Oyediran, 1979)[7] periodically even though their leadership overall was worse than the civilian administrations they had toppled. From my personal experience, in 1996 I escorted my 16-year-old son to the American embassy in Lagos for his immigrant visa. At the interview, since he was young I thought I could assist him answer some of the questions he had to answer but the lady who was interviewing him asked me whether he could speak English language and he answered that he could speak the language fluently. So I did not need to assist him. He was asked why he wanted to go back to the U.S as a citizen. One of his responses was that he regretted to have been born in Nigeria. I was astounded and I said son, I was born and bred here and I am not ashamed or regretted to have been born in Nigeria. If I your father was not ashamed to have been born here why should you? His answer was, that is you Dad. Judging by the number of Nigerians seeking immigrant visas at the embassies and consulates of America, Europe, and Russia etc in Nigeria for the past 20 years with the hassles they went through with desperation; one would normally suggest that their nation state has failed them. The political elites have jettisoned the call to embrace the principle of justice as fairness of (John Rawls, 1999: 52-53) or apply the utilitarian principle of maximization the greatest good for the greatest number of people to reduce poverty and misery of most Nigerians. It is not out of place or out of the ordinary that the crisis in the Niger Delta over the years and particularly in recent times is an expression of the inability of the country to respond positively, vibrantly and robustly to the common good, which they morally and ethically deserved. In other words, the principle of distributive justice that proposes equitable distribution of the wealth of the nation invariably is seen by many Nigerians to be lopsided. There is the need for the government to embrace good governance to assuage the stray nerves of the Niger Delta people and all Nigerians, if the country is to flourish and remain united. The most probable means of achieving it is to evolve a dynamic and authentic democratic culture. It is a democracy that produces leadership by example which takes the welfare of its people on the front burner of its policy. It is leadership of action and not of rhetoric and corruption. It is leadership that believes in education that empowers and makes its people to flourish. It is the leadership that recognizes Nigerian spirit of resilience and pride of nationhood. It is the leadership that believes that the future begins with good policies that will give right direction to enhance the quality of life of the people and the generation to come. The democracy Nigerians needs is that which respects and sustains the constitutional arrangement of governance, which is the hallmark of a good state.

Democracy grows and develops in a society that believes in its ideals and values namely, freedom or liberty, due process, the rule of law, justice and fairness. How this can be achieved is left for Nigerians to decide. They have to decide the kind of democratic culture of their own which of course will not be a laughing stock to themselves and the rest of the world at large but rather the one that engenders quality of leadership with vision and action.

This democratic culture is part of what I consider to be an embodiment of a sound culture, which Bernard Eugene Meland (1953: 120) has aptly expressed thus:

A sound culture, we might then propose, is: (a) democratic in its organization of life; (b) concern for the well-being of its citizens, that is, attentive to the standard of living particularly as this applies to health, comfort, and security; (c) and adequately industrialized to facilitate the production and distribution of goods so that both democracy and human well-being might be assured.

The value of philosophy to national interest is to draw the attention of the leaders to Nigerian basic needs not only by providing logical arguments but also employing moral persuasions. It is the duty of philosophers to train both the present and future leaders so that when it is their turn to lead, philosophy becomes their guide or at least a point of reference when decisions that involve human well-being or the supreme good are to be taken. The current waves of corruption, electoral frauds, kidnappings, disregard to due process and the rule of law etc are impediments to national development.

Conclusion

I began this Chapter with an introduction and moved on to look at the original condition of Niger Delta from a metaphysical and empirical perspective comparatively however, with the Biblical story of creation. I set in motion the idea that the universe in which man found himself including the inhabitants of the Niger Delta could not have been its owner because other living organisms were the original habitants and human beings are simply co-tenants. Be that as it may, I am not unaware of the fact that the authority to dominate the universe that the traditional belief of the people ascribes to the injunction of a Supreme Being is nothing but a means to justify their abuse of the environment in any form they like. The impression I have created is that the claim that the indigenes of the Niger Delta own the land has no moral claim except of course, by virtue of being rational agents or by association having been the dominant individuals and groups on the land. By application I only observe that humans do not own the universe they simply co-exist with nature. We came to this world with nothing and at death each one goes back likewise. So who owns the world? If the universe as we know it is not owned by man then, why killing ourselves over natural resources?

The main thrust of my argument is the identification of the root cause of the problem or crisis in the Niger Delta and who are responsible for it and the solution I proffer is a political system inherent in an authentic democracy that embraces the moral and philosophical ingredients of good governance that produces a good state. The people of the Niger Delta area had to resort to violence because Nigeria is not practicing an authentic democracy, which is people friendly and result oriented. The view of J. Olubi Sodipo on Nyerere's Ujamaa and its relevance to human society anywhere and everywhere that shares some moral principles with an authentic democratic culture collaborates what contributes to a good state.

> The basic ideals of the philosophy are human dignity and human equality and these ideals involve the elimination of ethnicity, ignorance and poverty, the promotion of mass participation in government and the provision of employment and decent life to all citizens (Fadahunsi and Oladipo ed., 2004:45).

The problem or the crisis that is man made, as it in the case of the Niger Delta and elsewhere, in my opinion, requires a solution which can be found by man alone using his natural faculty in which morality and philosophy play a vital role.

References

Ake, Claude (1981), *A Political Economy,* New York: Longman.

Meland, Bernard Eugene (1972), *Faith and Culture*, London: Feffer & Simons.

Nkrumah, Kwame (1978), *Consciencism*, London: Panaf.

Ogungbemi, Segun (2007), *Philosophy and Development*, Ibadan: Hope Publications.

Olaniyan, Richard (1982), *African History and Culture,* Lagos: Longman Nigeria.

Rawls, John (1999), *A Theory of Justice Revised Ed.* Cambridge: The Cambridge Belknap Press of Harvard University Press.

Sodipo, J. Olubi *Philosophy and the African Prospect* in Ayo Fadahunsi and Olusegun Oladipo ed. (2004), Ibadan: Hope Publications.

Stapleton, Brian (1967), *The Wealth of Nigeria,* London: Longman.

Wolfers, Arnold (1975), *Discord and Collaboration: Essays on International Politics*, Baltimore: John Hopkins University Press.

NOTES

1. See Louis Pojman, (1997), *Environmental Ethics: Reading in Theory and Application*, Boston: Jones and Bartlett Publishers.

2. See Plato, (1975), *The Republic* Translated by Francis Cornford, New York: Oxford University Press.

3. CF, Aristotle, "Justice" in *Justice and Equality*, ed. Bedau, A. Hugo (1971), Englewood Cliffs: Prentice- Hall.

4. CF, Thomas Hobbes, (1978), *Leviathan*, London: Collier Books.

5. CF, John Locke, (1965), *Two Treaties of Government*, New York, A Mentor Book, and John Stuart Mill, (1962), *Utilitarianism*, Glasgow: William Collins.

6. Kwame Nkrumah and Obafemi Awolowo were the most vibrant advocates of socialism in West Africa.

7. See Oyeleye Oyediran, ed. (1979), *Nigerian Government & Politics under Military Rule (1966-1979)*, London: Macmillan Press.

* Segun Ogungbemi (2010) "The Conflict in the Niger Delta Region and National Interest" in *Oil Violence in Nigeria: Checkmating its Resurgence in the Niger Delta* (ed.) Victor Ojakorotu and Lysias Dodd Gilbert, Saarbruken, Germany: Lambert Academic Publishing, 167-180.

Part Two

POLITICS, CUSTOMS AND SOCIAL VALUES

CHAPTER 4
Pan-Africanism And Nationalist Consciousness

Introduction

Nothing is good in itself as self-esteem. Therefore, when one has self-esteem one normally takes pride in oneself and in his identity and cultural values that are morally warranted. In the case of Africa, the mantra of African oneness and the spirit of unity that orchestrate a progressive vision and mission from the initial Pan African Movement without adequate interrogation of the impact of Nationalist orientation of ethnic consciousness with the attendant colonial interests in Africa constituted a weakening verve in the actualization of sustainable development of the continent.

My approach to the issue of Pan Africanism and African Nationalist Consciousness in relation to its primary goals and objectives with regard to sustainable development of the continent is both ethical and philosophical. It begins by raising some fundamental questions about its concepts of socio-cultural and political attainable ideals within Africa. Did Africans ever conceive themselves as united groups of people before the advent of European incursion to the political set up by Africans in the continent? If they did, how did slave trade and colonialism thwart their spirit of unity and oneness? Or was it not the case that the Africans before slave trade and colonialism never conceived themselves united given the language barriers, tribal or ethnic conflicts and wars, political and economic interests of the medieval emperors, lack of adequate means of communication and transportation within the continent, poor road network systems etc? Furthermore, were there adequate means of education and training to engrain and foster the spirit of unity among various and diverse ethnic groups? It cannot be denied that ignorance of the length and breadth of the continent including the knowledge of multifarious ethnicities in the continent was pervasive. Of course, there was and still is greed, like any other races in the world, for wealth and power at the expense of unity on the part of African leaders which had made Africa what it was in the past and what it is to some extent today. Recognizing the fact that Pan Africanism and Nationalist Consciousness were political and social ideals of African elite, intellectuals in America and Europe with objectives to liberate or emancipate the Black race and the entire continent from slavery and colonization and to restore the pride and dignity of the people, I have argued in this chapter that given some pragmatic suggestions on how the spirit of African oneness and unity in contemporary Africa or Africa in the 21st century can achieve sustainable development within the web of globalization, which I conceive to be the pride of being African is worth pursuing.

Africa before Trans-Atlantic Slave Trade and Colonialism

Any discourse on the subject of Pan Africanism and Nationalism will normally have at least a brief overview of the historical antecedent of the condition of the continent before going into the anthropological, social, political, economic, philosophical, religious, aesthetic etc exploration of what a scholar or an intellectual wants to discuss. I am not unaware of great works done on Africa by Basil Davidson, Samuel Johnson, F. K. Buah, J.F. Ade Ajayi, Philip D. Curtin, Adu Boahen, Toyin Falola, Kwame Nkrumah, Walter Rodney, Ali Mazrui, Claude Ake, Oluwafemi Mimiko, Frank Willet, William Bascom, John S. Mbiti, J. Olubi Sodipo and amongst others from their various and diverse intellectual perspectives.

Africa is the second largest continent in the world next to Asia with the land mass of 11,704,000 square miles or 30,312,000 square kilomiters.[1] It is estimated that there are over 800 indigenous different languages spoken in Africa[2] which undoubtedly would have made it very difficult to interact easily and foster unity and security needed for development. In spite of this, it is indubitable that in Africa before the coming of the Europeans right from the Neolithic age through the medieval eras, the imprint of development of different parts of the continent was remarkable. For instance, "The tropical African Neolithic, in contrast, gave rise especially to the advanced mixed agricultural tradition of the Western Sudanese savannas, where at a later date the great medieval empires of Ghana, Mali, and Songhai rose and fell."[3] Africa was known for her natural resources. For instance, Ghana was considered " a country where gold grows like plants in the sand in the same way as carrots do, and is plucked at sunset…The ruler of Ghana was considered the wealthiest of all kings on the face of the earth on account of the riches he owns and the hoards of gold acquired by him...that even dogs which guided the king while he sat in state wore collars of gold and silver."[4] Adu Boahen considered all this as mere exaggeration although there were evidences that the ruler of Ghana in the medieval was very wealthy.[5] One wonders that from the middle ages Africans could not pool their resources together and unite for the advancement of the continent. Was this as a result of greed on the part of the leaders of different empires or a mere ignorance of the need to harness the resources together to build a united continent? The glorious past of the continent cannot be swept under the carpet because that is where African descendants normally would have drawn inspirations for the task of carrying on the unfinished task of their forebears. The unfinished task of the forebears, in this case, is the unity and development of the continent. From the Neolithic age to the medieval and to about the 16th century or before trans-Atlantic slave trade, Africa and Africans were respected for their achievements when compared with Europe and other parts of the world.[6] Be that as it may, Africans were ill prepared for what became known of the negative description of Africa as a Dark Continent. Yes, Africa became "A Dark Continent" to those who did not have the knowledge of the geography of its location. The dark description of Africa by the Europeans was primarily to justify their exploitation of the continent. The continent has never been a dark space considering the amount of sunshine everyday and moonlight as nature dictates.

Africa became the place where Trans Atlantic slave trade flourished for about 300 years. Understandably to students and scholars of history that was the dark part of her history. The event to re-write her history was made by her own descendants in the diaspora and those in the continent. Arguably, it is the outcome of slave trade that led to Pan Africanism and African nationalism. Africa was prone to exploitation by the simple fact that Africans did not see themselves as a 'homogeneous' group whose interest was primarily unity, security and sustainable development. But that is not unique to African alone. It is a natural order found in other continents namely, Europe, Asia, North America and South America. It seems to me that the generosity and kindness of Africans to foreigners was crucial to their vulnerability to people they trusted and took care of as foreigners or strangers without knowing their negative intentions. The strangers were wolves in human clothing! Could this be due to ignorance on the part of Africans? It could probably be the case or simply a limited natural and human unawareness?

The origin and nature of the spirit of Pan Africanism and Nationalism

The spirit of Pan Africanism is grounded primarily in the psychological, historical, and social condition of a race dislodged from its root as a result of slavery and colonization. The nostalgic feelings of loss of freedom and the disengagement of the interactive relationships with one's kith and kin in a new life of servitude and loneliness in foreign lands, under normal circumstances would elicit a psychological yearning for a return to one's homeland. To both Africans on the continent and in the diaspora, it is generally believed that "Africa remains the 'homeland' that has facilitated the construction of the identity of blackness."[7] It is on this *homeland belief syndrome* that Africans, wherever they are, take pride of their belongingness. On the origin of Pan-Africanism, Ndabaningi Sithole writes:

> Formulated Pan-Africanism owed its existence to the Negro and African intellectuals. While the desire for things black or African was conceived in the hearts of millions of inarticulate Negroes and African masses, the intellectuals saw to it that this desire was carefully analyzed, reasoned out, and given the fullest articulation. They gave it direction, and a good programme, and continued to give it full backing until it became a universally recognized force to reckon with. They gave this deep desire, this aspiration in the black soul, a theory, which did not fail to move the hearts of those who loved and prized human freedom above everything else, and they gave it a practice that moved many into positive action to realize freedom for the black man.[8]

In a similar vein J.I. Dibua writes:

> Most scholars agree that the origin of Pan-Africanism can be traced to the era of the European slave trade when enslaved Africans, whether en-route to the New World or already in the New World, grieved and longed to reunite with their kin on the African continent. This implies that the origin of Pan-Africanism is related to the activities of African descendants in the diaspora.[9]

Dibua explains further:

> Michael Williams, however, has argued that the origin of Pan-Africanism can equally be traced to the African continent during the period of the slave trade. Africans in Africa who lost relatives

and members of their ethnic groups to slavery 'manifested a pristine desire for Pan-African unity by grieving for their relatives' safe return to Africa.' [10]

From the foregoing, Pan-Africanism, rather the spirit of Pan-Africanism, is primarily the manifestation of the dynamic and collective 'power' of Africans who went through the traumatic experiences of slavery and their yearnings for freedom and human dignity that they had lost. It is significant to note that the 'seed' of Pan-Africanism was 'sown' in Africa and 'germinated' in the Americas and Europe. What a paradox one may say but the reality of it is what became the source and inspiration to African-Americans in the diaspora and Africans on the continent of Africa that revolted against slavery, racial discrimination, oppression, colonialism, imperialism etc and the restoration of African freedom and dignity. The protagonists of Pan-Africanism generally belonged to two categories namely, Africans in the diaspora and Africans on the continent of Africa. One of the leading figures and the founders of Pan-Africanism was Marcus Garvey. He was a man who understood his background in the sense of the historic condition that made him to be in West Indies, a foreign land and his disconnection from his African root. And beyond that, he was well aware that to attain manhood, one of the necessary but not sufficient conditions is freedom of the mind that enables one to think rationally and to plan one's own destiny. In other words, education was a key component of self-discovery and without which Africans in diaspora would continue to live in misery, poverty and servitude. To free themselves from their social condition of bondage, Africans in the diaspora had to activate their innate human capacity to reason in order to demand for equality, freedom and justice. Garvey explains:

> The Negro is no cast-off, it is true that within the last few centuries white men have enslaved us, and scattered millions of us in the Western world, but we are still a majority of our continent-Africa, we are in the majority in the territories of the Caribbean, and we are a sizeable minority in the United States of America. We must now completely free our minds to think in terms of full manhood and to guide our own destiny.[11]

Garvey's Pan-Africanism was misconceived and misconstrued particularly his *Call to Africa*. To those who misunderstood him and his *Back to Africa Movement*, the idea of *the Call to Africa* meant that all the slaves still alive in the Western world and their descendants should go back to Africa because that was where they belonged and still is where they really belong. He explicates that what he meant by the *Call to Africa*:

> But what is the truth of the whole matter? The Back to Africa Movement is rather a simple, natural, logical and spiritual "Call to Africa". A spontaneous prompting, an irrepressible urge has found its birth in the minds of the Sons of Africa in all places of the earth in which they dwell. Silent, unheralded, swift and mysterious, out of the depths of their misery and suffering, out of their woes and despair has arisen an indescribable cry, a wail of lamentation- indefinable, yet heard, understood, interpreted, defined and reproduced in the clarion call of Garvey; reverberating and re-echoing in the now clear and unmistakable language of an oppressed and down-trodden people who cry for deliverance, and has at last moved the Omnipotence of the Deity into action.[12]

The charismatic posture of Garvey coupled with his power of oratory that accosted his speeches on freedom and liberation of African peoples from the oppression and exploitation of the white race made him to be at loggerhead with authorities in the Western world. Dibua writes:

> Perhaps the best-known Pan-Africanist advocate who espoused the emigration sentiment was Marcus Garvey. Although his movement has been unfairly portrayed as being primarily concerned with the "Back to Africa" philosophy, Garvey was not just an emigrationist; he was thoroughly Pan-Africanist. His United Negro Improvement Association (UNIA) was committed to the promotion of the unity of people of African descent in all parts of the world, the restoration of the dignity of the black person, the economic empowerment of black individuals, and the liberation from the vestiges of colonialism. … The effectiveness of Garvey's Pan-Africanist ideals and anti-colonial sentiments were such that his movement and the Negro World were banned in British colonies.[13]

To the Western world, Garvey was a radical Pan-Africanist whose ideas were capable of fueling agitation for freedom, equality, and justice in Europe and the Americas where Blacks had been subjected to all forms of ill treatment and humiliation. Similarly, Garvey's contemporaries in the United States of America felt that his radical approach and the *Call to Africa* could not help their situation because most of the descendants of freed slaves could not trace their way back to Africa. More importantly, of what use would it be after the Blacks had been used for the development of the United States of America only to leave when it was time for harvest? Ali A. Mazrui argues, "the making of America was inseparable from the impact of people of African descent."[14] The question is: Would it not be better to take a more moderate approach to get their worth and service where their ancestors and they themselves had served? It would be foolhardy to leave certainty for uncertainty. The certainty in this case is the United States of America and the uncertainty is Africa where they did not know anybody. In addition, Africa was conceived to be poorer than the United States of America. So what sense would it make to leave a place that is economically more buoyant for a continent where poverty and ignorance stirred one in the face? A notable and more moderate contemporary figure of Pan-Africanism in the United States of America was W. E.B DuBois. According to Dibua, "DuBois believed in an intellectual-led gradualist Pan-African movement.... The feud between DuBois and Garvey made the Pan-Africanist movement split into two rival camps, the radical camp (led by Garvey and the (UNIA) and the moderate camp (led by DuBois)."[15] It is significant to note this idea of split between the so-called *radical* and *moderate* camps of Pan-Africanists because it manifested itself among African nationalists. It will be discussed later. There were several Pan-African congresses held. According to Kwame Nkrumah the first President of independent Ghana, "The First Pan-African Congress was held in Paris in 1919...Fifty-seven representatives from various African colonies and from the United States of America and the West Indies attended...The second Pan-African Congress was held in London in 1921."[16]

The most significant of all the congresses held before 1945 was the one in 1945 in Manchester. Nkrumah explains:

> Pan-Africanism and African nationalism really took concrete expression when the Fifth Pan-African Congress met in Manchester in 1945. For the first time the necessity for well-organized, firmly-knit movements as a primary condition for the success of the national liberation struggle in Africa was stressed. The Congress was attended by more than two hundred delegates from all over the world. ...The foundational purpose was identical: national independence leading to African unity.[17]

Furthermore Nkrumah writes, "Instead of a rather nebulous movement, concerned vaguely with black nationalism, the Pan-African movement had become an expression of African nationalism."[18] This takes us to the next category or group of Pan-Africanism. They were African leaders namely, Nkrumah, Jomo Kenyatta, Nnamdi Azikiwe, Julius Nyerere, Nelson Mandela, Milton Obote, Samora Machel, Leopold Sedar Senghor, Sekou Toure, Robert Mugabe[19] among others. The leading figure among them was Nkrumah of Ghana. The agenda of African leaders was profoundly the independence of African countries from their colonial masters. In other words, political independence of all African States including elimination of *apartheid* in South Africa was on front burner of their agenda. Secondly, unification of Africa plus security and economic emancipation of the continent were considered paramount but all these could not be achieved without freedom and independence of all African countries. It was political freedom first and all others would be added later. The tone of Pan-Africanists in Africa became a nationalist agenda. Abiola Irele explains, "The practical divergence between the Pan-African ideal and the concrete objectives of African nationalism which began to take place as soon as the latter took the form of independence movements, took what one might call a 'territorial turn'."[20] The basic issue, it seems to me, was the fact that African unity could not be fought first because the colonial masters had partitioned the continent among themselves - Britain, France, Portugal, Spain, Belgium, Germany and Italy. When one looks at the size of the countries of these foreign powers that ruled over Africa one is compelled to ask: What went wrong with a giant continent like Africa that exposed herself to this kind of political and economic plunder and savagery of the Europeans?

Since the continent was never homogenous and governed as such by Africans in the past and during the colonial era, each African leader had no choice but to put Pan-Africanist sentiment apart and faced the reality of the liberation of his people first and foremost - the sovereignty of his country.

Before most African countries attained independence, Nkrumah had begun the agenda of unifying Africa together. But his effort was punctuated because his approach to achieve it was considered *radical* and perhaps he did not tarry enough to allow a country like Nigeria to attain independence to be carried along before embarking on such an important African project. The group to which Nkrumah belonged was the Casablanca bloc which comprised the following countries, Ghana, Guinea, Mali, Libya, Egypt, Morocco and the Algeria.[21] If African Pan-Africanists and Nationalists were set out to free all African countries from political and economic invaders of Africa, one wonders while Nkrumah would invite Egypt, Libya, Morocco, and Algeria bearing in mind of the illegal occupation of the region by the Arabs? The colonization of North African countries[22] by the Arabs that predated the trans-Atlantic slave trade is equally condemnable as the colonization of other African countries by the Europeans? As a matter of fact, one of the primary assignments of African Nationalists ought to have been the liberation of North Africa from the domination of the Arabs. Arabs in North African countries have no moral justification to condemn Europeans for colonizing Africa when they, the Arabs, were and still are guilty of the same offense.

The Monrovia group that was considered moderate and sometimes conservative comprised Nigeria, Cameroon, Liberia, Togo, and Ethiopia, [23] among others. The bone of contention was political and economic. Both the *radical* and *moderate* groups wanted African unity but in what form or what nature would it take? The *radical group* wanted a strong political union of the continent while the *moderate group* opposed it. The *moderate group* wanted economic cooperation among member states "while moving gradually toward some form of loose political cooperation."[24] Of course "Each of these groups had its own idea about the form that Africa unity should take as articulated in their respective charters. Paradoxically, the events that were to lead to the demise of these two groups and the subsequent formation of a body representing all African countries started at Lagos conference."[25] It was in 1963 in Ethiopia that African nationalists were able to solve this division that almost tore them apart and a new body was formed as Organization of African Unity, OAU, which became the mouthpiece of Africa. But today the body that was formed in 1963 as, OAU, has metamorphosed to African Union, AU, in 2001. It is significant to note that Pan-Africanism and African Nationalism is the same coin of different sides. The former grew from the outcry of injustices and inequality of the treatment of African descends in the diaspora and the expression of missing their 'Home' that is Africa while the latter received inspiration and support from the former to fight for the independence of their countries from the European domination. The convergence in both struggles culminated in the formation of OAU, now AU, an organ established by African leaders that speaks jointly in support of African interests either within the continent or in the comity of nations. The independence of African countries became the milestone or epitome of achievement of both Pan Africanists and African Nationalists. Toyin Falola explains:

> Independence brought the joy of nationalism to its peak. Various figures became instant heroes and household names as freedom fighters and political leaders. The intelligentsia captured the moment in diverse ways: in writings, in the decolonization of school systems, arts, and culture, and in great confidence as citizens of 'free countries.' Universities established cultural and African studies

centers, and the professors radiated absolute confidence. Young men and women were motivated with Africans as their heroes - leaders like Obafemi Awolowo, Kamuzu Banda, Jomo Kenyatta, Sekou Toure, and Kwame Nkrumah. Millions of young men and women could attend school and travel, that is, 'become modern.' Many new national flags proclaimed the fresh feeling; external embassies announced the new status for the world to see; Africans walked tall, boasting to one another that a new dawn had arrived.[26]

At this juncture we must be reminded constantly that one of the instruments that brought African leaders and political heroes to the limelight that influenced their achievements and courage was western education. In this regard, we cannot forget the immense contributions of the mission schools in Africa.

African Oneness and her Unity in the 21st Century

The philosophy of African oneness is the affirmation and confirmation of uniqueness of African identity and self-esteem of being an entity of the Black race whether one is in Africa, the homeland or in the Diaspora. It is a facticity that one cannot deny no matter the situation or condition one finds oneself. It is a 'given' which nature has bestowed on anyone who is from the Black race. This African oneness carries with it a responsibility to reject inferiority and intimidation and affirms the dignity of Blackness. It is this spirit of oneness that inspired Pan-Africanists and African Nationalists to seek a total liberation of the enslaved and colonized Africans from their oppressors. The spirit of Blackness and oneness expresses the psychological and philosophical power of resilience and the articulation of moral and ethical imperatives of freedom and human dignity because all human beings were born equal. But African oneness is not the same thing as African unity neither is it synonymous with it. African unity is rather an effort by Pan-Africanists and Nationalists to unite all African countries to form a political and economic power under one umbrella and be named United States of Africa. But there are inevitable and serious problems with this tall ambition. Can Africans unite under one umbrella called United States of Africa with the domination of Arabs in North Africa? How reasonable is it to trust an Arab who becomes President of this body bearing in mind the danger of subjugating Africa and her peoples to Islam and total domination of Africa by Arabs? This kind of behaviour manifests itself in Sudan that has led to bloodbath of innocent Africans. But the people of Southern Sudan were determined to have their freedom and national sovereignty, which they finally got on July 9, 2011.

There are other perennial problems with the idea of a unified States of Africa. One of them is language. Language is power that strengthens and fosters unity. If we take United States of America, for instance, the fact that most of the people living in the country came from different backgrounds with different languages notwithstanding, the official language is English. Similarly, in China the most populous nation on earth, her people speak one language. In Britain, France, Germany, Portugal, Spain etc that formed European Union will not form a United States of Western Europe and use English Language as their official language. A language is a treasure of national identity, which should not be lost. So in Africa, the second largest continent in the world, where we have over 800 different languages, which language will be used as a national and official means of communication?

One other critical factor that is germane, in my view, is the form of government that a United States of Africa will embrace. Will it be a democratic socialism or a democratic capitalism or what? Considering the kind of leadership we have in Africa at present who among them will be elected as President of the United States of Africa? Chinua Achebe has this to say:

> If you take someone who has not really been in charge of himself for 300 years and tell him, 'O.K., you are now free,' he will not know how to begin. This is how I see the chaos in Africa today and the absence of logic in what we're doing. Africa postcolonial disposition is the result of a people who have lost the habit of ruling themselves, forgotten their traditional way of thinking, embracing and engaging the world without sufficient preparation. We have also had difficulty running the systems foisted on us at the dawn of independence by our colonial masters.[27]

The observation of Achebe describes the kind of political class and leadership as inexperienced cannot be disputed. As a matter of fact the nationalists diagnosed African leadership and social and political ailments and prescribed different means of cure but each attempt became more deadly than the disease. Falola writes:

> Focusing on variously on the 'National Question' ethnicity, integration, and so on, studies have tended to assume that nationalism and ethnicity are irreconcilable. The strategy of analysis has been to seek the means to destroy ethnicity, assuming that this will promote nationalism. Advocates of military rule, centralized socialist planning, and the one-party states have all reacted partly

> out of the fear of ethnicity.... Everywhere, the one-party state was a crude reincarnation of colonial authoritarianism. The desire to build a strong nation became a justification for destroying the citizens themselves. Rather than solve the problems of ethnicity, it has led to the intervention of the military.... In taking the countries backward, they have also taken many lives, since the competition for power is so destructive as to provoke civil wars. Millions of people have died in Nigeria, Somalia, Rwanda, Burundi, Sierra Leone, Chad, Niger, Zaire and the Sudan as leaders, both civil and military, fight to the bitter end for power.[28]

From the foregoing, African leaders have plunged their countries into political turmoil that led to conflicts and wars with many lives lost and property worth billions of dollars destroyed. Many remained till today in refugee camps. For instance, Ivory Coast, Libya, Tunisia, Somalia, Sudan, etc. where political unrest has caused a total dislocation of their people who already have been traumatized by poverty, diseases, and ignorance. In recent time, Dambisa Moyo observes:

> Between 1981 and 2002, the number of people in the continent living in poverty nearly doubled, leaving the average African poorer today than just two decades ago. And looking ahead, the 2007 United Nations Human Development Report forecasts that the sub-Saharan Africa will account for almost one third of world poverty in 2015, up from one fifth in 1990 (this largely is due to the dramatic developmental strides being made elsewhere around the emerging world).[29]

What Africa needs most today are good leadership and good government. The political class that is fully conscious and committed to the sustainable development of Africa using human and natural resources that are abound in the continent to achieve this goal. The need to have credible leadership that is accountable to the people is now. Africa cannot afford to have a United States of Africa until the people are well educated in the art of governance. What we have in Africa is adequately captured in Aristotle's understanding of man and his politics.

He writes:

> For man, when perfected, is the best of the animals, but, when separated from law and justice, he is the worst of all; since armed injustice is more dangerous, and he is equipped at birth with arms,

meant to be used by intelligence and excellence, which he may use for worse ends. That is why, if he has not excellence, he is the most unholy and the most savage of animals, and the most full of lust and gluttony. But justice is the bond of men in states; for the administration of justice, which is the determination of what is just, is the principle of order in political society.[30]

Without disciplined leadership that has respect for law and justice, African leaders will continue to rule as if they own their countries and no outsiders should interfere in the domestic affairs. The political rulers in Africa like Mugabe of Zimbabwe, Laurent Gbagbo of Ivory Coast, Gaddafi of Libya whose regimes had been brought down by revolution are typical dictators who were not accountable to people they governed.

Conclusion

The present and future of the people on the continent of Africa must pursue peace and good leadership and not political ethnicity that is being used to hold on to power by African political class and leaders. And more importantly, the need for massive education and training of the teeming population of African children and youths including the girl-child is imperative. A pragmatic form of education with discipline, respect for human values and good governance, hard work, accountability and ingenious creativity and service delivery, among other social values should be some of the basic principles to be embraced in their institutions because they contribute to character formation and moral development of children and youths.

Unless there is a huge investment in human capacity building in education, there cannot be enviable oneness and development. It is when Africa has produced human materials of responsible behavior that the continent will be able to have a new political leadership that is properly schooled in the art of governance.

From the new elite of the masses they will decide the form of governance that is suitable for the continent. What is being conversed for here is that Africa in the 21st century must develop leaders that will consider their call to serve as a rare opportunity and not their right to loot the treasury of the State. Rather, to use their positions to serve the continent to achieve sustainable development and in my view, is the right way to go in the new age. And more importantly that is a form of patriotic behavior that adds value to African self-esteem and pride because as it is currently, the AU, the mouthpiece of Africa is weak because its members have not built a virile independent nation of political stability and economic viability to warrant global respect. Africa needs new leaders of 21st century positive mindset with vision and mission to rekindle African self-esteem and make Africa a great continent.

Notes and References

1. See Dennis Austin, "Africa." in *Collier's Encyclopedia,* Volume 1, 1983, 192-193.
2. See Joseph Greenberg, "African Languages" in Collier's Encyclopedia, Volume 1, 1983, 243-247.
3. Dennis Austin, "History" in Collier's Encyclopedia, Volume 1, 1983, 225-247.
4. Adu Boahen, *Topics in West African History,* (London: Longman, 1966), 5.
5. Adu Boahen, *Topics in West African History,* 5.
6. See Walter Rodney, Adu Boahen, and Toyin Falola
7. Toyin Falola, *The Power of African Cultures,* (Rochester: University of Rochester Press, 2003), 274.
8. Ndabaningi Sithole, *African Nationalism* 2nd *ed.* (London: Oxford University Press, 1968), 70.
9. J. I. Dibua, "Pan Africanism" in Toyin Falola (ed.), *Africa The End of Colonial Rule: Nationalism and Decolonization Volume 4,* (Durham: Carolina Academic Press, 2002), 29.
10. Ibid.
11. Amy Jacques Garvey & E.U. Essien-Udom (eds.), *More Philosophy and Opinion of Marcus Garvey,* (London: Frank Cass and Company Limited, 1977), 132.
12. Ibid 133-134.
13. J. I. Dibua "Pan Africanism" in Toyin Falola, 30-31.
14. Ali A. Mazrui *http://igcs.binghamton.edu/igcs_site/dirton12.htm.* Retrieved on 3/11/2010.
15. J. I. Dibua in Toyin Falola, 32.
16. Kwame Nkrumah, *Africa Must Unite,* (New York: International Publishers, 1963), 133.
17. Ibid., 134-135.

18. Ibid., 135.

19. Ehiedu E. G. Iweriebor, "Trends and Patterns in African Nationalism" in Toyin Falola Africa, (ed.), *Africa The End of Colonial Rule: Nationalism and Decolonization Volume 4*, 8.

20. Abiola Irele, *The African Experience in Literature and Ideology,* (London: Heinemann, 1981), 121.

21. See Kwame Nkrumah, *Africa must Unite, 143-145.*

22. See Kola Folayan "The Arab Factor in African History," (Inaugural Lecture Series 60, University of Ife, March 15, 1983).

23. Kwame Nkrumah, *Africa must Unite, 143.*

24. J. I. Dibua in Toyin Falola, 43.

25. Ibid., 45.

26. Toyin Falola, *Nationalism and African Intellectuals*, (Rochester: The University of Rochester Press, 2004), 109.

27. Chinua Achebe," Nigeria's Promise, Africa's Hope" *New York Times*, January 15, 2011.

28. Toyin Falola, *Nationalism and African Intellectuals,* 118-119. See also, Martin Meredith, *The State of Africa: A History of Fifty Years of Independence,* (London: Free Press, 2006).162-308, 485-573.

29. Dambisa Moyo, *DEAD AID: Why AID Is Not Working and How There is A Better Way for Africa*, (New York: Farrar, Straus and Giroux, 2009), 5.

30. Quoted in Louis Pojman, "Moral Saints and Moral Heroes" *Third Annual James Bond Stockdale Leadership and Ethics Symposium Post-Symposium* (San Diego: University of San Diego, 2000), 17.

* Segun Ogungbemi, (2014) "The Spirit of Pan-Africanism and Nationalist Consciousness: The Way Forward in the 21st Century" in *Pan-Africanism, and the Politics of African Citizenship and Identity* (ed.) Toyin Falola and Kwame Essien, New York: Routledge/Taylor and Francis Group, 202-214.

CHAPTER 5

Poverty In Africa: Its Causes And Moral Solutions

Introduction

Africa is a multinational and multicultural continent with people of pluralistic beliefs like other continents in the world. The nature of poverty in the continent must be approached with a liberal understanding of the attitude of Africans to poverty. From my research and dialogues with academic and intellectual colleagues sometimes one is not aware that he is poor until he has seen other climes where life is more abundant. This is sequel to my experience having lived in and visited several African countries. When I came to the United States of America in the 70s as a student and saw American lifestyle particularly the way and manner they wasted food on daily basis even till today, the infrastructural facilities and affluence displayed by the people which most Africans are unaware of, I came to a valid conclusion that most Africans were and are still poor. It is not necessarily because of conflicts and wars alone, I imagined were the causes of poverty in the continent but because of the level of Africa's technological advancement. The awareness of horrific nature of poverty ravaging Africa has been a source of national and international news in the United States of America, Europe, etc. The graphic pictures of malnourished children and their mothers carrying them on their backs and their fathers carrying the belongings on their heads and occasionally, the most fortunate among them put their loads on camels or donkeys. When you see some American celebrities on the television singing "We are the world. We are the children…let us start giving" it gives a resounding echo of the enormity of the need to save Africa from stricken poverty. In the last 50 years, conflicts and wars that erupted in some parts of Africa namely, Nigeria, Ghana, Liberia, Togo,

Sierra Leone, Ivory Coast, Mali, Cameroon, Angola, Sudan, Kenya, Democratic Republic of Congo, Uganda, Rwanda, Burundi, Ethiopia, Somalia etc., and Arab Spring in North Africa that resulted into destruction of property, displacement of people, loss of life and almost a complete desolation of villages and towns have worsened the level of poverty. What resonates the cause of these conflicts and wars and why they have become a recurrent decimal that remained unresolved to the extent that the whole world now sees Africa as a continent of pity? Must the foreign aid continue or must it stop? Does foreign aid contribute to poverty eradication in Africa or it has exacerbated the problem? Some scholars are divided on whether foreign aid should not be given to Africa while others say foreign aid is needed in spite of its attendant corruption or its abuse by political or government officials who divert some of it to their own purse.

I don't want to forget to mention natural causes of poverty and deadly diseases like drought, famine, smallpox, tuberculosis, etc. that are considered natural evil in religious and liberal ethics but the most vicious of all, in my view, is the moral evil that is human made. Therefore my focus here is moral evil namely, conflicts and wars, lack of good leadership and governance, greed and corruption, ethics of foreign aid, Africa's destiny and the imperative of aid. The import of this work, apart from assessing the moral evil with flurry of graphic news of victims across the length and breath of the continent, I have given some philosophical and moral arguments that are pragmatic and if followed, I believe, it will take Africa to a new haven of cutting edge technology and hopefully, world class prosperity.

Africa in my view, is not different from other climes that have waved their flags of good-bye to poverty and demonstrate their penchants for wealth and prosperity, aided by modern science and technology. The phenomenon of poverty and its corrosive effects on humans anywhere and everywhere is antidevelopment and antigrowth, which humans ought to fight and conquer. Now let me begin with some of the conditions of the state of affairs in Africa that have made Africa a pitiable continent since independence.

Conflicts and Wars

Wherever you have human beings living together there is always the tendency to have conflicts. It could be a domestic conflict - a conflict between husband and wife. There are conflicts within a macro society and the major cause invariably is injustice - inequitable distribution of wealth, positions and power among others. It can even be the insensitivity of the leadership to the growing yearning of the people over mismanagement of resources, abuse of power on the side of governments or the ruling class in the society. Conflicts can erupt as a result of land disputes among tribal or ethnic groups or as a result of foreign invasion. When conflicts cannot be resolved amicably, invariably it can lead to war. In short, conflicts and wars have been part of human existence everywhere in the world. What becomes inhuman about conflicts is that when they cannot be resolved and the aftermath of wars is human misery, poverty, starvation, death, devastation and degradation of environment.

Africa was not originally partitioned into countries, as we know it today. The partitioning of Africa was the handiwork of the Europeans namely, Britain, France, Portugal, Belgium, Italy and Germany in 1884 at the Berlin Conference. Colonization of Africa by these foreign powers has contributed to the incessant conflicts and wars since independence of African States. One would have expected the leaders of the new African States to work together to free Africa from poverty but that is not the case. Rather, African leaders have plunged the continent into political chaos and untold hardships of the citizenry. From 1960-2011 there have been about 60 instances of conflicts and wars in Africa. Let me give a few instances in Africa where conflicts and wars have impoverished the people and made the continent a pitiful State. I think the right place to begin is Nigeria being the most populous African State in the continent.

It is fair to say that Nigeria is not innocent when it comes to political violence and war. Let me mention the case of Biafra and the Federal government of Nigeria. On January 15, 1966 there was a military mutiny led by five army majors namely, Patrick Chukwuma Kaduna Nzeogwu, Emmanuel Arinze Ifeajuna, Donatus Okafor, Chris Anuforo and Adewale Ademoyega against a constitutionally elected political leaders of the Federal Republic of Nigeria. Out of the five soldiers who were majors in the Nigeria army, four of them were Igbos and one Yoruba. Major Chukwuma Kaduna Nzeogwu spearheaded the execution of the coup. The Prime Minister, Sir Abubakar Tafawa Balewa, the Premier of Northern Region, Sir Ahmadu Bello Sadauna of Sokoto, the Premier of Western Region, Chief Samuel Ladoke Akintola, Federal Minister of Finance, Chief Okotie- Eboh but no Igbo politician either at Federal or Regional governments was assassinated. The coup was generally conceived as 'Igbo coup' since most of the coup plotters were from the Igbo ethnic group. Among all the political leaders killed none was from Igbo ethnic group. Although the coup leaders denied that ethnic cleansing but its execution made people to have doubts about their overall intention. They claimed that their intention was to get rid of corrupt politicians and to cleanse some of the systemic socio-political ills. But from events that unfolded in Nigeria in the 60s it was difficult for people to close their eyes to the issue of Igbo ethnic intentions. The reprisals that followed in the North in which many innocent Igbos were killed made this belief more plausible. Lt. Colonel Odumegwu Ojukwu an Igbo felt that the pogroms against his people in the North and the gruesome murder of the first Military Head of State of Nigeria, Major-General Aguiyi-Ironsi an Igbo were disproportionally unjustified. More importantly nothing seemed to assuage the people of the North from killing innocent Igbos. Therefore Ojukwu and other Igbo leaders felt that the disproportionate reprisal was aimed at exterminating the Igbos of then Eastern region; if there was no acceptable political solution to it. My intention is not to write history of the Nigerian civil war (1967-1970) but rather to explain how it contributed to poverty and misery of the people and its psychosocial impact on humanity. During the war there were no forms of arable farming, no commercial activities, schools and tertiary institutions were closed, sounds of barrels of guns and bombs gripped the minds and created fear of the unknown to the Easterners in the defunct Eastern Region. There were starvation, malnourished children everywhere; dead bodies littered the streets and bushes, frustrations on the faces of fleeing parents etc. expressing human tragedy, misery, anguish and absurdity of existence. At the end of it all, several millions of lives were lost but the casualties were more on the side of the Igbos. Many people still harbor the agony and pain of the war till today. In other words, the agony of the war still remains in the psyches of many of the survivals and in history books in private and public libraries and archives. It seems to me that above all, the harrowing experiences of the survivals of the war are still being felt by generations of the Igbos both at home and in the diaspora.

This human tragedy also affected Steve Jobs as it was reported in his biography. He says:

> In July 1968 *Life* magazine published a shocking cover showing a pair of starving children in Biafra. Jobs took it to Sunday school and confronted the church's pastor. 'If I raise my finger, will God know which one I'm going to raise even before I do it?'
>
> The pastor answered, 'Yes, God knows everything.'
>
> Jobs then pull out the *Life* cover and asked, 'Well, does God know about this and what's going to happen to those children?' 'Steve, I know you don't understand, but yes God knows about that.'

Jobs announced that he didn't want to have anything to do with worshipping such a God, and he never went back to church.[1]

From the foregoing, Jobs' reaction tells another dimension to the Nigerian civil war. It reminds us that the world is a global village as a result of advancement in science and technology. We are reminded by Jobs' emotional reaction that human political and social inordinate ambition in any part of the world if not controlled has far reaching consequences elsewhere. Beyond Jobs' emotional distress after seeing photos of Biafra starved children it undeniably appealed to human moral consciousness. It is therefore, in my view, morally compelling for Nigerian political elites to embrace spirit of tolerance and avoid any provocation that is capable of leading to conflicts and warfare in future.

Africa has produced some leaders who have penchant for social and political violence as a means of getting to the seat of power and authority, There are also elected leaders and military juntas who perpetually wanted to remain in office without relinquishing power. Among such leaders was the former President Laurent Gbagbo of Ivory Coast or Cote d'Ivoire who lost an election but refused to hand over to Alassane Ouattara on the ground that Ouattara did not win the election. The truth of the matter is that he simply did not want to leave after ruling for ten years. He did not want to leave voluntarily until he was pushed out shamefully by foreign powers particularly, France. Unfortunately, he plunged the country into an unnecessary horrendous war that led to the death of many of his countrymen and women including children. The loss of property and psychological pain that his people suffered during the war was unimaginable.

The conflicts and senseless wars that took place in Africa are too many and far between. The kind of brutal murder of innocent men and women, children and the elderly not to mention the destruction of property, maiming and raping of women that had taken place in Somalia, Uganda, Burundi, Rwanda, Liberia, Sudan, among others cannot be morally justified. One wonders what the perpetrators of conflicts, violence and wars stand to gain. According to Toyin Falola:

> Warlords profit from political instability, turning it into advantages to create 'chiefdoms.' In such places, the emergence of warlords was preceded by wars, conflicts for power, or even the collapse of the states. Some warlords wish wars never end, as they benefit from what has been characterized as the 'market of violence,' a situation of permanent lawlessness.[2]

Joseph Kony a Uganda warlord is a typical example of the group who sees violence as a means of livelihood regardless of what rational and moral agents think about the immorality of their 'trade'. The military and their allies both inside and outside Africa are in my view mostly responsible for the crises that led to wars in Africa. Military leaders who toppled and forcefully removed democratically elected leaders like the former Prime Minister Tafawa Balewa of Nigeria in 1966, former President Kwame Nkrumah in Ghana, former President Patrice Lumumba in Congo Kinshasa among others because of their political and economic interests caused a setback in development which has made the continent to be wallowing in poverty.

Normally, human beings are made to live in corporate existence if they are to flourish and be happy. The natural environment given to humans has all the natural resources and if harnessed and distributed equitably the world will have no record of poverty stricken societies which Africa is notoriously known for. Poverty in this context according to Kolawole Olaniyan is "characterized by poor education, unemployment, bad health, and lack of access to basic services, which many in civilized society take for granted. Some may argue that the only poverty that counts is malnutrition, but scientific evidence suggests that even where basic needs are being met; relative poverty is bad for health and child development."[3] (*Punch* April 9, 2012.) Whatever yardstick used as indices to measure the level of poverty in Africa, the natural design of the continent is not meant that it should be poor. Rather, Africa and Africans like other human beings are made to contribute to the wealth of the rest of the world for human prosperity and sustainable development. In other words, as Nigel Dower argues:

> A fair distribution of the world's resources requires at the very least that all should have enough to meet basic needs. But for many people a fair distribution of the world's resources requires a lot more than this. It requires that many things, which are done in the world of international trade, and economic activity should be changed because they are in themselves unjust. What is done in and to developing countries may be seen as unjust, because of the exploitation of resources and of cheap labour.[4]

While Dower's argument is based on principle of justice, the natural state of Hobbesian state of nature is pragmatic.[5] Going by the historical events shown in Africa one does not need to be told whether Hobbes is right or not.

The road to peace, eradication of poverty and stability in Africa is good leadership and followership because the current condition of majority of Africans as rightly noted by Falola is that, "Poverty is so endemic that the best solution is not just in economic reforms, but in changing the nature of politics. Many realize that without good leaders and stable politics, their contract with poverty will be eternal."[6] If African leaders spend most of their productive times and resources fighting senseless wars, when will they have time for good governance that will benefit their people and remove Africa from the world economic index of poverty? What is the best way out?

Leadership and good Governance

Since independence of most African States, the continent has produced quality educated elites not to mention those who had their education under the colonial period whose primary mission and goal was to provide leadership and good governance to alleviate the burden of under-development of their people in Africa. Does having qualified educated elite necessarily provide Africans good leadership and good government in Africa? Of course not, but what it does is to provide a baseline of a necessary but not sufficient quality leadership and good governance. Africa needs well-educated people with 'civility' to productively govern the continent. But genuine or authentic leadership must acquire other sterling qualities in order to fulfill the yearnings and goals of African heroes/heroines who fought for the emancipation and independence of Africans from the bondage of colonialism. Contemporary Africans, in my view, must look for leaders who meet Joseph Allen's description and other scholars and intellectuals:

> The work of a political leader is a high calling - a vocation. Those who have pursued it with few moral scruples have given the name 'politician' an insulting connotation. But a political community cannot thrive without good leadership, and its leaders are by definition politicians – managers of political conflicts…. The calling of a politician is to seek to help the members of the community to express their covenant with one another and with the world beyond their borders.[7]

Linus Okorie believes that leadership from a professional perspective is "the ability to influence, motivate, and inspire a group of people towards a particular direction by inspiration, not intimidation or manipulation."[8] In other words conceptually and pragmatically "it is leadership that believes that the future begins with good policies that will give right direction that will enhance the quality of life of the generation to come."⁹ Having defined leadership as I have shown, what is good governance? Good governance is a sum total of provision of quality of life for the citizenry namely, food, shelter, clothing, good health care delivery, access to quality education and basic infrastructure and free Africans from her present predicaments.

The State of leadership and good governance in Africa

On October 1, 2010 Nigeria celebrated her 50th Independence anniversary with a hiccup of bomb blast adjacent to the venue of the celebration in Abuja. The nature of independence is freedom. The expression of that freedom in a violent manner as witnessed in Abuja - the capital of Nigeria on that day was antithesis to social and political values of a civilized nation. That incident was prophetic of what to expect in Nigeria within the next decade. The bomb blast on October 1, 2010 was morally condemnable but beyond its condemnation by all normal and rational human beings worldwide the impact of the economic realities on the populace was of greater importance. What has Nigeria done for Nigerians as a corporate nation? In other words, what benefits since independence did the citizens derive from her independence? This question can be answered either as an individual or as a corporate entity. What I want to underscore is the social and political responsibilities of the central government since independence to its people and how they have benefited from it? Furthermore, the issue is how accountable are the ruling class to the electorate? Are Nigerians better or worse off since independence? According to Kolawole Olaniyan:

> The grim disclosure on February 13, 2012 by the National Bureau of Statistics that more than two thirds of Nigerians-112 million individuals are living below the poverty line....
>
> Perhaps this terrible truth should not have been unexpected given the country unenviable rank in the widely publicized UNDP's Human Development index for 2011. The HDI is a summary measure for assessing long-term progress in three basic dimensions of human development: a long and healthy life, access to knowledge and a decent standard of living. Nigeria has for years remained in the low human development category – ranking 156 out of 187 countries and territories measured.¹⁰ (*Punch* April 9 2012).

What exemplary leadership has the ruling class demonstrated or the political office holders that is worth emulating by the masses? Going by what is naturally observable in our environment, the infrastructural decay stirs us in the face. Our roads are in terrible and deplorable condition, electricity is in short supply, potable waters are rarely available, and unemployment of our youth contributes to social vices, which undermine national security. The education sector appears to be the worst in decades and the health care services are not spared of negligence. All these contribute to the general apathy in the country. What has the ruling class done for Nigerians? On October 28, 2010 Festus Iyayi from University of Benin gave a concise evaluation of the Nigerian ruling class. He writes:

> The Nigerian ruling class thus has no connection with production and industry; it exports raw materials for cash in much the same way that of our generations of rulers exported slaves for beads and mirrors. Although it claims capital as its god, it cannot bring capital into existence through its own efforts. It is dependent, servile, lazy, and unimaginative. It is frightened of hard work, has a short term orientation and seeks immediate gratification.
>
> Until recently, each member of the House of Representatives was paid N27.9 million every quarter or N110 million a year as constituency allowance. Recently they voted to increase the amount to N45 million per quarter or N180 million a year. Until recently too, each Senator was paid N45.5 million every quarter or N182 million a year as constituency allowance. Senators also voted to be paid N90 million per quarter or N360 million per annum as constituency allowance. The constituency allowance of the President of the Senate is N400 million every three months or N1.6 billion a year. This currently translates to N4.44 million a day. When increased by the same rate as that of Senators, the Senate President will be receiving N3.2 billion annually or N8.8 million per day as constituency allowance. The Speaker of the House of Representatives currently receives N3.84 million per day or N350 million every three months or N1.4 billion per annum as constituency allowance. When increased by the same margin as that of members of the House of the Representatives, the Speaker will be pocketing N2.3 billion annually as constituency allowance.[11]

I believe Iyayi did not generate the above information and figures without a verifiable source. In collaboration with Iyayi, the former Governor of Central Bank of Nigeria, Lamido Sanusi says, "25 percent of the Federal Government's budget was spent on the National Assembly."[12] When Sanusi accused the Federal lawmakers of earning jumbo pay, the reaction of Nigerians was swift with rage and condemnation because the lawmakers appeared to be insensitive to the suffering of the masses.

Is it true that the ruling class has not come up with economic policies of their own to enhance the industries of the country? On the issue of Constituency Allowance: Why did the Revenue Mobilization Allocation and Fiscal Commission approve the excessive pay for the lawmakers? From the response of the people, "What the revenue commission approved is different from what the body (National Assembly members) approved for themselves."[13] If that be the case: Why did the officials of the Economic and Financial Crimes Commission spare them from being arrested? On the Constituency Allowance: Is it really the function of the lawmakers to engage in Constituency projects? Having collected the allowance: Who monitors the projects the lawmakers have executed in their various constituencies? In my discussion with the former Speaker of Ondo State of Assembly, he said that any lawmaker who collected money for Constituency projects and executed them himself is a lawless lawmaker and a rogue. And finally, if 469 lawmakers spend 25 percent of the national budget- that is ¼ of the national budget, haven't they taken more than their share of the *national cake*? The National Assembly has a culture of allocating money to themselves without due process and approval. The Nigerian public deserves to know particularly how the legislators came about their jumbo pay. I share the view of Joseph Adeyeye on how the revenue of Nigeria should be spent if the common man and woman are to derive any benefits from their investment in democracy. According to Adeyeye:

> We need to insist that our leaders realize that there are better uses to which we can put our money. Our roads and education are two areas that could benefit from money saved by slashing our legislators' obscene income. According to the Federal Roads Maintenance Agency, we only need N70bn annually for the next five years to repair our major roads.
>
> Our needs for such savings in education are even greater than for roads. We have some catching to do, and the earlier we get started the better. ...the Programme for International Students Assessment, a test run by the Organization for Economic Cooperation and Development, released the result of a global test in reading, mathematics and science for 15 year-olds. The results show that Chinese students did far better than North American and European pupils. It was a shock to many. But educators who have kept an

eye on China's massive investment in education in the last decade were not surprised. China, they say, have been pumping jumbo billions into her educational system for years, preparing a successor generation to take her society to the next level. That, I tell you, is a better way to spend jumbo billions.[14]

What Adeyeye has said on how the excess money paid to the legislators ought to be invested in more profitable ventures particularly education is what a responsible government should do. Former President of Nigeria Olusegun Obasanjo at the 4th Academy for Entrepreneurial Studies conference in Lagos berated the Legislators by saying "Today, rogues, armed robbers are in the state Houses of Assembly, and the National Assembly. What sort of laws will they make?"[15] It is right to raise the type of question Obasanjo asked but he being the former civilian President of Nigeria for eight years- 1999-2007 why did he not stamp out corruption in the country? It is true he instituted commissions for instance, Economic and Financial Crimes Commission (EFCC) that appeared effective but critics noted that he used the commission to silence or punish his political opponents and enemies.

Greed and Corruption

The issue of corruption is not new to most African States namely, Nigeria, Kenya, Zaire now Democratic Republic of Congo etc. But the most commonly publicized is that of Nigeria. So let me discuss that of Nigeria. Corruption in Nigeria is like an unwritten document yet it is more pragmatically vivid in every facet of life in the country. Hardly can you go anywhere in Nigeria without seeing its ugly head. It appears to be a permanent feature of human nature defiant of cure. That does not necessarily imply that all Nigerians are corrupt. But there are two basic areas of corruption I want to address namely, *official corruption* and *political corruption*. The first is mostly identifiable among government officials. They are the ones who award huge contracts and get kickbacks. It was recently reported that the Federal government of Nigeria had spent between 1999 and 2007 over 24 billion US dollars on electricity[16] and yet the country is intermittently in darkness. The situation is so porous to the extent that "over 830 factories, according to the Manufacturers Association of Nigeria"[17] have closed their industries while others simply relocated to Ghana where the supply of electricity is more stable and reliable. Some members of the Federal House of Representatives have accused its leadership of corruption, for instance, Dino Melaye and his group in the lower house of legislation accused the former House Speaker, Dimeji Bankole of spending 9 billion[18] naira without accounting for it. The case was investigated and

Bankole was found to have committed any wrongdoing. Some of State Governors both past and present in the last 10 years have been accused of mismanagement of their state revenues namely, James Ibori former Governor of Delta State who had served a jail term in Britain for money laundering, Joshua Dariye, former Governor of Plateau State, Alao Akala, former Governor of Oyo State, Gbenga Daniel, former Governor of Ogun State, etc. We cannot lose sight of corruption in the corporate organizations i.e. the banking industry and the multinationals i.e., Halliburton, Shell etc. It is not the case that the law enforcement agencies have not done anything to arrest and prosecute some of the perpetrators of *official corruption* in the country. As a matter of fact, some of them have completed their jail terms namely, Tafa Balogun, Olabode George among others. In the case of Olabode George, the Supreme Court after several years declared him innocent of the charges against him.

If members of the National Assembly unilaterally approved for themselves some remuneration beyond what Revenue Mobilization Allocation and Fiscal Commission had given to them, does it not amount to *official corruption*?

During the 2007 election many registered voters in different parts of the country were not allowed to cast their votes because some politicians brought their thugs to scare away the people. The leadership of People's Democratic Party which was the ruling part in Nigeria told all Nigerians that the 2007 elections was 'a do or die affair'. Being 'a do or die affair', their strategy was to use all the necessary means including rigging and intimidation of their opponents at the polls to win the elections. As it turned out in 2007 elections, Peoples Democratic Party (PDP) had the majority of the votes throughout the country. But those who felt aggrieved by the outcome of the elections went to appeal the election results. Prominent among them are Peter Obi, Anambra State, Rotimi Amaechi, Rivers State, Adams Oshiomhole, Edo State, Olusegun Mimiko, Ondo State, and Kayode Fayemi, Ekiti State, Rauf Aregbesola, Osun State,[19] among others who eventually won their cases in courts and consequently became governors of their States. If you calculate the loss of time and money spent on cases appealed in courts, unless one has the resilience and means, one would not engage in the exercise of getting justice from the judiciary as laid down in our constitution. In our political system there are those who became *institutionalized political godfathers*. They have money and influence so they dictate and choose among the political aspirants of their parties without regards for competence and acceptability by the society. Because Nigeria has many poor, uneducated, and unemployed youth, they are easily bought with money. They are used as thugs and agents of political rigging. The irony of it all is that these young and energetic individuals forget that the children of the politicians they do their bidding are kept away from the scene of political danger if at all their wards/children are in the country. The common practice of the politicians is to send their children abroad for higher training or engage them in different entrepreneur skills in overseas.

Political corruption has its damaging effects on the psyche, economic and social life of the people. Today, Nigerian youth hardly see any need for dignity of labour. The incessant kidnapping in the country, yahoo-yahoo, armed robbery and other vices committed largely by the youth in an effort to get rich quick do not portray Nigeria well in the comity of nations. The politicians in their lifestyle make the youth to see politics as a way of getting easy money without the rigor of labour. The sense of human value has diminished because they can be easily recruited to assassinate any political rivals insofar as they are 'well paid' for the job. Let me reiterate that the level of corruption in Nigeria may not as high in other parts of the continent but hardly can you find any country that is not corrupt.

There is this story of a Kenyan politician in the Kenyan political ruling party, Kenya African National Union (KANU) who was given a huge amount of money for campaign in his constituency. The Kenyan Shillings new notes given to the politician was to attract the rural poor. Unknown to the rooky politician the new notes were not genuine but they were allowed to be used for elections in the rural areas where the local people would not know because of their illiteracy. Instead of using the money for the purpose for which it was given to him he diverted it to his own personal use. He went to an Indian auto shop to buy a brand new Mercedes Benz. The Indian auto car dealer did not suspect that the politician used fake money but as soon as he realized it, he called the politician to return the car for some mechanical adjustments and if he failed to bring it immediately, it could lead to more damage that would cost him a lot of money to repair. The politician was compelled to return the car for repair. As soon as he brought the car the Indian auto dealer retuned his fake money to him. The politician could not complain openly because he knew the implications. When he secretly inquired from one of his political colleagues he was told that it had been one of the means to get votes. So the money was never for a personal gain. When the election was over and the ruling party won, the practice in Kenya when I was there was to mop up the fake currency notes from the public and have them destroyed.

The case of Mobutu Sese Seko is another example worthy of note. He was the President of Zaire, now The Democratic Republic of Congo, who enjoyed the support of Western Europe and the United States of America particularly when

Ronald Reagan was President because he was their ally, a Moderate and not a Communist. It was during the Cold War and Mobutu was their political African bride. Mobutu was richer than his country Zaire. When Zaire had a financial debt of about 5 billion US dollars, Mobutu was in excess of financial liquidity to the same amount his country's debt burden.[20] His people were suffering from poverty while Mobutu and his political friends were living in excessive affluence.

The ethics of foreign Aid

The ethical proposition that will be pursued here is based on the premise that since Africa has all the necessary resources both human and natural, why must the rest of the world help the people to eradicate poverty in the continent? Why must the global world assist a continent that spends most of her resources on conflicts, wars and a huge military buildup that normally they do not need? Why must the rest of the world be concerned about a continent that her political elite only pay a lip service to development and good service delivery? Should the rich nations help the poor in Africa in spite of corruption and waste of resources that are witnessed in the States of Africa? Do we have any moral obligation to the poor in Africa? These are some of the probable and cogent questions that any moral agent will raise on the need to give aid to Africa in the 21st century. There are many scholars who are divided on the issue. For instance, Dambisa Moyo in her book *Dead Aid* has argued that foreign aid to Africa may have intended to accelerate development of the continent but the reality on ground is just the opposite. The aid given to Africa rather than making the continent to be progressive it is retrogressive. Moyo explains, "More than US$2 trillion of foreign aid has been transferred from rich countries to poor over the fifty years – Africa the biggest recipient, by far."[21] Normally such huge investments in form of aid to Africa would have transformed the continent to a world class paradise but it is not so. To drive home her case, Moyo compares Africa with other countries that have made impressive progress. She writes:

> Consider this: in the past forty years at least a dozen developing countries have experienced phenomenal economic growth. Many of these, mostly Asian countries, have grown by almost 10 per cent of GDP per year, surpassing the growth rates of leading industrialized economies, and significantly reducing poverty. In some instances, poorer countries have leaped-frogged the per capita income levels of leading developed economies, and this trend is set to continue: by some estimates, star emerging-market performers such as Brazil,

Russia, India and China are projected to exceed the economic growth rates of nearly all industrialized economies by the year 2050. Yet, over the same period, as many as thirty other developing countries, mainly aid-dependent in sub-Saharan Africa, have failed to generate consistent economic growth, and have even regressed.[22]

If aid does not contribute to the enviable development that Africa needs, what then will work in its place? Moyo believes that direct investment is the prescription. By direct investment Moyo means that industrialized nations should build industries, factories, companies etc. in the continent that will create jobs for majority of people in Africa. If there is massive employment of African able-bodied individuals throughout the States of Africa, there will be no need for aid. After all, giving aid to African leaders empowers them and weakens the populace because they use such aid to corrupt the society, suppress opposition and make people to see them as some sort of semi-gods. When industries are built significantly in Africa it will contribute to better infrastructural development and improve the living standard of the people.

Dower has a different view about giving aid to poor countries. He believes that giving aid is a means to an end but realistically it cannot eradicate poverty. He believes that some form of aid may not work but there is other form of aid that works, "particularly that of voluntary agencies."[23] Furthermore, Dower argues:

> Caring is an unquantifiable dimension to moral responsibility. But if we have a proper appreciation of the facts of world poverty, of our global moral identities, of the moral seriousness of responding to extreme suffering, of what quality of life really consists in, and of the duty of caring as much as we can consistent with our quality of life, then we will care as we ought.[24]

I think it is not true that all forms of aid are not needed in Africa. I remember the American Peace Corps which really helped Nigerian students in the 60s and for those who could not get jobs as young men and women because of the level of their education, working for corps members was fun and it gave them some financial benefits because some of the corps members helped to pay their fees in high schools. The end result made some of them to get to the academic and economic ladder today. The significance of that moral obligation has its multiplying effects in our education sector. Some of them became professors while others became businessmen in their varying degrees. The truth of the matter is that I am one of the chief beneficiaries. We live in a moral space and within that moral confinement there is a compelling factor to help people who are economically disadvantaged which one cannot ignore considering one's background. We cannot ignore the role UNICEF has played in Africa and elsewhere in the world in combating deadly diseases like measles, polio, whooping cough, smallpox etc. Similarly we cannot forget missionary activities in Africa and perhaps elsewhere because they exemplify to some extent, a form of charity organization with the aim to educate and train Africans, which its end result is to alleviate poverty, even though their primary assignment is to evangelize for Jesus the Christ. Both the religious and secular nonprofit organizations have in no small measure contributed to what is, in my view, a foreign aid.

It may be difficult as Dower rightly noted to eradicate poverty in poor countries but I believe, contrary to him, that it is possible if most African elites determine to do it. Yes, they can! Peter Singer one of the distinguished ethicists in the United States of America believes that we live in a global community in which our moral obligations must be to the need of us all. He observes that the major reason why aid is not working as it should is because donor countries, for instance, the United States, France and Japan attach strigent conditions that make the recipient countries do their biddings, whereas Nordic countries "give to countries that are poor but have reasonably good governments that will not misuse the resources given."[25] Singer proposes that if Americans give at least 1 per cent from their annual income as aid to poor countries it will inevitably contribute to eradication of poverty in the world. He argues that doing so is a moral obligation, "To fail to give it shows indifference to the indefinite continuation of dire poverty and avoidable, poverty-related deaths."[26] To Singer, we must realize that it is time for all nations to embrace the ethics of inclusiveness and one universal existence for all humans. Does the concept of one world not conflict with free market economy and existential freedom? Why must the rich nations want to join developing nations to share the wealth of those industrial countries? Did Africa contribute to the wealth of the industrial nations to warrant such a moral demand? Of course scholars will be quick to say yes, Africa had in the past and even now continues to enrich the rich nations considering the case of slave trade, colonization and their imperialistic postures in the continent. Africa is not only in need of aid from the rich nations but also reparations that are overdue to the continent. We may not pursue that agenda here for now but it is worth noting. There is one fundamental moral or ethical question to the idea of one world that I want to bring to the fore. Is there any justice in such a concept of global community or global commonwealth?

This question and those raised before are some of the convoluted questions we probably have to answer individually given the nature and complexity of sociology of humans. But no matter how we try to answer the questions, the cardinal issue is social and moral justice should be our guide.

Africa's Destiny and the imperative of Aid

At the independence of African countries from colonialism the general vision of African leaders was to eradicate poverty. Kwame Nkrumah at independence of his country, Ghana writes, "We must abolish poverty, ignorance, illiteracy and improve our health services."[27] Today that vision to eradicate poverty, ignorance etc. is nothing but a mirage. More Africans are poorer than at independence as a result of poor leadership and lack of commitment to political promises of the ruling class. But since independence, Africa has produced rich men and women some of them were Heads of States during the military dispensation while some are today civilian Presidents of their countries, the question is; ought they not to contribute to the eradication of poverty in Africa in line with the vision of African leaders at independence? If some rich Africans invest their money in foreign countries to enrich themselves, why is it difficult for them to plough back some significant parts of their profit to Africa that is the source of their wealth to eradicate poverty in the continent? After all as the Yoruba say, *Nitori talika ni Olodumare fi da Olowo* meaning, it is because of the poor the rich were created by Olodumare- the Supreme God. Therefore, it is expected that wealthy Africans take the lead. Why must the rich nations take the lead rather than some rich men and women of Africa? Normally the destiny of Africa is in the hands of Africans both rich and poor. If African Presidents, political office holders, academics, entrepreneurs, industrialists, investors, professionals, and among others who have seen the kind of development in Europe and America, which makes life comfortable for their people the moral question is: ought they not to think that such development be replicated in Africa? Does Africa have to be poor in the midst of all the apparent abundant wealth? The questions raised here are fundamentally moral and ethical issues that cannot be ignored if Africans are serious about the need to eradicate poverty in their midst.

It is important to recognize the role women can play in the eradication of poverty given their natural dynamics. Educating women with its attendant freedom in contemporary Africa is a necessary condition to fast track development. In developed countries including, to some extent emerging economies, women get employed more than ever before because modern science and technology has made their empowerment knowledge driven. In other words, knowledge economy in the 21st century is key to women empowerment and without quality education it is hardly achievable. The more women get into the political mainstream with an upper hand in the affairs of national economy the better, given their numerical strength. Women have natural endowment for care, empathy with passion to eradicate poverty in Africa.

For Africa to take her destiny into her hand there is need for emphasis on scientific and technological advancement. It may require using all the human resources at home and abroad. Let us take a hypothetical look at contemporary Africa and ask all Africans in Europe and America to be led by a spirited African who has the capacity to make a forward march towards eradication of poverty in the continent. Will Africans on the continent cooperate with this revolutionary agenda? The leadership of a spirited African will determine the form in which the revolution will take. Will the people in Africa want their breadwinners living in Europe and America come home that is, leaving certainty for uncertainty? But these problems can be overcome when people know that the sacrifice will ultimately serve their overall interest. Assuming the hypothetical strategy works and a revolutionary leader brings about the needed prosperity and development to overcome the trauma of poverty in Africa, will that not be better alternative than waiting for a world government suggested by Singer?

But more importantly, Africans must ask their leaders why the money used to buy arms in other parts of the world could not be used for infrastructural development and eradication of poverty in the continent? Where are the inherent traditional values of African brotherhood gone in the social, political and psyche of African leaders that can enhance the quality of leadership and good governance? Since independence of African countries, the examples I have given from social, political and moral space in Africa show that there is hardly any difference from bad leaders in the past who contributed to poverty of Africa and the new generation of political and ruling elite who have exacerbated the impoverishment of the continent. In my view the moral imperative of performing duty for duty sake and not using human beings as means only but as ends in themselves of Immanuel Kant[28] seem not to have relevant application when it comes to eradication of poverty in the continent. For a moral action of universal application in the global community, the deontological ethics of Kant that is humanistic serves the urgent need to eradicate poverty.

Conclusion

The major ethos of my argument is how to eradicate poverty in Africa and the strategies or methods that could aid achieving self-sustainability. The moral concern is that giving aid to Africa is not the solution to end poverty in the continent. What is mostly needed as I have argued is to put an end to conflicts and wars because the money spent on buying arms could be used to build infrastructural facilities that will provide quality education, health care delivery system, job opportunities and economic growth and development. Furthermore, there is the need for good government, peace and tolerance that will enhance sustainable development. Above all, the concept of one world in which natural and human resources will be used to eradicate poverty not only in Africa but also throughout the world is laudable but is it achievable given the state of nature? What Africans should do is to look inward and take her destiny into her hand.

There are at least 22 billionaires in Africa and if they subscribe to this moral appeal to eradicate poverty in the continent, it is doable. It must be noted that in recent years some wealthy Africans philanthropists for instance, Moshood Kasimawo Abiola, Aliko Dangote, Mo Ibrahim amongst others have contributed to the eradication of poverty in their localities in terms of giving scholarships to poor students, creating job employments for the youths but these are few and far in between considering the large population of unemployed youths and high rate of illiteracy in the continent.

A clarion call to bring Africans home from Europe and America to join hands together is the right way to go in my view. If Africans both at home and the Diaspora get together and work assiduously recognizing that at the end of the day, if the hypothetical suggestion works, it will be to the interest of everyone and not just the poor but all categories of people in the society will be served. The moral fabric of care and the ethical imperative to leave the world better than we found it in the midst of wealth is the panacea to eradicate poverty in the global economy.

Notes and References

1. Walter Isaacson, *Steve Jobs* (New York: Simon & Schuster, 2011), 14-15.
2. Toyin Falola, *The Power of African Cultures* (Rochester: University of Rochester Press, 2003), 109-110.
3. Kolawole Olaniyan, "Need for government to outlaw discrimination against the poor," *Punch*, April 9, 2012.

4. Nigel Dower, "World Poverty" in *A Companion of Ethics*, ed. Peter Singer (Oxford: Blackwell Publishing, 1993), 274.

5. Thomas Hobbes, *Leviathan* (London: Collier Macmillan, 1978), 100.

6. Falola, 122.

7. Joseph Allen, *Love and Conflict* (Nashville: Abingdon Press, 1984), 282.

8. Linus Okorie, "Leadership deficit, cause of corruption in Nigeria" *Punch*, April 26, 2012.

9. Segun Ogungbemi, "The Imperative of Good Governance in Nigeria" Faculty of Arts Journal 5 (2008): 431.

10. Olaniyan, April 9, 2012.

11. Festus Iyayi, "Nigeria: The ruling class, challenges of development and electoral reforms," *Punch*, October 28, 2010.

12. John Ameh and Adelani Adepegba, "Sanusi refuses to back down," *Punch*, December 8, 2010.

13. Emma Anya, Sesan Olufowobi and Abimbola Adelakun," RMAFC meets today over controversial jumbo pay," *Punch*, December 20, 2010.

14. Joseph Adeyeye, "Our jumbo democracy" *Punch*, December 10, 2010.

15. Olusegun Obasanjo, "Rogues, armed robbers in N'Assembly," *Punch*, May 23, 2012.

16. See MD Yusuf, "Crises of Governance in Nigeria (2) *Punch*, December 8, 2010.

17. Editorial, "2011 Budget and Capital Project," *Punch*, December22, 2010.

18. John Ameh and Friday Olokor, "Melaye, colleagues return to House of Reps," *Punch*, December 9, 2010.

19. See *Punch*, December 9 and 10, 2010.

20. See Dambisa Moyo, *Dead Aid*, (New York: Farrar, Straus and Giroux, 2010), 22.

21. Moyo, 28.

22. Moyo, 29.

23. Dower, 275.

24. Dower, 282.

25. Peter Singer, *One World* (New Haven: Yale University Press, 2004), 191.

26. Singer, 194.

27. Kwame Nkrumah, *Africa Must Unite* (New York: International Publishers, 1975), 118.

28. See Lewis White Beck, trans. *Immanuel Kant Foundations of the Metaphysics of Morals* (Indianapolis: Bobbs-Merrill, 1978), 1

CHAPTER 6

Traditional Customs And Values In Contemporary Political Behavior In Nigeria

...a truly public-spirited person should accept public office not for what he can get for himself – such as the profit and glamour of but for opportunity which it offers him of serving his people to the best of his ability, by promoting their welfare and happiness. (Chief Obafemi Awolowo)

Introduction

Long before the coming of the Europeans, African oral traditions that are still extant plus African works of art remind us that African traditional customs and values were held with awe in every ethnic group in Nigeria. This claim became valid in written documents by the early historians, anthropologists, colonial officials[1] etc. The starting point is what are the traditional customs and values? Of what significance are they to contemporary Nigerian politics? Considering some of the negative impressions given by the colonialists of African traditional values and customs: Do we have any moral justification to prove that they are relevant to contemporary political power play in the country? I want to argue from moral and ethical perspectives that African customs and values are very relevant in Nigeria even though the present politicians who are generally either Christians or Muslims claim not to have much to do with African traditional customs and values. The moral values that are inherent in the traditions do not allow indiscipline without penalty. Generally speaking, the idea of stealing public funds, election rigging, corruption etc. that has characterized the political behaviors of Nigerian politicians would have been minimized if they had followed the traditional customs and values that have far reaching consequences if breached or violated.

The Nature of African Traditional Customs and Values

To begin with I need to clarify a notion generated when one speaks or writes on an idea that is captioned 'African' as I have done in this chapter to mean all Africans whereas it is impossible to do so if it means all Africans without qualification. The truth of the matter is that I cannot claim to have the knowledge of what is believed and practiced by every ethnic group in Africa bearing in mind of over 800hundred languages spoken in the continent which are based on different ethnic groups. Whenever I talk or write "African" it means a general representation and not necessarily a specific notion that is found among all Africans unless otherwise stated. So when I talk about African traditional customs and values I am simply making a general representation of the beliefs and practices of the traditional Africans from where we derive our existence and culture. In other words, I want to discuss African customs and values from three basic perspectives namely, (i) Social-utility values, (ii) Ethical and moral values and (iii) Existential and individualistic values. The question that is expected which will be addressed is what is the causal connection between these philosophical values and contemporary behaviors of Nigerian political class and political office holders?

(i) Social-Utility Values

Any meaningful discourse on African social-utility values must derive from the historical past of Africans, which predated the intrusion of Europeans to the continent. I have used the term social-utility values to refer to some traditional institutions which Toyin Falola calls, "Age-grades societies, secret societies, chieftaincy systems, and the indigenous religious priesthood...."[2] The use of traditional attires by Africans reveals the distinctive nature of who the Africans are and in modern times their countries. Furthermore the use of local or indigenous languages serves as a common thread to weave the society together as a remarkable bond of identity and unity. The folktales, social and religious festivals, songs, pity sayings, hunter dirges, chant names and all forms of African oral traditions found their expressions first and foremost in the local or indigenous languages. The inherent social-utility values found in all African cultures may not necessarily be limited to Africans alone, it could be the case that it is universal in general terms among all primordial cultures in Europe, Asia, Latin America etc which signifies that homo sapiens have some cultural similarities. The striking and most interesting part is that in spite of modernization, traditional social-utility values remain as a social fabric from where the contemporary Africans take their pride.

(ii) Ethical and Moral Values

Living together requires obedience to the rules and norms set by the society for peace and harmony to reign supreme. The learning process of ethical and moral values in an African society is in stages beginning from home, age grade, traditional institutions, and religious groups among others. In Africa, great importance is placed on "respect for elders, the authority of husbands over their wives, the need to work hard, and the habit of generosity to members of the kin group and the larger community."[3] Certain ways of life that are not in conformity with the social norms are regarded as taboos or aberrations. Any infringements of the laid down rules and taboos attract sanctions. For instance, honesty, truthfulness, faithfulness, accountability to the social groups when put in any place of authority is a hallmark of discipline, maturity, responsibility and respect. Until the introduction of Western culture of writing, African modes of knowledge of ethical and moral values were essentially oral. But since the advent of modern writing one can argue that the theoretical and practical knowledge of African ethics and moral values are what I call ethics of common sense or ethics of care[4] and divine command which is otherwise known as religious authoritarianism. In both forms, moral commitment to each one is sacrosanct. How do I mean? Let me illustrate what I mean from the society I am most conversant with- the Yoruba ethnic group in Nigeria. In Yoruba traditional society before Western civilization became dominant the custodians of corporate moral and ethical values were the monarchs and their chiefs. The people saw the adherence to the social norms by the monarchs as leadership by example. In other words, whenever the monarch who was and still is traditionally called *Oba igba keji Orisa*, meaning the monarch who is in second command to the god keeps to the social principles of justice and maintains peace and order, he enjoys the support and loyalty of his subjects but if, however, the monarch behaves contrary to the social or traditional norms there are some measures of discipline to make him retrace his steps otherwise some grave consequences may follow. If he becomes recalcitrant, that is, if he does not respect his chiefs who advise him on social and religious issues that are contrary to the general opinions, his behavior would be regarded as a moral and religious violation of the society. The first step to let the monarch know that he is no longer living by example is for his chiefs to boycott his palace commonly called *afin*. If he fails to right the wrong then he will be asked to commit suicide which the Yoruba call *won si igba* *fu*⁵. In a situation like this the monarch has no choice than to commit suicide. On the violation of common sense ethics for instance, stealing, breaking an oath etc there are sanctions for the offender sometimes it is retributive and sometimes it is by divine sanction. If one steals something or one makes an oath and fails to live by it the means for retribution is inherent in the moral principle of justice. If there is denial on the part of the accused swearing by an instrument of the gods for instance, a metal, which is an instrument of *Ogun* the god of iron, war and justice can be a means to punish the accused; and if he is innocent nothing adverse will happen to him. If, however, he has sworn falsely on Ogun the consequence could be fatal. He may be involved in a ghastly motor accident that can cause him to have multiple injuries or it can lead to his untimely death. Some gods may be more benevolent in which case the culprit may not die if he returns the stolen object. A case in point is the one that happened in my hometown, Idofin-Isanlu in Yagba East Local Government Area in Kogi State, Nigeria. There is a deity called *Origba*. The ontological characteristic of this deity is that its costumes are sacred and being so means they cannot be tempered with anyhow without severe consequences. There was a melodrama in the town in the early 90s when some robbers came to steal the costumes of the *Origba*. As the costume was taken away from its Shrine, which till now does not have any security lock, unlike the mission Churches where the electric generators were carted away, there was a sudden strike of lightning that frightened the robbers and they took to their heels and left the costume of the *Origba*. It is expedient to say here that the stealing of the costume of the Origba and the spontaneous reaction that made the robbers to return it was an act of offensive provocation. The exhibition and the execution of the power of the *affecting presence*⁶ were ontologically manifested. When the robbers were not able to cart away the costume of the *Origba* the rage and ravaging powers of the *affecting presence* were assuaged. The whole town was alerted that a strange phenomenon had happened and there was the need for the priests to appease the deity. The robbers could not disappear with the costume of the *Origba*.⁷ There was no evidence that the robbers were injured or killed since they returned the stolen goods of the deity. The truth of the matter is that the robbers have learnt a moral lesson that the deity does not tolerate stealing and that the divinity is at alert keeping vigilance over his property. Perhaps what the robbers could not know is that if they tried it again there may be no second chance of a safe escape.

The common sense ethics or ethics of commitment is different from the Western ethics of *oughtness* or *isness*, ethics of duty for duty sake or categorical imperative of Immanuel Kant.⁸ The traditional ethics or moral paradigms of the Yoruba are pragmatic and they are meant substantially for the general good of the corporate existence of the community. The essence of moral values and their applications within the traditional construct provides a unique praxis of communalism and social justice.

(iii) Existential and Individualistic Values

There cannot be a society without individuals and there cannot be any individual without a society. As much as each is not totally exclusive of each other the moral values that become composite and nurture individuals to become morally worthy of being associated with African communities provide the ground for self-assertiveness of being proud as Africans. But we are constantly reminded that before anyone becomes part of any social and political community he or she is first and foremost an individual. An individual with freedom or liberty that is equal in substance and value. Whatever anyone has within the corporate existence it is not a corporate property but that of an individual. According to John S. Mbiti, "The individual can only say: 'I am, because we are; and since we are, therefore I am.' This is a cardinal point in the understanding of the African view of man."[9] Mbiti may be right if his argument is limited to his ethnic group in Kenya but if he meant to say all Africans without exception he is probably wrong. The *cogito ergo sum*, I think therefore I am of Descartes in his *Meditation 11*, is a proposition which has universal application; one wonders why Mbiti finds it difficult to accept its truism. Rather, he chooses a corrupt version of it and applies it to Africans because he thinks they are nothing but a bundle of corporate entity whose members cannot think individually. For instance, the Yoruba believe that in the primordial existence *Ori* the *being* of the individual freely makes the choice to come to this world before Olodumare, the Supreme Being who is believed to be the foundation of everything that is. The *Ori*[10] chooses his parents, career, age groups, partners, and a set of values before coming to the world. While on earth the individual goes ahead to fulfill what his Ori had chosen in the primordial existence. He is expected to choose any among over 400 deities created by Olodumare who are, Orisanla, Ogun, Osanyin, Yemoja, Sango[11] etc, to worship and do his bidding in life. He has the free will to choose and abandon any of the divinities he feels is not serving his ultimate interests. Only human beings have ability and capacity of thinking and making rational and sometimes irrational choices based on their inherent values. And that is why they are morally held accountable.

From the foregoing or against the backdrop of the traditional customs and values that I have explained in a nutshell; it provides a moral base to examine the political behavior of the Nigerian political office holders. As it is said in Yoruba *bi omode ba subu a wo waju sugbon bi agba ba subu a wo ehin lati mo oun to gbe subu*, meaning if a child falls down, he will look forward but if an elderly person falls down he will look backward to know the cause of his fall. The political class and the political office holders in Nigeria are saddled with the responsibility to advance the progress and development of the country like people in the developed world because the world is a competitive stage where every country is running a race to probably be the best. Is Nigeria in the race? What are the requirements needed to be in the race and what are the causes for being in the race and not being able to win? Answers to these questions will be responded to in the course of this discourse.

Running a race

Running a race is neither a new concept nor a new phenomenon in human existence. It has its historical antecedent from antiquity insofar as it relates to Homo sapiens. How do I mean? For instance, when the first inhabitants of Nigeria came to what becomes today our geographical root; it was not in their thinking that they were in a race of global competitiveness. It was to them perhaps a normal existence in which individuals or groups as it were came to face the exigencies of their existential life. It is indubitable that they did not know much about the existence of other races in the world apart from their environment and the immediate surrounding neighbors.

Similarly, when we were born, none of us realized that we came to live in a world of competition. The two examples illustrate what I mean by running a race of *unconscious* activity. There is yet another dimension which is running a race of *conscious* activity. This can be domestic, academic, business, trade, politics, sports, games, entertainment industry, warfare, etc.

Whenever human beings engage in a race of *conscious* activity the ultimate goal is success. To engage in any of the above *conscious* activities requires focus, self-determination, hard work, perseverance, resourcefulness etc. It is like going to a battlefield. You can imagine the risks and tragedies they entail. Running a race as in sporting activities with intention to win normally requires being well fed and medically and psychologically fit. A person suffering from malnutrition or psychological disorder is not fit to take part in sporting activities. Whichever *conscious* activity one partakes in, there are always some challenges or obstacles along the line. But the competitors nevertheless weigh the options of either competing or not competing. And when they make the choice to compete as in the political race in the country particularly during elections they dare the consequences because of its inherent glorious values if they succeed. The elections that produced winners like President Goodluck Ebele Jonathan, Governor Raji Babatunde Fashola, Governor Isa Yuguda amongst others and those who won in the Upper and Lower Houses of legislations in their constituencies without rigging are good examples of running and winning a race.

Let me; however, draw our attention to the ugly dimension of running a race of *conscious* activities from the observation of one of the most astute British philosophers, Thomas Hobbes. According to him, in the state of nature, human beings engage in three things that lead to conflicts namely, competition, security and glory.[12] And if human beings are to be at peace there must be a Leviathan or a magistrate who will control the inordinate ambitions of man, if not, it can lead to war and self destruction.[13] We will see later how relevant his idea is to the contemporary competitive social and political activities in our society.

The Global Village

What exactly is this concept of global village and its relevance to us? The idea of global village is a late 20th century phenomenon that is predicated on the revolutionary change brought about by science and technology. It is about our changing world[14] in culture, politics, economics, technology, health, education, information and communication, vision and mission that contribute to the meaning of human existence. Philosophers aptly observe that nothing is permanent as change. A revolutionary change in science and technology is essentially a means to seek a better way of knowing who we are, what we are, and what we can derive from our cultural relationship as Homo sapiens. There is a requirement for being an integral part or being active players in the global village. The current active players are industrial nations namely, United States of America, Russia, Britain, France, Japan, Germany, etc plus those that are classified as emerging economies like China, Brazil, India, South Korea, etc. From what we know, Nigeria is not an active participant in the global race. What is clear is that the impact of globalization spreads across all nations including Nigeria although it is not yet a nation. Nigeria is a country of different nationalities namely, Yoruba, Ibo, Hausa, Kanuri, Ijaw, etc. Therefore, as the sage Chief Obafemi Awolowo rightly noted that "there is no such thing as a Nigeria nation…"[15] Similarly, Professor Wole Soyinka says that Awolowo was the first person who "designated Nigeria a mere 'geographical expression'"[16] with different nationalities. The events we witness in terms of governance and leadership in Nigeria are a clear index that the country is truly not yet a nation and that explains in part why the country only feels the impact of globalization rather than being an active participant in the global power of industrialization. Let us consider some of the events witnessed in the governance of Nigeria by the ruling class and the elite that suggest Nigeria's inactive player in the global village.

Governance and Responsibility

On 1st October 2010 Nigeria celebrated her 50th Independence anniversary with a hiccup with the news of a bomb blast adjacent to the venue of the celebration in Abuja. The nature of independence is freedom. The expression of that freedom in a violent manner as witnessed in Abuja - the capital of Nigeria on that day is antithesis to social and political values of a civilized nation. It was not the incident of the bomb blast perhaps that interested most Nigerians on that day, however unfortunate and morally condemnable it was. Rather, it was and still is: What has Nigeria done for Nigerians as a corporate nation? In other words, what benefits since independence do the citizens derive from her independence? This question can be answered either as an individual or as a corporate entity. Nigeria at 51 since independence the current wave of violence perpetrated by Boko Haram, a religious sect that claims responsibility for the bombing of several places in Northern Nigeria including the United Nations' building in Abuja on 26th August, 2011 and killed 23 people and wounded many people is a clear indication of the indignant attitude of the sect against the political ruling class and to a larger extent most Nigerians. What I am really getting at is the social and political responsibilities of the central government since independence to its people and how Nigerians have benefited from it? Furthermore, the issue is how accountable are the ruling class to the electorate? Are Nigerians better or worse off since independence? What exemplary patriotic leadership the ruling class and the elites have demonstrated that is worth emulating by the masses? Going by what is naturally observable in our environment, the infrastructural decay stirs us in the face. Our roads are in terrible condition, electricity is in comatose, potable waters are in short supply; unemployment of our youth contributes to social vices which undermine national security. The educational sector appears to be the worst in decades and the health care services are not spared of negligence. All these contribute to the general apathy in the country. What has the ruling class done for Nigerians? On October 28, 2010 Festus Iyayi from University of Benin gave a concise evaluation of the Nigerian ruling class. He writes:

> The Nigerian ruling class thus has no connection with production and industry; it exports raw materials for cash in much the same

way that of our generations of rulers exported slaves for beads and mirrors. Although it claims capital as its god, it cannot bring capital into existence through its own efforts. It is dependent, servile, lazy, and unimaginative. It is frightened of hard work, has a short-term orientation and seeks immediate gratification.

Until recently, each member of the House of Representatives was paid N27.9 million every quarter or N110 million a year as constituency allowance. Recently they voted to increase the amount to N45 million per quarter or N180 million a year. Until recently too, each Senator was paid N45.5 million every quarter or N182 million a year as constituency allowance. Senators also voted to be paid N90 million per quarter or N360 million per annum as constituency allowance. The constituency allowance of the President of the Senate is N400 million every three months or N1.6 billion a year. This currently translates to N4.44 million a day. When increased by the same rate as that of Senators, the Senate President will be receiving N3.2 billion annually or N8.8 million per day as constituency allowance. The Speaker of the House of Representatives currently receives N3.84 million per day or N350 million every three months or N1.4 billion per annum as constituency allowance. When increased by the same margin as that of members of the House of the Representatives, the Speaker will be pocketing N2.3 billion annually as constituency allowance.[17]

I believe Iyayi did not generate the above information and figures without a verifiable source. In a similar vein the Governor of Central Bank of Nigeria, Lamido Sanusi said, "25 percent of the Federal Government's budget was spent on the National Assembly."[18] When Sanusi accused the Federal lawmakers of earning jumbo pay, it buttressed what Iyayi has said in the above quotation. The reaction of Nigerians was swift with rage and condemnation because the lawmakers appeared to be insensitive to the suffering of the masses. Be that as it may, let us examine what Iyayi has said about the ruling class of our country. Is it true that the ruling class has not come up with economic policies of their own to enhance the industries of the country? Are they really ignorant leaders who can be easily deceived like our forebears who sold their people to slavery? Above all, are they indolent and intellectually stagnated? If they are: Didn't the electorate know before they were elected or did the electorate not elect the lawmakers? On the issue of Constituency Allowance: Why did the Revenue Mobilization Allocation and Fiscal Commission approve the excessive pay for the lawmakers? From the response of the people, "What the revenue commission approved is different from what the body (National Assembly members) approved for themselves."[19] If so: Why have the officials of the Economic and Financial Crimes Commission spared them from being arrested? On the Constituency Allowance: Is it really the function of the lawmakers to engage in Constituency projects? Having collected the allowance: Who monitors the projects the lawmakers have executed in their various constituencies? In my discussion with the former Speaker of Ondo State of Assembly, Oluwasegunota Bolarinwa said that any lawmaker who collected money for Constituency projects and executed them himself is a lawless lawmaker and a rogue. And finally, if 469 lawmakers spend 25 percent of the national budget- that is ¼ of the national budget, haven't they taken more than their fair share of the *national cake*? It is the same lawmakers who spent ¼ of the national budget on themselves who for political expedience hurriedly passed the bill of monthly minimum wage of 18, 000.00 Naira only only for Nigerian workers? Do they behave as rulers accountable to their people or they are there without regards to the principle of accountability to those who elected them? Are there not better ways to spend the national revenue than allowing the lawmakers expend it on themselves? We have the right to know how many bills our lawmakers have passed in the last one year and how relevant they are to their constituencies. We have the right to know how the legislators came about their jumbo pay. And we have the right to tell them how the national revenue should be spent. I share the views of Joseph Adeyeye on how the revenue of Nigeria should be spent. He writes:

> We need to insist that our leaders realize that there are better uses to which we can put our money. Our roads and education are two areas that could benefit from money saved by slashing our legislators' obscene income. According to the Federal Roads Maintenance Agency, we only need N70bn annually for the next five years to repair our major roads.
>
> Our needs for such savings in education are even greater than for roads. We have some catching to do, and the earlier we get started the better. ...the Programme for International Students Assessment, a test run by the Organization for Economic Cooperation and Development, released the result of a global test in reading, mathematics and science for 15 year-olds. The results show that Chinese students did far better than North American and European pupils. It was a shock to many. But educators who have kept an

eye on China's massive investment in education in the last decade were not surprised. China, they say, have been pumping jumbo billions into her educational system for years, preparing a successor generation to take her society to the next level. That, I tell you, is a better way to spend jumbo billions.[20]

What Adeyeye said on the excess money paid to the legislators ought to be invested is education and health sector of the economy is what a responsible government should do. Education, I mean quality education is the right of all Nigerians because that is the secret of power and development. Several years ago when President Obama was the President of United States of America; I listened to him challenging the principals of schools in the United States to come up with ideas and programmes that would improve the quality of education in their country. Don't forget that United States was and still the Super power in the world today. If the former President had that kind of passion for quality education for his country to enhance its leadership in the world, how much more Nigeria that was and still grappling with under-development?

Corruption and Development

Corruption is so endemic in Nigeria to the extent that it is synonymous with the people and the country. It will be an exaggeration to say that every Nigerian is corrupt without being specific with the word; corruption and in what context one can say that it is rampant or endemic. What I want to talk about specifically here first is official corruption in Nigeria and those who engage in it are the elites who have access to government in power and funds directly or indirectly. For instance, when members of the National Assembly unilaterally approved for themselves some remunerations beyond what Revenue Mobilization Allocation and Fiscal Commission had given to them, obviously that amounts to official corruption. The act of approving an unauthorized largess by the National Assembly to their members is morally and legally reprehensible. It was later reported in one of the print media that the newly constituted revenue commission would take a holistic view of the jumbo pay of the lawmakers.[26] The country has been waiting anxiously to know what the new commission members would do to correct the already imbalanced remunerations of the political office holders to assuage the outrage of Nigerian public over the excessive pay of the legislators.

There are others who are not members of the National Assembly who behave as if they are above the law because they are insulated from arrest and prosecution on the basis of their connections with those in authority. But the moment they are no longer in the good book of those in authority or their godfathers are no longer in power they become more vulnerable to arrests, prosecution and imprisoned if found guilty. It is when that happens that the public will be inundated with all sorts of stories and allegations of their criminality of corruption with forceful actions from law enforcement officials.

I have observed, with keen interest that most people arrested for corruption in Nigeria have been as a result of political vendettas or political persecutions of the opposition that government in power would usually claim to be fighting corruption notably during Obasanjo administration and also currently under Buhari administration.

It is not always the case that Nigerian law enforcement agencies have not done anything to arrest and prosecute some of the perpetrators of official corruption in the country. As matters of fact, some of them have served their jailed terms namely, Cecilia Ibru, Olabode George among others. But the fact remains that much more has to be done to stem the endemic official corruption in the country. Let me say inter alia that the legal battle that took place afterwards at the Supreme Court exonerated Olabode Gorge.

Let us consider the second form of corruption - political corruption. We are all aware of what happened in recent elections in the country when many registered voters in different parts of the country were not allowed to cast their votes because some politicians brought their thugs to scare away the people. For instance, the leadership of a particular political party told all Nigerians that the 2007 elections was "a do or die affair". Being "a do or die affair", their strategy was to use all the necessary means including rigging and intimidation of their opponents at the polls to win the elections. As it turned out in 2007 elections, Peoples Democratic Party (PDP) had the majority of the votes through out the country. But those who felt aggrieved by the outcome of the elections went to appeal the election results. Prominent among them were Peter Obi, Anambra State, Rotimi Amaechi, Rivers State, Adams Oshiomhole, Edo State, Olusegun Mimiko, Ondo State, and Kayode Fayemi, Ekiti State, Rauf Aregbesola, Osun State,[27] among others who eventually won their cases in courts and consequently became governors of their States. If one calculates the loss of time and money spent on cases appealed in courts, unless one has the resilience and means, one would not engage in the exercise of getting justice from the judiciary as laid down in our constitution. In our political system there are those who became *institutionalized political godfathers*. They have money and influence so they dictate and choose among the political aspirants of their parties without regards for competence and acceptability by the society. Because Nigeria has many poor, uneducated, and unemployed youth, they are easily bought with money. They are used as thugs and agents of political rigging. The irony of it all is that these young and energetic individuals forget that the children of the politicians they do their bidding are kept away from the scene of political danger if, at all their wards/children are in the country. The common practice of the politicians is to send their children abroad for higher training or engage them in different entrepreneur skills in overseas.

Because the politicians want to compete in the elections and win, they resort to the state of nature in their behaviour not knowing that it can always lead to conflict with the attendant result of brutality and destruction. What joy and satisfaction do we derive in destroying ourselves? Ade Ajayi an erudite historian writes:

> Perhaps one reason why there is so much violence, aggression and instability in our day-to-day life is that we have so little consciousness of a time perspective. We act and react as if there is only today, no yesterday, no tomorrow. We seem to care so little about the past; we have no enduring heroes and we respect no precedents. Not surprisingly, we hardly ever consider what kind of future we are building for our children and children's children.....

> The nation suffers which has no sense of history. Its values remain superficial and ephemeral unless imbued with a deep sense of continuity and a perception of success and achievement that transcends acquisition of temporary power or transient wealth. Such a nation cannot achieve a sense of purpose or direction or stability, and without them the future is bleak.[28]

Martin Meredith re-echoes the position of Ajayi as a general phenomenon in Africa:

> After decades of mismanagement and corruption, most African states have become hollowed out. They are no longer instruments capable of serving the public good. Indeed, far from being able to provide aid and protection to their citizens, African governments and the vampire-like politicians who run them are regarded by the populations they rule as yet another burden they have to bear in the struggle for survival.[29]

The precarious situation in which the political ruling class has plunged the country requires a rethink of an imperative recall to our traditional past of customs and values to savage the nation. The former Vice-Chancellor of Obafemi Awolowo University, Ile-Ife, Osun State Nigeria, Professor Wale Omole, at a book launch in Lagos called for a cultural revival. According to him, "In searching for the meaning of our existence, many have lost it by putting wealth first. But the truth is that wealth brings problems. There are thorns between roses. Therefore, real peace and happiness can be achieved not by achievement or pleasure but by serving others in every area of life"[30] A similar call to African leaders was made by the Sultan of Sokoto, Alhaji Muhammad Sa'ad Abubakar III at Jodidi Annual Lecture Series of Weatherhead Centre of Harvard University, Boston, Massachusetts in the US recently that suggested "five categories of values that would aid African politics for a dynamic framework for governance and a veritable yardstick for assessing political behaviour and action....these are: knowledge, primacy of justice, fight against corruption, dignity of labour and uplifting the status of women."[31]

Since independence, the development of this nation has been going at a snail speed not because there are no natural and human resources but that the leadership and political office holders have not lived up to the expectations of the people. The leadership and the political office holders plus the military incursion to the governance of the country whose religious affiliations are either Christianity or Islam have failed to live by the oath of office because both the Bible and the Qur'an they use for swearing their allegiance to the nation have no power of the *affecting presence* unlike the traditional modes of oath taking of allegiance which carries penalties on default by the people who take the oath. In other words the traditional values that make people to live uprightly by taking an oath using any of the traditional instruments of the gods like iron or any metal which is believed to be potent with power under *Ogun* the deity of iron in Yoruba land for instance, will make those who come from that political and geographical zone to swear by it when swearing their allegiance of office leadership at any level. Before the foreign religions came to Africa there hardly any ethnic groups in Africa without some traditional methods of making their leaders accountable to the people. The instance of the Yoruba given above is a good example. The fear of sudden or gradual punishments by the gods on whom a false political or religious office allegiance is made serves to control their political and religious behavior. If *Christian-democracy* and *Islamic-democracy* of swearing an allegiance of office that makes the people to fear and live up to the expectations of the people then it is better to go back to our root of doing things traditionally right. We need to go back to the *Traditional-democracy* of oaths taking regardless of one's religious affiliation. If this method is put in place perhaps the looting of national treasury by our leaders and political office holders will be drastically minimized because they probably don't want to try to test the anger of the gods when they know they have politically and economically misbehaved or abused their oaths of office. The retributions for the abuse of office by the elites and government officials are absent in the country because people know that the Bible and the Qur'an they use to swear in their oaths of office cannot cause them any harm. The principles of moral behavior, equity and social justice that are inherent in African traditional customs and values - ethics of care or common sense ethics are calling for attention because that is probably one of the major causes of Nigeria and Africa in general for underdevelopment.

Conclusion

Given the parameter of the idea of reversing the mode of taking oaths of office by using traditional instruments associated with the power of the gods to punish any erring political office offenders: Is there any philosophical or scientific evidence or proof that it can work in contemporary Nigeria? Is it true that because the corrupt political office holders go away with impunity after they have sworn oaths of office for good service delivery to the nation with Qur'an or the Bible that is why corruption is endemic? Or it is the case that Nigerians have not put the best of their human resource products in power and hold them responsible or accountable for the development of the country? Is it not a sign of scientific or philosophical bankruptcy that is behind the idea of reversing to an old-fashioned tradition or idolatry that never put the country in the front burner of success and progressive development before the advent of Western civilization? Why should anyone particularly a philosopher in the 21st century make such a suggestion? The questions I have raised above are probably what anyone objectionable to the course of going back to our traditional customs and values will support, particularly using any ontological and metaphysical objects to moralize political office holders in the country. These are some of the mind-bogging questions that deserve consideration in this discourse. The calls made by Ajayi and the Sultan of Sokoto for the need to consider the values in our historical past which are still extant today are indicative that the current political disposition of the country is in need of help. I am not unaware that the position of the Sultan on the call for the inward looking to our traditional values is primarily Islamic because the Sokoto Caliphate of their ancestor, Uthman Dan Fodio was an Islamic scholar of his time. The import of his call to the tradition of his people in the North is evident of the deviation from the tradition that his ancestor met on ground which was probably not all Islamic but the indigenous moral values he simply used Islam to propagate and perpetuate it.

The two foreign religions - Islam and Christianity that have dominated our ways of doing things morally and be held responsible, their followers have set the nation on the platform of incessant greed as demonstrated by the contemporary leaders and political office holders with impunity. The attendant result is the multiplying effects it has on the massive unemployed youths who are more interested in money without working vigorously for it. In other words, the idea of dignity of labor has no bearing in the psyche of the youths whereas in our traditional-democracy of values it exists.

Philosophers are part and parcel of the ancient, modern and the contemporary. His job is to set in motion philosophical arguments that can contribute to the progress of their society. Socrates, Plato and their generation did not lose sight of the importance of the Greek traditions and the gods, for instance, Zeus. Philosophers are to present philosophical and moral arguments that would be of values to the progress and sustainable development of their society and the world at large. To be part of the global village we need to showcase our moral values that have significant import of the *power of the affecting presence* just as the Church and the Mosques with the Cross and the Crescent individually and respectively has and manifested in their orientation of social values. It may have impact on the followers in the West and all the Arab world but since they are alien to us they are not necessarily effective, what works effectively as I have argued is the traditional modes of applying moral sanctions to the defaulters of the national responsibility. As far as I know amongst the Yoruba in Nigeria it is very rear for anyone to swear falsely on Ogun, the god of iron, war and justice, or Sango, the god of thunder or Sanpona, the god of smallpox with impunity. It is probably ingrained in their psyche and overtime it became part of the fears that contribute to the moral virtue that has united the people together. Whether it will work in the same way it did in the past and among the rural populace or not is yet to be publically tested in all the political spheres in the country. But the issue is since it had worked among the Yoruba traditional society there is no reason to doubt its efficacy. Since they hold tenaciously to the belief of the power of the gods it is morally logical to assume that it works for them. Just as the ethnic groups in Nigeria do not undermine the *power of the affecting presence* of the gods so also is their commitment to their traditional attires and languages. Africans in their beautiful native attires particularly during ceremonies and festivals showcase their distinctive cultures. The most notorious display of African attires in offices and international conferences, workshops and summits are by far made by Nigerians everywhere both at home and abroad. One would have imagined that such an exuberant display of native outfits by Nigerians also include the traditional customs and values of morals in public offices and private organizations where they work. Perhaps there will be no need for any calls for rebranding the bartered image of Nigeria because the good and glorious image of the country will remain sacrosanct. The rebranding of contemporary image of Nigeria within and outside the nation in a more effective manner in my view is for the leadership and political office holders to have a 180 degree turn to traditional moral values of honesty, hard work, discipline, respect for elders and traditions, etc. If Nigerian leaders put on the garments of traditional values like the gorgeous traditional attires they wear for any occasions with pride and dignity it is more effective way of rebranding the image of the nation than any form of political propaganda that will involve budgetary spending that will end up deepening the cancerous corruption that is already pervasive in the country.

The Federal Government of Nigeria should de-emphasize jumbo pay to political office holders and re-emphasize service delivery, performance and corruption free business enterprises as one of the only bases to reward its public and private servants. In the past, Alfred Ilenre explains, "The legislator was virtually a part-time official. The salary of the ministering the first Republic was lower than that of a professor. The permanent secretary earned more than a cabinet minister. The head of service earned more than the prime minister. Politicians were seen as being on national service."[32]

There is need for deification of the ideological national project-*National Interest* like any of the traditional gods and robe it with all the attributes that will make the *being* have the awe and respect that all Nigerians regardless of status will admonish. The inherent fear that any form of negative behavior towards the deities by any Nigerian will attract severe sanctions or punishments just as it is done during their service or veneration or worship. The deification of the *National Interest* as resonated in the cannon and symbol of *the affecting presence* inherent in its metaphysical *being* with the attendant authority and power serves to enhance the unity and development of the country - a land of abundant opportunities and privileges. It is, in my view, to this *deified being- National Interest* that we should have our corporate allegiance of loyalty, commitment and faithfulness. As Joseph Allen rightly argues, "Political loyalty is a topic not rightly confined to reciting the Pledge of Allegiance and waving the flag. Genuine love for one's country on the part of a public official takes the form of faithfulness in regard to the responsibility of one's office on behalf of the citizenry."[33]

There is nothing unusual for our resolve to go back to our traditional customs and values as a means to heal the nation of the contemporary immoral decadence accentuated by our public office holders and political leaders. As the Yoruba adage mentioned before that *bi omode ba subu a wo waju sugbon be agba ba subu a wo ehin lati mo nkan to gbe won subu*, meaning, if a child falls down he looks forward but if an elder falls down he looks backward to know the cause of his fall. The suggestions I have made and defended are meant to resonate the wisdom in the adage and if properly adhered to Nigerians will not be spectators in the global race of development.

Notes and References

1. See details in the bibliography of the works of some historians, anthropologists and colonial officials etc in Segun Ogungbemi (1984) *The Yoruba Conceptions of Human Nature: A Philosophical Approach*, University Microfilms International Openlibrary.org/authors/OL287263A., 198-202. See Toyin Falola, *The power of African Cultures*,(Rochester: University of Rochester Press, 2003),97-105.

2. Toyin Falola, *Culture and Customs of Nigeria*,(Westport: Greenwoods Press, 2001), 25.

3. Falola, 26.

4. See Ogungbemi, "An African Perspective on the Environmental Crisis" in *Environmental Ethics: Reading and Application,* (ed.) Louis Pojman, (Boston: Jones and Barttlet Publishers, 1994), 203-209. The concept of ethics of common sense is also discussed in my article, "The Role of Africa in World Resources and Reserves" *Journal of Philosophy and Development* Vol.10 Nos. 1&2, 2008 Ago-Iwoye, 139.

5. See Ogungbemi, *The Yoruba Conceptions of Human Nature: A Philosophical Approach*, 141-145.

6. I borrowed the concept of the "Power of Affecting Presence" from the work of Robert Plant Armstrong, *The Power of Presence*,(Philadelphia: University of Pennsylvania Press, 1981).

7. Segun Ogungbemi, *A Critique of African Cultural Beliefs*,(Lagos: Pumark Educational Publisher, 1997), 39.

8. See Immanuel Kant, *Foundations of Metaphysics of Morals*,(Indianapolis: Bobbs-Merrill Educational Publishing,), 1978.

9. John S. Mbiti, *African Religions and Philosophy*,(Garden City: Anchor Books, 1970),141.

10. E. Bolaji Idowu, *Olodumare: God in Yoruba Belief*, (London: Longman, 1962), 174.

11. Idowu, 71-106.

12. See Thomas Hobbes, *Leviathan* (London: Collier MacMillan Publishers, 1978), 99.

13. See Hobbes, 100.

14. See Peter Singer *One word* (New Haven: Yale University Press, 2002), 1.

15. Obafemi Awolowo *People's Republic* (Oxford; Oxford University Press, 1968), 237.

16. Wole Soyinka, "Between Nation and Space" wolesoyinkasociety@yahoo.com March 3, 2009.

17. Festus Iyayi; "Nigeria: The ruling class, challenges of development and electoral reforms," *Punch*, October 28, 2010.

18. John Ameh and Adelani Adepegba, "Sanusi refuses to back down," *Punch*, December 8, 2010.

19. Emma Anya, Sesan Olufowobi and Abimbola Adelakun, RMAFC meets today over controversial jumbo pay," *Punch*, December 20, 2010.

20. Joseph Adeyeye, "Our Jumbo Democracy" *Punch*, December 10 2010.

21. See MD Yusuf, Crises of governance in Nigeria (2) *Punch*, December 8, 2010.

22. Editorial, "2011 Budget and Capital Project," *Punch*, December 22, 2010.

23. John Ameh and Friday Olokor, Melaye, Colleague return to House of Reps," *Punch*, December 9, 2010.

24. See "EFCC to Arrest Six more Ex-Governors" *Punch*, October 7, 2011.

25. Kunle Akogun, "Halliburton Bribe Scandal" *This Day* February 11, 2011. See www.google Halliburton Nigeria for more information on the scandal and how the Federal Government ended up with the case.

26. See Everest Amaefule, "Jumbo Pay: RMAFC queries top officials "*Punch*, December 21, 2010.

27. See *Punch*, December 9, and 10, 2010.

28. J. F. Ade Ajayi, "Towards a More Enduring Sense of History" Quoted from Toyin Falola, *Nationalism and African Intellectuals,*(Rochester: University of Rochester Press, 2004), 239-240.

29. Martin Meredith, *The State of Africa* (New York: Free Press, 2006), 688.

30. Toluwani Eniola, "Ex-VC urges cultural revival at a book launch" *The Nation*, September 28, 2011.

31. "Sultan to African leaders: emulate Caliphate's founding fathers" *The Nation*, October 5, 2011.

32. *The News*, June 21, 2010, 23.

33. Joseph L. Allen, *Love & Conflict* (Nashville: Abingdon Press, 1984), 271.

CHAPTER 7

Yoruba Nation: The Desire For Self-Determination

Introduction

Generally speaking, nature has designed a physical geography of Oduduwa State/Nation in the present states of Nigeria comprising Okun people in Kogi State, all the Yoruba in Kwara State and the Southwestern States, Lagos, Ogun, Ondo, Osun, Ekiti and Oyo. The natural estate of the Yoruba is blessed with many natural resources with abundant human capacity to harness them for their development to the standards obtainable at least in Western Europe. The political structure inherited from the British and its subsequent 'military constitution' and Northern hegemony have made the advancement of the Yorubaland almost invariably impossible. It has become more compelling under the present Buhari administration that blatantly refused to listen to the voice of reason that his government favors Fulanization and Islamization of Nigeria with attendant banditry, kidnappings, raping, maiming, ransom payment, killings, destruction of properties and land grabbing with impunity. These are insecurity indices that threaten cohesive national existence. I have provided a common sense argument that is predicated on a generative concept of renaissance meaning, all Yoruba monarchs, elites, intellectuals, scholars, artisans both at home and in diaspora have collectively lost faith and hope in the slogan, 'ONE NIGERIA' that is indivisible and hence decided to demand for self-determination and corporate existence called Yoruba Nation. When there is no good government or a government in power has made the country to become a failed state; anarchy becomes inevitable. Therefore living in the Hobbesian state of nature, in which 'life is brutish, nasty and short', becomes a reality. The Yoruba intellectual principle of common sense reasoning teaches that self-preservation is the first principle of human existence and self-determination is the cure hence the Yoruba are justified in their demand for Yoruba Nation.

With strong optimism, spirit of patriotism and dynamic faith and commitment to the unity and progress of Nigeria: some of us who came to the United States of America for further studies completed our programs and obtained, Master's degrees and Doctorates in the 1980s. Amongst these are Moses Ekundayo Adeyemi, Thomas Olabode Ogunrinun, Ezekiel Onaolapo Okeniyi, Bamidele Solomon, Julius Sunday Afolabi, Joseph Biodun Balogun, David Tuesday Adamo and I, who decided to return home after our studies, to contribute to human infrastructure needs of the country. I believe we were probably not the only patriotic academics and intellectuals with such determination amongst the diasporas in America and Europe. I only mentioned those that I knew then. We were academic and intellectual foot soldiers who volunteered to lay down our lives in order to make Nigeria a great nation. But little did we know that the country that has a motto, 'Unity and Faith, Peace and Progress' was built on a faulty architectural structure and the Nigerian founding fathers were not unmindful of it as Chief Obafemi Awolowo warned in 1947 in his book entitled, *Path to Nigerian Freedom*, "Nigeria is not a nation. It is a mere geographical expression. There are no 'Nigerians' in the same sense as there are 'English,' 'Welsh,' or 'French.' The word 'Nigerians' is merely a distinctive appellation to distinguish those who live within the boundaries of Nigeria and those who do not."[1] Similarly, the first Prime Minister of Nigeria, Alhaji Tafawa Balewa writes, "Since 1914, the British Government has been trying to make into one country, but the Nigerian people themselves are historically different in their backgrounds, in their religious beliefs and customs and do not show themselves any sign of willingness to unite…Nigeria unity is only a British intention for the country."[2] The fear that Nigerians were not willing to unite as one was to serve their imperialistic agenda. It was indeed, in my view, a faulty foundation. "But the foundation of Nigerian political structure has never been metaphysically built in the mind of their leaders and followers and predictably as long as the mindset remains unchanged the country will continue to go in a vicious circle."[3]

Be that as it may, we believed that a faulty structural foundation could be reinforced using architectural and intellectual skills to do it. Unfortunately, political gymnastics and somersaults that took the center stage over the years particularly from 1986-2021 made it impossible to fix the faulty foundation. I will discuss some of the political malaises subsequently that saw the country gradually disintegrating with unstoppable velocity.

The concept of Yoruba nation

Yoruba State derives its source from the mythical and historical accounts of the ancestral patriarch of the Yoruba, Oduduwa. J. Omosade Awolalu explains, "According to some myths, Oduduwa is seen both as a primordial divinity and as a deified ancestor"[4] Akin Alao also narrates a myth that "Oduduwa descended from heaven charged by Olodumare, the Lord of Heaven, to establish the kingdom of the earth….One major conclusion from this tradition is the claim that Ile-Ife was not just the source for the Yoruba people but also the cradle of all mankind through the process of creation."[5] In summary, E. Bolaji Idowu explains, "Today, he (Oduduwa) is acknowledged by the Yoruba as the progenitor of their race; as the tradition has it, he begat several children who in due course became the progenitors of the various clans which, taken together, are the Yoruba people."[6] It is indubitable that whichever traditions either mythical or historical one believes it is a general consensus among the Yoruba that Oduduwa; from time immemorial, was their progenitor. I have therefore used Oduduwa state and Yoruba nation interchangeably; referring to the same people occupying a geographical location and having cultural, religious, linguistic, social and political beliefs and practices. Given the natural design of physical geography of Oduduwa State/Nation in the present states of Nigeria it comprises Okun people in Kogi State, all the Yoruba in Kwara State and the Southwestern States, Lagos, Ogun, Ondo, Osun, Ekiti, Oyo and the Itsekiri in Delta State. The natural estate of the Yoruba is blessed with many natural resources with abundant human capacity to harness them for their development. The population of the Yoruba in Nigeria is over 30 million excluding those that are in West Africa, Europe, America, Brazil, Cuba, Haiti, Jamaica, Tobago/Trinidad etc. As a matter of fact there are more Yoruba people in the diaspora than those residing in their ancestral home in Nigeria.

The first initiator of Yoruba Renaissance for self-determination

It is logical to argue that the seed of Yoruba renaissance was planted by Chief Obafemi Awolowo given his revolutionary and vigorous pursuit of providing free education and health infrastructure to the Yoruba in the defunct southwest region.

One of the virtues of education is ability to discern meaningful and purposeful course in life. It is revolutionary in nature. One of his followers and pioneers who singularly demonstrated the need for the Yoruba to fight for self-determination was Modiyu Adeniyi Osinowo, a 27-year-old headmaster of a primary school in Lagos. Having seen how Chief Obafemi Awolowo was shabbily treated during the celebration of Nigerian Independence in 1960 at Tafawa Balewa Square Lagos, he sought for how to redress the abnormality.[7] Awolowo had shown his displeasure over his invitation cards and seat at the venue to the Prime Minister, Sir Tafawa Abubakar Balewa. According to Awolowo,

> I stated, with all emphasis at my command, that in any ceremony or function connected with Nigeria's Independence, I was prepared to give precedence to only Dr. Nnamdi Azikiwe, and himself as Prime Minister of the Federation. If they were around, I would give precedence to three other outstanding nationalists, namely, Ernest Ikoli, Oba Samuel Akinsanya, and H.O. Davies – all of whom were great pioneers in the agitation for Nigeria's self-determination. I would not give precedence to anyone else. But the invitation cards sent to me put me in the same bracket as Junior Ministers and Civil Servants.

In the canon of Yoruba morality of *Omoluabi* it stipulates, *owo die die lara'nfe*, meaning; people of honor deserve respect and what Awo has reacted to is a demonstration that he has not been given his due respect and honor at that august ceremony. It is an aberration, which is morally and culturally offensive.

Osinowo could not tolerate such a blatant disrespect and humiliation of Chief Obafemi Awolowo in such a monumental occasion of which he was one of the architects and builders of the country. Consequently, he decided to exercise his fundamental human right to protest what he considered as injustice. His demand, "Let's have our own Pakistan. If they could rubbish Awo like this sooner or later, they would be defecating on our heads…let's have our own sovereignty."[9] Having our own 'Pakistan' refers to the breakaway or separation of Pakistan from India. Osinowo was assassinated five years after his protest in 1960; thus became the first martyr for demanding for Yoruba self-determination.

Is restructuring of Nigeria a prelude to Yoruba self-determination?

Is the political structure of Nigeria a contributing factor to the current agitation for disintegration? Is there any justification for this demand? I have used the word 'justification' as a compelling and moral warrant for the Yoruba self-determination to disintegrate from the unholy alliance with Nigeria on the ground that the union from the perspectives of the agitators is no longer profitable for their mutual corporate co-existence. The non-profitability of this alliance was gradually and systematically a build-up from the creation of the country itself by the British imperialist which before independence in 1960, Nigeria was divided into three regions namely, Northern, Western and Eastern. Northern region has the largest landmass and population than each of the other two regions. The country was initially a federation of three regions operated under a constitutional federalism that made each region semi-autonomous. By this arrangement, each region was using its resources and wealth for the development of its region. For instance, from 1955-1966 the government of Western region introduced and implemented free education policy, free healthcare services, industrial infrastructures for development and employment, establishment of sports facilities, radio and television – the first in Africa among others. By 1957, Western region had gained its self-regional governance from the British while waiting for the other two regions to do the same in preparation for the country independence in 1960. The role played by the Tafawa Balewa administration in the political crisis in the Western region under the premiership of S.L. Akintola and the arrest of Awolowo for treason and felony that led to his imprisonment in 1963 eroded confidence in the unity of Nigeria amongst his loyalists. Furthermore in the First Republic when Awolowo was in prison, the Federal Government created Mid-western region in 1964 from Western region without creating more regions from Northern and Eastern regions. This was seen as a political mechanism to weaken the influence and power of Awolowo and his political party – Action Group (AG). "The internal political crisis of 1962 in the Western Region affected the national political space and contributed to the fall of the First Republic in January 1966."[11] In spite of those political stumbles, the Yoruba still remained committed to the unity of Nigeria. Now what is the last straw that broke the Carmel's back that made the call for self-determination to be politically, morally and logically warranted? Is this call for Yoruba nation supported by most Yoruba at home and in the diaspora? From current happenings, it seems too early to be determined.

The re-birth of Yoruba Renaissance for self-determination

Major General Muhammadu Buhari (Retired) was the nominee of All Progressive Congress (APC) political party for president and supported by majority of Yoruba politicians and the electorates both in 2015 and 2019 with the mandate to give Nigerians good governance. With Professor Yemi Osibajo serving as the Vice-President, Nigerians were assured that better things were in the offing to alleviate their suffering. Being a Yoruba man, the Yoruba were optimistic that given his pedigree, Osinbajo would assist the President to accomplish the political party's mandate to bring 'Change' and move to the 'Next Level'. The electorates like ordinary trustworthy people did not ask critical questions about how they were going to bring change and its implications; and what happens if the change does not add any meaningful gains to their lives? Their first term in office did not bring the anticipated change the public expected but the politicians made them to believe another mantra, the 'Next Level' that people don't really understand. Today if you ask fellow Nigerians who weighed 140:Ibs during former President Jonathan government 2009-2015 but now weigh 90:Ibs under President Buhari administration whether they are better off today or worst off? Some of them would probably bring the photos they took during each administration and ask you to judge for yourself. This is just at the level of human stomach infrastructure. It is not the case that they were voluntarily losing weights but an attestation of a true manifestation and concrete reality of economic trauma that the mismanagement and administrative incompetence of President Buhari has subjected them to. Many of us living in diaspora keep wondering what kind of Buhari/APC 'Next Level' is that? In other words, so far, instead of good governance it is starvation, hunger and misery without empathy.

Buhari administration has succeeded in dividing the country along the line of religion and ethnicity by making Fulani ethnic group his priority in terms of privileges and appointments. He has favored the Fulani herdsmen who wantonly destroy farmlands of people across the country without compensation. They actually became unnecessarily violent and deadly. Nigerians are reeling under the yoke of 'Buhari nepotistic democracy' where Miyetti Allah Cattle Breeders Association of Nigeria whose acronym is MACBAN, known to be a terrorist organization by the majority of Nigerian nationalities but a cohort of Buhari administration whose many of its members are into banditry, kidnapping, killing, rapping, ransom payment and land grabbing in Nigeria. This savagery is not in consonant with Yoruba principle of peaceful co-existence. Today, Nigeria has found itself in the Hobbesian state of nature: a state of anarchy where everyone is for the preservation of his life because life is "solitary, poor, nasty, brutish and short."[12] Given this state of nature with all manners of evil machinations infesting the country without hope for peace and security: is it not time for the Yoruba ethnic group to seek for self determination of their ethnicity since it is their inalienable right?

It is about sixty years after Osinowo was murdered; his spirit for Yoruba nation metamorphosed in Professor Banji Akintoye and Yoruba elites both at home and in diaspora. It also ignited like wildfire amongst most of lower level educated and uneducated Yoruba youths in cities, towns and rural communities. Professor Akintoye is currently the leader of the 're-visited renaissance' for Yoruba self-determination or Actualization of Yoruba Nation, which is otherwise called Oduduwa Republic. The difference between Osinowo's revolution for Yoruba nation and that of Akintoye's agenda is that the former was an individualistic response to what he saw as an insult to Chief Obafemi Awolowo a Yoruba revered leader while the latter is a response to a sum total mismanagement of crisis that involves grabbing Yorubaland by the Fulani herders carrying deadly weapons and ammunition to kill Yoruba sons and daughter who challenge them for encroaching on their farms and destroying their daily livelihood.

Akintoye has made it unequivocally clear to the Nigerian public and rest of the world that the movement is unstoppable. "I want to advise the Nigerian State that the Yoruba self-determination struggle under my leadership shall continue to be peaceful and orderly…. We are matching on, and like valiant soldiers without a dint of fear. I make bold to put it to the Nigerian State that no one can stop an idea whose time has come."[13] Professor Banji Akintoye has announced on Television and social media at different times to the whole world that the Yoruba World Congress has joined the Unrepresented Nations and Peoples Organization UNPO in order to exercise their fundamental rights for self-determination. According to UNPO:

> UNPO Welcomes New Member: Meet The Yoruba World Congress!
>
> General Assembly of the Unrepresented Nations and Peoples Organization saw the UNPO welcome five new members. The fourth new member to be welcomed was the Yoruba World Congress (YWC), representing the Yoruba people of West Africa. The YWC

has joined the UNPO because they want the Yoruba people to be able to exercise their right to self-determination, which they aren't able to do as a part of Nigeria.

The Yoruba people number over 44 million, making them the largest homogeneous people in Africa. The majority of this population (around 40 million) is located in Nigeria, where the Yoruba make up 15.5% of the country's population. Most Yoruba people speak the Yoruba language, which is the most widely spoken Niger-Congo language. They share the same language and culture. Yoruba identity is primarily linguistic rather than ethnic, and they include both Christian and Muslim Yoruba.

The Yoruba people occupy a clear territory and have their own distinct nation. When Nigeria became an independent country, little consideration was given to the Yoruba people's distinctiveness and separateness from the other peoples of Nigeria. As a part of Nigeria, the Yoruba people have suffered under governments that are fundamentally hostile to them, and which have allowed countless attacks on the Yoruba people to happen with impunity. The UNPO believes that the Yoruba people should be allowed to exercise their right to self-determination, as they have a valid right to do so.

Currently, the Yoruba region is the wealthiest in Nigeria, containing 8 Nigerian states (5 of which are in the top 10 wealthiest of the 36 states in Nigeria), including the economically important state of Lagos, which itself alone would be the 5th largest economy in Africa, were it independent. The region is extremely rich in natural resources, the exploitation of which makes up the largest part of the economy. Agriculture is also an important part of the economy.

The YWC have joined the UNPO to see what avenues are available to have their voices heard to assist in their quest for self-determination. YWC is an amalgamation of many Yoruba self-determination groups offering authentic representation and defense of the values, rights and demands of the Yoruba indigenous people.

The UNPO warmly welcomes the YWC to its membership and looks forward to working with the Yoruba World Congress over the coming years.[14]

When Professor Akintoye said that an idea that whose time has come, nobody could stop it[15], the backing of the UNPO of the agenda for Yoruba self-determination has, in my view, demonstrated his leadership competence to an appreciable proportion. There have been two instances that could have made the Yoruba to have their own country: the first is the 'Natural architectural design' of the geographical location of the Yoruba people that is blessed with a large population and rich cultural and linguistic values; and made possible by the Providence. The second one was when Western Region got its Regional self-government in 1957. The Western Region Government under Chief Obafemi Awolowo administration could have decided not to join the rest of the two regions, which were not ready for independence and declared its region Yoruba nation or Oduduwa Republic. Perhaps the British government would have been happier since Awolowo was seen as a thorn in their flesh for agitating for Western Region self-government and independence of Nigeria. Could it be because the idea was perhaps in the formative period?

As Akintoye is breaking the frontiers of success internationally his strategy to have the full backing of Yoruba at home is to me a Herculean task. Is he getting majority of Yoruba people at home consciously aware? What orientation/strategy has he put in place apart from social media and television interviews? Does his idea of Yoruba self-determination resonate well with Yoruba politicians and political class? Do the Yoruba youths key into the idea of disintegration of Yoruba people from the rest of Nigeria? Will this agitation not lead to war or social unrest? Who is going to finance this huge project called Yoruba State? Will the Yoruba in diaspora be allowed to participate in the referendum considering their huge financial and intellectual contributions? These are some of the questions that I think are begging for answers as the struggle for the realization of Yoruba nation or self-determination is gaining ground in the country. Is there no alternative to Yoruba pullout from Nigeria? I believe the Yoruba World Congress is not unmindful of the issues I have raised and perhaps they are equally working towards resolving them in their strategic planning.

From the home front, we have seen activities of the foot soldiers making strident efforts to sensitize people from state to state in Yorubaland. The most visible among them all is Chief Sunday Adeyemi, popularly called Sunday Igboho, a Yoruba activist and freedom fighter. The Odua People's Congress under the leadership of Chief Iba Gani Adams, the Are Onaokakanfo of Yorubaland amongst others has been observed to be active in this awareness crusades. It suffices to say that many Yoruba traditional leaders, Chiefs, Obas etc support this idea privately and surreptitiously because of security, economic and political implications.

Is restructuring an alternative to Yoruba self-determination?

What is restructuring? Why are political officeholders, political class and political elites talking now about restructuring? Why is the idea of restructuring so convoluted that any debate on it leaves the public to be more confused? Is it because there is no agreeable definition that everybody understands without equivocation? What do they want to restructure and for what reasons, and more importantly whose interest will it serve most? In other words, will the Northerners agree if what most people accept as justice and equitable solution but their own interest is not made paramount as expected? Similarly will restructuring be a panacea to disintegration at this time when the idea of Yoruba self-determination has reached a point of no return? Even if all these questions are adequately answered and at the end of the exercise no solution; will the effort not tantamount to exercise in futility with all the money and time spent?

Let me begin with a philosophical question that I believe will unravel the questions I have raised above. Is restructuring a property or something that is contingent on a substance that is fundamentally the essence of political corporate existence? Must the political elites, academics, intellectuals and professionals, labour unions leaders, and youth leaders not focus on cognitive intuition and principles of equity and social justice; written in an unambiguous language that is not voluminous and cumbersome to read but systematically outline the duties and functions of a democratic government that guarantees freedom, liberty, rights and justice? I mean a constitution of the people by the people and for the people. It is a transparent constitution that will guarantee good governance, harmony, patriotism, loyalty, peace and unity.

It seems to me when people debate the issue of restructuring, they are consciously referring to certain provisions in the 1999 Constitution as amended that should be amended or expunged because it does not enhance national interest as if it is their 'property'; Northern leaders are always quick to defend it because it is their 'property' and not the property of those who want to 'restructure' provisions in it. And truly, there is no need to argue with them because what you consider as not equitable in it is what give them privileges and advantages over the rest of the political zones. Therefore, it is not worth the time of people who understand the mindset of the political officeholders and political class of the people who belong to the Fulani hegemony. This is similar to what the Republicans in the United States are doing by supporting conspiracy theories that Democrats are working against the interests of American white nationalists.

I am not unmindful of the current efforts being made by National Assembly to review the 1999 constitution as amended and the position of Professor Akin Oyebode who avers:

> I am sorry to disappoint the National Assembly members that the exercise they have commenced is needless because you can't amend a forged document. We don't have a constitution, what we have is a military arrangement and the earlier we know this, the better for our country. Let me say that when a document is irredeemably faulty, there is no amount of amendment that can make it work. The time is right to put an end to the lie that we are operating a republic, we are only pretending to be.[16]

Featuring on the Channels Television's Politics Today on Monday, May 24, 2021, Professor Itse Sagay argues that the 1963 Republican Constitution should be the one to be amended and made relevant to the yearning of the generality of the citizenry. "If we had that, with amendments here and there to make it accommodate states rather than regions which we used to have, I think all these agitations will die down and everybody will be happy."[17] I doubt if everyone will be happy because the proposed new constitution will not have unitary provision where power will be at the center to control national revenues in favor of the North.

Both Oyebode and Sagay are eminent professors of law and their constitutional prognosis of Nigeria is at variant to each other. Oyebode has argued that any amendment of the 1999 constitution as amended is a fruitless exercise while Sagay has suggested an amendment of the 1963 Republican Constitution to reflect the prevailing realities on ground now. I want to remind Sagay that 1963 Republican Constitution was a product of colonized Nigerians with colonization hanger overs whereas the present dispensation is dominated by sons and daughters born after independence whose concepts of constitution they want will be radically different from their forebears with colonization mentality; like the idea of British parliamentary system. I have proposed a complete set of ideas that will lead to a new constitution that emanates from the people by the people and for the people. That is what I defined as People's Constitution. But wait a minute, will it satisfy northern political oligarchy and will it also stop the agitation of Yoruba self-determination? My simple answer is: let the people decide. But going by the view of Akintoye that when the time of an idea has come nobody can stop it, it is very unlikely that they will back down from their agitation of a country of Yoruba people-Oduduwa State/Yoruba nation. In other words, it appears the amendment of either 1963 Republican Constitution or the 1999 military constitution as amended is too late in the day because it is like trying to force a couple who have already divorced themselves after they have shared their property and waiting for the court to pronounce their dissolution. It is like the case of Bill Gates and his wife in the United States of America. There is no court in America that will force them to remain as husband and wife. Human beings are not inert objects that can be tied or glue together by force. Sooner or later they will free themselves from the unholy alliance. That is the reality on ground today in Nigeria; the Yoruba are saying they have had enough of their union with Nigeria.

Agitation for Yoruba nation without war

The fear of war is the fear of death with all the associated tragedies when war breaks out. One of the philosophers who has given a graphic picture of war was Thomas Hobbes. According to him:

> For war consisteth not in battle only, or for the act of fighting, but in a tract of time wherein the will to contend by battle is sufficiently known: and therefore the notion of time is to be considered in the nature of war, as it is in the nature of weather…. Whatsoever therefore is consequent to a time of war, where every man is enemy to every man, the same is consequent to the time wherein men live without other security than what their own strength and their own invention shall furnish them withal. In such condition, there is no place for industry, because the fruit thereof is uncertain: and consequently no culture of the earth; no navigation, nor use of the commodities that may be imported by sea; no commodious building; no instruments of moving, and removing such things as require much force; no knowledge of the face of the earth; no account of time; no arts; no letters; no society; and which is worst of all, continual fear; and danger of violent death; and the life of man, solitary, poor, nasty, brutish, and short.[18]

Against this backdrop of graphic fear of war and death as expressed by Hobbes; the experiences in African countries for instance, Nigeria, Liberia, Sudan, Sothern Sudan, Central African Republic, Rwanda and Libya have made many Nigerians to think for better options which a rational agent would consider and advise agitators for disintegration of the country at this precarious period of uncertainty. There is a critical issue that needs to be considered and that is, the question of how Nigerians decided to be governed as one entity before and after the First Republic. Did the Yoruba fight a war before becoming part of Nigeria? I have not come across any literature or historical accounts that enumerated the war the Yoruba fought before they were accepted as part of Nigeria. If the Yoruba did not become a member of the union called Nigeria by way of warfare: why should their agitation for disengagement cause fear of war? Why the apprehension and pessimism after Akintoye has assured them that there will be no war because UNPO supports a peaceful separation and not by means of war? The intellectual persuasion of pen and dialogue is more powerful than the barrels of guns and missiles. Chief Gani Adams, the Aare Onakakanfo of Yorubaland has argued with utmost optimism that the realization of Yoruba nation is worth dying for. Speaking in Lagos on Wednesday, May 26, 2021 he argues, "I want to say it here that the struggle to seek a new nation is the legitimate rights that we are determined to live and die for and we wouldn't waiver in our beliefs and determination to liberate our race."[19]

Conclusion

The development of Western Region in the 50s and 60s was equal to none in the country in terms of human and infrastructural developments. For instance, in the area of human infrastructure, they had functional free education program, free health for children, pregnant women etc plus implementation of minimum wage policy. The infrastructural development was phenomenal during Awolowo administration: the Western Nigeria Television (WNTV) the first in Africa, the 25-storey building called the Cocoa House, Liberty Stadium with floodlights and many other industrial structures; later called Odua investments that provided job opportunities for people. All these observable developments endeared Chief Obafemi Awolowo to the Yoruba people. This reminds me what one of my lecturers at University of Ibadan told us in class in the 70s that had it not been the free education of Awolowo, he would have not known the four walls of classroom in his life. Given an interview on Channel Television titled, 'Politics Today' Seun Okinbaloye asked Professor Sagay which way to go on the current debate on Constitutional Review Agenda? What is pertinent here is his reference to Chief

Awolowo when he was a student in those days at Ibadan. According to Sagay, the three regions then were in competition with one another and what he knew was not the Federal Government but Ibadan and Chief Obafemi Awolowo, which was the 'golden age' of Western Region, and by extension: perhaps Nigeria. It was the golden age not by sentiment but like other rational human beings, the Yoruba people proportion their political and economic advancement according to evidence. The Yoruba people in Nigeria believe in their ability to rule and govern themselves using the platform and roadmap of Chief Obafemi Awolowo administration and to improve on its trajectory within the cutting edge of science and technology like any of the developed countries in the world. Having found themselves in a federal political structure that guaranteed their collective peaceful co-existence with other ethnicities in Nigeria in 1960 and 1963 constitutions but due to military incursion into political governance with decrees to legitimatize their government, a unitary system was foisted on the country; and before they finally handed over to a civilian administration in 1999 it was not without a military constitution known as 1999 Constitution. The constitution has remained a cog in the wheel of progress and peaceful co-existence of most Nigerians. In the last six years of President Buhari administration, his Fulani ethnic group believes that they own the ancestral lands of all Nigerians; and they are ready to force the landowners out of their territories. This is a bitter pill the Yoruba and many Nigerians are not ready to swallow which President Buhari is forcing down their throats. He has told the nation that people should learn to live together in peace but he has not told his Fulani ethnic group to peacefully approach landowners to give them lands for cohabitation together with their herds. It must be noted that before now, there had been Fulani herdsmen living peacefully among the communities that granted them temporary space to live and do their legitimate business everywhere in Nigeria. They use sticks to control their herds as they graze around but the Fulani militiamen that invade people's land by force tender their cattle not only with sticks but also with deadly weapons and ammunition to kill anyone who dare to stop their animals from grazing on their farmlands. The Chairman of the Yoruba security outfit codenamed Amotekun in Oyo State, General Ajibola Togun (rtd) was reported as saying that, "The Fulani that I grew up to know were the native Fulani. But these ones causing problems are non-Nigerians. They are from Futa Jallon, Mali, Burkina Faso, Chad, and Niger Republic."[20] The Buhari administration has treated these foreign Fulani militiamen regardless of their ruthless and terrorist behavior with impunity. As a matter of fact, the Federal Government has a policy to create a Rural Grazing Area (RUGA) everywhere in the country for them. Nosa Igiebor writes, … "the Buhari we see is irredeemably ugly. One who's mortgaged his presidency to the defense and protection of Fulani militants of all stripes. He speaks for them. He pampers them. He even bribes them with multibillion naira schemes like RUGA (rural grazing areas) and National Livestock Transformation Plan."[21]. The Yoruba have rejected the RUGA policy because it amounts to forcing them to give their ancestral lands to foreigners. Why is Buhari administration more concerned about private business of these Fulani than the citizens of the country who own the lands? This unjust treatment of the Yoruba has convinced the people that the Federal Government has a sinister plan that must be restricted and the best solution is to seek their self-determination. And I believe it is a just demand in order to prevent any further bloodletting and other forms of criminality in Yorubaland. I am not unaware of the idea of restructuring as a plausible solution to dissolution of the country. President Buhari has repudiated any form of restructuring contrary to what is in the 1999 constitution as amended. President Buhari says, "Those calling for separation or restructuring are very naive or even mischievously dangerous.... My appeal to each and everyone here is to try and educate their children. We are better as a nation, there is no way we can be separated."[22] From the foregoing, President Buhari has foreclosed any form of acceptable solution to outrageous injustice with brutality and carnage his Fulani ethnicity has subjected fellow Nigerians into with impunity. His administration has impeded progress of other ethnic groups in Nigeria and particularly the Yoruba people. The envisaged progress in human capacity building and basic infrastructural development that the Yoruba under the Awolowo administration in the Western Region had begun became elusive. The Yoruba are now saying enough is enough of this retardation of progress. As the adage goes in Yoruba, Orisa bo gbemi, wa fi mi sile bo bami, meaning if Orisa does not bring prosperity to one's life, he should leave one alone. The Yoruba also believe that when one embarks on an existential expedition that is not yielding an expected result, a rational being should disengage on the fruitless journey and retrace his steps. The Yoruba people in Nigeria and in diaspora are prepared to build their own country for the present and future generations who will be proud of their traditional, cultural and identity values; and be respected in the comity of nations. The will to self-determination is the right choice and it is ontologically imperative. It is a moral and legitimate obligation that the heroes of our time will bequeath to this generation and generations yet unborn.

ENDNOTES

1. Obafemi Awolowo, Path to Nigerian Freedom(London: Faber and Faber, 1947), 47-48.

2. Nigeria: Tafawa Balewa and Other Prophesies' This Day 28 February 2020.

3. (Segun Ogungbemi "Removing the Debris" in Indigenous Knowledge Systems and Development in Africa eds. Samuel Ojo Oloruntoba, Adeshina Afolayan and Olajumoke Yacob-Haliso, (Gewerbestrasse: Palgrave Macmillan, 2020), 66-67.

4. J. Omosade Awolalu, Yoruba Beliefs and Sacrificial Rites (London: Longman Group Limited, 1979), 25.

5. Akin Alao 'Politics and Government' in Culture and Customs of the Yoruba ed. Toyin Falola and Akintunde Akinyemi(Austin: Pan-African University Press, 2017), 597.

6. E. Bolaji Idowu, Olodumare: God in Yoruba Belief(London: Longman Group Limited, 1962), 23

7. The News '60 years ago: How Awolowo was humiliated at Independence, but Balewa intervened' Thursday, October 1, 2020.

8. Ibid.

9. The Man Who Saw Tomorrow' https||preview.redd.it (reddit)

10. Ibid

11. Akin Alao, ibid, 601

12. Thomas Hobbes, Leviathan(London: Collier Macmillan Publishers, 1962 edition), 100.

13. tori.ng 'No One Can Stop Oduduwa Nation- Prof. Banji Akintoye' Monday 03rd May , 2021.

14. UNPO Newsletter: August 20, 2020.

15. tori.ng 03rd May , 2021. 'No One Can Stop Oduduwa Nation- Prof. Banji Akintoye'.

16. Tribuneonlineng.com 'Constitution review: You can't amend forged document, Oyebode tells NASS' May 25, 2021.

17. Mouthpiece Nigeria, 'Nigeria should scrap its constitution, adopt 1963 Republican Charter'-Sagay, mouthpiecengr.com 24 May, 2021.

18. Thomas Hobbes Leviathan, 100.

19. tori.ng Thursday 27th May, 2021. 'We are Ready To Die In Order to Actualize Oduduwa Republic'-Gani Adams,

20. tori.ng Thursday, June 3, 2021 "Fulani Militiamen from Mali, Niger Republic, others have infiltrated most South-West forests"

21. TELL May 31, 2021, "Chronicle of a failed 'Messiah'

22. tribuneonlineng.com June 19, 2021 "No government will cede its authority to people that are not elected- Buhari"

CHAPTER 8

Marriage For A Meaningful Existence

Introduction

Marriage customs and practices are predominantly human affairs although our experiences with natural habitats suggest that there is a very close affinity between male and female in social relationships for instinctive procreation purposes. This chapter is not about non-human 'marital relationships'. It is about human institution of marriage that has defined the phenomenon of existence and its various forms of development. I will examine four different forms of marriage namely, monogamy, polygamy, companionate, and gay marriage and how each of them promotes a meaningful existence.

There are, however, some interesting questions that people normally ask when the issue of marriage is discussed: What is marriage? How did it begin and for what purpose? Is marriage a rite of passage between a male and female or an institution for gender partnership? Is marriage limited to a relationship between a male and female alone? Why do people prefer one form of marriage to the other? What are the social, moral, religious and political implications for choosing any form of marriage? How do we make the institution of marriage conceptually and practically meaningful in the new generation? I am aware that questions about marriage cannot be exhausted and I don't pretend that the above questions are the only ones to be asked.

There has always been tension within the social, political and religious strata of human society about what informs the preference for a particular choice or form of marriage. For instance, toward the end of the 20th century and at the turn of

21st century the western world has penchant for gay marriage. Whereas in most African countries gay marriage is considered an abomination, while polygamy is culturally accorded a noble practice. Does any form of marriage provide necessary and sufficient condition for a meaningful existence? A curious mind will ask: What constitutes a meaningful existence in marriage? My intention in this discourse is to attempt to respond to all these questions on the model of marriage as a human institution that I have set out to espouse, noting its significance for underpinning a meaningful existence.

Marriage as a Divine Institution

One is not sure when marriage was first instituted before the advent of religion but whenever it took place, it was probably first and foremost for procreation purposes. Social and cultural anthropologists and scientists have endeavored to unravel the origin of human existence but what became their findings are empirically inconclusive. For instance, Richard E. Leakey wrote that Charles Darwin suggested, "that human forebears might be found in Africa."[1] If this hypothesis is true, it necessarily follows that Africa is where human procreation began and hence the development of micro human society. But how did marriage become instituted and for what reasons and purpose? Did the first man on the planet earth institute it or it was instituted by a divine command?

Given the nature of African social and cultural narratives of human existence it could be the case that as John S. Mbiti writes, "God is the explanation of man's origin and sustenance: it is as if God exists for the sake of man."[2] And if that were the case, then Africans would probably not hesitate to look back and assert that the Supreme Being who is conceived to exist for their purpose is the one that instituted marriage from time immemorial. The proposition of marriage as an institution ordained by the Supreme Being means in the religious and social context that it has a moral and legal authorization to cement conjugal relationships between a man and a woman for both of them to become husband and wife for the promotion of procreation, social values, happiness, identity, economic prosperity, and metaphysics of immortality, etc., which are the hallmarks of rational beings.

Mbiti further explains, "For African peoples, marriage is the focus of existence. It is the point where all members of a given community meet: the departed, the living and those yet to be born… Therefore, marriage is a duty, a requirement from the corporate society, and a rhythm of life…."[3] From the western world,

Russell writes, "Marriage differs, of course, from other sex relations by the fact that it is a legal institution. It is also in most communities a religious institution, but it is the legal aspect which is essential."[4]

In western culture, it is Christianity that made marriage a religious institution using the Biblical narrative of how God acted in human history through the mythical story of Adam and Eve. Adam was living in a solitary confinement in the Garden of Eden. At the opportune time God decided that Adam should be free from loneliness to a social corporate existence. So, God embarked on the first surgical operation in human history by applying a *metaphysical anesthesia* that made Adam to fall asleep for the duration it took his Creator to get a woman from one of his ribs. In this narrative God did not ask Adam for his consent whether he wanted a wife or not. But the beauty of it all is that Adam became a family man free from loneliness in his solitary confinement.

Thus in the Old Testament we have the first Biblical m*arriage act*, Genesis 2:24-25, "Therefore shall a man leave his father and his mother, and shall cleave unto his wife: and they shall become one flesh."[5] I believe all Biblical scholars are aware that the above quotation was not part of the original text because there were no father and mother from where a man could leave behind and cleave to his wife. There were three people involved in the above narrative; i.e., God, Adam and Eve. But even the wife, who was a divine gift to Adam, in retrospect, was a symbol of good and evil that he could probably not fathom. The marriage ceremony that was performed by God in the Garden of Eden was for some specific purposes; i.e., helpmeet, companionship and procreation so as to replenish the planet earth.

This is the primary domestication of Old Testament theology of marriage. The birth of Christianity however provided additional function of marriage. Joseph Allen explains, "One way of characterizing what the marriage relationship is like is to identify the purposes or goods that it should serve. The Christian tradition has identified several, among them (1) procreation, (2) companionship, (3) the restraint of sin, and (4) the sacrament."[6] The sacrament that was not originally part of the Old Testament theology of marriage has given more religious glamour to the institution of Church marriage.

From the foregoing, I have attempted to establish the origin of marriage from African and Western perspectives, which was primarily a divine and social institution. Is marriage only a divine institution? Marriage is not just a divine institution; it only provides the basis for its existence and the primary functions in human history. The real actors in marriage are the human beings who are expected to find its worth and values.

Marriage as a human institution

If the proposition that the male and female who first existed became husband and wife were true, it is, therefore, plausible to believe that their form of marriage was not classified. As human population increased, the social dimension of marriage began to emerge. Thus the idea of introduction, "bridewealth"[7] and actual wedding ceremony becomes a social requirement that makes the living together of husband and wife morally and legally warranted.

In Nigeria, this form of marriage is called traditional marriage or customary marriage. It is called traditional marriage or customary marriage because it follows the traditions, social customs and norms laid down by the forebears and whatever is done in the process must be in accordance with the traditions and customs of the people. E. Bolaji Iyekolo writes, "marriage …is a union between two families, the bride's and the bridegroom's parents and their relations. It goes beyond just the marriage between a man and a woman, but demands reciprocal support from both families."[8]

When marriage is conducted in the traditional and customary manner, it receives normative blessings from the parents of the bride and the bridegroom, families, extended families, and friends. In all customary marriages nobody forgets to invoke the blessings of the departed ancestors because their joy is to have progenies who will remember them.[9]

Since traditional or customary marriage is more of family relationship, conflicts between husband and wife are in most cases resolved by extended family members. Due to this form of social relations divorce is never encouraged, because elders from both families of the husband and wife get involved and amicable solutions are found; this is more so when the marriage is blessed with children. The blessings of children in most cases serve as a healing balm to estranged relationship.

However, in a sterile marriage sometimes divorce becomes inevitable, because the family of the husband will encourage him to have another wife who expectedly will give birth to children. When the first wife can no longer bear the horror of shame of being barren, she leaves the man and possibly travels to a more conducive environment.

In many traditional societies the inability to produce children by a couple is always the fault of the wife and not that of the husband. But modern medical science has proved that the fault could come from either the husband or the wife or both. Therefore the family needs some medical advice and suggestions that could resolve their problem of barrenness. This later development in human medicine, in my opinion, has little or no effect on the traditional mind that sees married women as the cause of infertility. My intention is not to discuss the issue of divorce here but to note it as an unacceptable norm in traditional or customary marriage in Africa.

The advent of western colonization introduced another form of marriage that is radically alien to African customs that are based on equal rights and freedom between married couples. Russell explains, "there must be a feeling of complete equality on both sides; there must be no interference with mutual freedom; there must be the most complete physical and mental intimacy; and there must be a certain similarity in regard to standards of values."[10] It is a marriage institution that seeks to protect the rights of both spouses in the court of justice. This form of marriage gains popularity among the elite who have been exposed to western education and are in either private or public institutions, away from their traditional family homes. The married couples normally take an oath of allegiance in court and once it is done it becomes bidding. The oath of allegiance in either customary marriage or court marriage is a commitment that obligates each party to certain responsibilities that are meant to enhance unity and harmonious relationship. The success of any form of marriage depends on the commitments and faithfulness to marriage obligations.

Monogamy

Monogamy is a marriage relationship between a man and a woman that is generally described as "one man, one wife."[11] We do not know how it first began but whenever the idea of getting married to an opposite sex was introduced as a social relationship, it may be among the first form of marriage in human history. It is also the most predominant form of marriage among other forms of marriages known in human social relationships. Some religious intellectuals or scholars would probably argue that the story of Adam and Eve could have been the first example of monogamy in human history.

On a critical look at the story it is plausible to argue that what actually took place in the Garden of Eden in form of marriage was nothing but an introduction of *incest* because the woman was made from the body of Adam. Thus, Adam was the father of Eve and Eve was the daughter of Adam; therefore, in a nutshell, Adam married his own daughter. As I have argued earlier, the story of Adam and Eve as narrated in the Old Testament was a myth about the origin of human existence as conceived by the Israelites. There was no evidence that a man called Adam or a woman called Eve ever lived as historical figures. The name Adam means man and Eve means woman. Therefore, they could not be the first ancestors that practiced monogamy in human history.

My supposition is that for monogamy, given the initial human population, it is logical to believe that it is the first form of marriage in human existence that was meant to respond to the immediate natural and social needs of the couple. The first natural order between husband and wife is sexual relationship that could lead to procreation and development of family. In other words, monogamous marriage seems probably to have been the original basis of human family relationship and as population increased certain social values emerged.

To this end, human beings in Africa prioritize his/her interest on economic or material values in addition to other metaphysical interests. The pursuit of personal and social values adds to his/her proportional or aggregate sense of what constitutes a meaningful existence. It seems to me that what possibly counts as proportional or aggregate values are: longevity, children, wealth, and good legacy. Russell argues, "A marriage which begins with passionate love and leads to children who are desired and loved ought to produce so deep a tie between a man and woman that they will feel something infinitely precious in their relationship...."[12] As noble as this proposition is, Russell does not tell us the number of children to be desired and loved. He is probably right by saying that children serve a unique bond of affection and intimacy to a married couple.

If having children is so significant in marriage as it has been emphasized in this narrative, is it possible in a monogamous marriage to satisfy the desired number of children a couple should have bearing in mind the health hazard to the woman? All depends on the number of children the couple really want to have. But it must be borne in mind that at the developmental stage of human forebears, perhaps pastoral life was their primary occupation, and the need for more children to increase the labour force was desirable.

In modern time, monogamous marriage has gained popularity among the elite in Nigeria in consequence of the influence of western culture that emphasizes the principle of one man one wife that has become a cliché, which is conceived as 'me and my husband'. Even though this form of marriage is an ideal to the elite, because it fosters a deep friendship, unity and harmonious relationship, it allows mutual engagement for purposeful relationship that obligates both parties to live according to the marriage vows. It also makes the couple to have proper future planning in terms of the number of children to have and their well being that will enhance and promote happiness.

As lofty as all this may be, Russell sounds an ethical warning, "in a rational ethic, marriage would not count as such in the absence of children. A sterile marriage should be easily dissoluble, for it is through children alone that sexual relations become of importance to society, and worthy to be taken cognizance of by a legal institution."[13] We have four issues that Russell has raised here i.e., children, social expectation, barrenness and divorce. The most important are children and social expectation, because they are what contribute to human values. Children are the necessary ingredients in marriage and when a couple does not have them it is like a wife who makes a pot of soup without its important ingredients. A home without children is dull and uneventful, a situation that in most cases leads to separation or divorce. This does not imply that having children alone can make a married couple to remain inseparable. What it means, I believe, is that children provide a durable synergy between their father and mother for a peaceful home.

As one lays emphasis on the importance of children in a monogamous home, it is imperative to address what Allen calls, "bringing them up to responsible maturity."[14] This means giving the children sound education and providing an enabling environment that will make them to be fulfilled in life. To be fulfilled in life is hereby construed to mean contributing meaningfully to human capacity building and promoting human happiness. In other words, I think Allen is simply saying that it is of no value to have children parents cannot provide their necessity of life, which will enable them to survive in a competitive society and to become morally responsible to their fellow human beings. The position of Allen is for an ideal situation where parents have the basic needs to meet the upbringing of their children. And secondly, the philosophy behind childbearing of each individual and societies differ. For instance, in many African societies, parents believe that having many children is a sign of divine favour and it is expected that parents who have them must rejoice whether they are rich or poor. Some even would suggest that since God gives children to parents he will surely provide for their needs, hence they should not worry too much about how to find the support for their children. What is most important to most African monogamous marriages is having children that society will be able to identify as their contribution to its population and development no matter its magnitude.

Polygamy/Polygyny

Let me erase the impression some of my American male friends have about polygamy in Africa, because it sounds weird to them. Their general belief is that African men have multiple wives and that is why they have many children. That explains one of the reasons why they are poor, hence the need for foreign aid to take care of their basic needs, including education. I used to tease them that if any of them followed me to Africa, I would give him five to six wives. They would say really! And then laughed themselves to frenzy.

Of course, they are ignorant of the number of men and women who actually are involved in polygamous marriage. But their problem was that they were not curious enough to investigate whether the information they had about polygamy in Africa was true or false. Perhaps it was not that of importance to them. According to the World Bank, the percentage of female population in sub-Sahara Africa in 2013 is 50.02 and the male is 49.98. The difference between the female and male in terms of percent differential is 0.04.[15]

The word 'polygamy' means a marriage relationship that involves a man having more than one wife. It is a marriage form that deals with minority women who are in need of husbands even though they know that the man is already married hence, polygamy is a "plural marriage."[16] While polygamy on the one hand is conceived as 'plural marriage', polygyny on the other is defined as a practice where a man marries "two or more wives."[17] I am aware that these marriage forms are practiced in Africa and America particularly among the Mormons, Church of the Latter Day Saints, believers in the States of Utah, Arizona, Colorado etc.[18]

The two forms of marriage are significant because they express three factors in human sexual relationships. The first is the desire on both parties to respond to the call of nature to procreate, the second is to have wives and their children for agrarian labour force (for economic reasons), and finally to remove social stigmatization because in many African societies, a woman wants to have a husband as a symbol of crown over her head in order to earn respect in the community. But the most important in these sets of social values is having children.

Maillu elaborates, "Having children has been seen and understood as a kind of natural insurance policy against the unseen bad circumstances which might rob a person of his loved one, of his shelter, food and company. It is a move to ensure that when you weep, there will be, or there is likely to be, someone who matters to see your tears."[19] Yes, it is psychologically significant to understand the metaphor of having a child to see the tears that run down the cheeks of any of his parents who weeps. In addition to this is, "The fear of getting old without a child is comparable to the fear of going to war without weapons. The fear of falling sick without a child, the fear of dying without a child, the fear of extinction – such fears are, indeed, crippling and traumatic experiences to many people."[20]

Maillu is simply expressing an African experience, which may not necessarily be relevant in more advanced countries where medical services take care of most of the fears. The idea of extinction is a genuine concern to Homo sapiens and that is why polygamous or polygynous marriage forms attempt to allay the fear.

Companionate marriage

The simple definition of this marriage form is marriage of convenience. According to Merriam-Webster dictionary, companionate marriage is "a proposed form of marriage in which legalized birth control would be practiced, the divorce of childless couples by mutual consent would be permitted, and neither party would have any financial or economic claim on the other."[21] It is a marital arrangement to satisfy specific interests, including the libido of both partners, until such a time they both willingly decide to end the relationship. In other words, it is a marriage of *wait and see*, which has no solid commitments or profound obligations.

This idea of mutual relationship between consenting male and female adults deviates from the conventional moral principles or cultural and social norms of marriage in society. The occasion of modernization and democracy in Europe and America made people to have penchant for the new freedom and rights. And in the course of exercising freedom and rights, companionate marriage became charitable among young adults[22] without any recourse to the inherited Christian marriage doctrine and values.

The ethics of companionate marriage allows easy disengagement without going to court or to make compensation necessary when the two consented to end the relationship. In other words, the relationship has an inbuilt divorce mechanism to allow each partner to go freely without any misgiving. The only problem there is: what if one partner does not want to consent putting an end to the relationship because of the psychological trauma that will result from the technical divorce. The agony of being stigmatized as fairly used man and woman in the eye of the public will be undeniably difficult to erase. Another enigma in this form of marriage is if children are involved in the relationship: who takes care of them? How does this form of marriage deepen human, social and cultural values? In other words, how does companionate marriage contribute to a meaningful existence?

Same-sex marriage

Homosexuals all over the world are a minority whose idea of marriage differs significantly from the conventional practice of male and female marital relationship. Marriage, in their view, ought to be based on love, rights and choice of the individuals whether it is between a man and woman or between the same-sex. It is an expression of falling in love. And when two people are in love, it is difficult, if not impossible to separate them. If monogamists and polygamists do not feel ashamed of being husband and wife, why should homosexuals feel ashamed of same-sex marriage? So, same-sex marriage is a union between the same sex; that is man and man, woman and woman in a "holy" matrimony.

There is a scenario that is not yet addressed here. We have a woman-to-woman marriage; one is husband and the other wife - female husband. It sounds odd and a contradiction in terms. It is indeed a misnomer, which has become fashionable as a result of modernity. May we not confuse this idea of female husband with what is practiced in some African communities? There is a strong kinship system in Africa that recognizes married women who are economically and politically powerful in their communities who marry women in order to raise children in their own family lineage. Such women are called female husbands. Michelle Zimbalist Rosaldo elaborates, "Among the Lovedu...for instance, a woman may win power, status, and autonomy by taking over her husband's estate or by accumulating capital and marrying wives (the Lovedu have queens who, in the ritual aspects of marriage, perform in the role of a man)."[23]

Jane Fishburne Collier writes that among the Nuer ethnic group female husband is a common phenomenon.[24] Nkeonye Otakpor told me that female husband is practiced in some parts of Igbo land in Nigeria. The idea of female husband is a misnomer as well as a contradiction in terms. Yet, it accurately describes a marriage institution peculiar to some Igbo communities West of the Niger as well as East of the Niger.

What it means is that a childless woman is culturally permitted to marry another woman. The childless woman plays the role of a husband. She is entitled to the rights and privileges of a husband within the cultural context. This arrangement enables her to maintain her position in the household. It helps conduct her burial ceremonies without rancor and unnecessary quibbling.

Let me reiterate again that there is a difference between an African idea of female husband and the Euro-American lesbian practice. In the case of same-sex marriage in Europe and America it is a subtle revolutionary movement that became noticeable towards the end of the 20th century, which became a concrete reality in the 21st century. The voice of gay people became louder and politically forceful in Western countries to the extent that they became recognized by law to engage in marriage, hence the term same-sex-marriage. The Church in those countries where same-sex marriages are allowed by law is divided because some of the ministers and members of the congregation are involved in homosexuality. However, the Catholic Church remains opposed to homosexual activities including same-sex marriage. That is why, in Nigeria, the Catholic Archbishop Diocese Abuja, Cardinal John Onaiyekan says that gay marriage or same-sex marriage is against the will of God and the stance of the Catholic Church is "irrevocable."[25]

In many African societies homosexuality is generally conceived as immoral and it is against the natural law, because it makes procreation naturally impossible. Therefore same-sex marriage is an abomination and a threat of human extinction. For instance, in Uganda, before the antigay law, homosexuals were subjected to inhuman treatment in public places and sometimes paid the supreme price of punishment. According to Alan Cowell:

> Brushing aside Western threats and outrage, President Yoweri Museveni of Uganda significantly strengthened Africa's antigay movement…signing into law a bill imposing harsh sentences for homosexual acts, including life imprisonment in some cases…. 'Africans never seek to impose our view on others; if only they could let used alone,' Mr. Museveni said, alluding to Western pressure to reject the bill.[26]

Similarly, in Nigeria, Cowell reports, "In Nigeria, Mr. Jonathan's approval of the similar legislation there inspired mob violence against gays in areas including the capital, Abuja."[27] But before Jonathan administration homosexuals had been practicing their sexual acts secretly because of fear of harassment from the public. They did not want to come out openly to demand for their rights because doing so could provoke negative reactions from the public. As far as African traditions are concerned Western civilization has a limit when it comes to any form of rights that is against the acceptable social and marital norms. That is why most African leaders did not want President Obama of the United States and world leaders to lure them into the idea of granting same-sex marriage a legislative support in the continent.

It is morally unreasonable to subject gay people wherever they are to inhuman treatment. They have inalienable rights to exist and not to be stigmatized anywhere in the world including African countries. President Museveni and former President Jonathan did mellow down their strict stance on homosexuality in their countries due to foreign pressures particularly from United States of America and Britain.

Some critics of gay marriage wonder the kind of moral values same-sex marriage is promoting and why they think in the 21st century it will contribute to a meaningful existence? The only significant contribution to a purposeful life same-sex marriage attempts to propagate is that no matter what people say about your lifestyle as long as you know your rights, demand for it as long as it takes, perhaps someday people of rational conscience in your community will pause a moment and reason with you and fight on your behalf until the needful is done.

Relationship between marriage and a meaningful existence

The relationship between marriage and a meaningful existence has to be put in perspective. Are we talking about marriage in terms of its traditional conceptions, roles and objectives as it relates to meaning and purpose of life? Or are we concerned about its existential, ethical and epistemological argumentations and clarifications to satisfy intellectual curiosity of the 21st century mind? Both ways of looking at marriage and its purpose and meaning in an authentic life are imperative in view of modernity and its implications for human existence.

Russell raised a fundamental issue of happiness or unhappiness in marriage, "When we look round the world at the present day and ask ourselves what conditions seem on the whole to make for happiness in marriage and what for unhappiness, we are driven to a somewhat curious conclusion, that the more civilized people become the less capable they seem of lifelong happiness with one partner."[28] The observation of Russell is probably true in Western world.

I want to postulate a premise on which to properly situate the primary and ultimate objective of human existence that necessitates marriage differently from what Russell says and the early two institutions of marriage already discussed. The propelling factor of human existence is happiness. Therefore, marriage in whatever form it takes is primarily to enhance human happiness. The psychological impetus of happiness becomes the cutting edge in human multifarious activities that lead to compendium of achievements.

The role of human procreation is meant to increase human happiness and to prevent human race from extinction. Therefore, happiness, whichever way it is conceived, is definable only in reference to a meaningful existence of which marriage takes preeminence. Any form of marriage that does not consummate to having children only leads to a short-term happiness. But those who have children always have emotional happiness when they are back from school. And when the time comes for them to go back to school particularly, those who are in boarding institutions, parents generally have certain percentage of their happiness removed until when they come back. Most married women who have children endure a lot of discomfort and domestic abuse from their husbands for the sake of the children. In most African societies, one is accorded respect for being married and more importantly if the marriage is blessed with children. A noisy home occasioned by the presence of children brings more happiness than a solitary existence without children. Those who have penchant for children hardly complain about their disturbances.

From the foregoing, companionate and same-sex marriages that cannot lead to human procreation do not contribute to an ultimate meaningful existence. Therefore, the engagement in marriage that qualifies as a meaningful existence is the one that maximizes happiness through procreation and safe human existence from extinction. I am not unaware of the current moral and legal issues of lesbian, gay, bisexual and transgender (LGBTQ) identity and their notion of marriage. While I believe in inclusiveness of all forms of marriages, the challenge of procreation remains existentially significant. The question of happiness in a meaningful human existence without marriage and children is undoubtedly in my mind a moral, ethical and epistemological issue and not a scientific one. If having children becomes the ultimate value in marriage in terms of its meaningfulness to individuals and corporate existence, same-sex couples can adopt children just like barren women.

Conclusion

I believe that any form of intellectual discourse on marriage as either a divine or human institution or both which is relevant to the contemporary space must be understood in terms of its maximization of happiness and meaningfulness to human existence with emphasis on procreation to save humanity from extinction. This notion of human value as exemplified in this paper recognizes the import of religious concerns and its due respect for human procreation and happiness, but it dissociates itself from its theological hermeneutics. This is aptly explained by Richard Taylor, "The meaning of life is from within us, it is not bestowed from without, and it far exceeds in both its beauty and permanence any heaven of which men have ever dreamed or yearned for."[29] Since human beings found themselves in this precarious existence they have no option than to find what could make their existence worth living. And my contribution to it is found in happiness, which marriage and children are its ethos.

Endnotes

1. Richard E. Leakey *The Making of Mankind* [New York: E.P. Dutton, 1981], 13.

2. John S. Mbiti *African Religions and Philosophy* [Garden City, New York: Doubleday & Company, 1970], 119.

3. John S. Mbiti *African Religions and Philosophy*, 174.

4. Bertrand Russell *Marriage and Morals* [New York: Horace Liveright, 1970], 130.

5. The Holy Bible, [Nashville, Tennessee: Crusade Bible Publishers, 1970], Genesis 2:24.

6. Joseph Allen *Love & Conflict: A Covenantal Model of Christian Ethics* [Nashville: Abingdon Press, 1984], 223.

7. Toyin Falola *Culture and Customs of Nigeria* [Westport: Greenwood Press, 2001], 121.

8. E. Bolaji Iyekolo *The Peoples of Okunland* [Lagos: Concept Publications, 2006], 92.

9. John S. Mbiti *African Religions and Philosophy*, 175.

10. Bertrand Russell *Marriage and Morals*, 143.

11. John S. Toyin Falola *Culture and Customs of Nigeria*, 12.

12. Bertrand Russell *Marriage and Morals*, 142.

13. Bertrand Russell *Marriage and Morals*, 156.

14. Joseph Allen *Love & Conflict: A Covenantal Model of Christian Ethics*, 224.

15. www.tradingeconomics.com population: female -% of total in sub Saharan world.

16. David G. Maillu *Our Kind of Polygamy* [Nairobi: Heinemann, 1988], 1.

17. John S. Toyin Falola *The Power of African Cultures* [Rochester: University of Rochester Press], 259.

18. See Elizabeth R. Rose Polygamy in the American Southwest – Child Brides, Polygamous Communities, www.polygamy.com.

19. David G. Maillu *Our Kind of Polygamy*, 5.

20. David G. Maillu *Our Kind of Polygamy*, 6.

21. Merriam-Webster Online Dictionary, 2015.

22. Bertrand Russell *Marriage and Morals*, 156-157.

23. Sherry B. Ortner, "Is Female to Male as Nature is to Culture" in Michelle Zimbalist Rosaldo & Louise Lamphere eds., *Woman Culture and Society* [Stanford: Stanford University Press, 1974], 37.

24. Jane Fishburne Collier, "Women in Politics" in Michelle Zimbalist Rosaldo & Louise Lamphere eds., *Woman Culture and Society*, 95.

25. News Express Nigerian online, Catholic Stand Against Homosexuality Irrevocable – Onaiyekan, http://www.newsexpressngr.com/news/detail.php?news=13332 [accessed August 27, 2015].

26. Allen Cowell, "Uganda's President Signs Antigay Bill", New York Times, February 24, 2014, http://www.newyorktimes, [accessed on February 24, 2014].

27. Allen Cowell, "Uganda's President Signs Antigay Bill", New York Times, February 24, 2014.

28. Bertrand Russell *Marriage and Morals*, 135.

29. Richard Taylor "Does Life Have a Mean*ing?*" in *The Meaning of Life: Questions, Answers and Analysis*, Steven Sanders and David R. Cheney, eds., [Englewood Cliffs, New Jersey: Prentice-Hall, 1980], 85.

* Segun Ogungbemi (2016) "Marriage for a Meaningful Existence" *Caribbean Journal of Philosophy* Vol. 8, N0 1, 83-103.

CHAPTER 9

African Women At The Receiving End

Introduction

From time immemorial women have been at the receiving end of unwholesome treatments by men and nature. There are two principal issues in human existence that both male and female consider extremely important in Africa namely, ancestry and inheritance. The issue of rights becomes insignificant in Africa insofar as the place of women is concerned if by rights we mean women having equal privileges, opportunities, freedom and treatment as men. It appears as if women have no other choice than to live in the world of men in spite of some of their gruesome treatments particularly during conflicts and wars. The question is: what is the origin of women being treated as means and not as ends in themselves? Is there any moral justification for treating women as means only? The idea of treating women as means only in this context means that they are beings of instrumental values only and not as beings having both instrumental and intrinsic values. This chapter examines the causes of treating women as means only. It also raises some fundamental moral and ethical reasons why in the 21st century women ought to be treated as equals with men and if there is any justifiable or any moral warrant not to treat women as equals, it ought to be to their best interest as in the case of military operations or any other human activities that will endanger their lives at a particular situation. The moral and ethical approach, which this chapter takes as a plausible means of giving women their rightful place as equal partakers in the universe of humans is, in my opinion, the most logical and reasonable.

Man and Woman Relationships

Generally speaking, 'women are essential commodities' in Africa. Man is not considered complete or matured without a woman. A bachelor or a spinster is not fully integrated into the society until he or she is married. One of the major reasons why a woman is valued in Africa is her ability to procreate and contribute to man's social, domestic and economic needs. To Africans, women contribute to personal, social and psychological happiness of men. An African environment without women is desolate and does not appeal to man's habitation. Within African cultural setting for a woman to be married she is expected to meet certain traditional values namely, chastity, circumcision, good behavior mostly, respect, etc. Although modernization has influenced some of the traditional virtues that a marriageable woman must meet before getting married, one of the most difficult aspects of the traditions is female circumcision or female genital mutilation. It is believed that if a female is not circumcised she will be promiscuous which is infidelity in marriage. Female circumcision generally in Africa is part of initiation before marriage. A woman that is not circumcised is not mature. But the practice of female genital mutilation is in practical terms to the *interest* of man even when the practice has led to untimely death of many women. In recent times the HIV/AIDS pandemic made the practice unacceptable and condemnable because the traditional instruments used for circumcision are not sterilized. The World Health Organization, human rights activists, in the western world and Africa engaged in fierce campaign against female circumcision. In spite of the intervention of modernization the practice of female circumcision still persists mostly in rural communities because it is considered virtuous for a woman to be circumcised.

Having stated the importance of women to men in Africa the question that follows is: why are women not considered equal to men? In other words, if women are considered all that valuable to men why don't they receive equal treatment like men? Why can't a women claim equal rights in the society as men? Why can't women have equal say in matters that affect their lives like men in the family and community like men? The questions raised are germane and they can be answered within the cultural and customary traditions in which both men and women live in Africa. In other words, given the nature of different ethnic groups in Africa one cannot be very assertive but there are general overviews of women from which one can give a fair and general answers to the questions raised above. Even then as I have said earlier culture and traditions play a significant role in the way and manner women are conceived and treated in Africa. Toyin Falola writes:

Culture definitely plays a role in many of the experiences of women, as well as the hardships they complain about. Gender inequality can be rationalized by culture. Gender roles and reward allocation may be based on old beliefs. Within households, even if gender roles are complementary, men are regarded as heads of households while a woman has relevance as a mother and wife. She keeps traditions and kinship alive by bearing children and socializing them. As a bearer of children, she acquires respect within the household; as bearers of male children, she acquires prestige and ensures the stability of her marriage and the continuity of kinship and its traditions.[1]

In a patriarchal society that Africa generally speaking is, the form of culture and traditions are determined by and large by men and women play marginal roles in matters of significant importance. That is why some scholars have identified women with *nature* and men with *culture*. Michelle Zimbalist Rosaldo explains:

> Insofar as men are defined in terms of their achievement in socially elaborated institutions, they are participants, *par excellence*, in the man-made systems of human experience. On a moral level, theirs is the world of "culture." Women, on the other hand, lead lives that appear to be irrelevant to the formal articulation of social order. Their status is derived from their stage in a life cycle, from their biological functions, and, in particular, from their sexual or biological ties to particular men. What is more, women are more involved than men in the "grubby" and dangerous stuff of social existence, giving birth, and mourning death, feeding, cooking, disposing of feces, and the like.[2]

Similarly, Ernest Katahweire noted that in Kinyankole culture in Uganda women were inferior to men.

> ... A woman was, on the one hand, regarded as unimportant and incomplete in her home. She was supposed to be inferior to the husband; and part of her training was geared towards enabling her to regard and treat males, including her brothers, as superior. She had to always accept as a sign of good manners what her husband said.[3]

From the foregoing there appears a paradox, on the one hand as I have argued that women are *complete* or *mature* and on the other they are integral part of men and without them a man is not conceived complete in the society as if women are mere human materials only to be used to satisfy the need of man. Rosaldo puts it more succinctly, "Women may be important, powerful, and influential, but it seems that, relative to men of their age and social status, women everywhere lack generally recognized and culturally valued authority."[4] The idea of gender inequality should not be predicated on traditions, cultures and natural state of women. As a matter of fact Simone de Beauvoir believes that nature does not define who a woman is. She argues from the standpoint of an existentialist. "It is not nature that defines woman; it is she who defines herself by dealing with nature on her own account in her emotional life."[5] The import of her position will be discussed later because of its significance.

The geographical nature of the continent made Africans to be basically agrarians. Before the advent of modern science and technology there was not much an average farmer could do to feed his family if he had to succeed in feeding and maintaining the family adequately well. Two things became imperative for man in Africa. One, he needed more women as wives to assist him on the farm and secondly the wives were to bear children who would help on the farm. He needed female children for two principal reasons. First the need to assist the domestic chores in the household was extremely important and secondly, to give out one's daughter in marriage in the society, which subsequently enhanced his economic condition and social status in the community. In spite of what I have said about the importance of having girls in the household, there is equally the need to have boys to be adequately command respect among men in the community. Having male and female children is the most ideal for man in Africa because of its intrinsic and extrinsic values. David G. Maillu, a Kenyan argues:

> Having children has been seen and understood as a kind of natural insurance policy against the unseen bad circumstances, which might rob a person of his loved one, of his shelter, food and company. It is a move to ensure that when you weep, there will be, or there is likely to be, someone who matters to see your tears. Yet a child is much more than that. As the Luo community of Kenya puts it, to have a child is to have a mirror for looking at your back. Over and above, your child is a reflection of yourself in whom you see, study, understand and realize yourself. A child is a parable of your own life; a parable that tells you, 'Look here, this is you and these are your

works.' Having a child makes you take leave out of yourself in order to have an outside view of yourself, which should be, by itself, an exciting experience.[6]

I have quoted Maillu at length because of the significance of his view in relation to the value man in Africa attaches to having children which in retrospect expresses the values of women in African society because without them the pride, hopes and aspirations of man to life would have been thwarted. Three things, it seems to me appear to be the bedrock of Maillu's argument namely, man's psychological ego, material investment and reward in human, and ancestry. There is another dimension to the scenario of having male children in Africa. Inheritance of landed property and leadership in one's family has made male children more important than female children. In most African communities women have no share in the landed property of their father. It is believed that once you are a woman you are expected to get married and be with your husband. It is not expected of a woman whether married or not to have a say about their father's landed property. The landed property is considered an eternal inheritance that must be culturally protected and women dare not partake. The belief is that women have no inheritance in the universe of men. For a woman to secure a respectable position when she is married having male children is a necessary condition. If she fails to have at least a male child for her husband in most cases it can be a good excuse for the man to take another wife. A story was told of how a woman who had four girls without boys went against a medical advice not to be pregnant again because of her poor state of health. Instead of heeding to the advice because she did not want her husband to take another wife and to prove she was capable of giving birth to a male child got pregnant and at the point of delivery she died including the baby. There is another pathetic example that happens most often among the Yoruba in Nigeria. Some married women who have given birth to female children for their husbands and no male children are of the habit of consulting oracles through some traditional priests who have the secret knowledge of appealing to the gods and ancestral spirits to give male children to desperate women. A story was told of a woman who already had given birth to female children decided to give it a trial. She was told that it was possible for her to have a male child but the one available for her if she actually wanted one would make her unhappy all her life. The woman said as long as it is a male child she did not mind all the discomforts and consequences of the choice. She was to meet some demands, which were basically sacrifices to appease the god. After she had met the demands she became pregnant and gave birth to a male child. The true story is that the woman from the time she gave birth to the boy she has not had peace of mind. All her petty business got ruined and the boy remained a thorn in her flesh. The man she wanted to satisfy abandoned her and she was left in anguish, poverty and wretchedness. One would normally not encourage a woman to pay such price for the sake of having a male child as in the case of the first example but in Africa it seems inevitable for a woman to please her husband and the society at the expense of her life. The second example portrays the woman as an irrational being who knowingly made a choice that would make her miserable in life. But suffice to say that there are some, if not many, married women who irrationally behaved like the two examples given to satisfy men in their various rural and to some extent urban communities in contemporary Africa.

The influence of Christianity on Africa also exacerbated the conceived notion of women as valuable objects but subordinate to men. The story of Adam and Eve in Genesis chapters 2 and 3 is a glaring example. For those who might not be very familiar with the mythic event in the book of Genesis where Adam was made to be the sole agrarian administrator in the Garden of Eden. Being the sole administrator of his environment, Adam had power and authority over his domain. But perhaps unknown to him he was a naked creature whose existence depended on eating fruits without meat, fish, carbohydrate etc and living a life of solitary confinement with unquestionable obedience to his Creator who commanded him to eat from the fruits of the garden except the one in the centre of the garden. The day you eat out of the forbidding fruits he was told, "thou shalt surely die." This mythological theology of the nature of man as depicted in the Mosaic understanding of the beginning of Jewish civilization is instructive. It was a civilization of relationship between a Super-power-Unseen-Being and a finite-being at the receiving end whose flourishing existence would depend permanently on the prerogative of mercy of the Unseen Transcendent Being. But unknown to Adam that the fruit of the forbidden tree was a new civilization lurking behind his unfolded ignorance and freedom. The outcome of their action led man not to accept his condition any longer. This is the genesis of man's transcendence, which is the outcome of human discovery of philosophy, science and technology our *eternal now*. The other side of the myth of Adam and Eve in the Garden of Eden is the natural state of the woman in relation to man in terms of superiority of the latter over the former which some anthropologists and interestingly feminists have explained from the perspective of *nature* and *culture*. The difference between Adam and Eve was very clear from the onset in the sense that the woman was valuable to the man however, in terms of power and authority; she was made subservient to the man. In the New Testament the relationship of a married woman to her husband is a life of submissiveness because Eve in the Old Testament was made to be submissive to Adam the husband. The Christian Holy Scripture teaches that the husband is the head of his wife which symbolizes authority and power over the woman. Furthermore in the New Testament a woman is considered a weaker vessel and to be in that category of *being* normally she cannot be treated equal with man. The import of Christian doctrine of women corroborates the way women in African culture are conceived, valued and treated as a companion, domestic administrator, baby boom factories etc which make them identified with *nature* while men are identified with *culture*. The two concepts i.e., *nature* and *culture* have to be clarified because of what they mean in our understanding of man and woman relationships and, of course, the distinctiveness of each identity.

Nature and Culture

The idea of associating nature and culture to the subordinate role of women to authority of men is symbolic. One of the most brilliant exponents of this position is Sherry B. Ortner. The view that women are closely related to nature is primarily due to their motherhood functions like childbearing, nurturing, training and domestic responsibility without which a child cannot survive if left for the father. Ortner explains:

> Woman's physiology, more involved more of the time with 'species of life'; woman's association with the structurally subordinate domestic context, charged with the crucial function of transforming animal-like infants into cultured beings; 'woman's psyche,' appropriately molded to mothering functions by her own socialization and tending toward greater personalism and less mediated modes of relating-all these factors make woman appear to be rooted more directly and deeply in nature.[7]

If woman is symbolically associated with nature how is man related to culture? Are women not part of culture bearing in mind the fact that they are the social foundations of what men are? How can culture be truly defined which will not be women inclusive? In response to these questions the explanation of Ortner seems to clarify it all. According to her, "The culture/nature distinction is itself a product of culture, culture being minimally defined as the transcendence, by means of systems of thought and technology, of the natural givens of existence."[8] What has come to the fore is that women are part and parcel of culture in the sense that they play a middle cause in human development. This middle status of women definitely becomes the problem of women because it enables men to exploit and treat them in some ways as *means* only and not as *ends* in themselves.

There is another clear distinction between women and men, which defines women from the perspectives of nature which is termed *'feminine psyche'*. Ortner explains:

> It is important to specify what we see as the dominant and universal aspects of the feminine psyche. If we postulate emotionality or irrationality, we are confronted with those traditions in various parts of the world in which women functionally are, and are seen as, more practical, pragmatic, and this-worldly than men.... the feminine personality tends to be involved with concrete feelings, things, and people, rather than with abstract entities; it tends toward personalism and particularism.[9]

The underling factor about men as *culture* is the fact that they are more adventurous, objective about life and not as emotional on issues as women. It is no surprise that when a man is found quarrelling or fighting or beating a woman people who are around the scene normally say: *Don't you know she is a woman?* But it is generally considered an aberration in Africa for a woman to beat a man or a wife to beat her husband. Furthermore it is true that men as *culture* however without men and women there cannot be a society but it is men that dictate the structure and governance of the society. Men in most cases provide all the necessary logistics and strategies that lead to security and protection that both men and women need for survival. It is important to note that culture is dynamic and the propelling factor is men and women simply play a supportive role. Most critics of male chauvinism cannot, it seems to me, deny this. Does this justify women being treated as unequal in human society? Bertrand Russell noted that generally speaking women have been unequally treated when compared with men. He argues, "In most civilized communities women have been denied almost all experience of the world and of affairs. They have been kept artificially stupid and therefore uninteresting."[10] Furthermore Russell argues, "A woman had in no period in her life any independent existence, being subject first to her father and then to her husband?"[11] If *nature/culture* in relation to woman and man symbolically described and pragmatically demonstrated as I have explicated, it necessarily follows, that women world wide and particularly African women are nothing but *tools* for men to use for their satisfaction.

Africa is bedeviled by social conflicts and wars, which have been occasioned by misrule and mismanagement of resources by African leaders who over the years are predominantly men. At every turn of events that lead to conflicts and wars women and the children are the worst victims whereas they are invariably innocent. The innate aggressions in men coupled with greed are in most cases responsible for most of the conflicts and wars and of course, ethnicity and external forces. Social, political and religious unrests in Nigeria, Liberia, Uganda, Somalia, Rwanda, South Africa and Sudan among others have contributed to loss of life and property and women and the children usually became the major victims. One cannot forget occasional natural disasters like droughts, famine and rain storms in some parts of the continent i.e., Ethiopia, Mali etc that have led to evacuation of the environment and the major victims were women and children. Women have natural attachment to their children unlike men. When the children cry it is the mothers that first attend to them. So when natural disasters strike it is women that bear the brunt more than their male counterparts.

The Imperative to Change the Negative View of Women

Let me begin from a philosophical point of view because that seems to have a moral import to challenge the patriarchal attitude of men toward women. Plato got it right when he argues that when it comes to natural talents some women are superior to men just as men are not equal in natural disposition of talents. This is made explicitly clear by Plato when he argues, "that a man and a woman have the same nature if both have a talent for medicine; whereas two men have different nature if one is a born physician, the other a born carpenter...there is no occupation concerned with the management of social affairs which belongs either to woman or to man, as such."[12] It is necessary to clarify the meaning of nature as used by Plato from the one already discussed under nature and culture. The meaning of nature as used by Plato simply means talent and it ought not to be confused with the one already discussed above. There is something we need not gloss over from the story of Adam and Eve. It was Eve that made Adam to eat the forbidden fruit which opened the intellectual mind of the man. If that be the case women ought to have been appreciated with the daunting courage to liberate men from ignorance and bondage in the Garden of Eden. It is the act of the woman that brought human civilization, science and technology and not the dogma of obedience of the man. It is in this regard that I agree with De Beauvoir that it is not nature whichever way it is conceptualized that defines woman; it is first and foremost the case that she is the one who defines herself.

Coming to Africa, it seems African women cannot be treated in isolation. The trauma of childbirth, nurturing and training of their children must be conceived as a natural talent which men don't have. The unjust treatment inherent in the affairs of women has no moral justification whatsoever. For instance, land and property inheritance that are denied women simply because of their gender has no convincing moral basis. What a man can do, perhaps a woman, if given the same opportunity, can do better. The denial of education of girl child in many rural and urban African communities is unacceptable because it is through education that the natural gift of intelligence can be actualized. It is through education that modernization, as we know it today brought a lot of opportunities and challenges. It is education and civilization developed in Europe and America that brought uneven development in the world to the extent that the industrial nations consider themselves superior. That is why African countries are generally referred to as developing countries whereas the industrial countries are considered developed nations. The power of knowledge is the backbone of science and technology that both male and female have the talents and to deny women the opportunity to excel in the areas of expertise is like a cog in the wheel of progress. Train a woman, we are told you train a nation. It is not just any form of education that lacks accumulation of skill and theoretical knowledge in philosophy, science and technology etc as in some of religious institutions in Africa. Ortner is right when she says, "Ultimately, both men and women can and must be equally involved in projects of creativity and transcendence. Only then will women be seen as aligned with [*culture*], in culture's ongoing dialectic with [*nature*]."[13]

For women to have equal treatment with men, having education is not enough they should have freedom of choice in most of their life endeavors. The cultural tradition that prohibits women from taking certain vocations like military, paramilitary, and politics etc that are considered the preserve of men because of the high risks involved do indeed rob women of their ability to compete and have their gallantry tested. The choice to be what individuals want in life ought to be the prerogative of both men and women as long as it is not inimical to social cohesion and progress. Insofar as women are unduly restricted their possibility to transcend is circumscribed. It is an irony of mythic event that Eve who made Adam to set himself free in the Garden of Eden that his male descendants who encapsulate her female progeny. Assuming Eve is watching her descendants under the yoke of enslavement caused by Adam's descendants she would probably see them as ingrates. Of course if she had the power to intervene she would probably not hesitate to do so. I am aware of the fact that the Genesis account of man and woman corporate existence in the Garden of Eden is a myth but every myth has some lessons it wants to disseminate. Generally, myths are a form of information that is not intended to be taken literally. They are to be interpreted by demythologizing the raw import of its presentation to unravel the moral, theological, aesthetic and philosophical meanings.

The traditional belief of ancestry and keeping one's lineage in the patriarchal system in most African societies that is predominantly men is not in line with the principle of equality and justice. If women give birth to both male and female children it is morally reasonable that the lineage ought to be of both sexes- male and female as it is being done in the United States of America.[14] In a similar vein the tradition which stipulates that only through the male progeny can men be immortalized should be considered naive and rejected. Modern society counts on the achievements of individuals in the state to immortalize them rather than through their descendants.[15] For instance, in Africa there are several women who have achieved notable positions in the academia, politics and other professional bodies namely, Professor Adetowun Ogunsheye the first female Professor in Nigeria and currently the president, African Gerontological Society (Nigeria)[,16] Professor Grace Alele Williams, the first female Vice-Chancellor in a Nigerian University and President Helen Sirleaf of Liberia, the first African female president, Winnie Mandela former wife of President Nelson Mandela a dynamic and charismatic South African political struggle fighter among others. May I say in parenthesis that I am not unmindful of the great strides some African women had made politically in terms of leadership before the advent or the intrusion of the Europeans. S. O. Arifalo writes, "In the pre-colonial traditional Nigerian societies, female participation in political life was limited. The few who participated included the legendary Queen Amina of Zazzau (Zaria), who was reputed to have ruled over an empire, Ile-Ife's Moremi and Queen Idia of Benin."[17] There were some women who were monarchs in Yorubaland namely, Olowu and Teboye in Ile-Ife, Eyearo, Eyemoi and Amaro in Akure [18] etc. But as Arifalo rightly observed the above "examples were exceptions rather than general rule."[19] Yes, it could be an exception rather than a general rule but it was also a case of women revolution against ineptitude of men to lead at the material time. It couldn't have been a case of leadership dictated by age, which Oyeronke Oyewumi by inference has argued in her book, *The Invention of Women: Making an African Sense of Western Gender Discourses* to support how leadership is not based on gender in Yoruba land. Furthermore, the idea that contemporary feminist movement, which has permeated Africa, could not have been entirely Western cultural influence as Oyewumi has argued.[20] The revolution that made women to lead even when men were incapable to do so in the instances that I have given above demonstrates that at an appropriate time African women could fight for their rights without the influence of Western civilization. The ability of those women who acted gallantly to save their people was a response to the exigencies of the time just like the Civil Rights movement paved way for feminist movement in our time.[21] When women are saddled with responsibilities generally, experience of their performances has shown that they are more prudent than and not as corrupt as men particularly as domestic and political office holders. Perhaps that was one of the reasons why Paul Kagame the President of Rwanda has more women in his cabinet.[22]

Conclusion

If women are as valuable to humanity as expressed in this paper it becomes reasonable to treat them as equals with men. To do otherwise is mere injustice. A culture that negates the treatment of women as equals simply because of their physical nature, belief of male superiority over female, denial of education, freedom of choice and action is capable of stagnating development. Culture and customs are dynamic institutions susceptible to change. As Falola rightly noted that, "Culture and customs reflect the people's creativity, their adaptation to environments, and the impact the external world has had on them."[23] The adoption of Beijing Declaration about 20 years ago as a global policy towards gender equality and involvement of women in all facets of development is part of this cultural change. It is an indisputable fact that the impact of modern civilization on contemporary Africa has contributed to the little change about the potentials of women which is significant enough to give them more opportunities and set them free from the traditional harsh life to which they have been subjected for a long time. And I believe treating women as means and end only in themselves is the surest way to enable them to contribute more meaningfully to the sustainable development of Africa. And to achieve this objective, it is expedient and morally imperative for men to have the political will to make it realizable.

Notes and References

1. Toyin Falola, *The Power of African Cultures* (Rochester: University of Rochester Press, 2003), 51-52.

2. Michelle Z. Rosaldo, "Woman, Culture, and Society: A Theoretical Overview" in *Woman, Culture & Society* eds. Michelle Zimberlist Rosaldo and Louise Lamphere (Stanford: Stanford University Press, 1974), 30-31.

3. Ernest Katahweire, "The Position of Women in Kinyankore, with particular reference to the Church of Uganda in Ankole" *The African Mind: Journal of Religion and Philosophy in Africa* no. 1 (1989):208.

4. Rosaldo, 17.

5. Simone De Beauvoir, *The Second Sex* (New York: Penguin, 1987), 69.
6. David G. Maillu, *Our Kind of Polygamy* (Nairobi: Heinemann, 1988), 5.
7. Sherry B. Ortner, "Is Female to Male as Nature to Culture?" in Michelle Zimberlist Rosaldo and Louise Lamphere, 84.
8. Ortner, 84.
9. Ortner, 81.
10. Bertrand Russell, *Marriage & Morals* (New York: Liveright, 1970), 27.
11. Russell, 29.
12. Francis Macdonald Cornford, trans., *The Republic of Plato* (New York: Oxford University Press, 1979), 152-153.
13. Ortner, 87.
14. See Toyin Falola, *Culture and Customs of Nigeria* (Westport: Greenwood Press, 2001), 118.
15. See Russell, 32.
16. See, "First female professor deplores poor treatment of the elderly", *Punch*, February 15, 2010: 1&11.
17. S.O. Arifalo, "The Evolution of Nigerian Women in Politics" in *Essays in Contemporary Nigerian History* Eds. S. O. Arifalo and Gboyega Ajayi (Lagos: Foresight Press, 2003), 99-100.
18. See Arifalo, 100.
19. Arifalo, 100.
20. Oyeronke Oyewunmi, *The Invention of Women: Making an African Sense of Western Gender Discourse* (Minneapolis: University of Minneapolis Press 2001), 12-14.
21. Ali A. Mazrui, "Pan Africanism and the Origins of Globalization" First Lecture, 2001, [online], available from http://igcs.binghamton.edu/igcs_site/dirton12.htm 11 March 2010.
22. CNN "Rwandan President Speaks Out," 2010. Available from http://www.cnn.com/video/#/video/world/2010/03/17/rwandan.president.amanpour.cnn 4 April 2010.

* Segun Ogungbemi, (2011) "African Women at the Receiving End" in *Beyond Tradition: African Women in Cultural and Political Spaces* (eds.) Toyin Falola and S.U. Fwatshak, Trenton: Africa World Press, 1-10.

Part Three

PHILOSOPHY OF RELIGION

CHAPTER 10

Knowledge, Beliefs And Values

Introduction

The remarkable elements that reveal a distinctive nature of humans from all other beings are basically knowledge, beliefs and values. The three constituent elements are epistemologically and ethically integrated into human creative activities, which form the basis of human culture. While this is so, although it is not static, yet it has instrumental, intrinsic, and enduring appreciation that is embedded in values. It is my interest to engage in the epistemic discourse of knowledge, beliefs and values as power inherent in human creative activities. The ability of humans to exhibit this is also manifested and demonstrated in the work of art that understands knowledge in terms of acquaintance and competence that has contributed to human understanding of African beliefs and values as treasures of African genius. I further interrogate the ingenious creativity of African work of art as power of invocation and power of virtuosity that naturally constitute positive values. Let me say from the onset that knowledge and beliefs as explicated in this chapter are creative values that nurture and guide human actions. My primary objective was to limit my concentration on knowledge as acquaintance and competence as related to African work of art but some remarkable events that will be explained later made me to expand the scope to include other cognitive and scientific aspects of human beliefs and values. This must not be taken as a research that dwells primarily on scientific knowledge. That is beyond the scope of this research. Let me begin to explicate the three concepts of knowledge, beliefs and values.

Knowledge

The starting point in our understanding of knowledge is to give a brief explanation of the nature of knowledge by raising some pertinent questions. What is the nature of knowledge? Or what are the constituent elements of knowledge? Or what are the categories of knowledge? What is knowledge? How do we know we have knowledge? What makes knowledge a value or what makes knowledge a property of value? There are so many questions one can raise with regard to knowledge because of its importance to human understanding of himself or herself and the environment. According to Antony Flew, "Philosophical questions about the nature of knowledge belong either to epistemology or to the philosophy of mind. The two groups of questions may be roughly separated by saying that the first group concentrates on the nature of knowledge, whereas the second concentrates on the nature of the knower."[1] There are two basic epistemological schools of thought namely, Rationalism and Empiricism. The rationalist argues that a priori knowledge which employs deductive reasoning gives us a sole foundation of what we know on Reason alone while the Empiricist argues to the contrary that a posteriori knowledge based on Experience is what gives us true knowledge and that Reason is its errand boy. The debate on what epistemologically gives a priority to each of these arguments in Western philosophy from Plato to the present remains an interest to students and scholars of philosophy. There is, however, the third nature of knowledge that emanated from both Reason and Experience, which is called scientific knowledge. Stanley M. Horner and Thomas C. Hunt explain, "It is a widely held view that science is basically an inductive-empirical method for obtaining knowledge. There is some justification for this popular assessment, because scientists do put great store in specific facts, observations, and sense data."[2] Having given the basic three areas of knowledge above, the question is: What is knowledge? How do we acquire knowledge? Can we be sure or absolutely certain that we know something? To know something requires an understanding of the object of what is known. For instance, if one says he knows God the object of what is known in this case is God. An interesting question that is likely to follow is: How do you know God? He may say I read it in the Bible or in the Qur'an and I believe it? Or he may say God reveals Himself to him in his sleep. Another question that has to be answered is: How are you sure or certain it is God that revealed Himself to you in your sleep and not some sort of a being called the Evil-genius? I have used this example not with the intention of proving whether the knower and the object of what is known are verifiable but rather to show the intricacies in propositional knowledge. Whichever way we look at the concept of knowledge, the most important to us in this discourse is the fact that human beings are saddled with the problem of knowledge.

From the foregoing, I want to argue that human beings are the only creatures properly endowed with creativity to exercise their faculties of knowledge in ways that have revolutionized their environment. Knowledge in this regard, I want to submit, is an intrinsic and extrinsic value that separates humans from brutes when properly and morally applied. Because humans are creative beings with values, knowledge becomes power-house with which to unravel what appears a mystery and to liberate them from fear and ignorance.

To acquire knowledge requires education and training. By virtue of being humans, nature has given everyone a genetic trait that is inherited but as Socrates argues, according to Louis Pojman, that we are clouded by ignorance and what is needed at any level of human development is "a suitable guide, a teacher, to bring out the best in us, to question and guide us like a mid-wife inducing labor, until at last we give birth to knowledge. The teacher has no truths of his own to impart, but to help us to recover knowledge which we must have learned in a previous existence."[3] What this means is the idea that we were born with innate ideas or intuitive knowledge. John Locke a British empiricist argues that no human beings have innate ideas, what we acquire in terms of knowledge is from experience and environment.[4]

If knowledge is creativity developed by human faculty whichever manner or method it is acquired, as I have noted, it is inherently treasured value we cannot ignore at any level of human development. I am concerned in this discourse with the traditional Yoruba knowledge of science and technology and work of art that gives express credence to the above understanding of the nature of knowledge without necessarily thinking that the theoretical explanation as espoused thus far is purely a Western concept. The reason for this presupposition is that in my view knowledge is universal.

We have preponderance of evidence in Africa amongst indigenous professionals of medical science using incantations for healing. For instance, if a scorpion stings one or someone is having a terrible headache, an incantation is one of the most effective remedies for immediate relief and healing provided its procedures are followed. This form of traditional healing process is what I call *Yoruba scientific medical speech-act-healing*. This form of primary healthcare had been in existence and frequently used before the western orthodox medicine and it is still being used till today. Professor Ademola Dasylva is of the view that the mode of incantation is not a mere spoken words alone but rather getting to know the *inner-person* and the ability to call the *inner-spirit* which has a direct link with the particular part of the body that needs to be healed.[5] The power to enact this form of efficacious scientific-medical healing among the Yoruba that I am most conversant with deserves a universal or a global recognition and patriotism. Another example is the significance of the river goddess of Osun in Oshogbo, Osun State in Nigeria where barren women who make appeal to the goddess for children during her yearly festival become pregnant and have babies within a year. This form of scientific-medical solution to barrenness cannot be undermined among the Yoruba in Nigeria. Professor A.B.T. Byaruhanga-Akiiki calls this form of healing of barrenness as *theology of healing* since it involves a deity.[6] The scientific-medical verifiability that the pregnancy and the eventual birth of the baby demonstrate a by-product of the powers of Osun goddess and the woman which make it not only, a *theology of healing*. It is in my view a synergy between metaphysical and empirical forces. In other words, a physiological process of human reproductive system enacted by spiritual powers/energies to provide results in favor of the family that asked the *Consultants* for help. The goddess is metaphysical/spiritual being and the woman and the baby are empirically identifiable entities.

When it comes to the Yoruba work of art, I consider its knowledge as acquisition and competence. It is a skill learned or a creativity that disseminates some form of information towards improving or influencing the quality of life of people(s) who have interaction or contact with the artwork or work of art. I will discuss this issue later after I have given a brief theoretical explanation of beliefs and values.

Beliefs

What is the nature of belief and its relationship to knowledge? Is belief the same thing as knowledge? What makes belief a value? Pojman explains that, "A belief is the outcome of a thought. Belief-acquisitions are internal 'yesings', assentings, which we can consciously experience."[7] H. H. Price writes, "Belief is often contrasted with knowledge, as in 'I do not know where he lives in Bradford'. Knowledge is what we aim at in all our enquiries and investigations. But often we cannot get it. Belief is a second best."[8] We cannot have knowledge without having some form of belief. But such belief has to be defined or explained within the context it is being used. How do I mean? For instance, I have knowledge where Adekunle Ajasin University is located in Ondo State in Nigeria because I teach there. It necessarily follows that I believe there is a University called Adekunle

Ajasin University and I know its location in Ondo State. However, if someone says he read in the newspaper or in a geography book where Adekunle Ajasin University is, he may not claim to know it for certain. He simply has an idea where the University is. All he can say is that he read in such and such place or someone told him where the University is said to be located. He cannot claim to have absolute knowledge of its location. But his belief is that there is a University called Adekunle Ajasin University Akungba-Akoko in Ondo State, Nigeria.

We must also bear in mind that belief is attitudinal. That is to say my belief of a proposition is occasioned by my attitude towards it. For instance, if someone comes to me and says when he dies he will go to heaven. He may not be able to provide any logical proof to substantiate his belief but talking about it and living according to the tenet of his belief becomes attitudinal. This form of belief is not saying that we must believe according to evidence or we must have self-introspection of what we believe. To the believer, subjecting his or her belief to a philosophical or a scientific analysis is to betray and ridicule the object of his belief. In other words, asking for more and more evidence until a proposition is believed is unnecessary. For a believer to be provocative, a man or woman of faith/belief does not need such irreverent philosophical or scientific evidence.

There is other aspect of belief that is more profound among the religious people, which needs to be addressed; and that is faith. Belief and faith to the religious people are used interchangeably. The works of H. H. Price, *Belief* and Louis Pojman, *Religious Belief and the Will* among others are of significant importance to this discourse. These scholars have given a more profound analysis and exposition of belief and faith, which ordinarily I should not say much about it except for the sake of clarification and for the sake of those who might have not read their works, it is necessary for me to explain the relationship between belief and faith. When belief is conceived in terms of faith it does not necessarily ask questions because it is what God has said or what the man of God says is the gospel truth and anyone who questions the veracity of the belief or faith becomes 'irrational' or is seen as an enemy of faith. By the very nature of faith which St. Paul in the New Testament defines as "the substance of things hoped for, the evidence of things not seen"[9] therefore subjecting it to epistemological scrutiny to the believer is unwarranted. Generally speaking, in Nigeria and particularly among the religious zealots or religious fundamentalists, it is sacrilegious or profane to question the basic tenets of their belief or faith because it is a "precious value". In philosophy of religion and philosophical theology such is conceived as *irrational faith* or unreasoned belief or "just believe" as Celsius, the first critic of Christianity accused the early Christian believers.[10] I have dwelt on belief/faith in the field of religion because that is where it is most prevalent. This takes us to the next concept – values.

Values

When we talk of value(s) we mean something that is good or something that has worth. I have maintained from the onset that knowledge and beliefs are values because of their intrinsic and extrinsic worth to humans. There are different ideas and beliefs about values. We have, for instance, material, spiritual, academic, intellectual, social and moral values etc. The sum total of human values is generally conceived as cultural values. In the study of axiology, moral theories including ethics, the theory of value has dominated a large proportion of what morality is all about. But first, how is the theory of value defined? According to Flew:

> A theory of value is a theory about what things in the world are good, desirable, and important. Such theories aim at answering a practical rather than a purely theoretical question since to conclude that a state of affairs is good is to have a reason for acting so as to bring it about or, if it exists already, to maintain it.
>
> Within the context of moral philosophy the central problem is the relation between the moral rightness of certain actions, for example, telling the truth and the non-moral value of certain state, for example, happiness.[11]

Considering human values from the perspective of propositional or ethical studies will limit the scope of human values. To this end, my concern is to conceive human values as diverse as humans scattered around the globe. I am aware that relativism becomes a relevant discourse once human values are conceived as diverse because of our backgrounds, environment, social status, tastes, aesthetic principles etc. Our priorities in life are based on their values or the values we placed on them. Some people place their values on having many children so that when they grow old the children will look after them since in Nigeria we do not have nursing homes where the aged can be taken care of. There are others who place their values on intellectual and academic pursuit like Toyin Falola for human capacity building and development. While some others place their values on material wealth by acquiring houses, cars, aircrafts, etc for their comfort, happiness and satisfaction. Within academia there are scholars who place their values on the accumulation of artifacts because of certain satisfaction they derive from it. There are those who derive inspiration and academic satisfaction in the study of philosophy which itself is a value. All that I have said about the plenitude of values is a characterization of humans as conscious and creative beings. If humans are not conscious and creative, their sense of values and the general utilization of their ability to enhance the quality of life will not be attainable.

The nature of Yoruba work of art

Before I begin to give some philosophical exposition of Yoruba artwork, let me make a general supposition of the universality of art. Plato reminds us of two composite natures of art namely, divine art and human art. By divine art, he means art that is made by nature and human art is made by man.[12]

The term African work of art or African art or African aesthetics or artifacts or artwork means the same. Furthermore, I am concerned with the traditional work of art, which is otherwise known as classic traditional art. This is the work of art that was in existence before Euro-American contacts. It is an "undiluted work of art" which was not meant primarily for commercial purposes.

Our Knowledge of Yoruba aesthetics stems from two major sources namely, the local artists as presented and preserved in Yoruba culture and scholars who have written on the significant contributions Yoruba aesthetics have made to human civilization. Prominent among the scholars were William Fagg, William Bascom, Henry Drewal, John Pemberton, Kevin Carroll, Suzanne P. Wenger who became known as Aduni Olorisa, a devotee of Osun the river goddess in Oshogbo, Osun State, Nigeria, Robert P. Armstrong, Frank Willett, Robert Farris Thompson, Eyo Ekpo, Wande Abimbola, Wole Soyinka, John Tunde Bewaji, Samuel Ade Ali among others have made African art in many ways a major Africa's contribution to human civilization. The knowledge disseminated by the artists in poetry, music, dance, songs, painting, sculpture etc in all forms of subtle language of aesthetic science of its own prove significantly the talents of the genius who consciously or subconsciously engaged themselves with how best to understand the nature of existence and the foot print of the dynamics of human spirit on the environment that became his own. This takes us to two dimensions of knowledge-based argument of the ontological and empirical spheres of Yoruba aesthetics with regard to its contents and forms. The two are in my view not necessarily diametrically opposed but rather complementary if properly understood. Writing on African art, Dele Jegede explains:

> Since African art functions at various levels – for the living and the dead, physical and metaphysical, secular and sacred, legislative and judicial, social and educational, symbolic and aesthetic – it is art for life's sake. While we may admire and appreciate its forms and expressive qualities, it has a primary function, which is often central to the social and religious values of the cultures that produced it.[13]

The work of Theodor W. Adorno explicitly expresses the inseparable fact of form and content in his book titled *Aesthetic Theory*:

> Art negates the categorical determinations stamped on the empirical world and yet harbors what empirically exists in its own substance. If art opposes the empirical through the element of form – and the mediation and content is not to be grasped without their differentiation – the mediation is to be sought in the recognition of aesthetic form as sedimented content.[14]

The Yoruba work of art exemplifies the uniqueness of both forms and contents in the execution of artistry. To understand the genius at work one needs to be broadly exposed to the philosophy, psychology and culture of the artist who is in the world of diffused cultural dilemma on the one hand and on the other trying to make sense in explaining what it means to be aesthetically human. From the foregoing I don't want to give an impression that African art as we know it today was conceived as "art for art's sake" rather it was art for specific occasions to serve a pragmatic or an ontological purpose to enhance and maximize the quality of life of individuals or community or both. It, however, depends on the end to which a particular work of art is set to serve, for instance, pottery and its geometric designs could be for a commercial purpose or for a ritual to ward off evil forces and bring peace, unity and prosperity to individuals and the society.

I have benefited from the clarification of Yoruba work of art by my teacher, Professor Robert P. Armstrong particularly his idea of aesthetic of invocation and aesthetic of virtuosity and how they contribute to human knowledge and values.

Aesthetic of Invocation

In my study of Yoruba work of art I became more intimately impressed with the sculptures because of their aesthetic expressions. The spirit of transcendence and creativity of the artists keeps the imaginative mind wondering the import of the reality in human existence they have graphically demonstrated without necessarily putting it in book volumes yet an individual or individuals perceiving the works can make volumes out of them. According to Armstrong, Yoruba aesthetics are divided into two different components as a result of two cultural traditions under which it has influence namely, Yoruba society and European-American culture. Within Yoruba culture Armstrong argues that the artwork is viewed as having powers of invocation, which I call aesthetics of invocation and powers of virtuosity that is otherwise here called aesthetics of virtuosity. I will discuss each of these conceptions under its subdivisions. Let me begin with his conception of powers of invocation. What does he mean by powers of invocation? Armstrong explains:

> In all cultures certain things exist which, though they may appear to be but ordinary objects, yet are treated in ways quite different from the ways in which objects are usually treated.
>
> Consider, for example, a wedge-shaped stone about two inches in length and no more than one and a quarter inches at its widest part. The casual observer may think it to be no more than a stone brought to its present shape by the natural processes of wearing away that time brings about. More sophisticated viewers will observe that it has been worked to such a shape. But whatever the case, it is unlikely that either observer will be prepared for the honors paid to such a stone in a Yoruba village in west central Nigeria, by a Shango priest, who will bow before it, clapping his hands and reciting praise poems to it. What is this thing? Is it a god? Is it a relic of some special merit? Does it own power? Is it a work of art? Perhaps to the questioner's great surprise, each of those questions may be answered affirmatively: the stone celt is in some respect or other of divinity, meritorious, powerful, and a work of art; or, more properly, it belongs to that order of phenomena of which what we call "works of art" are but a suborder.[15]

Let me corroborate what Armstrong has said above with another concrete example. In my hometown, Idofin-Isanlu in Yagba East Local Government Area in Kogi State, Nigeria, there is a deity called *Orìgba*. The ontological characteristic of this deity is that its costumes are sacred and being so means they cannot be tempered with anyhow without severe consequences. In this town there are two old mission churches namely Sudan Interior Mission (SIM) now known as Evangelical Church Winning All (ECWA) and the Baptist. In order to serve the God of Christianity fervently the worshipers went to buy two electric generators to give them light every evening they wanted to worship the Benevolent, Omni-Powerful and

Omni-Present Being. There was a melodrama in the town in the early 90s when some robbers came to steal the two electric generators the same night and one of the costumes of the *Origba* in the broad daylight. The two electric generators that belonged to the above named mission Churches were successfully stolen but the unfortunate happened when they made attempt to go away with the *Origba* costume. As the costume was taken away from its Shrine which till now does not have any security lock unlike the mission Churches where the electric generators were carted away, there was a sudden strike of lightning that frightened the robbers and they took to their heels and left the costume of the *Origba*. It is expedient to say here that the stealing of the costume of the Origba and the spontaneous reaction that made the robbers to return it was an act of toxic provocation. The exhibition and the execution of the power of the *affecting presence* were ontologically manifested. When the robbers were not able to cart away the costume of the *Origba* the rage and ravaging powers of the *affecting presence* were assuaged. The whole town was alert that a strange phenomenon had happened and there was need for the priests to appease the deity. The costumes of the deity according to Armstrong in this case are potent with *power of presence* whether it is invoked or not. The robbers could not disappear with the costume of the *Origba* but that cannot be said about the two electric generators of the two Churches whose God is too *merciful* to act![16]

What is affecting presence? Armstrong explains, "It is factually true that the affecting presence is not in its distinctive and definitive sense a symbol, though it may, and indeed often does, also bear symbolic attributes. Rather it directly presents affect. It is only in this sense, namely that form does incarnate affect, that it may be said that there is a universal aesthetic."[17] There is an academic contention whether the sculptures, which we call African work of art, are symbols, or representations or presentations. For instance, Susanne K. Langer considers sculptures as symbols and that the functions of the symbols are representational.[18] From what Armstrong has said, however, in the above quotation, the affecting presence of the sculptures are presentations and not symbols or representations.[19]

It suffices to say that when the sculptures were taken to Europe, America, Asia and other parts of the world outside the continent of Africa, the deities they present were not taken along with them.[20] But the fact remains that when the sculptures are in foreign lands, the descendants of Africa in the diaspora whose ancestors went with the artifacts, made the worship of the deities namely, Ogun, the god of iron, war, peace and justice, Sango, the god of thunder, Yemoja, the goddess of water and fertility, Esu Elegbara, the god of indeterminacy etc an integral part of their cultural heritage.[21] Therefore, wherever the gods are worshiped in those foreign lands like Brazil, Jamaica, Haiti, etc the sculptures that present the forms and the contents of the art demonstrate the *power of the presence* especially during their festivals or anytime they are invoked.

To place the values of the *affecting presence* in perspectives within the political system in Nigeria, one would have loved to see all our political office holders use any of the objects of the gods to swear during their oath taking exercise. If this had been done perhaps the level of corruption that is endemic in the country would have been minimized or non-existent because like the example of the *Origba* given above, it would be foolhardy to swear falsely holding the symbol of a deity when one knew that the *power of the affecting presence* would consume him or her. Rather than using our African form of oath taking, Nigerian political and office holders to use the Bible or the Qur'an which they know will not harm them even if they behave contrary to the terms of office and responsibility. It is this abandonment of our cultural values and the embrace of foreign cultures with their religious values and practices that perhaps have exacerbated the recklessness of immoral behaviors of African leaders while in and out of office. The implication therefore, is that there is a definitive morally-in-built value in Yoruba aesthetic of invocation which ought not to be ignored. What this implies, in my candid opinion, is that it is high time we resolved to embrace the moral values exemplified in African cultural values.

Aesthetic of Virtuosity

When we talk about African aesthetic with particular reference to sculptures, as having power of invocation and power of virtuosity it becomes a phenomenon of dualism as perceived by the cultural spectators. To the genius of the works of art there is no dichotomy between the forms and its contents. But to the foreign admirers of the sculptures like Armstrong and others, the contents within the cultural environment from where the works derived their existence, the sense of their values differentiate what the works represent to the indigenous people. That is why Armstrong classified sculptures from Africa as having powers of invocation and powers of virtuosity. To Africans, Armstrong writes:

> Although in our culture we do not make sacrifices of blood to such special things, yet we too have analogous "objects." To them, Americans and Europeans and Japanese – for example – also offer "sacrifice." We may or may not write poems to them, but we lavish our resources upon their purchase and upkeep. And we house them

in some of the grandest structures our culture produces, designed by our most gifted architects and executed in the most expensive of materials. But it is not only the housing of such works that is expensive. There are also the services they must have: insurance, guards to protect them against vandalism and theft, conservators to cure them of their ills and to maintain them in the greatest degree of health, specialists to mount them and place them in dramatically disposed and lighted displays.[22]

From my observation of those objects in the galleries and museums outside Africa Armstrong is right in his description of the cultural bifurcation assessment of the way and manner the sculptures designed for traditional concerns are treated in its homeland and in the foreign land because the intentions for which they were made to serve were never the same. Anyone who has visited individual home collections of African sculptures as I did at Armstrong's house in Down Town Dallas, Texas, United States of America, Museum of Mankind in London, United Kingdom and Art Galleries in other parts in Europe, America etc will not dispute what Armstrong has said. Due to the influence of modernization the sculptures and other works of art of individuals, social and national interests in Nigeria and other parts of Africa do indeed receive similar care and treatment. Dele Jegede writes, "Many who are privileged to view African art works in museums are touched by their visual presence, their aesthetic power, and their formal attributes."[23] Let me say in this regard that the preservation of Africa works of art by the Cultural Heritage Museum University of Ibadan, Ibadan, Oyo State, Nigeria deserves mention for its aesthetic worth and expression.

John Ayotunde Isola Bewaji gives a general view of African sculptures, which captures a more profound way of conceiving the nature and purpose of their state of being. Bewaji explains:

> Thus we can say that sculptures are important in the artistic terrain of Africans. They are often grandiose, noble, intimate, intricate and even disturbing. They help to record history as they chronicle their times and epochs and they serve mementos and memorials, endearing monuments to, and of the time, as well as commemorating for posterity and for self achievements or the travails of the people as they journey through the ages – that is, as they undergo the necessary transition through space and time. And sculptures are also capable of serving to express the architecture of the people, in

that the conglomerate of power may dictate that certain methods and materials be used in building certain edifices. These are ways of adapting creativity to life and living.[24]

The import of African sculptures as explained by Bewaji in the cultural context is very true but one can add that the fact that the genius of the production of the artwork did not write down their ideas does not rob them the philosophical exposition of their world view which contain their metaphysics, epistemology, ethics, syndetic logic, religious, scientific and technological understanding of man and his environment. Scholars of contemporary African Philosophy must be conversant with this fact when it comes to giving a definitive nature of African Philosophy. If this had been done there would probably be no intellectuals or scholars or elite who would be in doubt of the existence of African Philosophy. As Toyin Falola rightly noted, "Art appreciation provides people with leisure activity as they visit museums and monuments. Furthermore, it contributes to modern living and the economy, as people decorate homes and offices with artwork."[25] With preponderance of evidence of what African works of art has contributed to knowledge within Africa and outside the continent, one wonders why its study does not become a major integral part of study in our various institutions of learning in Nigeria.

Conclusion

I began with a view to bringing to focus that knowledge, beliefs and values are essentially a by-product of human creativity. It is because of the level of human consciousness and ability to transcend some their limitations that make creativity a distinctive feature of the genius in us. I have given an insight of what knowledge, beliefs and values are in relation to our views of African aesthetics particularly sculptures as aesthetic of invocation and aesthetic of virtuosity. The principles of truth telling and honesty that are emphatic in traditional Africa culture as expressed in the beings which the sculptures present and any acts of betrayal or abuse of what they stand for can invoke the wrath of the gods. The political office holders as I have mentioned jettison this value, which invariably explains the rampant corruption in our country today. In other words, if our leaders had not devalued the currency of our traditional culture of accountability and embraced the principles of justice engendered in our cultural heritage perhaps Nigeria would have not been listed as one of the notoriously corrupt nations. One of the challenges that we must constantly remind ourselves is the subjective existential import the artwork presents with its affecting presence. As Armstrong argues, "The work of affecting presence holds the mirror up-not to nature but to man. The world is caused to bear the supreme fact of man's presence in it. It is owing to this achieved end that the affecting presence is presentational."[26] What makes *affecting presence* affecting therefore ostensibly, in my view, is human creativity.

The enrichment of human creativity is fully expressed in culture. The diffused nature of culture in the case of Africans in the continent and Africans in the diaspora is better understood in their common background as people of Black race and of African heritage. The strange phenomenon of trans-Atlantic slave trade and colonialism which brought about a divergent polarity and loss of freedom on both sides – the Africans in the continent and diaspora, not withstanding, the feelings of belonging to a continent and race plus the attendant sense of dignity, freedom and human worth which has been facilitated by knowledge, beliefs and values inherited in African culture, the mode to transform the continent after independence to a more robust developed State in all ramifications is the most urgent call to service on the part of all African descents wherever they are.

Notes and References

1. Flew Antony, *Dictionary of Philosophy* (New York: St. Martin's Press, 1979), 180.

2. Stanley M. Honer and Thomas C. Hunt, *Invitation to Philosophy: Issues and Options* (Belmont: Wadsworth, 1982), 80.

3. Louis Pojman, *Religious Belief and the Will* (New York: Routledge & Kegan Paul, 1986), 14.

4. John Locke, *The Empiricists: An Essay Concerning Human Understanding* (Abridged) (Garden City: Anchor Books, 1974), 9.

5. Ademola Dasylva drew our attention during my presentation of this paper at the conference to the power of the speech–Act to mean something more than the ordinary usage of words but something that requires an understanding of the art of incantation that has power to deal with the inner-spirit and the place in the body that requires healing.

6. See A.B.T. Byaruhanga-Akiiki, "The Theology of Medicine" in the *Journal of African Religion and Philosophy Vol. 2. No. 1 1991*, Kampala, 23-33.

7. Louis Pojman, *Religious Belief and the Will*, 19.

8. H.H. Price, *Belief* (New York: Humanities Press, 1969), 72.

9. See Hebrew 11: 1.

10. Dodd's, *Pagan and Christianity in an Age of Anxiety* (New York: Norton and Company, 1970), 120-121.

11. Flew Antony, *Dictionary of Philosophy*, 338.

12. Albert Hofstader and Richard Kuhns, (ed.), *Philosophies of Art and Beauty: Selected Readings in Aesthetics from Plato-Heidegger* (Chicago: University of Chicago Press, 1976), 46.

13. Dele Jegede "African Art" in *Africa Vol.4* Toyin Falola (Ed) (Durham: Carolina Academic Press, 2002), 282.

14. Theodor W. Adorno, *Aesthetic Theory* (Minneapolis: University of Minnesota Press, 2006), 5.

15. Robert P. Armstrong, *The Powers of Presence* (Philadelphia: University of Pennsylvania Press, 1981), 3.

16. Segun Ogungbemi, *A Critique of African Culture Beliefs* (Lagos: Pumark, 1997), 39.

17. Robert P. Armstrong, *Wellspring* (Los Angeles: University of California Press, 1975), 13.

18. See Susanne K. Langer, *Philosophy in a New Key* (Cambridge: Harvard University Press, 1980), 26-102.

19. Robert P. Armstrong, *Wellspring*, 21-24.

20. I agree with Ademola Dasylva during my presentation of the paper that when the sculptures were taken to foreign lands, it is important to emphasize that the divinities they "present" remained in Africa.

21. See Roger Bastide, *The African Religions of Brazil* (Baltimore: John Hopkins University Press, 1978.

22. Robert P. Armstrong, *The Powers of Presence*, 4.

23. Dele Jegede "African Art" in *Africa Vol.4*, 281.

24. John Ayotunde Isola Bewaji, *Beauty and Culture: Perspectives in Black Aesthetics* (Ibadan: Spectrum Books, 2003), 142.

25. Toyin Falola, *Culture and Customs of Nigeria* (Westport: Greenwood Press, 2001), 77.

26. Robert P. Armstrong, *Wellspring*, 81.

* Segun Ogungbemi (2020) "Knowledge, Beliefs and Values" *Caribbean Journal of Philosophy* Vol. 12, No. 1, 2020, 36-50.

CHAPTER 11

Belief In
God

Introduction

For sometime now, the philosophical impulse or the inspiration to write on this subject has given me some restless moments simply because however popular or unpopular some of my views may be in an environment in which what one says about God in terms of genuine philosophical interest is generally misinterpreted as anti-religious or an expression of atheism which is considered in this part of the world as anti-social. Having given lectures on philosophy of religion to my students at Bishop College Dallas, Texas in the United States of America, Ogun State University now Olabisi Onabanjo University, Ago-Iwoye Ogun State, Lagos State University Ojo Lagos, Adekunle Ajasin University Akungba-Akoko, Ondo State Nigeria, Moi University Eldoret, Kenya and a public lecture on Religion in 1992 at Makarere University Kampala, Uganda all in Africa, my experience in all the places I have mentioned and my discussions with both intellectuals, clergy men and colleague scholars in and outside the discipline of philosophy made it compelling to make my position clearer on religious belief that has such an irresistible, psychological or spiritual power on the adherents.

To believe in God warrants a religious proposition that is predicated on faith. Therefore any discussion on the existence of God from the vintage view of the believer must be seen from the veil of its perspective. But the claim of religious propositions, in my view, to be assertive and authoritative in our understanding of who we are, what we are, and our mission in the universe both empirical and metaphysical must be philosophically interrogated. It becomes more imperative to investigate with the searchlight of rational and empirical instruments at our disposal to know the foundation and justification of a belief in God. The reason for justification of religious belief is necessitated by our understanding of the universe in modern times due to modern philosophy, science and technology, which has made our view of the world to be a global village as a result of communications networks.

The Existence of God

In my inquiry about God, the first point of call is the front door of *Reason* and *Empiricism* and not faith. How do we know that God exists? Or is there any concrete evidence from the vantage point of Reason that gives logical and moral proof that God exists? This is a million dollar question that requires a deep investigative mind to reflect on. It is not like a question your child will ask and you give it a spontaneous response without a second thought or reflection. For instance, if you tell your child that God made him and he replies by asking, who made God? We must not lose sight of one important fact about religious belief that it is an individual enterprise. Some have simple faith without necessarily undergoing all the treacherous trouble of any philosophical analysis to justify the basis of their belief in the existence of God, for example, conservative Christians, fanatic Muslims, traditional religionists etc, while some remain unconcerned about the existence of God not to talk of its justification because it serves no existential interest or purpose to them i.e., atheists. There are however, some who have taken delight in the analytic, intuitive and pragmatic exploit of Reason to arrive at a rational and moral warrant that have aroused more philosophical arguments, for instance, philosophers, process and philosophical theologians among others. In my search for a rational argument for the existence of God apart from reading and training in theological institutions in Africa and United States of America, I have been duly influenced by my teachers namely, Shola Olukunle, Schubert Ogden, Louis P. Pojman, and great authors on the topic, namely, St. Augustine, Thomas Aquinas, St. Anselm, Rene Descartes, Soren Kierkegaard, David Hume, Immanuel Kant, Ludwig Wittgenstein, H.H. Price, Paul Tillich, Anthony Flew, William James, Richard Swinburne, John Macquarrie, Bertrand Russell, Kai Nielsen, John Hick, Gary Gutting, Alvin Plantinga, John Smith, among others. All my teachers and all the great authors that I have mentioned or not mentioned only gave me an insight of the complexities and intricacies that are involved in unraveling one's argument for the existence of God and to help me develop my own understanding that I can rationally defend as self-evident.

The question of how do I know that God exists has to be answered within some human existential background. How did the idea of God originate? The answer to this question has become the foundation on which its acceptance by the believer, is morally and epistemologically warranted. David Hume's book, *The Natural History of Religion* gives a clue as to how the belief in God came to being. He argues that the belief in God as we know it today was initially polytheistic and not monotheistic.[1] He postulates that the belief in God did not arise from the wonders of the natural aesthetics but rather from human exigencies and his ability or inability to cope with them. Hume explains:

> We hang in perpetual suspense between life and death, health and sickness, plenty and want; which are distributed amongst the human species by secret and unknown causes. These *unknown causes,* then, become the constant object of our hope and fear; and while the passions are kept in perpetual alarm by an anxious expectation of the events, the imagination is equally employed in forming ideas of those powers, on which we have so entire a dependence.[2]

Furthermore Hume argues:

> Any of the human affections may lead us into the notion of the invisible, intelligent power; hope as well as fear, gratitude as well as affliction. But, if we examine our own hearts, or observe what passes around us, we shall find, that men are much oftener thrown on their knees by the melancholy than by the agreeable passions. Prosperity is easily received as our due, and few questions are asked concerning its cause or author. …On the other hand, every disastrous accident alarms us, and set us on enquiries concerning the principles whence it arose: Apprehensions spring up with regard to futurity: And the mind, sunk into diffidence, terror, and melancholy, has recourse to every method of appeasing those secret intelligent powers, on whom our fortune is suppose entirely to depend.[3]

I have quoted substantially from Hume because any form of retrospect on religious belief needs a reasonable background that captures a vivid picture of the condition that necessitated the imaginary, invisible and intelligent power or being who became the object of worship in polytheistic or monotheistic religion. In Judeo-Christian tradition, the origins of religion espoused by Hume have a clear similarity in the sense that polytheism seems to have been the basis of human religion because the name ELOHIM in Judaism means several Gods. However with the development of human thought and the understanding the writers of the Holy Bible came to a conclusion that YAWEH who revealed himself to them is one God and not many or several Gods. It seems to me that Islam took its root from this monotheistic notion of God who is referred to as Allah, just like Christianity took its root from Judaism. The three religions originate from a common ancestry, Abraham. They are called Abrahamic religions or Abrahamic faiths.

The three religions offer humanity the knowledge and origin of human existence who is God and therefore, God exists. Christian doctrine teaches that God is known by revelation, nature, the Bible, human conscience and finally through Jesus the Christ. Radical theologians/scholars have not found any of the above means of knowing God to be self-evident. There are most often ambiguity and contradictions in the Bible for instance, in Exodus Chapter 20 Moses claimed to have received the Ten Commandments from YAWEH with specific rules punishment: thou shall not kill, thou shall not commit adultery etc. But it is the same YAWEH who instructed Samuel who anointed Saul as the first King of Israel and subsequently in 1 Samuel 15: 1-9 asked him to go and kill all the Amalekites including innocent children and animals for an offence, which that generation knew nothing about (Judges 10:12; 1 Sam. 15:2). Similarly, in the book of Deuteronomy 22: 23-24 it says, if a woman is betrothed to a husband and another man has a carnal knowledge of her and the woman cried out and nobody came to her rescue the man should be stoned to death. But what do we find in the book of Matthew 1:18, Mary was betrothed to Joseph and she was impregnated by the Holy Spirit, which resulted into the birth of Jesus; but the Divine went away with impunity. However, secular theologians have defended the birth narratives of Jesus as recorded in Matthew and Luke as an event that was not authentic and necessary when it comes to the significance of Christology. They have argued that if the birth narratives of Jesus were that significant the closest friends of Jesus namely, John, Peter, James including Paul who wrote extensively on the Church whose Head is Jesus the Christ would have recorded it.[4] To a rational mind the issue that is at hand is the contradictory aspect of the law that came from the Divine and recorded in the Holy Bible.

If human conscience gives credence to our knowledge of the existence of God then there would have been no need for any evangelical crusades, and all the missionary enterprises in various parts of the world would have been unnecessary. Can we always rely on human conscience for validation of authentic knowledge, beliefs and moral actions without disappointing consequences? For instance, I witnessed live a horror on the Channels Television on October 17, 2005 in Lagos. There was an 11-year-old boy called Samuel who was accused of child kidnapping. The boy claimed innocent of the charge but the crowd would not accept his claim of innocence. He was forcefully dragged on the ground and mercilessly beaten while passersby and interested onlookers were watching with amusement. The police post was a stone throw from the scene and nobody called the police to the heinous crime of this inhumanity to man. The conscience of the people seemed to have been out of tune with law and order in the city. When Samuel realized that his appeal of innocence fell on deaf ears of his accusers and the spectators he had only one more option. He took his appeal to the Omnipotent, Omniscient and Omnipresent God to save him from the maltreatment of his fellow men but the Heavenly Father appeared unconcerned like his accusers. In other words, when Samuel cried out and said, 'God save me' that was the highest appeal to the Maker of all things who could come to his aid. More so the crowd understood the religious language used by Samuel since he thought his fellow men and women were religious and the appeal could prick their conscience. The greatest shock that Samuel did not expect from his fellow citizens of conscience was a flow of gas/petrol on his body and fire that set him ablaze. As I watched it, my heart bled and I became speechless. It was one of the worst events that I thought could happen in Nigeria. As I pondered on the drama that ended the life of Samuel, I raised the question, was the moral precept no longer written on the hearts of these men and women? Of course, public outcry made the police to fish out those perpetrators of the wicked act but Samuel was not allowed to see how justice had been done in his case.

A similar event that shook the whole world was the terrorists' attack on the World Trade Centre in New York on September 11, 2001. It questioned the significance of human conscience as a living testimony that God exists. To most people, the conscience of the terrorists that masterminded the plan and its execution would have told them that a place like the World Trade Centre in New York with all its edifices and aesthetic splendors plus its relevance to human economy deserves preservation and not destruction. But the conscience of the terrorists saw it differently. To them, it is not the life of their fellow human beings working in the buildings of the World Trade Centre or its significance to human economy that matter but a zealous religious vengeance that lurked behind their action. The two live stories that I have given were the most horrific and worst cruelty of inhumanity to man I have seen in recent times. How can conscience that has its origin from the Divine do those two opposing activities that are incompatible with moral reason? All these clear-cut contradictions and absurdities found in the holy books make the events to be incredulous fairy-tales. It is no surprise that during the Enlightenment in Europe and the United States of America where Christianity had made a lot of impact on its civilization, the Biblical stories about creation, revelation, miracles, commandments, salvation, and eschatology among others were subjected to critical reasoning. It became necessary to make the belief in God more credible and acceptable to the modern man. This gave rise to different philosophical arguments to prove the existence of God namely, ontological, cosmological, and teleological and other forms of logical arguments.[5] But rather than proving the existence of God or belief in the Deity credible but also the logical arguments end up creating more moral contradictions, confusions and doubts than convictions that are intended by their exponents. This was made explicit in part by H B Acton, one of the exponents of Immanuel Kant's philosophy. He writes:

> Kant argued that no theoretical proofs could be provided to demonstrate that God exists, that the will is free and that the soul is immortal…. Furthermore, we cannot obtain empirical knowledge of God, freedom and immortality, since they transcend anything the senses could reveal. But the idea of a creator who has so ordered the world that a single interconnected series of purposes is at work in it has served as an impetus for the advance of knowledge and a unified conception of the world. Although we cannot know that there is any object corresponding to it, the Idea of God helps to regulate our search for knowledge.[6]

Although Kant was entirely entitled to his Platonic Idea and its application to the existence of God theoretically, it has in no way solved the implicit epistemic and moral foundation and justification that it is intended to solve. According to Charles Hartshorne, "God didn't make the world in the literal, simple-minded sense that people have talked about; no world could be made in that simple-minded sense…. Creatures have to make themselves. That's the only way they can be made."[7] Some scientists have argued contrary to Kant that the universe as we know it has no purpose.[8] Of course, Kant and contemporary creationists would not accept that the world as we come to know it was not created by God with a purpose.

There is yet another area of philosophical contention with regard to the logical proofs for the existence of God. In all the logical proofs for the existence of God, the idea that He is all-good, all-powerful, all-knowing etc does not justify his existence. The apparent presence of evil either natural or moral in the world has exacerbated a negative impression on the plausibility of the existence of God.

Russell was probably correct when he said that God is to blame for all human predicaments. If God has all the positive attributes with its attendant possibilities then it becomes extremely difficult to exonerate him from all the sufferings of man. As a matter of fact, man from our own understanding had at no time requested God to create him. And if he did, he would have not allowed himself to be subjected to the kind of intolerable environment he is currently living. After all man must be intelligible enough to know the kind of conducive condition that suits his plan and purpose in life having seen the kind of world of splendor his creator lives assuming the descriptive picture of the abode of God were true. Even if man does not know as much as his creator, it is necessary for his creator to realize that the kind of environment that is good for him is equally good for his creature. Normally, it seems to me that nobody wants poverty, sufferings, diseases and death. Just as an earthly father cares for his child within his limited means and resources; and as much as he could possibly do to avert the vicissitudes in existence so that he can flourish, one would expect a more robust care from the Divine who apparently is more buoyant with unlimited resources at his disposal. Those issues raised are reasons why the believers hold tenaciously to believe in God because they claim he can answer their prayers no matter how long it takes and even if their prayers are not answered here on earth, there is hope for a better place in the hereafter. To nonbelievers such belief is nonsensical. Is it really nonsensical or a misunderstanding of religious language? In other words, skeptics, agnostics, atheists etc who doubt or deny credibility of religious beliefs in God simply do so because they do not understand religious language.

Understanding Religious Language

What is religious language? Is it different from a commonly spoken language or speaking in tongues? According to Wittgenstein, religious language of believers has an apparent internalization than its ordinary usage and meaning. He calls it religious language-game. To Wittgenstein, the language-game of believers requires an understanding of its entry-departure-transition rules. For instance, if you go to a church and you see the picture representing Jesus Christ and the kind of reverence and awe that it is given to it, as an ordinary man who is not religious, it will not make any meaning to you. You may not understand how an ordinary picture can have a regulatory impact in the life of the believer. In other words, Wittgenstein is saying that since we do not understand the language-game of the believer, not in terms of its linguistic structure but in terms of the experiences associated with it, the non-believer cannot criticize it. Let me give a recent event that captures vividly the view point of Wittgenstein. Some of us who did not know Pastor Eskor Mfon before he passed away several years ago; but we heard or read of his demise through the printed media; *TELL* Nigeria's Independent Weekly, May 28, 2007 that he had been a charismatic Church Minister of the Redeemed Christian of God (RCCG) City of David, Dideolu Estate, Victoria Island extension, Lagos Nigeria. At his funeral the General Overseer of the Church, Pastor Enoch Adeboye made this religious statement.

> Eskor did not die of sickness. What happened was that sometime in April, God showed Eskor a glimpse of heaven – the glory and the grandeur of it. He was captivated by it. He longed to be there. Since then, I tried to persuade him to remain with us on this side of life so that he could continue the great works he was doing. But he refused my entreaties. So Eskor merely responded to the alluring wish to be on the other side of eternity.[9]

Pastor Adeboye was speaking a language-game his followers understood and it resonated with them in accordance with their belief in the celestial world. However, the correspondent of TELL who did not understand his religious language conceived it differently because he did not belong to their religious community. According to him, "Adeboye's words as soothing and comforting as they were could not pacify thousands of people who had come to pay their last respect to Mfon, as they wept bitterly."[10] In this event Wittgenstein would say that a non-believer could not understand the religious language-game of Adeboye and so we cannot criticize him.

Of course, no philosophical mind would accept the above view of the man of God and the language-game theory of Wittgenstein. Pastor Adeboye being the General Overseer of the religious organization, should normally have been the first person to lead his followers to the celestial world. But how come his subordinate Mfon could be so willing to go to the world beyond, realizing the kind of economy of his country and the need to take care of his family and give his children the nurture and affection they would badly need? In view of Adeboye's religious explanation and cause of death of Mfon, it cannot stand the test of Reason. On empirical and medical sense, the family opted for an autopsy test done on the remains of Mfon rather than the metaphysical hypothesis of Adeboye. Some months later, the cause of death of Pastor Mfon was made public. He was medically confirmed that he died of colon cancer.

So far I have given in a nutshell some critical problems that stand on the way of accenting to a religious proposition that bothers on the veracity of a belief in God. Is there any other plausible ground on which one can possibly argue that it is reasonable to believe in God? Perhaps the argument of human capacity or methodological conservatism that is based on religious experience and achievements is worth discussing for its persuasiveness but not necessarily convincing.

Religious Experience/Achievements

There is no denying the fact that belief in God has to some varying degrees brought about both psychological, economic, social, political and religious improvement to man. The belief in God has made man to view himself as not being alone without a superior companion. When trouble or affliction comes man believes the unseen superior being is always there to be consulted. If he receives a positive response it elevates his spirit. Man believes that for him to overcome his manifold problems the belief in a superior being is a necessary and sufficient condition. To overcome fear of the wild and dreaded universe man needs God at his disposal whether he sees the superior being or not. The trajectory of human progress and development became the ethos of his civilization and contemporary cutting-edge technology of digital century cannot be divorced from positive contributions of religious belief in God. For instance, Christianity and its great doctrines of love and missionary activities have improved human capacity in terms of education, architecture, trade, industry and commerce. In the United States of America, Christianity is the basis of its development of capitalism. In Africa, the manifestation of the power of the Christian God was demonstrated by the activities of the missionaries using orthodox medicine, education that brought about a better understanding of their environment, infrastructure that improved their standard of living among others. The propelling force behind the activities of the church in human development is a loving and merciful God. This way of looking at the belief in God can appropriately be described as religious methodological conservatism because it justifies the belief in the existence of God on the ground of what the belief has demonstrated. It is not only in Christianity that the belief in God has contributed to the well-being of man. To some certain degree the belief in the Supreme Being in African Traditional Religion before the advent of Abrahamic faiths and other foreign religions from other continents gave the traditionalists the courage, wisdom and understanding of how to live in partnership with the environment. But colonization and its Western civilization and religion worked against a fair assessment of the impact of African Traditional

Religion on the social, economic and political integration of the Africans. Be that as it may, religion be it Christianity or African Traditional Religion or any form of religious beliefs in which the existence of the Supreme Being is justified embraces the principle of methodological conservatism which Gary Gutting calls "*truth-independent* justification of beliefs."[11] What this argument wants to show is that having seen those activities that brought about human development as enumerated above the question is what other justification do we need to prove the existence of God? That is to say, belief in the existence of God has been justified on the basis of the transformation and cordial relationship between man and his Creator if not what man enjoys now would have not been possible.

To accept this religious view is to shut the door of doubts of the skeptics. Has the argument of religious experience based on the functions and achievements of religion demonstrated that God exists? The answer to this question will depend on what one accepts as necessary and sufficient evidence? To most people who believe in the existence of God, what counts as sufficient evidence is what has brought about positive change in their lives that has made them to maximize the greatest good for their well being. And since the belief in the existence of God has achieved this utilitarian goal, it is irrelevant to ask for further justification; the foundation of what has made life more meaningful to them. To the religious conservatives, only those who are intellectually arrogant will be asking for more evidence. But to the skeptics, the argument for the existence of God cannot be justified on religious experience and its socio-functional achievements because they are two different things entirely. If the issue of the existence of God is like the physical farmer and his empirical farm, the problem of justification of the owner of the farm will not be all that difficult. The farmer can be easily interrogated to know whether he is truly the owner of the farm or not. If anyone is in doubt of his claim, a third party that knows about it can be asked to substantiate the claim; and once one is convinced of the veracity of ownership, the need for justification has no basis any longer. But insofar as a metaphysical Being who is not seen physically and yet he is said to be the foundation of whatever is in the universe and beyond surely needs a justification if the belief is to be authentic. What then can count as authentic evidence that God exists?

Four pragmatic warrants necessary for believing in God

I believe any authentic justifications of belief in God must meet some, if not all these four criteria; that are indubitable. They are here otherwise referred to as pragmatic warrants.

1. God's appearance must be more public and universal not merely private and individualistic so that there will be no doubt or ambiguity about what he says or does and particularly, what he reveals or commands whenever there is a discourse about him. If this happens, there will be no need for papacy, archdeaconry, and all other evangelistic titles that are commonly used in the service of God.

2. The universality of belief in God must be indubitable in any form of linguistic descriptions. There should a universal religious language common to all human races that is understood by all.

3. The moral principles of God must be such that it enhances the well-being of man rather than to worsen his condition in his natural estate: planet earth.

4. The natural human habitats should be his eternal now where God could visit as a resort to interact with his creature similar to mythical Garden of Eden and not in the hereafter to avoid any hopeless impression of immortality in the unknown world beyond. This reminds me of the argument of the Wager by Pascal.[12] According to him, it is better to wager than not to wager because it could be the case that after death one may get to heaven and if one does not believe in God while on earth he has lost the chance of being in the heaven. And on the other hand if at the end of the day there is no God one does not lose anything. Of course, an illogical reasoning cannot persuade one because to believe in God requires a total commitment and a double-dealing believer has no place in his kingdom. At any rate a God of moral principles would normally extend his personal commitment to all humans to ensure their happiness and not their suffering regardless of their belief in his existence or non-existence. Therefore this impartial moral nature of God that is germane in believing in his existence becomes imperative.

The four pragmatic warrants for believing in God are the minimal criteria that make it credible, in my opinion. In other words, the belief in God has further given credence to moral and epistemological warrants that justify his existence. If, however, the belief in God fails to meet the above minimal criteria, it necessarily follows that it is not credible to believe in his existence. It is rather better to be an existentialist-agnostic or a weak atheist onlooker in a world crippled with religious uncertainty and deceit.

Is belief in God not a human invention?

Beyond any justification of the belief in the existence of God it is worth considering Hume's postulation of historical condition of man that made him to conceive a higher being he could relate with in his solitary condition. Hume is probably right that the idea of God is a by-product of human imagination rather than a concrete reality. Anthony Kenny puts it more succinctly:

> If there is no God, then God is incalculably the greatest single creation of the human imagination. No other creation of the human imagination has been so fertile of ideas, so great an inspiration to philosophy, to literature, to painting, sculpture, architecture, and drama.[13]

It is necessary to reflect on the plausibility of the "Ground" of human religious invention. Did man make God in his own anthropomorphic image contrary to what is written in the Bible that God created man in his own image? This theological proposition brings to the fore the nature of human transcendence. It is a fact that human beings are rational agents endowed with self-consciousness or self-awareness in the state of beings in the cosmos. Their survival depends largely on how aptly they utilize their transcendent intelligence in the world. Because self-preservation is key to human species, therefore to fight extinction becomes a daily do or die struggle or affair. As far as human knowledge reveals from human and physical geography, the planet earth is the only habitable for humans to live in and flourish because natural resources are there for them to tap and use for their existential ambience and comfort. The more they are confronted with dead and fear the better they use their innate scientific and technological faculty to transcend. In a nutshell man has become a *creator* of his own *creatures* by developing artificial intelligence or robotic engineering or biomedical engineering of *beings* to enhance his quality of life. His creativity and innovations are becoming unstoppable because that is the nature of transcendence. All socio-religious, socio-cultural, socio-economic and political activities are towards improving and preserving *self* because that is his *eternal-now*. Is a philosophical-scientific-humanism not replacing human spirituality? What is human spirituality? Is there any form of relationship between a philosophical-scientific-humanism and human spirituality? There is a general belief that man is more than a physical being. He is theologically a spiritual substance meaning a soul but philosophically conceived as the mind. In both schools of thought the soul/mind is intangible and capable of independent existence outside the body. In philosophical theology, human soul/mind is conceived as divine because he emanates from God. Man seeks to placate God with allegiance and obedience to his directives for harmonious relationship because he believes that nothing becomes possible for him without the permission of God: an existential facticity of the true nature of human existence. Therefore, human spirituality is a sum total belief that man is not only a physical being but also a spiritual entity; a dualism of some sort whose existence is perpetually dependent on God. For want of appropriate terminology it is a *transcendental dualism* or an *ontological dualism*, which is antithesis of philosophical-scientific-humanism. Properly understood, philosophical-scientific-humanism is a human understanding of his nature as monism a substance devoid of spirituality. Man is the creator and architect of his humanity. He does not hold allegiance to any superior intelligent Being. He found himself in a universe of beings and his primary objective is to consciously formulate his own principle of life: self-preservation. There is no empirical being superior to him in the cosmos of beings. He is the transcendent master planner and engineer of his own life. There is no *eternal-life* but *eternal-now* in the universe he lives and continuously recreates for his existential comfort, happiness and satisfaction. That is the only empirical world he has a scientific understanding of its humanity, which is verifiable. Therefore the belief in God is a product of human imagination. In other words, without man, God does not exist. Man is an empirical and verifiable genius!

Conclusion

I am aware that those who have a religious belief particularly, theists will consider my argument bias and provocative. But the truth of the matter is that by taking any philosophical position it will inevitably have some elements of bias. The issue therefore is whether the bias is logical and morally justifiable? I think the argument I have advanced to arrive at certain pragmatic criteria that belief in God must meet to be logically and morally warranted, is persuasive and convincing.

For those who believe that man cannot set up any criteria to justify belief in God, my position is to remind them that the condition that made religion to be prominent in the life of man is existential and not metaphysical. In so far as the terrifying exigencies of life that Hume proposed as the reason man conceived God in his imagination and without man the knowledge of God would be elusive is undeniable. In my own opinion, we cannot justify the existence of God without first examining the conditions that necessitated its belief. Due to advancement of human knowledge of science and technology and its improvement on human well-being in this digital age, only time will tell whether belief in Abrahamic God is not simply buying time before it becomes irrelevant. In other words, the more affluent man becomes the less he thinks about God. With the advancement of human biomedical technology or biomedical engineering or robotic engineering, it is likely possible that diseases and death that threaten human existence and which make people find succor in God will be overcome. And when that happens, it is anticipated that the new civilization would have brought about the apex realization of human ingenuity and creativity as the creator of his world, the *eternal-now*, which is the goal of human existence.

* Segun Ogungbemi (2007-2008) "Belief in God: A Religio-Philosophical Analysis" *Orisun: Journal of Religion and Human Values*, Department of Religious Studies, Olabisi Onabanjo University, Ago-Iwoye, Ogun State, 6-7, 1-15.

CHAPTER 12

A Comparative Study Of Olodumare
The Yoruba Supreme Being And Judeo-Christian God

"Nothing will so enlarge the intellect, nothing so magnifying the whole soul of man, as a devout, earnest, continued investigation of the great subject of the Deity."¹

Introduction

There is a prevalent belief among the Yoruba that Olodumare the Yoruba Supreme Being is the same with Judeo-Christian God. The idea of equating Christian God with Olodumare has been principally the intellectual works of Bishop Ajai Crowder who translated the Bible to Yoruba and Professor E. Bolaji Idowu a liberal theologian whose book: *Olodumare: God in Yoruba Belief* has contributed to this doctrine. Is it true that the Christian God is the same as Olodumare the Supreme Being? Do they share the same universal power and authority over all the created beings from the metaphysical- primordial existence to the physical existence where human beings are very dominant? In other words, do they share common attributes namely, omnipotence, omnipresence, omniscience etc that have become a definitive theological characteristic of a being called God?

My research findings using a philosophical theology method suggest some elements of similarities but in essence they are not necessarily the same. It has also established the claim that before the introduction of foreign religions in Yorubaland the people have had a philosophical concept of the existence of Olodumare, the Supreme Being.

Essential Definitions and Clarifications

Let me begin with some definitions/terms of names and concepts for the purpose of clarity, (1) Olodumare: the Supreme Being, (2) God, (3) theology, (4) natural theology and (5) philosophical theology.

(1) Olodumare: the Supreme Being,

Some prominent Yoruba scholars in the field of religion and theology namely, J. Olumide Lucas, E. Bolaji Idowu, J. Omosade Awolalu among others will be our guide in defining the name Olodumare who is often given a superlative expression as Olorun Olodumare, the Supreme Being or simply the Deity. According to Idowu:

> What the Yoruba have in mind when they speak the name Olodumare, call upon the Deity in prayers, or approach Him in worship, is expressed by all the descriptions taken together. The name Olodumare has always carried with it the idea of One with Whom man may enter into covenant or communion in any place and at any time, one who is supreme, superlatively great, incomparable and unsurpassable in majesty, excellence in attributes, stable, unchanging, constant, reliable.[2]

Lucas in his book, *The Religion of the Yorubas* writes that Olorun in Yoruba traditional thought has a refined characterization. "He is credited with omnipresence, omniscience, and omnipotence."[3] Awolalu is of the view that Olodumare is the Supreme Being having numerous attributes some of which have been mentioned by Lucas and he adds that the Deity is "the Creator, the Ruler of the universe and the Determiner of destiny."[4] In a nutshell, the Yoruba idea of Olorun Olodumare can be defined as the Supreme Source of everything that is both metaphysically and empirically or otherwise. He is the Supreme Being or the Deity, the eternal, the Creative genius, the Being of beings, the foundation of morals and principle of justice, the One and the only Supreme and the Absolute who controls everything in existence.

(2) God

According to Van A. Harvey's *A Handbook of Theological Terms* "God is, in Christian Theology, both a proper name and an abstract noun for deity."[5] This implies that God is conceived in anthropomorphic and metaphysic absoluteness in power and authority. Writing in the same vein, John Macquarrie in his book, *Principles of*

Christian Theology conceives God in relation to the cosmos and argues that "God" cannot be conceived apart from the world, for it is of his essence (letting-be) to create; God is affected by the world as well as affecting it, or creation entails risk and vulnerability; God is in time and history, as well as above them."[6] God properly conceived and defined from this perspective becomes squarely the mental work and attitude of existential beings because without beings, God cannot be known outside the context of human existence. This means that the understanding of God by humans is an expression of his relationship, which is bilateral. It is a relationship that is both mutually beneficial to the Infinite and finite beings that believe in him with reverence, awe, in worship and adoration.

(3) Theology

We have come to a field that is so diverse due to human conceptions of God, the Deity and how to communicate its various and diffused perspectives reasonably enough to its community of faith. Macquarrie, in my view, has given a comprehensive and less ambiguous definition of theology. According to him, "Theology may be defined as the study which, through participation in and reflection upon religious faith, seeks to express the content of this faith in the clearest and most coherent language available."[7]

Theology is human creative activity to express and educate the inner content of religious faith in God anywhere such belief is considered relevant to their individual and corporate existence. It is no surprise therefore to hear about different kinds of theology i.e., Systematic theology, Symbolic theology, Christian theology, Moral theology, African theology, Black theology, Biblical theology, Natural theology, Philosophical theology etc. These theologies are defined within the ambit of the theological interest of the theologians who engage in the intellectual enterprise of theologizing. Whichever way any of these theologies is defined it must have a general component of God and how human discourse of the Deity is communicated in the language that people understand.

(4) Natural theology

Natural theology according to Harvey "refers to the effort to construct a doctrine of God without appeal to FAITH or special REVELATION but on the basis of reason and experience alone."[8] Charles Hartshorne in his book, *A Natural Theology for our Time* defines natural theology as "a theory of divinity appealing to 'natural reason'- that is, critical consideration of the most general ideas and ideals necessary to interpret life and reality…" [9] Macquarrie explains that natural theology is "to supply rational proof of the reality of those matters with which theology deals."[10]

The constituent element of natural theology and its investigative method to validate the truth and reality of a religious proposition is within the bound of reason and empirical evidence. This is what led to various ontological, cosmological and teleological arguments for the existence of God. But rather than proving the existence of God, it has led to promoting skepticism and in most cases outright atheism. Hartshorne once told a story of his encounter with Rudolf Bultmann, an Existentialist and New Testament theologian where he asked him this question:

> What is the difference between the God of philosophy and the God of religion? His reply, which pleased me greatly, was, if I recall correctly, approximately this: 'The God of philosophy is anyone's God, the God of religion is your God and mine'. I should generalize a bit more widely, and say, the God of philosophy, or at least of metaphysics, is any creature's God, the God of religion is the God of humanity, or more concretely, our God now. [11]

The view of Hartshorne as expressed above which is probably in consonance with Bultmann will somehow generate a lot of debate. I am not convinced that philosophy has a God rather philosophy properly understood which both Hartshorne and Bultmann were aware uses reason and empirical methods of inquiry to validate the reality of God of religion just as it does with science, history, technology, ethics etc. The danger of philosophical inquiry is that it does not have a limit. It keeps asking for more evidence until one is completely exhausted with a compendium of reasons. The foregoing explains why over the years natural theology had engaged the intellectual world in matters related to God of religion to the extent that it ended up losing its disciples and its prominence in philosophical circles. What has become a concomitant of natural theology is philosophy of religion as it is being taught in colleges, liberal seminaries and universities.

(5) Philosophical theology

Philosophical theology seeks to make religious beliefs more reasonable without necessarily involving deductive and inductive reasoning to prove its contents of faith like natural theology. Macquarrie aptly expresses the definition and nature of philosophical theology. According to him, philosophical theology is:

> ...descriptive rather than deductive, but it performs the same function of providing a link between secular thought and theology proper. It lays bare the fundamental concepts of theology and investigates the conditions that make any theology possible. In doing this it also provides a defense of theology against its detractors, by showing that theology can claim to have foundations in the universal structures of human existence and experience. [12]

To elucidate more on philosophical theology Macquarrie writes:

> Philosophical theology seeks to show us what is the logic of theological discourse, or perhaps to show us whether it has a coherent logic at all. Only when these matters have been explored can we judge about the claims of theology, and have some reliable grounds for assessing whether it does in fact speak of matters that are of paramount importance for human life, or whether it is a tissue of confusions and errors, or whether it is baseless and illusory, like the pseudo-science of astrology. [13]

There are two major issues that we have to note in this discourse namely, that philosophical theology is descriptive and its aim is to present theological beliefs in a logical and coherent language. When theological or religious propositions are presented in this manner, it becomes reasonable and persuasive. In other words, philosophical theology is the arsenal with which to propagate the contents of religious beliefs because of its relevance to human existential experience of faith and values.

From the foregoing, how does the indigenous Yoruba theology of the Deity fit into these grandiose definitions and method of philosophical theology espoused in western scholarship? This question will be answered as the discourse progresses. But let me say that the comparative study of the Deity as conceived in traditional Yoruba thought and its counterpart in western theological tradition necessitates using a common theological method to make the comparison justifiable. I want to stress that all theologies, it seems to me, are grounded in assumptions or suppositions and if that is the case, using a common method of philosophical theology is the most appropriate to explain any aspect of its conundrums. For instance, the work of Antony Flew and Alasdair MacIntyre, *New Essays in Philosophical Theology*[14] is a revolutionary approach, which elucidates the content of theological doctrine using a philosophical vehicle of reason to respond to a changing concept of religious Deity and the paradoxes in the religious assumptions.

Yoruba Theology of Olodumare

Let me say from the onset that I have deliberately avoided giving any linguistic analysis of the name Olodumare because Idowu, Awolalu, and in Modupe Oduyoye's *Yoruba Religious Discourse* have done it among others. Besides, its intellectual exercise is convoluted and does not help adequately enough in the presentation of the theology of the Deity in the language that is lucid, clear and coherent. The theology of Olodumare or Olorun or any other names by which the Supreme Being is conceived in Yoruba is shrouded in several myths. This is understandable because the origin of the Deity is a mystery. If that be the case, which I think it is, it is therefore important to present the one that is most fascinating and relevant to philosophical theology.

The starting point is that Olodumare is a self existent Being and the foundation of all that exist. Idowu makes this more explicit:

> Someone who has made a careful study of all the material which our sources afford will have no hesitation in asserting that Olodumare is the origin and ground of all that is.... From all the evidence, which we gathered from the traditions, the Yoruba have never, strictly speaking, really thought further back than Olodumare, the Deity.[15]

The assumption that Olodumare is the source of existence of all things is the basis of this theology. The Yoruba's indisputable faith in this religious canon, one will argue, is shrouded in mystery but that is the nature of all theologies. This Deity does not make himself hidden in mystery, according to the Yoruba belief; he makes himself known in nature, traditions, revelation and human conscience, the seat of human moral values. It is through his revelation in different mediums the Yoruba conceive him as omnipotent, omnipresent, omniscient, omnibenevolent etc. Awolalu adds that the Yoruba know that the Supreme Being "is the Creator, the Ruler of the universe and the Determiner of destiny. The kingdom of this world is a theocratic one in which the Supreme Being is Himself the Head, while the divinities that have no existence apart from Him are His intermediaries and functionaries."[16]

The Yoruba have a mythological tripartite theocratic structure of existence. The first is the abode of the Supreme Deity, otherwise known as the world of the "highest Good" and the second is the cosmos of rational, intelligent, spiritual and existential beings and finally the universe where humans and other natural beings/things coexist with one another. The most concise and explicit explanation of this theological phenomenal world is what is presented to us in the concept of human destiny. Although Idowu argues that in the oral traditions of the Yoruba one is not very clear about the state of nature of beings in the pre-existent life; he however explains that in the oral sayings of the people there is sufficient evidence to show the foundation of Yoruba theology and human geography both encapsulated in the concept and philosophy of human destiny.

> The general picture, therefore, is of a complete "person" kneeling before Olodumare to choose or receive. When the rite before Olodumare is complete, the person starts on his way into the world. He arrives at the gates of between heaven and earth, and encounters the *On'ibode*- 'The Gate-Keeper'- to whom he must answer some questions before he passes through.[17]

Questions that the "person" coming to the world may answer bother on the reason why he has chosen to leave the theocratic world for the universe of beings/things that are naturally polarized with both good and evil for human existence. But the beauty of the choice of the individual to come to the world is the prerogative of being to exercise his free will and be held responsible or accountable for it. The theological explanation of the rational being "person" in the pre-existence must be understood beyond its local content of the explanation of the origin of the Yoruba. It seems to me that it explains the existence of the individual in the universal context. This explains human geographical locations on earth. That is, Africans in Africa, Chinese in China, Indians in India, British in Britain, Americans in America etc. Olodumare has never given preference in terms of love or affection to any particular race. It is a practical demonstration of his all-inclusiveness in the proposition of Yoruba theological canon of his benevolence or All-goodness. The Deity does not co-exist with any son. He has no son with whom he is "well pleased" who will be used as an atonement for universal sin. That is not part of Yoruba theology of Olodumare. In other words, the concept and theology of soteriology are not in tandem with the Yoruba theology of the Supreme Deity.

Furthermore, the demythologizing of the being of man espouses his missions and accomplishments. It explicates the mantras of existence and the transcendent nature of humans with ability to challenge natural forces both seen and unseen and transforms themselves within the vicissitudes of existence and rules the universe as they deem it. Reinhold Niebuhr makes it more explicit.

> The obvious fact is that man is a child of nature, subject to its vicissitudes, compelled by its necessities, driven by its impulses,

and confined within the brevity of the years which nature permits its varied organic form, allowing them some, but not too much, latitude. The other less obvious fact is that man is a spirit who stands outside of nature, life, himself, his reason and the world. [18]

Niebuhr is probably right by conceiving man as a child of nature but beyond that rationalistic view of man and his relationship with nature the underlying factor from Yoruba theology of God and man is that it is not man's disobedience that led him to his precarious situation in the universe. In other words, the concept of universal sin in Biblical theology is alien to the relationship between the Deity and man. For man to choose voluntarily to come and live on earth implies losing his infinite being in the theocratic existence to a finite existence where death is a fact of that existence.

The Supreme Being does not require any form of worship in any confined environment known as shrines or any place of worship. Olodumare, the Supreme Deity does not ask for any form of animal or human sacrifice for the forgiveness of sin. What man did in the pre-existent life was a rational choice to carve a world of his own within the prerogative power of the Supreme Being and to exercise his governance in a symbolic manner to mirror his limited authority after that of the infinite theocratic setup in the Supersensible world.

Olodumare and His Divinities

The Yoruba pantheon is theologically complex because of the myths pertaining to their existence, the uncertainty of their numbers and their individual functions. The general belief as contained in the traditions is that Olodumare created the divinities to serve as his ministers or messengers. The divinities do not have a separate existence neither are they independent outside the purview of the Supreme Deity. According to Awolalu, "The actual number of the divinities is not easily determinable; it has variously been estimated to be 200,201,400, 460, 600, 601, 1,700 or even more." [19] Jacob K. Olupona in his book, *City of 201 Gods: Ile-Ife in Time, Space and the Imagination* has argued that Ile-Ife the mythical home of human existence and the cradle of Yoruba civilization has 201 gods.[20] One can imagine how numerous the divinities are in all Yorubaland bearing in mind the large number of their towns and villages in Nigeria. What moral and logical reasons for Olodumare to have created many divinities? One may not be able to answer this question for the Supreme Being but one can only suggest a probable reason which is based on the growing number in population of the Yoruba and the need for the deities to take care more adequately for their domestic, social, economic, security, spiritual and psychological needs. The intention here, however, is not to dwell on the moral or logical reasons why the mushroom of divinities was created by the Deity for the people but to present within the frames of philosophical theology the most relevant of the gods to the contemporary intellectual space. In Yoruba theology the following are some of the principal divinities, (1) Orisha-nla, (2) Oduduwa, (3) Ela, (4) Orunmila, (5) Ogun, and (6) Esu. They are so designated because of their significance in the affairs of the Yoruba? This will become more vivid as we discuss each of them

(1) Orisha-nla

Orisha-nla is otherwise called Obatala the arch-divinity because of his position in the hierarchy of beings. Parrinder explains, "The most important of the Yoruba *orishas* is Orishala (Orisha-nla, the great god). He is also called Obatala, 'king who is great' or king in white clothing'" [21] Similarly Idowu writes:

> According to our oral traditions, Orisa-nla is very ancient. He was the very first to receive a definite characterization, and that will explain why he is described by some of our elders as the image or symbol of Olodumare on earth. Yoruba theology also calls him the off-spring of Olodumare in the sense that he derived immediately from him and that the attributes of Olodumare are revealed through him.[22]

Orisha-nla is generally conceived as a sculpture divinity because in Yoruba oral traditions Olodumare saddled him with the molding of human forms. After he had made human forms Olodumare put life into them but he did not allow Orisha-nla to have the metaphysical know-how. The import of this myth is that Olodumare is the giver of life and no other being has the secret and knowledge to impart life to humans. The Deity remains de facto the Creator of human beings. Besides, humans remain a special breed in the hand of the Supreme Being because all other animals in the universe were not created in the same manner. The essence of life i.e., intelligence, transcendence, creativity, spirituality etc became a special lot of human beings. All these carry with them responsibility and accountability because humans are answerable to the Supreme Being since they did not create themselves.

In the mythical Yoruba ontology of humans in which Orisha-nla was seen as sculptor divinity, it implies therefore, that any human defects or physically challenged individuals can be blamed on Orisha-nla and not the Supreme Deity.

That is why for instance, the albinos or the hunchbacks are regarded as *eni orisa*, the votaries of the Orisa. They are so called the votaries of orisa to provide protection to them. It is believed that if they are not considered as the votaries of the orisa there is tendency to harm or kill them but being a special creation of the orisa anyone who causes any harm to them will be visited with the wrath of Orisa-nla. The moral protection of the physically challenged beings as exemplified in the theology of Orisa-nla is an indication of the premium the Yoruba placed on the value of human sanctity.

Orisha-nla also mirrors the symbolic attribute of holiness of the Supreme Deity because he is associated with white clothing or objects. His devotees dress in white robes, which, signifies purity of mind and closeness to the Deity.

(2) Oduduwa

In the theological discourse of this deity one is confronted with two mythical traditions of his existence and accomplishments. There is one that presents him as a messenger of the Supreme Deity who usurped the responsibility of Orisa-nla in the creation of the universe and subsequently metamorphosed as a historical founder of the Yoruba and first god-king of Ile-Ife, the cradle home of Yoruba civilization. Kola Abimbola writes:

> It was the wish of Olodumare, the High Deity of the Yoruba, to create dry land…He therefore sent 400 Orisa to perform this important task. Olodumare gave the Orisa a parcel of dust from Heaven. He also gave them a chameleon and a hen. This hen had five fingers on each foot. Obatala was charged with the sacred duty of creating dry land from water, and it was to him that Olodumare gave all the items mentioned above. The Orisa descended to Oke-Ara ("mountain of wonders" which is near to what would later be known as Ile-Ife) with the aid of the iron chain supplied by Ogun. While on top of the mountain, Obatala drank too much palm-wine and went to sleep. His younger brother, Oduduwa, then acquired the implements given to Obatala by Olodumare, and created dry land from the primordial water. He sprinkled the sacred dust on the water, and wherever a grain of sand touched became solid. He then set free the hen, and the hen scratched the ground in all directions. Miraculously, the land started to expand and expand. Oduduwa then set free the chameleon to fell the solidity of the earth. The place where dry land was created from water, and from where the land

expanded, is called Ife. The verb "fe" means, "to expand". Oduduwa later became king of Ile-Ife...As a matter of fact; the Yoruba believe that all vegetation, all animals, birds and humans originated from Ile-Ife, therefore the cradle of mankind and all creation.[23]

I have quoted Abimbola at length because of its mythical and historic content, which I consider significant. What do we make theologically of this myth? The driving force behind this myth, it seems to me, is that the Yoruba have had their traditional belief of the origin of human existence and other creation before the advent of other religions. That Islam, Christianity and all other religious beliefs have no superior knowledge about the world better than the Yoruba. The belief in Oduduwa as a deity who transformed himself as a king provides the basis for human sense of self-governance rather than the theocratic system in the primordial existence. The politics of institutional monarchy that is evident in the myth is key to the way and manner the Yoruba structures their corporate life. This form of institutional monarchy is indigenous which has no foreign content. But the institution has no independent originality without being grounded in Olodumare the Supreme Deity. The monarchical structure of the Yoruba system of governance is a caricature of that of Olodumare in the Supersensible world. The emphasis in this theology is that human beings are not masters of themselves and the universe where they reside. The knowledge to govern or rule over their corporate existence is derived from the Ground of beings, Olodumare.

(3) Ela

This deity appears obscured in contemporary literature of Yoruba theology. But Idowu is of the view that, "The name Ela means "Safety" or "One who keeps in safety"; "Preservation" or" Preserver," "Salvation" or "Saviour."[24] In terms of the ministerial post assigned to him by Olodumare Ela is the 'Prime Minister' who has the wizardry of governing over a very turbulent society of beings. Idowu further explains that the deity called "Ela is the spirit of truth, rightness, and amicable living, working on earth to create and promote order, happiness, and understanding among the inhabitants of the earth."[25] As the promoter of peace and good neighborliness Ela is "opposed to the evil works of Esu and engages himself in obstructing him or undoing his evil deeds in the way a superior would."[26]

(4) Orunmila

In Yoruba traditional social life, Orunmila appears very close to the people because it is believed that Olodumare gave him the oracle of wisdom and knowledge with which to know the mystery of the world and the secret behind human success and failure. Hardly could anyone find in everyday life of the people occasions that will not warrant a consultation with the deity through his oracle called *Ifa* to know what is in stock for him. As Awolalu aptly notes, "As one who lives in and sees both heaven and earth, he is believed to be in position to plead with Olodumare on behalf of man so that unpleasant circumstances may be averted or rectified."[27] The belief of the Yoruba about their individual and corporate existence is that everyone must always be on guard because you never can tell what can befall you from time to time hence the need to ask from Orunmila through *Ifa* divination. That is why the Yoruba say, boni ri, ola le mo ri be, idi niyi ti babalawo fi nd'falojojumo, meaning, because of uncertainty in life that is why the man of secret knowledge consult his *Ifa* oracle daily. This self-consciousness of man and the need to make him relevant in the vast natural encumbrances is corroborated by Niebuhr who argues, "The truth is that man is tempted by the basic insecurity of human existence to make him doubly secured and by the insignificance of his place in the total scheme of life to prove his significance."[28] Olodumare was aware of all this but when man used his free-will and chose to come to live on earth, a provision to find his way in the wilderness of existence became imperative. So Orunmila and his *Ifa* oracle became the errand deity to handle the insatiable need of the Yoruba. It needs to be made clear here that from Yoruba traditions and my knowledge of the theology of the people the presentation and interpretation of *Ifa* as a deity in the theocratic structure of Yoruba cosmology are misleading. It is indeed theologically absurd to equate *Ifa* oracle with Olodumare, Obatala, Esu, and substitute Orunmila with *Ifa*.[29]

(5) Ogun

Ogun is conceived in Yoruba theology as god of iron, war, peace and justice. The Yoruba oral traditions present Ogun as one of the deities sent to create the earth and on their journey they encountered a difficult terrain and the deity was called upon to clear the way for them, which he did. To the Yoruba, Ogun plays a vital role in human existence. Awolalu explains, "He is believed to be the divinity of iron and of war and pre-eminently the tutelary divinity of hunters, the blacksmiths, the goldsmiths, the barbers, the butchers and (in modern time) the mechanics, the lorry and taxi-drivers – indeed all workers in iron and steel."[30] Properly designated in concrete terms, Ogun is the god of modern science and technology. Ogun must not be construed as a metal like iron and steel which are mere instruments of the deity. All the manufacturing industries are a product of Ogun. The monetary instruments and all forms of monies produced in naira, dollars, and pound sterling, euros etc are made possible by Ogun. All housing, hospitality and infrastructural industries belong to the genius of Ogun. The shrines, synagogues, temples, churches, mosques and all sacred places of worship owe their existence and sustainability to Ogun. Human beings cannot survive without the presence of Ogun and its instruments on the planet earth.

In Yoruba social and political system Ogun is seen as a deity of justice. Awolalu writes:

> It is also believed that Ogun stands for absolute justice so he is called upon to witness a covenant or pact between two persons or groups of people. At present, when a Yoruba who is an adherent of the traditional religion is brought to the law court, he is asked to swear on Ogun (represented by a piece of iron) instead of on the Bible or the Quran. This he does by kissing a piece of iron as he declares he will 'speak the truth, the whole truth and nothing but the truth'. The Yoruba believe very strongly that anybody who swears falsely or breaks a covenant, to which Ogun is a witness, cannot escape severe judgment, which normally results in ghastly accidents.[31]

From the forgoing, the principle of absolute justice remains in the domain of the deity. For social cohesion and transparent justice Ogun remains a deity the Yoruba trust in their daily transactions.

The presence of Ogun in the cosmological and theological proposition of the Yoruba belief is a manifestation of Olodumare's manifold phenomenon in materialistic and spiritual dimensions necessary to make human existence purposeful and meaningful. The mythologemic personality of Ogun represents the characterization of, in a graphic form, the nature of human existence that is constantly becoming.

A curious researcher will probably ask if these divinities actually exist and whether what the Yoruba believe about them is really true. If so why is it that their society is still backward? The question whether the belief is true or not is not predicated on economic and social development. Rather it is grounded in the cultural values of the people and it is reasonably worthy of their belief.

(6) Esu

Esu remains the most complex divinity in Yoruba theology of beings. Idowu writes, "What we gather from our sources is that Esu is primarily a 'special relations officer' between heaven and earth, the inspector-general who reports regularly to Olodumare on the deeds of the divinities and men, and checks and makes reports on the correctness of worship in general and sacrifices in particular."[32] Some of the most recent works on Esu are found in Kola Abimbola, Jacob K. Olupona and Toyin Falola (ed.) *Esu: Yoruba God, Power, and the Imaginative Frontiers* in which 20 prominent scholars have given their perspectives of this deity. In all, Esu Elegba, Elegbara etc are the names and indicators of the power of the deity and the awe, fear and respect the worshipers have for him. The characterization of Esu as both good and evil is what makes him to be loved and hated by the Yoruba. The dualistic nature of the deity symbolizes human coloration of moral virtues. Morally and theologically "Esu exists only mythically for the purpose of explaining the Yoruba exigencies and vicissitudes of life. It is in this regard that Esu has become a phenomenon of existence."[33] Esu, like all the other divinities in Yoruba belief, has no relevance outside the theological, moral and philosophical propositions of humans.

The most crucial question is how does one understand this complex theology of Olodumare with numerous divinities? Is this theology polytheistic or monotheistic? Idowu argues that the theology is monotheistic because there is only one Supreme Deity who manifests himself in different forms and functions through several mediums. It is therefore appropriate to consider it a monotheistic theology or as Idowu suggests a 'Diffused Monotheism.' He explains:

> For the purpose of a descriptive label, we would like to suggest such a startling thing as "Diffused Monotheism" this has the advantage of showing that the religion is monotheism, though it is a monotheism in which the good Deity delegates certain portions of His authority to certain divine functionaries who work as they are commissioned by Him. For a proper name we unhesitatingly say that there can be none other but "*Olodumareism*".[34]

It needs to be underscored that the model of existence from the primordial life was originally Oneness of the Deity and as time went on the Being-in-itself decided to form a multiplicity of beings from where the concept of family and corporate existence developed. There is hardly, in my opinion, a resounding joy and happiness in a monotonous life. Plurality and multiplicity add values to any form of existence including that of Olodumare. And perhaps that is what is inherent in Yoruba theology of *Olodumareism*. It is this rich theological doctrine of Olodumare that the missionaries and their followers did not aptly comprehend before they erroneously labeled the religious belief of the Yoruba polytheistic. The Yoruba theological discourse of Olodumare is all-engaging because it is not just about the Deity alone but pragmatically about humans and the phenomenon of existence.

Having presented the theology of Olodumare and his functionaries in Yoruba religious belief, let us consider how Christians conceive their God and see whether it is the same Deity that is worshipped by both traditional Yoruba and Christians.

Judeo-Christian God

The theological proposition on which Judeo-Christian God is conceived is predicated on his act in history in the life of the Israelites, the Jews and culminated in the universality of his love towards all humans through the sacrifice of his son, Jesus the Christ. The proclamation of 'God who acts in history'[35] of mankind resonated in the prophetic and evangelistic works of prophets in the Old Testament and the apostles in the New Testament that led to massive evangelistic engagements of the missionaries worldwide. But what do I mean by 'God who acts in human history'? How does he act in history and for what purpose? And more importantly why does God have to act in the history of mankind and particularly through the Israelites or the Jews? What is the need of his presence in the affairs of humans? These are some of the issues that are germane in this theological doctrine of God who acts in human history. Judeo-Christian theology presents in a nutshell, in my view, three distinctive theological traditions that will be discussed here namely, (i) primitive Mosaic theology, (ii) primitive Hellenistic/Protestant theology and, (iii) Existentialist theology. I have used the word 'primitive' to qualify the first two theologies not in a pejorative sense but only in relation to new development of human understanding in theological, philosophical and scientific world of modern man. Rudolf Bultmann puts it more vividly; "The contrast between the ancient world-view of the Bible and the modern view is the contrast between two ways of thinking, the mythological and the scientific."[36] It is this contrast that makes the first two theologies primitive in relation to the third form of theology. Let me discuss these three theologies in the lexico-graphical ordering.

i. Primitive Mosaic theology

Primitive Mosaic theology presents both polytheistic and monotheistic constructs of God as Elohim, denoting several gods "or when used in the plural of majesty for 'God' or 'deity'"[37] and Yahweh, meaning Jehovah which denotes one God respectively in the Old Testament (OT). In both names, God is seen as a creative genius that created the world out of nothing. After creating all that is, he created man in his own image (Genesis 1:26) and made him the boss in the universal existence.

Thus man arrogates to himself the dominant authority over the universe, which of course, has its own environmental consequences. In a similar OT tradition, Genesis 2^{7-25} gives another account of God's creativity that ushered in the beginning of human corporate existence and marital institution as demonstrated in the life and existence of Adam and Eve. It becomes very compelling to note that the conscripted pastoral life that Adam and Eve lived made them not to have creative knowledge or transcendence to enhance their corporate life. They were so ignorant to develop the kind of economic and entrepreneurial skill for self-existence and self-esteem. Adam and Eve had a restricted freedom with abundant unalloyed loyalty to their God. In Genesis 3, the robust relationship that existed between God and Adam turned sour when his wife ate the forbidden fruit and gave him to eat as well, that Yahweh had instructed Adam not to eat and the day he ate it death would become an inevitable reality for him. This singular disobedience led to his eternal damnation and expulsion from the Garden of Eden including his wife. Adam and Eve did not lose everything as they were forced out of the blissful Garden of Eden; they gained their freedom from servitude and knowledge of good and evil that prepared them for challenges in the new environment. They, however, became theologically stigmatized with what is doctrinally called the Adamic sin or a generic sin that has been a theological debate in Christendom. The theological presupposition is that the Adamic sin became a preparatory formula and justification for God to reconcile man to himself. In this theological discourse, God in his infinite grace and mercy took a decisive action in human history to redeem man and made him accountable, not only to himself and humanity alone, but also and above all, to his Creator. This primitive Mosaic metaphysical-mythological theology forms the basis of the eschatological hope for human eternal redemption as explicated by the Christian Church. To achieve this theological objective, God who acts in human history, as contained in the Pentateuch called Abram who later became known as Abraham, a pastoralist by vocation to leave his home base in Ur for an undisclosed destination. What God needed from him was faith and obedience and in return he would receive abundant blessing in terms of wealth, heir, and land. The land of Canaan was the place that would be given to him and his descendants. His children would be uncountable like the sand of the sea. Abraham had faith and his wife who was barren became pregnant and gave birth to a son called Isaac who became a test of faith. He was asked to sacrifice his only son, Isaac. Abraham did not hesitate to obey God's command and as he was about to sacrifice Isaac, a ram was given as a substitute and the young Isaac was spared of untimely death.

Isaac got married to Rebecca and they had two children Esau and Jacob. Thus Abraham, Isaac and Jacob became patriarchs of the Jewish nation and from them emerged a dynasty, King David, the Lion of Judah. I have simply given a brief chorological Biblical history that depicted the actions of God in history without discussing the polemics involved in that history. The conception of 'God acts in history' in relation to the story of Abraham has indeed portrayed Yahweh in a despicable manner that made him to be solely responsible for historical tragedy in Palestine and the Middle East till today. For God to singularly choose Abraham among all men in his time as a favoured individual became a perennial problem in human history. That is, the principle of favouritism of Yahweh as witnessed in the OT with its attendant consequences in history continues to exacerbate human misery. The existence of Abraham in human religious history is an existence of paradoxical tragedy. If one relates the claim of Prophet Mohammad, the founder of Islam who traced his ancestry to Abraham and, the experience of violence in many parts of the world traceable to this patriarchal family from time immemorial, it becomes worrisome, if the claim can be justifiably regarded, as coming from the heirs of Abraham and his creator, Yahweh, who is All-Powerful, All-Knowing and All-Good.

ii. Primitive Hellenistic/Protestant Theology

Primitive Hellenistic/Protestant Theology is based on the agenda of God to consummate his redemptive plan in human history. The New Testament (NT) provides this theological discourse. Here we are presented with a Triune conception of God. That is, God the Father- the Creator, God the Son- the Saviour and God the Holy Spirit- the Comforter acting in history of man. This looks like a polytheistic theology but in the explanation of the Church doctrine, it is purely monotheistic because it is the same Godhead displaying his manifold 'natural being' in mysterious ways that human cognition cannot fully comprehend. In the Hellenistic tradition, God the father sent his son to be born in human form as contained in the birth narratives of Jesus in two of the synoptic gospels, Matthew and Luke. Matthew 1^{18-25} and Luke 1^{26-35} recorded how the pregnancy of Mary who was betrothed to Joseph was the act of the Holy Spirit. As a curious researcher, one wonders, why the Triune God would engage in such an immoral act of impregnating someone's wife so as to bring salvation to all mankind? Why couldn't Matthew and Luke through the inspiration of the Holy Spirit inform them about the moral implications of their birth narratives of Jesus? Could God not use a more moral method to achieve his redemptive objective? After all, man never asked God to create him. To subject the process of his redemptive drama to ridicule as shown in the birth narratives in the Gospels of Matthew and Luke is theologically, morally and doctrinally embarrassing. Be that as it may, perhaps we may need to consider the inherent intention the birth narratives in terms of faith and human salvation. John, one of the closest disciples of Jesus, did not bother to write about his birth narratives so also Paul one of the frontline Apostles who propagated the gospel of Jesus the Christ. If the birth narratives of Jesus were that important they would have written significantly on it. But to a contemporary mind the best way to understand the intent of the birth narratives of Jesus is to demythologize it. Bultmann, in his book, *Kerygma and Myth*, demythologizes the miraculous conception of Jesus by a virgin within the context of, what it means, to a man of faith.

The ministry of Jesus is the hallmark of God's action in history. John 3^{16} is a proclamation and demonstration of God's love. Theologically, it is the most revolutionary in human history because it sets man free from the bondage of sin, fear and self-alienation from his Creator. But the gift of love that God has given to the world is predicated on acceptance by the individual to make salvation a reality for him or her. It is a life of faith and obedience to the teaching and preaching of Jesus. The Hellenist Christianity, which became the foundation of Protestantism, took the Kerygma, the proclamation "of the early Christian community to the life and death of Jesus of Nazareth…. The content of this proclamation was that the age of fulfillment promised by the prophets had come, that it had reached its climax in the life, death and RESUREECTION OF CHRIST."[38] The dynamics of the redemptive message as contained in the Kerygma became a missionary tool that promoted the witness to faith of those who believe.

iii. (iii) Existentialist theology

The advancement of science and technology in the 20th century provided some scientific and verifiable knowledge. Bultmann reiterates:

> The science of today is no longer the same as it was in the nineteenth century, and to be sure, all the results of science are relative, and no world-view of yesterday or today or tomorrow is definitive. The main point, however, is not the concrete results of scientific research and the contents of a world-view, but the method of thinking from which world-views follow.[39]

The new way of theological thinking therefore has to change in line with modern way of world-view if it is to be relevant to the needs of man. Bultmann argues:

> For the world-view of the Scripture is mythological and is therefore unacceptable to modern man whose thinking has been shaped by

science and is therefore is no longer mythological. Modern man always makes use of technical means, which are the result of science. In case of illness modern man has recourse to physicians, to medical science. In the case of economic and political affairs, he makes use of the results of psychological, social, economic and political sciences, and so on. Nobody reckons with direct intervention by transcendent powers.[40]

It is not only science and technology that has reshaped the thinking of human world-view, but more fundamentally philosophy. It has always made it more difficult to accept some of the biblical doctrines about God without moral or epistemological justification. Using a philosophical apparatus of reasoning, Friedrich Nietzsche argues, "From the start, the Christian faith is a sacrifice: a sacrifice of all freedom, all pride, all self-confidence of the spirit; at the same time. Enslavement and self-mockery, self mutilation."[41] For a modern mind to have faith in God and serve him with his entire life, his soul and with his material and spiritual wealth is nothing but religious slavery. When will he have time for himself and family if he does all that for the sake of pleasing God? Furthermore, to a curious mind it is theologically and doctrinally absurd to believe that a God was hanged on the cross? Nietzsche notes: "Modern men, obtuse to all Christian nomenclature, no longer feel the gruesome superlative that struck a classical taste in the paradoxical formula 'god on the cross.'"[42] That God died on the cross for all human races is theologically nonsensical. So, a new theology is needed to explicate the mysterious nature of God who acts in human history, taking cognizance of philosophical and scientific orientations of modern men and women. Existentialist theology of the 20th and 21st centuries has taken a bold step to engage modern men and women with a new hermeneutics of the Kerygma in order to make it meaningful and reasonable. It is in this regard that Bultmann introduces the de-mythologizing of the primitive theology of God. According to Bultmann, "To de-mythologize is to deny that the message of the Scripture and of the Church is bound to an ancient world-view which is obsolete."[43] In other words, the mythological components of the proclamation of the Biblical doctrine of God who acts in history for the emancipation of mankind through Jesus the Christ, needs to employ existentialist theological method, of de-mythologizing, to make the message existentially subjective and objective. Schubert Ogden explains:

> By saying that God acts to redeem mankind *only* in the history of Jesus Christ, he subjects God's action as the Redeemer to the objectifying categories of space and time and thus mythologizes

> it.... The claim 'only in Jesus Christ' must be interpreted to mean, not that God acts to redeem only in the history of Jesus and in no other history, but that the only God who redeems any history- *he in fact redeems every history*- is the God whose redemptive action is decisively re-presented in the word that Jesus speaks and is.[44]

What Ogden is saying is that Bultmann is limiting God's decisive act in history to only through Jesus the Christ and such a theology is unacceptable to the principle of universality of God who acts in all human history. But the question is: Does God have to act through Jesus to redeem mankind in all different human histories? While one will agree with Ogden on the universality of God, who acts in history, it may not necessarily be the case that it should be through Jesus the Christ. Rather, it could be the case that a God who acts in history is to be properly construed to mean in all ramifications his inclusiveness through the deities, prophets, priests, and ancestors.

Is Olodumare, the Supreme Deity the same as Judeo-Christian God?

Having discussed the Christian belief in God, his attributes and how he has acted in human history, can we equate him with the Yoruba concept of Olodumare, the Supreme Being? In other words, is the Yoruba concept of Olodumare the same as the Christian God? Or is the Christian God the same as that of the Yoruba? There are striking similarities in both beliefs as well as dissimilarities. The two theologies of the Divine Beings present them as invincible and yet active in human history in terms of similarity of attributes and creativity. According to oral and written traditions of the Yoruba, Olodumare is Holy so also in the Christian God in the Bible. Other attributes common to both Deities are omnipotence, omnipresence and omniscience, among others. In both Christianity and Yoruba indigenous religion, there is only one universal God who created heaven and earth. To the Christians, he is called Yahweh and to the Yoruba, he is Olodumare, the Supreme Being. With regard to their creativity the narratives of human creation and the universe are not similar. In one of the Yoruba mythologies of creation as already explained, Olodumare entrusted the making of human form to Orisa-Nla and after he had completed the assignment Olodumare went to put life into it and he or she became a living human being having consciousness and conscience.

The Christian God in Genesis 2:7 was similarly depicted as a potter who molded human form by himself and breathed into its nostrils and he became a living soul.

We also have in Genesis 1:26 where God created male and female in his own image rather than being a potter. Let me explain the two theological terms of 'make' and 'create'. To make in this theological context means producing something from a material substance while to create is a speech act that brings forth something out of nothing. The idea of creativity as conceived and used here has to do with the practical demonstration of the ingenuous ability of production that has become the hallmark of not only the Divine Beings but also of human beings.

The theological concept of Godhead i.e. God the Father, God the Son and God the Holy Spirit manifesting and acting in human history seems to suggest polytheism rather than monotheism. A similar case can be made against Olodumare who has a legion of ministerial agents i.e. Obatala who is otherwise known as Orisa-Nla, Ogun, Ela etc who are saddled with specific responsibilities in human history. It is theologically inappropriate to consider the two religions as polytheistic because the understanding here is that it is the same God or the Supreme Being manifesting his power and authority in the universe of humans as he deems fit. From this theological expression one can speak of both religions as monotheistic. Idowu however calls the religion of the Yoruba Diffused-Monotheism. There has never been any occasion that the Christian God or Olodumare deliberately created a permanent vacuum without relating either directly or indirectly with human beings. That is why in Christianity Jesus the Christ became the link between God and man. And in Yoruba theology Esu, Ela and all other divinities serve as linkages with Olodumare. But this does not mean that the Supreme Being cannot be reached directly by individuals or community when the need arises. Given all the similarities between the two Deities discussed above, can one say that they are the same? We may not be able to make a valid deduction without knowing their dissimilarities. The Christian theology of the generic Adamic sin, the preference and choice of a race, the Israelites over and above other races in the world, the birth narratives of Jesus, the sacrifice of God the Son on the cross for the universal salvation of all humans etc do not make moral and intellectual sense in Yoruba theology of Olodumare.

The incessant conflicts, violence, wars and senseless killings of innocent men and women including children encouraged and authorized by the God of Christianity for instance, in 1.Samuel 15, where Saul was asked to go and destroy all the Amalekites including animals. God in the OT made the Israelites to be warmongers rather than peace lovers of their neighbors. It is also true that when the Israelites disobeyed him they were punished and on several occasions taken into captivity. Such action in human history cannot be traced to Olodumare.

The Christian God acting in human history in the New Testament (NT) chose to send his Son to die for the sin of mankind and only through him alone can the reconciliation between him and man be resolved. And anyone who does not come through the Son, Jesus the Christ will be thrown to hell fire on the Day of Judgment. This belief forms the basis of the NT theology of grace and redemption. The examples given in the Biblical theology that presents God as acting in human history explicate the divergence between the Yoruba theology of Olodumare and God of Christianity. In Yoruba theology of Olodumare we have a perfect moral Deity who cannot be associated with impiety as seen in the Christian God. We have a Universalist Deity who is concerned with a democratic structure of the universe depicting the way humans should relate with one another and be happy. Of course, Olodumare given his activities in the cosmos of humans and the mode of his operations in the theocratic pantheon as we have seen, it is morally and logically improper to equate him with the Christian God. Byang Kato, a conservative Christian theologian got it wrong when he argues, "If any religion is as good as the other, why should one try to tell somebody to accept one way rather than the other? Yet that is the constant theme of the Bible – warning men to repent and accept the new and the living Way."[45] Kato believes that it is pseudo-theology to equate the Christian God with the Yoruba Deity because the Yoruba have no clear idea or concept of the Supreme Deity, hence they do not worship him.[46] Of course, being a conservative theologian and someone not versed in Yoruba theology of God, Kato, in my opinion, is absolutely wrong. From the foregoing, it is indisputable that the Yoruba have had the concept of Olodumare the Supreme Being from time immemorial.

Conclusion

I began with a proposition that Olodumare; the Supreme Being in Yoruba may have some similarities in terms of attributes and creativity with the Christian God however they are not necessarily the same. I have identified areas of authentic sameness but also dissimilarities, which make it compelling to reject the notion that the two Deities are the same. The examples given to prove that they are not the same on moral and logical grounds are not exhaustive. I have also argued that the Yoruba concept of God was not in consequence of their interaction with other cultures. In both theologies man becomes a common confluence between Olodumare and the Christian God who acted in human history. In other words, the whole theology of God in Yoruba belief or in Christianity is about man's metaphysical invention of a Superior Being or God hence without man the theology has no relevance or significance. It is from this perspective that the Yoruba belief in Olodumare and the Christian God has a converging purpose and meaning.

Notes and References

1. J. I. Parker, *Knowing God*, (Illinois: InterVarsity Press, 1973).
2. E. Bolaji Idowu, *Olodumare: God in Yoruba Belief*, (London: Longman Group Limited, 1962), 36.
3. J. Olumide Lucas, *The Religion of the Yorubas*, Lagos: CMS Bookshop, 1948), 34.
4. J. Omosade Awolalu, *Yoruba Beliefs and Sacrificial Rites*, (London: Longman Group Limited, 1979), 18.
5. Van A. Harvey, *A Handbook of Theological Terms*, (New York: Macmillan Publishing Co., Inc., 1964), 105.
6. John Macquarrie, *Principle of Christian Theology*, Second Edition, (New York: Charles Scribner's Sons, 1977), 121.
7. John Macquarrie, *Principle of Christian Theology*, 1.
8. Van A. Harvey, *A Handbook of Theological Terms*, 158.
9. Charles Hartshorne, *A Natural Theology of Our Time*, (Illinois: Open Court Publishing Company, 1967), x.
10. John Macquarrie, *Principle of Christian Theology*, 13.
11. Rudolf Bultmann, *Kerygma and Myth: A Theological Debate*, (New York: Harper & Row Publishers. 1961), 132.
12. John Macquarrie, *Principle of Christian Theology*, 39.
13. John Macquarrie, *Principle of Christian Theology*, 43-44.
14. Antony Flew & Alasdair MacIntyre, *New Essays in Philosophical Theology*, (New York: Macmillan, 1973 rep.).
15. E. Bolaji Idowu, *Olodumare: God in Yoruba Belief*, 18.
16. J. Omosade Awolalu, *Yoruba Beliefs and Sacrificial Rites*, 18.
17. E. Bolaji Idowu, *Olodumare: God in Yoruba Belief*, 174.
18. Reinhold Niebuhr, *The Nature and Destiny of Man: Volume I Human Nature*, (New York: Charles Scribner's Sons, 1941), 3.

19. J. Omosade Awolalu, *Yoruba Beliefs and Sacrificial Rites*, 20.

20. Jacob K. Olupona, *City of 201 Gods: Ile-Ife in Time, Space, and the Imagination*, (London: University of California Press, 2011).

21. Geoffrey Parrinder, *West African Religion*, (London: Epworth Press, 1973rep), 27.

22. E. Bolaji Idowu, *Olodumare: God in Yoruba Belief*, 71.

23. Kola Abimbola, *Yoruba Culture: A Philosophical Account*, (Birmingham: Iroko Academic Publishers, 2005), 120-121.

24. E. Bolaji Idowu, *Olodumare: God in Yoruba Belief*, 106.

25. E. Bolaji Idowu, *Olodumare: God in Yoruba Belief*, 103.

26. E. Bolaji Idowu, *Olodumare: God in Yoruba Belief*, 103.

27. J. Omosade Awolalu, *Yoruba Beliefs and Sacrificial Rites*, 23.

28. Reinhold Niebuhr, *The Nature and Destiny of Man: Volume I Human Nature*, 192.

29. See Kola Abimbola, *Yoruba Culture: A Philosophical Account*, 66.

30. J. Omosade Awolalu, *Yoruba Beliefs and Sacrificial Rites*, 32.

31. J. Omosade Awolalu, *Yoruba Beliefs and Sacrificial Rites*, 33.

32. E. Bolaji Idowu, *Olodumare: God in Yoruba Belief*, 80.

33. Segun Ogungbemi, "Esu: The Phenomenon of Existence" in Toyin Falola (ed.) *Esu: Yoruba God, Power and the Imaginative Frontiers*, (Durham: Carolina Academic Press, 2013), 86.

34. E. Bolaji Idowu, *Olodumare: God in Yoruba Belief*, 204.

35. Schubert M. Ogden, *The Reality of God and Other Essays*, (New York: Harper & Row Publishers. 1977), 164-187.

36. Rudolf Bultmann, *Kerygma and Myth: A Theological Debate*, 38.

37. The Interpreter's Dictionary of the Bible: *An Illustrated Encyclopedia*, (Nashville: Abingdon Press, 1982), 94.

38. Van A. Harvey, *A Handbook of Theological Terms*, 138-139.

39. Rudolf Bultmann, *Kerygma and Myth: A Theological Debate*, 37.

40. Rudolf Bultmann, *Kerygma and Myth: A Theological Debate*, 36.

41. Friedrich Nietzsche, *Beyond Good and Evil* Walter Kaufmann (trans.), (New York: Vintage Books, 1966), 60.

42. Friedrich Nietzsche, *Beyond Good and Evil*, 36.

43. Bultmann, R. *Jesus Christ and Mythology*, (New York: Charles Scribner's Sons, 1958), 36. See also Rudolf Bultmann, *Kerygma and Myth: A Theological Debate*, 3.

44. Schubert M. Ogden, *The Reality of God and Other Essays*, 173.

45. Byang H. Kato, *Theological Pitfalls in Africa*, (Kisumu: Evangel Publishing House, 1975), 104.

46. Byang H. Kato, *Theological Pitfalls in Africa*, 35.

* Segun Ogungbemi. (2016) "A Comparative Study of Olodumare, The Yoruba Supreme Being and Judeo-Christian God" Yoruba Studies Review Vol. 1: Number 1: Fall 2016, 41-64.

CHAPTER 13
The Challenges Of Boko Haram Insurgency In A Multi-Religious Space

Introduction

Nigeria has become more frequently known in the world news today than ever before because of an Islamic group known as Boko Haram insurgency that began as a mere religious sect, which nobody thought could cause so much damage to life, property and development in some northern parts of the country. In April 2014 the country woke up to a weird and bizarre reality of what the group belief system was and still is and its objectives. Its doctrine and 'philosophy' contradict what Nigerians do not expect from Islamic religion that teaches peace. The kidnapping of over 200 schoolgirls on April 14, 2014 at Chibok in Borno State, Nigeria and the initial inaction of the Federal Government to respond decisively in rescuing the defenseless children, further exacerbated the infuriation of Nigerians, world leaders, Human Rights Organizations, Women's Rights Activists, around the world, and terrified schoolgirls in several parts of Nigeria because as with any sovereign nation, it is the duty and the right of the people to be protected by their Federal Government and to feel safe. The condemnation of Boko Haram Islamic sect all over the world and the show of action to rescue the school girls have not yielded any fruitful results because most of them are still in captivity of their captors. It has become imperative to have a philosophical discourse in a religious pluralistic society like Nigeria to unveil the contents of faith, the relationship between faith and reason, its limits and the need to have tolerance, accommodation and respect for opposing views without resorting to conflict and violence. This chapter explicates the role of faith and reason in human understanding with respect to human rights, human dignity and value, which ought to be key in religious indoctrinations. This chapter also examines how the Islamic sect began, their leaders and supporters, and its aims and objectives in relation to the general concept of freedom, human rights, development and general well being of a nation with the view to providing pragmatic and moral solutions to the insurgency.

Boko Haram a religious phenomenon

Before the advent of foreign religions in sub-Sahara Africa particularly, Islam and Christianity, the indigenous religions were the majority. According to Toyin Falola, "Islam has a longer history in Nigeria than does Christianity. At the beginning, Islam was a minority religion, but it spread gradually and became the dominant faith in the north during the nineteenth century: the present century has witnessed phenomenal growth in Nigerian Islam."[1] It is arguably true that as a result of its expansion, it gave rise to various Islamic sects like Boko Haram.

Nigeria being a multi-religious, multicultural society and an emerging democratic country, its constitution allows freedom of worship. Having the freedom to practice one's religious beliefs does not necessarily mean causing harm to fellow Nigerians without recourse to court of law for adjudication. Even before now, religion has had its stronghold in the life of the people as if everything that happened or continues to happen must have a religious explanation to satisfy unanswered questions of human existence. It is this kind of attitude to religion that makes its practice viral in every imaginable dimension insofar the anticipated values that enhance the quality of life of both the individual and corporate existence is not endangered. Therefore the soil of religious pluralism in Nigeria enabled the seed of Boko Haram Islamic set to germinate, grow, and flourish in the three major Northeastern States namely, Borno, Yobe, and Adamawa. It also spread to the neighbouring States specifically, Bauchi, Gombe, Kano, Niger, Kaduna including Abuja the Capital Territory. Muhammad Yusuf who hailed from Na'iyyah countryside in Yobe State formed the group in Maiduguri the capital of Borno State in 2002. According to Ahmad Murtada:

> The real name of this movement is Jama'at Ahl us-Sunnah li'd-Da'wah wa'l-Jhad [The group of the people of Sunnah for preaching and Struggle]...The name "Boko Haram" is a Hausa name, which only the Hausa people understood and is a compound name comprised of Hausa and Arabic. The Hausa applied the term

"Boko" to Western forms of education so when the term "Haram" is applied to it the intent is: 'the Western education system is haram'. ²

Murtada further explains the real meaning of "Boko" which technically and linguistically in Hausa means, "traversing the Western education system of education is haram."³ Victor Iyanya gives his own vivid understanding of the historical background of Boko Haram and its meaning.

> The 'Boko Haram' movement actually began in 2002 like any other Islamic sect founded on puritanican ideology. Originally, it was known by the Arabic name, Jama'atu Ahlis Sunna Lidda'awati wal-Jhad, which means an organization of people committed to the Teachings of the prophet, with emphasis on the Jihad. However, the local residents of Maiduguri where it was formed considered the full name of this organization to be too long; hence, they came up with the word 'Boko Haram' which is actually a combination of Hausa and Arabic words. While the term 'Boko' is a Hausa word referring loosely to Animism, Westernization, or non-Islamic education; the word 'Haram' is an Arabic figurative expression, which means 'sin' or forbidden.⁴

The brief historical narrative of Murtada and Iyanya of the formation of Boko Haram in the above quotation contains some variations for instance, the original name and its corruption in Hausa and Arabic languages. This is so, perhaps because of the socio-linguistic backgrounds of both scholars but in essence the facts about Boko Haram they explicated remain validly the same.

The religious dogma of Boko Haram centers on the belief that they are sent to save people from the wrong indoctrination found in western education. The practice of Islamic injunctions as contained in the Sharia is sacred and biding on Muslims. Therefore, western education and its democratic system of governance, freedom, equality, human rights etc are not in tandem with the teachings of the Qur'an. Their leader, Muhammad Yusuf denounced the evolution theory of Charles Darwin and prohibited any form of education that has western coloration because it is sinful. To be a Muslim is to avoid any form of teaching that emanates from mission schools or colonial institutions. The mode of teaching acceptable to them is the recitation of the Qur'an. Muslims must not be this worldly but to be otherworldly. Any fashion or mode of dressing depicting western culture by women is haram, forbidden. That was why Muhammad Yusuf prohibited his followers from taking official employments in government institutions however, engagements in jihad and obedience to Sharia law by Boko Haram Islamic sect are conceived as divine command.[5] To establish Islamic Caliphate in the northern states of the country is a religious, social and political form of identity. This vision and mission of the movement has its historical antecedent. Falola explains, "The nineteenth century was to mark the height of Muslim influence, due largely to the successful jihad of Usman [Othman] dan Fodio, which triggered the establishment of Nigeria's first caliphate. The Sokoto-based caliphate was divided into emirates, and a single sultan oversaw all the emirs."[6] In modern times, Boko Haram is simply emulating Iran, Pakistan, Libya, etc, which are extremist Islamic nations.

Religion thrives predominantly more where there is abject poverty, ignorance, unemployment, social-disconnect due to poor leadership, social dis-orientation and hopelessness of the citizenry. This scenario is the characteristic of what has become most of the States in Nigeria where Boko Haram became a religious haven for its members. Considering the enormous military and economic strength of Boko Haram it is generally believed that there are some individuals and groups of sympathizers of the sect within and outside the country. The former President of Nigeria, Dr. Goodluck Ebele Jonathan on Sunday, January 8, 2012 informed Nigerians during the celebration of the Armed Forces Remembrance Day, held at the National Christian Centre, Abuja that "Boko Haram is everywhere, in the executive arm of the government, in the legislative arm of government and even in the judiciary. Some are also in the armed forces, the police and other security agencies."[7]

Similarly Murtada writes:

> President Goodluck Jonathan has frankly stated that there are factions who support the movement within the Nigerian government itself, yet neither he, nor any other minister or member of the government, have elaborated further. It is true that some members of the movement sold their property and informed women that they were getting prepared for jihad, this was in the beginning [i.e.2009].[8]

Did the President know the exact number of government functionaries that were in Boko Haram? Were they conservative or moderate Muslims and what roles did they play among the sect? If the President knew those that were members of Boko Haram did he ever invite them for dialogue to know on the level of their involvement among the group in terms of financial contribution, intelligence information gathering etc? At the time the President claimed to know those that were Boko Haram in his government, did it occur to him its threat to his administration and unity of the country? What had been done to make Boko Haram elements in his administration held accountable without violating their constitutional rights at the initial stage of their membership since they could become a potential danger to the country?

Iyorchia Ayu, former Senate President of Nigeria and the 5th Adekunle Ajasin University Convocation Guest Lecturer in 2014 gave an inside information of some of the supporters of Boko Haram. He writes:

> Reportedly, prominent businessmen and politicians in both Nigeria and Chad, in association with French companies, have invested heavily in the Chadian oil industry, and as a result, benefit from Boko Haram's destabilization of the North-Eastern part of Nigeria. It is widely believed that it is they who are the principal financials and arm suppliers to Boko Haram.[9]

The editorial of one of the leading printing media in Nigeria, *The Punch* of Friday, March 28, 2014 lent its voice on the concern for the Federal government to take a proactive action on the foreign supporters of Boko Haram. According to the editorial:

> The US officials insist that the dangerous Islamist sect has ties with al-Qaeda in the Islamic Maghreb, which operates in northwest Africa, Somalia's al-Shabab and al-Qaeda in the Arabian Peninsula. With the collapse of Libya after Muammar Gaddafi's death in 2011, and the routing of al-Qaeda rebels in Mali last year in a campaign led by France, Nigeria has witnessed a steady rise in the influx of arms being used by Boko Haram to perpetrate terror.[10]

With the preponderant of evidence established by the intellectuals and scholars above, it is obvious that Boko Haram Islamic sect has had its phenomenal plan to become a formidable threat to the unity and corporate existence of the country. The question is: was the government not aware from 2002 when the movement was gathering momentum in terms of their primordial theological training and evangelistic campaigns that they were capable of being violent? I intend to answer this question after we have examined their violent operations that define them as terrorists.

The genesis of Boko Haram's conflict/operations and targets

If Boko Haram Islamic sect began like any other religious group in the country without being violent, at what time of their religious teachings, preaching and operations did they become noticeably a roaring lion seeking, whom to devour? What prompted them to behave without recourse to the constitution that granted them freedom of worship? But the issue is: do they see themselves as Nigerians for whom the constitution is made to protect? And more importantly, do they know what the constitution of the country is all about and whether their corporate interest is guaranteed and their obligations to the State? If they are aware of all these issues raised, why did they decide to engage in insurrection of monumental scale of destruction of lives and property ever witnessed in the country? Was there any provocation that led to their revolt against the State? Murtada offers what seems to be the genesis of the insurgency of Boko Haram. He writes:

> Armed confrontations by those influenced by the da'wah of Muhammad Yusuf go back to the group's excursions along with violent clashes with police in 2003. The events started when some isolated ascetics in the village of Kannama in the town of Gaidam near Niger were deemed as having odd behaviour and the police were informed. The police investigated and found no problems yet the second time the police were informed about them for suspicious actions the police attacked them leaving some dead and injured. Police were viewed ordering members of this group, including their wounded cripples, to lie face down on their stomachs and then two or three shots were fired into them. This led to a group under the leadership of Shaykh Baba seeking revenge against the police who committed the killings.[11]

When all the conflicts between the police and the Boko Haram sect were going on in the northeast of the country, it was reported that their leader Muhammad Yusuf was in Saudi Arabia. He was however briefed about 'the Kannama jihad'.[12] And on his return to the country, he intensified his religious crusade, which attracted many youths and consequently made the northeast their operational enclave.

When Boko Haram ran foul of Borno State law that mandated motor bicycle riders in the State to use helmets, some of their members who were apprehended by the police were punished and a number of them seriously injured and a couple of them died. Muhammad Yusuf felt that the rights of their members were not protected by the law enforcement agencies of the State and he demanded for justice. And failure to get justice on time would lead to reprisals or simply jihad.[13] Initially, the strategic operations and targets of Boko Haram was Maiduguri where police stations and military installations were destroyed with many lives lost. On July 26, 2009 however, Muhammad Yusuf the leader of Boko Haram was killed but his death did not put an end to the ravaging onslaught of Boko Haram in the northeast. After the death of Yusuf Abubakar Shekau took over. He has been the most notorious leader of the group. Since he took over the leadership of Boko Haram, Nigeria has not known peace. For instance, on August 26, 2011 the United Nations building in Abuja was bombed and 26 people were killed. The kidnapping of Chibok secondary school girls on April 14, 2014 in Borno State caused the anger of the rest of the world. World leaders, Civil Rights Groups, and Nigerians condemned their barbaric act and called on the Federal Government of Nigeria to find means to rescue the girls. How could the insurgents have their way to a government institution when an emergency rule was imposed on Borno State including Yobe and Adamawa States? It is evident that there was a communication gap between the security agencies or a mere sabotage that paved the way for the terrorists to have their field day of terror. The hypocrisy of Boko Haram leadership that sought justice from the Federal Government as a result of police brutality on their members has now become the organization violating the rights of their victims-Chibok schoolgirls with impunity and defiance. It is often said that 'those who come to equity must come with a clean hand.'

The call to rescue the Chibok schoolgirls from their captors, so far, has not yielded any desirable fruitful results in spite the intervention of international bodies. The delay in getting the Chibok girls rescued was traceable to lack of spontaneous response of Jonathan administration when they were kidnapped. The unstoppable onslaught of the Boko Haram insurgency in several rural communities, towns and cities in Borno, Yobe and Adamawa States among other places in Nigeria with attendant loss of over 500,000 lives and millions of miserable displaced victims was and is still despicable.

The essence of good governance anywhere including Nigeria is to protect its citizens and promote their happiness. If Boko Haram terrorists have the audacity to cause the enormous casualties on their fellow Nigerians with unqualified social and psychological trauma as they have done and are still doing in 2021; the establishment of an Islamic Caliphate in the captured territories in the northeastern part of the country calls for serious concern over the sovereignty of the country. For Boko Haram to attempt to secede from Nigeria through unorthodox means is an act of rebellion.

The destruction of infrastructural development in the northeast and some adjacent states like Kano, Niger including Abuja Capital Federal Territory is monumental. The insecurity in the ravaging Boko Haram insurgency enclave has not limited its targets to the areas under their control but also to the entire country thereby resisting free movement of goods and services, which has economic effects on the domestic trades and services. Besides, where there is terror and insecurity, the essential commodity of peace cannot thrive. It is this lack of peace that made Boko Haram scorecard of terror to force the Independent National Electoral Commission to shift the dates of 2015 general elections from February 14, 2015 and February 28, 2015 to March 28, 2015 and April 11, 2015. This is the first time in the history of Nigeria that a religious sect has had such enormous impact that caused the derailment of elections of national interest. The import of democratic elections in any constitutional democracy is geared towards good governance and development. And what Boko Haram has done, in my view, is to negate that democratic process and deny Nigerians the right to good governance and development.

From the foregoing, Boko Haram has made itself a terror of metaphysical and empirical phenomenon. It is not an exaggeration, but an expression of fact, which resonates daily the experiences of Nigerians, that 'the fear of Boko Haram is the beginning of wisdom'. The question is: when will Nigeria and perhaps, the global community overcome this *Islamophobia* of Boko Haram?

Overcoming Boko Haram insurgency

If Nigeria is to overcome the way in which Boko Haram has bedeviled the envisioned development of the country: a three main approach needs to be employed. First, we must treat the religious symptoms from where the restiveness of the mind which necessitates an individual or group of individuals to seek spiritual and psychological remedies from the Source of beings. In the case of Boko Haram, Islam provides the roadmap for self-discovery and the spiritual solution to abate the inner dysfunction of self-worth. The cognitive part of the human mind to comprehend the teachings of Islam in the 21st century as dictated by science and technology and the need for a compelling imperative of hermeneutics to unravel the mindset of the discourse of jihad and sharia differently from its primordial understanding. This cognitive apparatus has two components namely, *freedom-from* and *freedom-to*. Theologically, *freedom-from* as it is being used here means, a rescue mission from the state of wilderness of ignorance. And *freedom-to* theologically, is a state of living in freedom without inhibiting the rights of others and to promote unity and harmony, which ultimately enhances good neighborliness. To be in the realm of *freedom-to* demands respect for divergent opinions with tolerance because nobody has the absolute truth, knowledge and understanding of the Holy Order. In the light of this, the Islamic proposition of jihad therefore means an inner struggle to overcome the exigencies of life and human sinfulness. It is diametrically opposed to the jihad of the 6th century Islam. It is counter intuitive for God, to ask anyone to go and kill a fellow human being because all men are created equal. As President Obama rightly says, "We hold these truths to be self-evident that all men are created equal. These are not just words. They are a living thing, a call to action, a roadmap for citizenship and an insistence in the capacity of free men and women to shape our own destiny."[14] Nonie Darwish, a frontline critic of jihad writes:

> In today's world of international law and human rights, things such as violent jihad, extortion of war spoils jizya money for protection, and giving 'temporary peace' in exchange for ransom, are major international crimes.... These are acts that the whole world has defined a long time ago as against international law. But committed jihadists and Islamists do not seem to get the message.[15]

Any jihadist agenda propagated particularly by the Boko Haram insurgents and their affiliates i.e., Al-Qaeda, Al-Shabab, and others whose intentions are inimical to human capacity development and growth must be seen as taking an overdose of theological medicine which is more deadly than the apostasy it is meant to cure. The mindset of individuals or group of individuals who are members of Boko Haram needs to be brought to the workshop of *Reason* for cleansing. In other words, the content of faith of Boko Haram that encourages suicide bombings because of its reward in the hereafter needs to be subjected to critical analysis. How can someone be concerned about the hereafter he has no absolute assurance of, when nobody has gone that way and come back to tell him the comfort of the place. Of what importance is suicide bombing to the Almighty God who granted individual the right to live on this planet earth? What joy does the Almighty God want to derive from this heinous crime that kills the individual suicide bomber and innocent people? The inner mind or the mindset of those who engage in this religious doctrine, suicide bombing has to be overcome because no society can flourish in an environment where the psychology of the religious is set against itself. It is socially and religiously counter-intuitive and counter-productive. The resounding message of faith within the bounds of *Reason* must be propagated to the Boko Haram insurgents to save them from their religious illusions and delusions. The second approach to overcome Boko Haram is to examine the political space of Islam within the context of the corporate existence of Nigeria and the appropriate system of governance that will assuage any form of injustice that is occasioned by marginalization or poor governance. In other words, has the constitution of Nigeria failed to address issues that made Boko Haram insurgents found Islamic Sharia more appropriate in its application to their political, social and religious needs? To advance our discussion further it is necessary to know what Sharia is and its purpose. According to Darwish:

> Sharia is the body of Islamic law. It deals with all aspects of day-to-day life, including politics, economics, banking, business law, contract law, marriage, divorce, child rearing and custody, sexuality, sin, crime, and social issues. It makes no distinction between public and private life, treating all aspects of human relations as governable by Allah's law. The Sharia laws are based on the Qur'an and hadiths (sayings and example of the Prophet) as well as centuries of debate, interpretation, and precedent. There are literally thousands of Sharia laws.[16]

From the foregoing, Sharia is a theocratic law made to govern the lifestyle of Muslims, which is subject to interpretations depending on the social and cultural milieu of the adherents. Is Sharia meant to be a universal law? Can Sharia be practiced in a democratic system of governance? In the case of Nigeria where there is no State religion, is Sharia biding on non-Muslims? Major General Muhammadu Buhari, former Head of State of Nigeria and currently the President of the country had said when he was the presidential candidate of APC, a political party in 2015 presidential election:

> Our constitution, which in many respects is similar to the American constitution, does not permit a state religion. The Sharia identified in the constitution is almost synonymous with customary law. It is only applicable in matters of personal status such as marriage, divorce and inheritance. This has been the case since the 1979 constitution. Just as no one can make any customary or any other religious law the law of Nigeria, so Sharia cannot therefore be the law of Nigeria.[17]

If majority of Muslims in Nigeria understand the constitution of the country and have been enjoying living in peace and harmony, how come Boko Haram sect feels indifferently? Marc-Antoine Perouse de Montclos explains:

> ...the radical form of Shariah that Boko Haram wants to impose does not correspond at all to the demand of a very large majority of Nigerian Muslims. By the same token, the sect appears to be extremely marginal.... Boko Haram used religious references to legitimize political grievances as a moral right. But it would not and could not transform into a party.... The story of Boko Haram thus leaves room for a more general discussion on the politicization of Islam and the Islamisation of politics. Despite the assumptions of the theory of a clash of civilizations between Muslims and Christians, Nigeria did not develop religious parties as such either Islamic or Christian Democrat.[18]

Considering the historical background of Islam, Benson O. Igboin gives a probable reason why Boko Haram opted for Sharia to legitimize their demand. He argues:

> Since the aim of the early Islamic community was to unite the growing community in religion, administration and legislation, around the historical figure-Prophet Muhammad; the militants find this historical need urgent in modern society because Islam is still growing and expanding although persecuted.[19]

What those behind the radicalization of Islam need to know is that there is no society that can continue to live in the historical past of its religion in the 21st century with the intention of imposing the anachronistic belief on the rest of the populace, without any recourse to human principle of fundamental rights and peaceful co-existence, which is key to engender harmonious relationships that will not end up in violent conflict. Therefore, Boko Haram militants and their supporters have violated the rights of innocent people in the northeast and other parts of the country. The leadership of Boko Haram and their allies should have used the constitutional means at their disposal since they have members of the House of Representatives in the National Assembly to champion their grievances or use a non-violent strategy, which is more humane and legitimate as a moral option. Everywhere in the world where non-violence had been used it has produced resounding results and their heroes/heroines recognized worldwide. Barbara J. Wien writes:

Nonviolent leaders and peace s/heroes can be found in every culture on every continent in every era. The cast of characters who have promoted and agitated for nonviolence through the centuries is too vast to feature here, but they include such figures as Jesus Christ (Palestine), Buddha (India), Saint Francis of Assisi (Italy), Henry David Thoreau (USA), Amadu Bamba Mbacke (Senegal), Jane Addams (USA), Badshah Khan (Pakistan), Gandhi (India), Martin Luther King, Jr. (USA), Mairead Corrigan Maguire, Betty Williams and Ciaran Mckeown with the Community of Peace People (Ireland) Nelson Mandela (South Africa), Rigoberta Menchu (Guatemala), Thich Nhat Hanh (Vietnam) and many others. However, rarely is the subject of nonviolence featured in the media, taught in schools, or presented in books.[20]

There are two important things Wien has drawn our attention to which can further deepen genuine social, religious and political relationships without coercion i.e.

i. historical achievements of several centuries that nonviolence as an alternative option to war and

ii. the need to include a nonviolent strategy method in our institutions' programs because doing so will give generations of young men and women a more humane option to peace than the coercive approach that leads to destruction of numerous lives and property.

If Boko Haram had taken a nonviolent approach in their pursuit for social and economic justice the world would have had sympathy for their rationale and moral course of action. No one is ready to listen to terrorists that are bent on causing mayhem thereby making life unbearable, and preventing economic prosperity in a country rich with natural resources and preventing infrastructural development because they want an Islamic state.

The third main approach to checkmate Boko Haram insurgency and any religious insurrections is for the Federal Government to have a more proactive and efficient military and security intelligence services. A situation in which Nigerian military were overpowered by the Boko Haram forces is a clear indication that the security of Nigeria is at risk. To secure the nation against internal and external aggression requires full preparedness of disciplined military forces at all times.

Nigeria used to be the economic and military regional super-power in Africa. The world was shocked when the country could not repel the forces of Boko

Haram in spite of the resources at her disposal. The Jonathan administration failed to properly prepare its administration for the security of the country and the citizenry. The invasion and destruction of some parts of northeastern Nigeria by Boko Haram terrorists with many lives lost and displacements of thousands of innocent people were indicative of national insecurity, which demanded urgent national attention.

Conclusion

There is no doubt that Boko Haram and all its affiliates have violated the rights of the citizens of Nigeria, particularly the 276 Chibok schoolgirls who were kidnapped as they were preparing for the West Africa School Certificate examinations. The Boko Haram extremists used violent means to demand for their rights instead of applying legal provisions in the 1999 constitution of the Nigerian State. There is no justifiable reason for Boko Haram insurgents to want to secede from the corporate unit of the country by the use of coercion or war without facing a more preemptive force by the Federal Government to crush their insurgency. If the leadership of Boko Haram had engaged in a nonviolent strategy as I have argued in this chapter, their grievances would have invoked sympathy. And more importantly it is apparently clear that no political and moral will on both sides of the divide to end the violence. The absence of political and moral will on both parts leads to distrust and without trust there cannot be genuine pursuit for peace. The application of Machiavellian principle to put an end to the brutal forces of Boko Haram appears to be the only solution the Federal Government has in its arsenals, to allow peace to reign particularly in the northeastern part of the country. With the help of security forces from her neighbors and the goodwill of international community the Nigeria military forces have been able to recapture all the areas taken by the Boko Haram, Islamic terrorists and freed thousands of their victims except the Chibok schoolgirls and others in the Sambisa forest in the northeast of Nigeria. One wonders why the Federal Government had not taken such a decisive action much earlier to checkmate the violent advancement of the insurgents.

The use of military force to repel religious violence, in my view, is not as humanly cost effective as the sound education to change the mindset of the people. Wole Soyinka's view in this regard is noteworthy, "It will serve to remind us that we are a people to whom tolerance is a norm, knowledge an eternal pursuit, and pluralism the foundation of our communal ethos. Such monuments will represent milestones of the human journey towards enlightenment, a shrine to the real martyrs of human civilization."[21] For the Federal Republic of Nigeria to preserve the collective social, moral, religious and intellectual values as espoused by Soyinka, in my view, a proactive means to provide basic infrastructural needs which include healthcare, clean water, food, and housing, free education for the populace, and a continuous effort to reduce corruption that hinders development. And more importantly, Nigerian leaders have to build strong and effective institutions that will prevent religious groups like Boko Haram from sprouting in different parts of the country and becoming a threat to national security.

Notes and References

1. Toyin Falola, *Violence in Nigeria: The Crisis of Religious Politics and Secular Ideologies,* (Rochester: Rochester University Press, 1998), 24.

2. Ahmad Murtada, *Boko Haram in Nigeria: Its Beginning, Principles and Activities in Nigeria,* www.SalafiManhaj.com (2013), 4.

3. Ahmad Murtada, *Boko Haram in Nigeria: Its Beginning, Principles and Activities in Nigeria,* 4.

4. Victor Iyanya, "Religious Bellicosity in Nigeria: The Case of 'Boko Haram' Islamic Sect," in *Or-Che Uma: African Journal of Existential Philosophy* Vol. 2. No. 1. 10-11.

5. Ahmad Murtada, *Boko Haram in Nigeria: Its Beginning, Principles and Activities in Nigeria,* 4.

6. Toyin Falola, *Violence in Nigeria: The Crisis of Religious Politics and Secular Ideologies,* 25.

7. This excerpt is from President Jonathan's speech at the Armed Forces Remembrance Day held at the National Christian Centre, Abuja, on Sunday 8 January, 2012.

8. Ahmad Murtada, *Boko Haram in Nigeria: Its Beginning, Principles and Activities in Nigeria,* 24.

9. Iyorchia Ayu, "The Break Up of Nigeria: Myths, Realities, and Implications," Being the 5th Convocation Lecture Delivered at the Adekunle Ajasin University, Akungba – Akoko, Ondo State, Nigeria on 5th November, 2014.

10. "Cutting off Boko Haram's Foreign Connection," in *The Punch,* Friday, March 28, 2014, 20.

11. Ahmad Murtada, *Boko Haram in Nigeria: Its Beginning, Principles and*

Activities in Nigeria, 6.

12. Ahmad Murtada, *Boko Haram in Nigeria: Its Beginning, Principles and Activities in Nigeria,* 7.

13. Ahmad Murtada, *Boko Haram in Nigeria: Its Beginning, Principles and Activities in Nigeria,* 8.

14. This quote is from Barrack Obama's speech in Selma, Alabama on March 7, 2015.

15. Nonie Darwish, *Cruel and Usual Punishment,* (Nashville, Tennessee: Thomas Nelson, 2008), 185-186.

16. Nonie Darwish, *Cruel and Usual Punishment,* 4.

17. This statement is part of Muhammadu Buhari's campaign speech during his presidential campaign before the 2015 general election in Nigeria.

18. Marc-Antoine Perouse de Montclos, "Boko Haram and Politics: From Insurgency to Terrorism," in Marc-Antoine Perouse de Montclos (ed.) *Boko Haram: Islamism, Politics, Security and the State in Nigeria,* (Leiden: African Studies Centre, 2014), 152.

19. Benson O. Igboin, "Boko Haram Sharia Reasoning and democratic Vision in Pluralist Nigeria," in *Interdisciplinary Political and Cultural Journal* Vol. 14 No. 1/2012, 77.

20. Barbara J. Wien, "The Promise of Nonviolence, a New Stage in Human Evolution, (Unpublished article, 2015), 1.

21. Lanre Adewole "Soyinka calls for 'Wall of remembrance' for Terror Victims" in *Nigerian Tribune,* Wednesday, 14 January 2015. 2.

PART FOUR

TRADITION, CULTURE AND VALUES

CHAPTER 14

Traditional Religious System

Introduction

The Yoruba are one of the most populous ethnic groups in Nigeria. According to Kola Abimbola, "It is estimated that the population of the Yoruba in West Africa is forty million. This makes them one of the largest groups in sub-Saharan Africa."[1]

The religion of the Yoruba is described as traditional or indigenous because it is not imported from any other culture. It is a religion handed over from the forebears from generation to generation, and it is one of the major religions in Africa and Nigeria in particular. Her rich cultural identity and values have engaged scholars and intellectuals across the globe in its study. This chapter will focus on the structure of the Yoruba belief system, the form of worship and veneration, the influence of Islam, Christianity and modernization and the import of the belief in the diaspora. This study concludes that the tolerance and accommodation of the Yoruba religious system brought about some enlightenment that has enriched the indigenous belief system although its firm grip on the society has waned considerably. Be that as it may, the import of the religion in the diaspora is monumentally significant because of its cultural identity and values.

The Structure of the Belief System

The foundation of Yoruba religious belief is Olodumare, the Supreme Being. It is this Deity who sets the agenda for all the created beings in the spirit world and humans on the planet earth. He surrounds himself with a plethora of divinities who serve as his ministerial agents; he directs them and the interests of humans. E. Bolaji Idowu explains

> The existence of Olodumare eternally has, for all practical purposes, been taken for granted as a fact beyond question. It is upon this basic faith that the whole superstructure of Yoruba belief rests. Then there are the divinities, especially the principal ones. All the indications which have come down to us are that they were all brought into existence by Olodumare that they might be His ministers in carrying out each in his own office, the functions connected with the creation and theocratic government of the earth.[2]

Toyin Falola explains further, "The Yoruba have constructed a hierarchy of spiritual forces, similar to their political hierarchy which gives immense power to kings, then chiefs, then lineage heads, with ordinary people at the very bottom. In this hierarchy, God is the supreme deity with the ultimate power, the creator of the universe, the final judge."[3]

Under the Supreme Being, the principal deities are Orisa-nla, Orunmila, Ogun, Eshu.[4] Other deities associated with nature are Yemoja the water goddess and Ile the earth goddess; deified individuals such as Sango the god of thunder, lightning, and storms; Orisa-Oko the god of agriculture; ancestors; and men and women.[5]

Olodumare has not only given the Yoruba the pattern of political structure and governance but also provided avenues by which human problems can be solved without necessarily calling on him for small matters. It appears there are as many deities created by Olodumare, collectively called *orisa*, to assist the Yoruba in their daily affairs as the initial population of the people. For instance, Jacob K. Olupona writes about 201 gods in Ile-Ife, the mythological home of the Yoruba and the cradle of their civilization.[6] If Ile-Ife has 201 gods or more, one will imagine the overall numbers of them in all the villages, cities, and towns throughout Yorubaland.

But it is not the number of the gods that matters; rather, it is their functions in human affairs. It is the belief of the Yoruba that every individual has freedom to choose any of the gods he or she feels can be of help to him or her. Sometimes, however, parents choose which of the gods or goddesses who would be most beneficial to their children. And if one is not too sure which god or goddess to choose, the system provides an appropriate channel of inquiry through the *Ifa* priest or *Babalawo* who is endowed with secret knowledge to determine the deity that will be favorably disposed to the success of the individuals in life.

In this structural belief system, *Ori* (the personality soul or the guardian spirit) is constantly appeased with appropriate sacrifices and veneration. The impression given by the Yoruba in their religious theology is that Olodumare and his ministerial agents made humans to be dependent on him. Therefore, fear, ignorance, and anxiety grip the human mind and subject the totality of human existence to the whims and caprices of Olodumare and his deities. Thus, the institution of worship and veneration becomes an avenue to advance the spiritual transcendence of the Yoruba with the propensity to enhance their perceived notion of meaning and purpose of life.

Worship and Veneration

In all religions, worship is conceived as a response to human understanding of his or her environment and the need to be in constant contact with the perceived superior powers that must be placated from time to time for the purpose of achieving authentic existence. E. Bolaji Idowu explains,

> Worship is an imperative urge in man.... Man perceived that there was a Power other and greater than himself, a Power which dominated and controlled the unseen world in which he felt himself enveloped; a Power which he therefore made out by intuition to be the "ultimate Determiner of Destiny." ...Thus worship in its rudimentary form originated in the spontaneous and extempore expression of man's reaction as he found himself confronted with the revelation which evoked in him as active response.[7]

To the Yoruba, worship has something to do with their perceptions of human existence, the existence of the Supreme Being, deities, and ancestors who are essential to their spiritual, social, and cultural life and for economic prosperity and longevity. J. Omosade Awolalu explains,

> Worship is a religious exercise, which involves the performance of devotional acts in honour of a deity or divinities. It presupposes a yearning for God and it is a means of glorifying the Source, the Sustainer and the End of life; it confirms man's acknowledgement of the Transcendent Being who is independent of the worshipper

> but upon whom the worshipper depends. Furthermore, the needs and limitations of ordinary human nature prompt men to seek a divine strength to sustain him in the fulfillment of his destiny here on earth. When man has lost the favour of the supernatural beings, it is through worship that he seeks to regain it.[8]

Worship is, therefore, a flourishing road map or a pathway to the deity, divinities, and ancestors exist for the Yoruba to follow and utilize as long as they live on this planet earth. The Yoruba nature of worship began as a private spiritual enterprise before it became a social and cultural public utility. In other words, it was the individual that first began the business of worship before it became a community activity. The deities who are collectively called *orisa* and ancestors appear to be the primary focus of Yoruba worship. This does not imply that Olodumare, the Supreme Being, is never accorded worship and veneration. Olodumare assigned the *orisa* the responsibility to serve human; they can become the primary object of Yoruba worship.

There are different places of worship in Yorubaland. There are individuals who have sacred places of worship in their homes and farms but the most prominent ones are the shrines. And it appears there are as many shrines as the numbers of the *orisa*, for instance, Ogun shrine, Obatala shrine, Eshu shrine, Sango shrine, Oke-Ibadan shrine, Origba shrine, and Osun shrine. The shrines are simple architectural designs, and, in most cases, they do not command aesthetic expression of beauty that we find in some other places of religious worship like temples, mosques, and churches.

Each of these *orisa* has his or her priests/priestesses and devotees. In Yoruba traditional religion, the *orisa* have their sacred days of worship and the big events are the festivals. It is important to note that, in all forms of traditional religious worship in Yoruba society, offerings, rituals, sacrifices, prayers, and supplications are of great importance. It suffices to say that each deity has its own appetite and taste that are recognized and adhered to by the devotees when occasions call for worship. Idowu explains,

> For instance, Orisha-nla delights in snails cooked in shea-butter… Orunmila normally prefers his rat and fish to anything else; the staple food of Sango is ram; Ogun relishes dogs and roasted yams and snail; while Esu will do anything for a cock. Every one of the divinities takes kola-nuts; the exception is Sango who would rather have orogbo ("bitter kola"). Secondly, there are certain foods or

drinks which are *tabu* to each divinity. For example, Orisa-nla does not drink palm-wine: it should not be taken near his shrine, and his worshippers should not touch it; Esu does not like palm-kernel oil: anyone who brings it near him is therefore asking for trouble upon himself or upon someone else.[9]

The food and drink items are normally used during either the sacred days of the divinities or during the festivals. Religious festivals are special occasions that attract a large number of people in the community including their neighbors and people of different faiths. During the festivals, dancers, traditional singers, and different masquerades wear colorful attire and showcase their talents. Most of the spectators who come for the festivals probably do so for social and economic reasons rather than its spiritual importance. Wande Abimbola writes,

> It may be argued with some degree of plausibility that the observance of some of the traditional festivals and, to a lesser extent, of the cults by the Yoruba in general is largely a sociological phenomenon rather than a religious one.... The significance of the festivals is seen...in terms of local trade and the phenomenon of religious co-fraternity generated by the festivals.[10]

The festivals synergize religious plurality among the Yoruba that further explains the elasticity of tolerance and accommodation in their society.

Veneration is occasionally conceived as worship, but in the real sense of the term, they are not necessarily the same. Veneration is a deep or profound respect for a being or an ancestor. It also involves devotion, supplication, and propitiation with intentions to have mutual relationship or to heal a relationship that has been broken. When it is conceived in this way, it is more or less confused with worship, which is more elaborate than veneration. Idowu believes that the Yoruba do not worship their ancestors: "'Ancestor Worship' is a wrong nomenclature for that which in fact is no 'worship' but a manifestation of an unbroken family relationship between the parent who has departed from this world and the offspring who are still here."[11] Awolalu holds a different view:

> From our observation of activities at the graves of the ancestors or wherever the ancestors are invoked, we are convinced that what is done is more than a circular rite or sheer veneration.... But at the ancestral shrine, there is a system or ritual which engenders the

> feeling that one is standing before an aged, revered being who is interested in the supplicants and who is capable of supplying their needs.[12]

Awolalu is probably right if a descendant of an ancestor goes to the ancestral shrine with his objects of sacrifice therefore what takes place there can be aptly described as worship. On the other hand, Idowu is actually talking about a kind of supplication or propitiation that happens at the grave of a departed ancestor, which is mere veneration and not worship. In other words, veneration takes place at the graves of the departed ancestors while worship strictly speaking is restricted to the shrines.[13]

The religiosity of the Yoruba and its ages-long institution of worship and veneration have shown their deep-seated spirituality as a means to security, economic prosperity, and social development. Were the Yoruba better off in their self-conceived spirituality before the British rule or Western civilization in Nigeria? What influence does foreign religions and modernization have on the indigenous religious worship? And to what extent does the resilience of the people help to sustain the influence of foreign religions and modernization?

Abimbola argues, "Yoruba Religion has a practical purpose. It is not merely concerned with faith and afterlife, but also with practical guidelines on how to live together in a diverse, multicultural, global, and cosmopolitan world."[14] It is significant to say that social and economic development of any group or groups does not necessarily depend on how religious a society is but rather on the level of their scientific and technological advancement. The industrial revolution of Western Europe, along with its aftermath of colonization of African ethnic groups, was anathema to the Yoruba's initial industrial advancement and progress. For instance, the technological advancement of the local blacksmiths who made domestic tools and jewelry, men and women who produced textile industries, and others reflect the ingenious creativity of the Yoruba before the advent of the British rule in Nigeria. In other words, before independence, the British found Nigeria a profitable place to market their industrial goods, which was detrimental to local industrial revolution that was beginning to take place, particularly among the Yoruba ethnic group.

Influence of Christianity, Islam, and Modernization

Any discourse on the influence of Christianity, Islam, and modernization on the indigenous religion of the people in Yorubaland must deal with its historical background. Awolalu gives a concise insight of the penetration of missionaries to Yorubaland:

> Christianity was introduced into the southern part of Nigeria as a result of the liberation of slaves from the New World toward the end of the 18th century. The liberated slaves who returned to West Africa and who had embraced Christianity in servitude preferred to continue Christian worship rather than return to the old traditional mode of worship. It was they who asked that pastors be sent to them from Freetown, Sierra Leone which was the "home" of the liberated slaves in 1842. In this way, Christianity began to challenge African traditional religion.[15]

Missionary activities in Yorubaland were not limited to evangelization that focused on a higher level of spirituality and religious superiority over the indigenous religion. They were also materialistic ventures inherent in education, medicine, administration, architecture, sports, etc. As Falola explains,

> The adoption of Christianity was not without its advantages, mainly the association with the symbols and power of Europe. It brought Western education, medicine, and opportunities for work in the formal economic sectors. It enabled a number of African chiefs and kings to use religion to promote international trade and consolidate their power. To the elite produced by the missionaries, it led to an assumption that they were equipped with knowledge to transform Africa. It provided an avenue to build social networks in the new cities: the elite and church members could share and circulate information about jobs, social services, public policies, and other things beneficial to them.[16]

One of the most devastating effects of Christianity in Yoruba society was the attempt to eradicate their cultural values and identity. Upon being a Christian, new converts must change their names either to biblical or European names, such as changing Toke to Ruth or Catherine or Dapo to Frank or Charles. Yoruba names that have cultural and historical meanings, such as Ogunlana (god of iron has paved the way) and Osagbemi (*orisa* has saved me), have been changed to Oluwaseyi (the Lord has made it possible) and Jesugbemi (Jesus has made me to prosper), respectively, to reflect the adoption of Christian faith.

It needs to be emphasized that the translation of the Bible to the Yoruba language was one of the effective strategies used to encourage literacy among both young and old coverts. People could read the Bible on their own. When they were not exactly sure what they were reading, their pastors could assist them, which ultimately deepened their knowledge of the Bible. The biblical narratives of love of God and his forgiveness of sin no matter its circumstances gave a psychological succor to a disturbed mind. The idea of freedom from fear and the courage to be oneself without dependence on the gods and other spiritual forces became a liberating proposition that led to the abandonment of indigenous religion. The belief that God offered his son Jesus the Christ on the cross as atonement for the Adamic sin that is biblically conceived as generic was sufficient for human redemption. Therefore, the idea of using human sacrifice to appease the angry deities to ward off metaphysically inflicted epidemic diseases like smallpox was a delusion and scientifically unwarranted. Therefore, the sacrifice of Jesus the Christ on the cross is the epitome of all sacrifices divinely authorized by God. Thus, the interventions of the missionaries and the British rule put an end to human sacrifice in Yorubaland.[17]

Having discussed the influence of Christianity on the indigenous religion in Yorubaland, one needs to consider Islam, which has become one of the major religions in Nigeria. How did Islam make inroads to Yoruba religious space? And what method did the Muslim clerics or missioners use to influence Yoruba belief system? Falola writes,

> The nineteenth century was undoubtedly the time when the Yoruba became a Muslim people. Islam was already established in a few urban areas, notably Ilorin, Badagri, Epe, and Lagos, but it was largely a minority religion for merchants, slaves, and traders, especially those of northern origin.... By the middle of nineteenth century, Muslims constituted a vocal minority in most Yoruba towns, but because they were not persecuted, Islam gradually developed gradually across the southwest. The allure of Islamic education, the increasing number of northern missionaries, and the increasing Muslim acceptance of the Yoruba traditional elite all helped to facilitate the spread of Islam.[18]

The Islamic method of evangelism among the Yoruba was different from that of Christian missionaries. Falola explains,

> Southwestern Muslims were less critical of Yoruba indigenous religion and political authority. Muslims did not encourage imams to displace the local kings or to turn the region into a theocracy. While the Muslims criticized what they called paganism, many aspects of traditional religions came to influence Islamic practices, or at least became tolerated to a degree that enabled people of different religions to coexist. Muslims did not call for al-Shari'a to displace local laws or to subvert local authorities.[19]

It is perhaps appropriate to regard the impact of Islam on Yoruba indigenous religion as *religious assimilation*, which synergized their mutual peaceful coexistence. The acceptance of Christianity and Islam by the Yoruba, in addition to their traditional religion, gives the impression of someone shopping from one religion to another to maximize his or her "self-centered opportunism" in the universe of *beings*.[20] One Yoruba adage says *onakan o'woja* (a marketplace does not have one entrance, it has multiple entrances). What the adage implies is that for anyone to achieve any goal in life, he or she has to approach it from different perspectives. And in Yoruba belief system, indigenous religions, Christianity, and Islam have provided valuable means to achieve lofty existential and corporate goals of life.

The influence of modernization on Yoruba tradition religion is another important aspect that is worth discussing. Modernization as conceived here is the effect of changes from the traditional concept of values and ways of doing things to the modern as a result of improved knowledge capacity and rationalization of the place of human being in the cosmos. In other words, "[i]t means a change in the attitudes, values, and expectations of people from those associated with the traditional world to those common to the modern world. It is a consequence of literacy, education, increased communications, mass media exposure, and urbanization."[21] The British rule in Nigeria introduced a new social, political, and economic landscape that brought western civilization to the doorstep of the Yoruba. British rule built the basic infrastructure of society, that is, roads, transportation system, education, modern medicine, housing, and electricity. The reduction of illiteracy and impoverished living standards actually alienated the enlightened among the Yoruba from their religious traditional and cultural values: "The 'new' African-wearing Western attire, bearing Western names, speaking and writing in European languages, and eating Western food-can now conveniently avoid traditional religion, opting instead for Christianity or Islam."[22]

Even traditional places of worship were not spared of modern architectural impact. Awolalu writes,

> The Ifa Temple at Ile-Ife, for example, is a huge edifice situated on Oke-Itase hill overlooking the city. The huge building compares favorably with any cathedral church in size. Similarly, the Osun shrines in Osogbo have been remodeled by Susanne Wenger, a European artist who has accepted traditional religion and who has become a devotee of a number of divinities worshipped in Yorubaland, particularly Osun and Sango.[23]

From the foregoing, the indigenous religion of the Yoruba is consistent in its adaptation to any influence that enriches the cultural belief system without necessarily surrendering all its authority and powers.

The Dynamics of Yoruba Traditional Religion

Given the impact of foreign religions and modernization, the dynamics or resilience of Yoruba indigenous religion remains a constant reminder that Olodumare, the Supreme Being, divinities, and the ancestors have not given supremacy to them. It must be borne in mind that no religion or culture is immune to change and nature has a built-in mechanism for change. Therefore, the Yoruba traditional belief system, given the propensity of change inherent in nature, is amenable to change; indeed, change is inevitable.[24] The dynamics of the belief system of the Yoruba are not only feasible in the homeland but also in the museums and galleries in Europe, Asia, and America. The artifacts referred to as symbols, representations, and presentations by social and cultural anthropologists describe objects of religious worship. They remind tourists from foreign lands that although their ancestors persecuted Africans, Africans are symbolically alive in their midst.

The curators, tourists, and individual collectors of these artifacts venerate them from time to time. Robert P. Armstrong, however, does not agree that Europeans and Americans consider African artifacts as objects of religious worship in the same sense of the Africans. Rather, they are "aesthetic of virtuosity and not aesthetic of invocation." What Armstrong considers the aesthetics of virtuosity is devoid of religious content of the belief associated with the artifact such as Sango, Eshu, or Ogun:

> the aesthetics of virtuosity originates in the freeing of the work of affecting presence from dependence upon the energies of gods and

other external sources, committing it instead to a dependence upon the more reliable though less mighty abilities of man. Its focus lies not in embodying who-ness or what-ness, but how-ness; not in managing power, but in perpetrating excellence; not in establishing the general, but in exalting the particular.[25]

What Armstrong is simply saying is that the affecting presence is the psychological consciousness of appreciating African works of art that make the Europeans, Americans and Japanese to expend such huge resources for the upkeep of African works of art in their domain. On the other hand, aesthetics of invocation is associated with the "nature of persons": "They have both social role and status. Further, they manifest some of the same needs as a person – they must be fed, bathed, and often clothed."[26]

The impact of Yoruba indigenous religion is not only seen in the Africans in the homeland but also in the diaspora. Toyin Falola explains:

> The Orisa tradition is one of the most visible aspects of Yorubaism with the Candomble practices in Brazil, made visible by devotees and the activities of Babalorixas and Iyalorixas. In Cuba, the Lucumi (the name for Yoruba) practice Santeria or Regia de Ocha. In Haiti, there is Vodun, an integral part of Nago culture. Egungun and Gelede have spread in Latin America and the Caribbean, even in such places as Trinidad and Tobago. In the United States, many variants of Yoruba religion have survived, especially in Louisiana and South Carolina.[27]

The incurable nature of traditional religion manifests itself in the life of the descendants of the Yoruba in the Diaspora. The fact that the religion has no evangelical apparatus like Christianity and Islam to propagate its doctrines, precepts, and cultural identity values, the metaphysical dynamics inherent in its festivals make it imperative for new converts to identify with the belief system. Some prominent Yoruba scholars and intellectuals in the diaspora are fervent admirers and ingenious believers in the power, authority, and cultural values of Yoruba religious belief system. First and foremost among them are Jacob K. Olupona, Toyin Falola, Michael Afolayan, Aderonke Adesanya, Tunde Bewaji, Kola Abimbola, Akintunde Akinyemi, and Dele Jegede. These scholars have given credence to Yoruba traditional religious values in their profound scholarship and publications. The homeland also includes academic devotees of Yoruba religion, namely, J. Omosade Awolalu, Wande Abimbola, Ademola Bewaji Dasylva, and Akinwumi Isola, among others. It is noteworthy to mention the inroads traditional religion has made in Nigerian colleges and universities, most notably in departments of Religious Studies or Religion and African Culture.

Few other fields of human endeavor reflect the persistent practice of African traditional belief than the art of medicine. As the Yoruba saying goes, *Ilera loro* (health is wealth). Where orthodox medicine has failed in the treatment of an ailment, the people find hope and solace in the power and efficacy of traditional medicine. Falola writes, "In 1978, the World Health Organization [WHO] called on African governments to recognize and use traditional medical practitioners. Some governments responded to this challenge, and a number of efforts have been made to reform and 'professionalize' the occupation of traditional healing."[28] The recognition of traditional medicine by the WHO is a testament to the dynamics of Yoruba indigenous medicine, which is associated with their religion.

Conclusion

This chapter has shown the importance and relevance of Yoruba traditional belief system given its historical past and contemporary values. It has demonstrated the challenges and encroachments of foreign religions, namely Christianity and Islam, and Yoruba's resilience in the face of these challenges. The influence of modernization has contributed largely to the reduction of adherents as a result of western civilization and its doctrine of secularization and industrialization, including employment opportunities and better standard of living. It is also argued that the deity, divinities, and ancestors in traditional religion probably appreciate the aesthetic ambience introduced to the Yoruba landscape.

It is not only the Yoruba in Nigeria who have identified with the traditional belief of the people but also those in the diaspora. The import of this is the fact of its spiritual and psychological appeal to the physical and material sensibility of its devotees. The cultural identity dimension is another imperative factor of its survival. Its traditional form of "liberalism" is exemplified in terms of endurance, patience, and peaceful coexistence with other religions, including western secularization, "has been the sine qua non of the existence of the Yoruba."[29] Thus, the dynamics of the Yoruba belief system has become a legacy that has endured the tides of time.

Endnotes

1. Kola Abimbola, *Yoruba Culture: A Philosophical Account* (Birmingham: Iroko Academic Publishers, 2006), 35.

2. E. Bolaji Idowu, *Olodumare: God in Yoruba Belief* (London: Longman Group Limited, 1962), 18.

3. Toyin Falola, *Culture and Customs of Nigeria* (Westport: Greenwood Press, 2001), 34-35.

4. See Toyin Falola (ed.), *Esu: Yoruba God, Power, and the Imaginative Frontiers* (Durham: Carolina Academic Press, 2013), 3-392.

5. See Segun Ogungbemi and Benson O. Igboin, "A Philosophical Analysis of Yemoja in Cross Cultural Context," in Nana Akua Amponsah (ed.), *Beyond the Boundaries: Toyin Falola and the Art of Genre-Bending* (Trenton: Africa World Press, 2014), 67-695.

6. See Jacob K. Olupona (ed.), *City of 201 Gods: Ile-Ife in Time, Space, and the Imagination* (Berkeley: University of California Press, 2011), 1-2.

7. Idowu, *Olodumare*, 107.

8. J. Omosade Awolalu, *Yoruba Beliefs and Sacrificial Rites* (London: Longman Group Limited, 1979), 98.

9. Idowu, *Olodumare*, 118.

10. Wande Abimbola, "The Place of African Traditional Religion in Contemporary Africa: The Yoruba Example," in Jacob K. Olupona (ed.), *African Traditional Religions in Contemporary Society* (New York: Paragon House, 1998), 54-55.

11. Idowu, *Olodumare*, 192.

12. Awolalu, *Yoruba Beliefs and Sacrificial Rites*, 64.

13. Segun Ogungbemi, *A Critique of African Cultural Beliefs* (Ikeja: Pumark Nigeria Limited, 1997), 4.

14. Abimbola, *Yoruba Culture*, 102.

15. Joseph Omosade Awolalu, "The Encounter Between African Traditional Religion and Other Religions in Nigeria," in Jacob K. Olupona (ed.), *African Traditional Religions in Contemporary Society*, 112.

16. Toyin Falola, *The Power of African Cultures* (Rochester: University of Rochester Press, 2003), 203.

17. See Awolalu, "The Encounter Between African Traditional Religion," 117.

18. Toyin Falola, *Violence in Nigeria: The Crisis of Religious Politics and Secular Ideologies* (Rochester: University of Rochester Press, 1998), 26.

19. Ibid., 27.

20. See editorial comment on Segun Ogungbemi's article titled "A Philosophical Reflection on the Religiosity of the Traditional Yoruba" in *Orita: Ibadan Journal of Religious Studies* 18. 2 (December 1986): 59.

21. Samuel P. Huntington, *Political Order in Changing Societies* (New Haven and London: Yale University Press, 1968), 33.

22. Falola, *The Power of African Cultures*, 207.

    1 Awolalu in Olupona (ed.), *African Traditional Religions in Contemporary Society*, 116.

23. See Jacob K. Olupona (ed.), "Major Issues in the Study of African Religion," in *African Traditional Religions in Contemporary Society*, 32.

24. Robert Plant Armstrong, *The Powers of Presence: Consciousness, Myth, and the Affecting Presence* (Philadelphia: University of Pennsylvania Press, 1981), 12.

25. Armstrong, *The Powers of Presence: Consciousness*, 10.

26. Toyin Falola, *The African Diaspora: Slavery, Modernity, and Globalization* (Rochester: University of Rochester Press, 2013), 131.

27. Falola, *The Power of African Cultures*, 211.

28. Wande Abimbola, "The Place of African Traditional Religion in Contemporary Africa: The Yoruba Example," in Jacob K. Olupona (ed.), *African Traditional Religions in Contemporary Society*, 58.

* Segun Ogungbemi (2017) "Traditional Religious Belief System' in *Yoruba Culture and Customs* (ed.) Toyin Falola and Akintunde Akinyemi, Pan African Press, 281-291.

CHAPTER 15

Esu The Phenomenon Of Existence

Introduction

Esu apart from being an agent of the Supreme Being, he plays the role of espionage in the cosmos of beings and humans. The belief that Esu manifests different and dynamic characters make people to think of him as unpredictable divine whose ambivalent attitudes cannot be denied but this should not obliterate the truth of his positive actions that endeared his worshipers to him. As a matter of fact some individuals are given names that show his benevolence. Such names as Esubiyi, meaning, Esu has given birth to this child, Esutosin, meaning, Esu is worthy of worship etc; are common names among the Yoruba. Contrary to some belief that Esu is an enemy of man like the Biblical account of the Devil or Satan I have argued rather that the moral characterization of Esu is a paradox of human disposition of polarity of existence. To this end, therefore, what is essential to know about Esu is the moral and epistemological lessons which sometimes, if not often, in the confused estate of human existence the Yoruba mythically explain the being of man and the governance of his universe in the phenomenon of Esu whereas there is no Esu whose existence can be logically, morally and epistemologically justified beyond human existence. In spite of this the question is: Why is Esu very important to humans in Yoruba belief? It seems to me that the existence of Esu is predicated on the Yoruba explanation of good and evil. But we may not be able to appreciate their explanation of good and evil and the significance of the mythological creation of Esu without a brief profile of the Yoruba.

The Yoruba

It is important to have an overview of the people whose belief of Esu we are about to study. The Yoruba are mostly found in South West of Nigeria now divided into six states namely, Lagos, Ogun, Oyo, Osun, Ekiti, and Ondo. There are also Yoruba people in Kwara, Edo, Delta and Kogi States. We also have many Yoruba in West African countries and outside the continent namely, Benin Republic, Togo, Liberia, and Sierra Leone. There are Yoruba in Cuba, Brazil, Haiti, Peru, Trinidad and Tobago, Jamaica, and the United States of America etc. One cannot have an accurate number of the Yoruba. As a matter of fact, it is an aberration if not a taboo in Yoruba belief to count the number of one's children. The idea of counting the number of people among the Yoruba is alien and it is traditionally or culturally condemnable. Perhaps this partly accounts for the problem of not having accurate census figures in Nigeria. I am aware of some works of scholars who have written from historical, philosophical and anthropological perspectives and gave different figures of the population of the Yoruba which is currently outdated as a result of better standard of living that has resulted in an upsurge in population growth in Nigeria. According to the recent work of Kola Abimbola "It is estimated that the population of the Yoruba in West Africa is forty million. This makes them one of the largest groups in sub-Saharan Africa."[1] If we consider the Yoruba in the Diaspora the population of the Yoruba will probably be sixty million. The essence of the numeric number of the Yoruba shown above is to show that they are not a small fraction whose philosophical and religious belief is insignificant. As a matter of fact the Yoruba are a nation of significant cultural, aesthetic, educational, entrepreneurial, and scientific relevant in all human ramifications. Therefore the study of their belief in Esu goes beyond the literal and conservative interpretations hence the need to examine it from philosophical and moral dimensions. But first, let us see the primordial existence the cosmological structure of the Ground of beings and humans as contained in Yoruba mythology of existence.

In the Primordial Existence

The Yoruba have several myths of primordial existence but in this chapter we are concerned about the most general where Esu is prominent. In the theocratic structure of the Ground of beings the Yoruba give us a superstructure of hierarchy of beings with defined responsibilities in form of division of labour in an administrative government. Here we have Olodumare, the Supreme Being presiding over all activities in and from his supersensible world and next to him are myriads of divinities and spiritual forces namely, Orisa-nla otherwise known as Obatala who was saddled with the creation of the universe and to make human forms for the Supreme Being to put life in them. But on his way from the supersensible world, he got drunk with palm wine and slept off. When Olodumare waited for Orisa-nla to come and report to him on the assignment given to him and no information of his whereabouts, he sent Oduduwa. Oduduwa got where Orisa-nla was and found him deeply asleep as a result of drunkenness; he did not wake him up instead he went ahead to perform the work given to him by the Supreme Being. When Orisa-nla woke up from his slumber and discovered that someone had performed the assignment given to him by the Deity, he was remorseful. The Deity overlooked his misdeed and gave him another assignment. He was to mould human form and after he had done so he should leave the place for the Deity to put life in them. Apparently the Deity did not want him to know the secret of life which he had imparted to humans. Another divinity of importance is Orunmila who was given the secret of wisdom or foreknowledge from which humans are to inquire particularly their destiny. Esu who is our primary concern is one of the major divinities among myriad divinities created by Olodumare, the Supreme Being to partake in the affairs of humans and the universe of beings.[2]

Esu and the Cosmos of Humans

The Yoruba understanding of the universe is that Olodumare, the Supreme Deity made humans the most dominant figure and charged them with some responsibilities. To be a dominant figure does not literarily mean that they can use the environment as they seem fit without any control. In other words, the universe created by the Deity and the relationship of human beings within the environment is that of peaceful co-existence unlike the Biblical story in which Adam was made to believe that he was the centre of the universe and everything created by God was for him to use as he liked. The governance of human universe in Yoruba belief is structured in partnership with the Supreme Deity, divinities, spiritual forces, and ancestral spirits. The natural phenomena namely, the earth, trees, forests, mountains and hills, rivers, seas, lagoons, winds and the like are personified. Because these natural phenomena have indwelt spirits they are potent with mysterious powers. What then is the role of man in an environment dominated by unseen forces with mysterious powers? How does he see himself in relation to his cosmos? Karin Barber explains: "Yoruba cosmology presents a picture of man, a solitary individual, picking his way… between a variety of forces, some benign, some hostile, many ambivalent, seeking to placate them and only himself with them in attempt to thwart his rivals and enemies in human society."[3] In one of my works I have argued that,

> man sees the purpose of his creation as the attainment of certain social and cultural values, such as: 1) to grow to maturity and be able to have a house, 2) to have many wives and children and grandchildren, 3) to have enough food and money as are necessary for the care of himself and his dependents, 4) to live according to the moral and social traditions of society, 5) to live a healthy and long life, and 6) to die a natural death in old age and be buried by his own children. By so doing he will become an ancestor.
>
> To achieve these life goals is a primary objective of man in Yoruba philosophy, because these values are intrinsically and extrinsically good. They bring satisfaction, and anyone who achieves them is considered successful.[4]

If man is to achieve the above set of goals in life he must recognize the importance of Esu. In other words, the awe of Esu is the beginning of wisdom and success. Esu has some distinct praise names namely, Esu-Elegba, meaning Esu who gets six pence and Esu-Elegbara meaning "the one with many manifestations."[5] Let me elucidate what the two praise names of Esu mean in the context of exigencies of life. When one goes to consult Ifa oracle, the babalawo, the Ifa priest whose expertise is needed to know what to be done to ward off the problem that one is encountering, the consultation fees required by Esu was six pence, a denomination of the British form of exchange during the colonial administration in Nigeria. Before the British however, the medium of exchange among the Yoruba was the cowries. During that time *egba* was the fees. Without giving Esu his first due, it was and still is very unlikely that any babalawo would do the consultation because Esu is the gate way to all the divinities and the Supreme Deity. Esu-Elegbara connotes the unpredictability nature of Esu in his capacity to manifest his multiplicity of his *being*. When Esu is described in this way he is seen as a trickster. According to John Pemberton, we must not consider the trickery "simply as deceit; it is a power."[6] What is the nature of this power? Pemberton explains, "Eshu, like Hermes, has the power to bind and release. With charms he produces sleep, breaks locks, and becomes invisible. He is described as being able to transform himself into a bird, become like the winds, or appear as other persons. He confuses recognition by throwing dust, blinking his eyes, and clapping his hands."[7]

In a recent public lecture on "Esu Elegbara: A Source of an Alter/Native Theory of African Literature and Criticism" Funso Aiyejina noted the dimension of trickery of Esu, "In Yoruba philosophy, Esu emerges as a divine trickster, a disguise-artist, a mischief-maker, and a rebel, a challenger of orthodoxy, a shape-shifter, and enforcer deity."[8] From the foregoing therefore, the essence of the trickery of Esu as a form of power or *ase* is a demonstration of the significance of his stewardship to man, divinities and above all Olodumare, the Supreme Being. Because of the importance of Esu to the Yoruba, Abimbola concludes, "Without Esu, the Yoruba cosmos would be in a state of perpetual conflict."[9] Does the existence of Esu bring law and order to human corporate existence in practical terms or he is an embodiment of fear, confusion and human psychic apprehension in human social and environmental encounters? E. Bolaji Idowu argues that, "The attitude of the Yoruba to Esu is generally one of dread…. This is because, by virtue of his office, he holds the power of life and death over them as posterity or calamity for them depends upon what reports he carries to Olodumare. Everybody seeks, therefore, to be on good terms with him."[10] If Esu is truly a steward and his function is to serve man why must he be held in fear and trembling? Why must man fear the steward as if he is the Supreme Being who has the overall control of human cosmos? Why did the Supreme Deity give Esu such an enormous power that almost rivals his own authority? How is it that Esu the steward, in the performance of his duty becomes a master of the people or divinities he has come to serve? In human existence it appears that nothing is as frightening to man as death. So if Idowu is correct that Esu holds the power of life and death it necessarily follows that it is dreadful. If the myth that arrogates the power of life and death to Esu is anything to go by then it follows that he is evil. It is this aspect of Esu that is probably the reason why scholars have found it difficult to give an appropriate or a plausible explanation and interpretation of his characterization. According to Samuel Johnson, a Yoruba scholar, "Esu or Elegbara- Satan, the Evil One, the author of all evil …"[11] Writing on Esu in the same vein, J. Olumide Lucas asserts, "…Esu, a deity who is sometimes malevolent, but whose malevolence has so preponderated over his beneficence that is now regarded by many as 'the Supreme Power of Evil' and the 'Prince of Darkness.' "[12] G. J. Afolabi Ojo writes, "Esu, more abstract in conception is the deity acknowledged as the supreme power of evil, evil in this sense comprising illnesses, diseases, suffering, misfortunes, accidents, calamities and catastrophes."[13] P. Ade Dopamu argues that Esu in Yoruba theology or religion is the same as the Biblical Satan or the Devil. ... "Esu or Satan or the Devil is the invisible foe of man because we do not have any physical, observable struggle with him. His activity is spiritual and so it is invisible. He works with souls of men. The soul is the seat of intelligence and it distinguishes man from other creatures."[14] If Esu has no physical and observable existence, how can he be an enemy of man? How does an entity we cannot ascertain his existence have such enormous influence on human souls more importantly that no one has ever seen a soul or souls? Philosophers and scientists will find it difficult accepting the view of Dopamu that the soul is the seat of human intelligence. As far as our understanding of human body is concerned, it is the brain that is the seat of intelligence and not a reified spiritual entity. Be that as it may, some prominent scholars have argued that Esu in Yoruba belief is not the same as the Biblical Satan or the Devil. Geoffrey Parrinder explains, "Since it is admitted by everyone that the favour of Eshu can be successfully invoked on behalf of his worshippers, it is evident that this is quite different from the Jewish-Christian Devil who, in traditional theology, is a purely evil force, can only do evil, and therefore would never be used to protect houses and villages as Eshu is."[15]

Similarly, Toyin Falola writes, "Esu can never mean the biblical Satan – their homelands and power are far different."[16] Idowu agrees that Esu in Yoruba religion is not the same as the Devil or Satan in Christian theology. He argues however that, "On the whole, it would be near the truth to parallel him with Satan in the book of Job, where the Satan is one of the ministers of God and has the office of trying men's sincerity and putting their religion to the proof."[17] I think Idowu is probably not correct in his theological comparison of Esu in Yoruba with the Biblical story in the book of Job. Liberal theologians do not consider the drama of trying a righteous man like Job a true event because it is absurd for God to suffer an innocent man. Esu in Yoruba does not have the portfolio of tempting humans with the intention to make become miserable as it is the case in the book of Job. As a matter of fact Esu would have failed in his duty as a messenger of the Supreme Being because one of his duties is to ensure there is justice and good rewards for those who have sincerely worshipped the Deity, divinities and men. How then do we resolve the conflicting characterizations of Esu by the above scholars? One of the best ways to solve the convoluted characterizations of Esu is to give the concept a philosophical and moral assessment. By doing so we will be able to establish the most plausible and authoritative of what is inherent in Yoruba conception of Esu. Abimbola has argued that Esu is not the Biblical Satan or the Devil. Furthermore Esu is not the cause of human predicament including death. He writes:

There are many differences between the Christian and Yoruba conceptions of evil. Evil in Anglo-Christian theology ultimately derives from one source, Satan. All evil acts, deeds, etc., ultimately result from the fact that Satan has a supernatural ability to overcome, persuade or entice humans and other entities into improper conduct. But in Yoruba religion, evil does not emanate from one source. Evil emanates from the evil supernatural forces called Ajogun. There is two hundred plus one of these forces in the cosmos. These forces are all separate and distinct entities, and as such they are individually responsible for a specific type of evil. The Ajogun have eight warlords: Iku (Death); Arun (Diseases); Ofo (Loss); Ega (Paralysis); Oran (Big Trouble); Epe (Curse); Ewon (Imprisonment); Ese (Afflictions). Hence, one can engage in some linguistic licence and claim that, while Christian theology has a mono-demonic conception of evil, Yoruba religion has a poly-demonic conception of evil.[18]

From the foregoing if we go by the explanation of Abimbola, it becomes clear that Esu in Yoruba belief is not responsible for evils in human society. The question arises: who made Ajogun? Or is Esu in Yoruba religion double as Ajogun and a Supervisory Counselor of Olodumare, the Supreme Being who has power to cause some havocs in human affairs? But generally, Esu as already mentioned is an errand divinity to serve the interests of man and other divinities. It is clearly a way of making sure in the cosmos of humans that there is orderliness and peace. But is it true that Esu is always on the side of orderliness and peace in human society? This will become vivid as we discuss Yoruba belief in good and evil which invariable to some extent traceable to Esu.

The Yoruba Sources of Good and Evil

There is a dualistic nature of moral values based on good and evil. Parrinder argues perhaps very wrongly that, "Dualism of good and evil is otherwise unknown to the peoples of West Africa, as the terms used are obviously of European origin…"[19] The idea of dualism of good and evil cannot be a preserved knowledge known by the Europeans alone as all men and women everywhere in the world have the faculty of comparison, deduction and induction. Moral values are deduced from that which is good and evil. It is a common phenomenon among humans to apprehend two major factors about human existence namely life and death both of which have moral values. As a matter of fact nothing is intelligible to man as his understanding of his existence in relation to both life and death. Human projects and values are subjected to the barometer of life and death which according to the Yoruba cannot be discussed without givingEsu his appropriate recognition. If humans are to know good and evil and do what is right and abhor what is wrong, there ought to be some guiding principles by which it can be measured. To the Yoruba, at the creation of human beings the Deity impacted a substance called *eri okan*, conscience to everyone. *Eri Okan* is an indelible imprint on individuals of the presence of the *being* of Olodumare, the Supreme Being. *Eri okan* is also referred to by the Yoruba as *ifa aya*, oracle of the heart, or *ojiji aiye wa*, the shadow of our world or life, or *olu bewo ohun ti ase*, the inspector of our deeds; and it carries with it a connotation of a secret judge of our deeds. Generally, it is the voice that speaks within, that urges us to right the wrong. It is the gentle voice that brings peace to our mind when we do the right thing expected of us. And when no one is around to witness our actions, the voice is there. It is that which encourages us to bear the burden of injustices even when people collaborate and witness falsely against us. Yes indeed, it is a partner who never forsakes us.

The Yoruba also give us another source of good and evil. It is called *Ori inu*, inner head or simply called *Ori*, the *existential being* of man. In the primordial existence, an individual *Ori* makes a choice of coming to this world for some specific reasons and to perform certain functions. It is the *existential being* of the individual that chooses his parents, race, colour, vocation, life span etc. And as an individual makes these various choices the *olu bode*, the gate man in the supersensible world standing and watching bears witness. Once the choices are made they remain irreversible as he or she proceeds to be in the world. On getting to the world the parents know exactly what to do. They are to go and find out from *Ifa* oracle through the *Ifa* priest what their child chose while coming to the world. At this point the *Ifa* priest must make sure that Esu is given the necessary propitiation for the parents to get an answer to their investigation. If the child made choices that are good the priest will inform the parent with a warning so that *omo araye* or *elenini*, the evil ones do not put a cog in the wheel of his progress. The evil ones in this context do not mean Esu but rather some fellow human beings. If on the other hand, the child came with a bad luck, which is considered evil the parents will ask the *Ifa* priest what to do to alter it even though they are aware that it is irreversible. To the Yoruba this kind of good or bad luck is called human destiny. The belief of the Yoruba is that humans must not accept limitations in whatever they do because they are transcendent beings. To a curious mind if one takes a cursory look at history and contemporary events in our world one will wonder why an individual in the primordial existence chose the kind of world or environment he found himself. Why would people in most African States choose poverty, social conflicts, wars and migrations from time to time? Why would the Asians choose geographical locations that are prone to earthquakes and other natural disasters? Or why would people with disability choose delight in being disabled? Given the nature of poor economic conditions and a high rate of unemployment in Nigeria plus poor leadership and governance most Nigerian youths would prefer going to America or Europe rather than living in their country. Surely if they were aware of their predicaments in Nigeria in the primordial existence they would probably not have chosen to be born in Nigeria. Let me unravel some of the ambiguities in the notion of choice making in the pre-existent life. It appears that the Yoruba are simply saying that individuals have their destiny in their hands and not in anyone else's. It is also to exonerate the Deity from anything that happens to individuals because he did not compel anyone to choose to come to this world. Everyone is solely responsible for his choice. The Yoruba philosophy is that 'your destiny is in your own hand'. But in the real sense of the matter can Olodumare be absolved from human predicaments since he is the creator of everything that is? In all this what role does Esu play in human choice making in the pre-existent life and his behaviour while on earth? Esu may have nothing to do with the choice making of individuals in the supersensible world but on getting to this world he has a role to play in almost everyday affairs of people. This is made explicit by an informant of George E. Simpson in his book, *Yoruba Religion and Medicine in Ibadan*; "…but one of these men claimed that Esu is, 'the brain behind all good things as well as all bad things', meaning that Esu interferes in all things."[20] If Esu is behind all good and evil and the Yoruba who became Christians attribute all misfortunes to the Biblical Esu both names suffer double tragedies. That is why Falola argues that, "As Esu got into the Bible and spread with Christianity, the old Esu [Esu in Yoruba] suffered in the process, with his name soiled and damaged, destroyed for ever."[21] It needs to be stated that it is not only Esu that has the power to do good and evil if one considers what other divinities do to human society. For instance, a story was told about the divinity of smallpox in my community, Idofin in Yagba Local Government, Kogi State, Nigeria which his anger caused the death of many people. Some of our towns and urban communities have witnessed some volcanic eruptions that destroyed almost all the people. One will not be surprised to see a chain of hills with deep valleys in Akoko land in Ondo State which suggested the kind of anger the spiritual forces that inhabited the area several decades ago exhibited. In spite of some of the examples I have given among many of them the names of the divinities have not been bartered as that of Esu. When one juxtaposes the number of natural events that resulted into the death of people and the daily accidents on our roads, occasional air disasters etc, Esu is generally held responsible. We must bear in mind that nothing is as dreadful and most frustrating as death. But beyond death being dreadful it affects man's hopes and aspirations. Louis Pojman makes this very explicit in his book *Moral Values and the Meaning of Life*:

> But in death all our desires are frustrated. All that we value is separated from us. We are removed permanent from all we value: our loved ones, conscious experience, our work, beauty, creativity, pleasure and the like. Hence it seems that death must be seen as both natural and as that which will be feared so long as people have goals and recognize the Grand Frustrator that death is.[22]

Of course, nobody wants to lose his loved ones and if Esu is seen as the facilitator of death he must be feared. There is something more fundamental in Yoruba theology of Esu beyond his nefarious activities we should acknowledge and appreciate. It is indubitable that the myth about Esu says more about human beings than the spiritual power that we have been considering. First, in the real sense of it can we establish the fact that Esu exists? The Yoruba will say that Esu does not have empirical and verifiable existence as human beings yet he exists. That is why he is worshipped on daily basis. But the fact that one worships a being does not necessarily mean that such a being exists. For instance, every Christmas festival we hear of Father Christmas but in actual fact no Father Christmas exists. But if you tell the children that have funs with Father Christmas that he does not exist they will tell you that he exists and that he gives them gifts. To convince you that he exists they may even show you the gifts they got from him if they have not been disposed with. To say that Esu does not exist is tantamount to say that Olodumare and all the divinities do not exist because no one has seen any of them physically. Be that as it may, how do we explain Esu in such a way that his conceptions rationally make sense? The way to understand the myth of Esu in relation to humans is through their experiences of who they are? and what they are? as beings who characteristically behave as Esu incarnate.

Esu a Yoruba imaginary invention

If the Yoruba have contributed any existential and philosophical understanding of our world it seems to me that nothing is as symbolic and imaginary as the invention of a deity that unambiguously exhibited our human character in all ramifications. The world in which Esu found himself is administratively arranged with a Godhead surrounded by his lieutenants with different portfolios. What can be as striking as the way in which the Yoruba administrative structure on earth shares a similarity with the one in the supersensible world? An Oba, meaning King who has his traditional chiefs each with his distinctive responsibility, heads the administrative governance among the Yoruba. For instance, we have *Balogun*, the head of the military whose responsibility is basically to safeguard the security of the town against any internal and external aggressors. He reports to his *Kabiyesi* the King from time to time on issues that affect his portfolio as the situation dictates just as Esu reports to the Supreme Being on his everyday activity.

The Yoruba philosophy of Esu is a descriptive characterization of man who is constantly in need of appeasement and nurture because of his insatiable wants and needs; this underlies the metaphysics of this belief. In addition, the mythic Esu reminds us of human greed not only as an individual but also as corporate entities and nations. It is greed that led Africans to sell their fellow Africans to slavery. It is greed that made America, Russia and the entire Europe engage in deadly weapons. It is greed that has led to senseless warfare in contemporary African countries.

The whole world is currently experiencing economic meltdown as a result of greed of some individuals and industrial nations. Our environment is not spared of human greed and exploitation of world natural resources which has resulted into environmental degradation, pollution, and the destruction of ecosystems. Some environmental scientists have argued that man is heading towards self destruction because human existence depends heavily on the environment to survive.[23] According to one of the world leading environmental scholars, Eugene P. Odum, "Without a quality environment, there can be no organized society or quality individuals."[24]

Going by the mythologemic[25] conception of Esu with its antecedence of goodness to his worshippers to the extent that some of them bear such names as Esugbemi, meaning Esu has made me to prosper or Esudare, meaning Esu has dispensed good judgment, the morality of this belief is reflected in the understanding of man as a being with goodness. That is why the Yoruba say *ara eniyan lore wa*. What this informs us is that all humans have inherent values that others can derive some benefits.

There is yet a metaphysical assumption of Esu that is phenomenological and existential in Yoruba belief that is imperative to note. Considering the nature of man generally speaking he is a being faced with polarity of existence. The existence of Esu in Yoruba religion exhibits a divinity that is always under tension because he is to make sure that the services he renders both to man and other spiritual beings are incongruent with the portfolio given to him by Olodumare. Given the insatiable wants of man Esu is under tension. If one considers the prayers of men and women on daily basis with the number of sacrifices to different divinities including the ones for Esu which he monitors, to satisfy them is almost an impossible mission to accomplish. So the Yoruba understand this kind of polarity of existence and explain it mythically. After all according to Robert P. Armstrong, "Myth is culture-specific, which is to say that it is established in a given manner and is of a given constitution definitive of a given culture. It exists in particular contours and tensions which are the form and process of being."[26] The power to explain human world view is naturally given to man who has the ability to express it intelligibly the way he can be understood and myth is an integral part of human natural constitution.

There is a moral dimension of the problem of good and evil underpinning the whole concept of the mythic Esu. The paradoxical nature of Esu coupled with some confusion that arose from Christian scholars who equated the Biblical Esu with that of the Yoruba seem to have a convergence when it comes to the issue of the problem of good and evil. On the one hand Esu is good but on the other he exhibits evil depending on the experiences of the people who have had a course to use him. But in reality in Yoruba culture there is the language of apposition. Some people are described as *omolu wa bi*, people of good character while some are regarded as *eda buruku*, evil or wicked persons. In Yoruba society we have preponderant evidence of both people of godly and diabolical characters. To an external observer, the conception of Esu in Yoruba religion is complicated[27] and one of the reasons for its complication is the multiplicity of imaginary divinities that have certain roles to play in human affairs and in this case, the problem of good and evil.

Conclusion

I have synchronized the myth and reality in the explication of Esu in Yoruba belief in a syndetic expression. While the Yoruba believe that Esu exists in reality, I have argued against the belief. The philosophical and moral imperatives in this work make Esu not to be an existent being. He exists only mythically for the purpose of explaining the Yoruba exigencies and vicissitudes of life. It is in this regard that Esu has become a phenomenon of existence. It is man *qua* man who has become an enigma, a riddle of existence that cannot be easily unraveled without going through the treacherous route of philosophy. But the truth of the matter is that Esu after all, in reality, is not the phenomenon of existence rather it is man.

Notes and References

1. Kola Abimbola, *Yoruba Culture: A Philosophical Account* (Birmingham: Iroko Academic Publishers, 2006), 35.

2. Cf. E. Bolaji Idowu, *Olodumare: God in Yoruba Belief* (London: Longman, 1962), 80-85.

3. Karin Barber, "How Man Makes God in West Africa: Yoruba Attitudes Toward Orisa", *Africa* 5/3 (1981), 729.

4. Segun Ogungbemi, "A Philosophical Reflection on the religiosity of the traditional Yoruba", *Orita Ibadan Journal of Religious Studies* XV111/2 (1986), 61.

5. Funso Aiyejina, "Esu Elegbara: A Source of an Alter/Native Theory of African Literature and Criticism" (Public Lecture, Centre for Black and African Arts and Civilization, Lagos, July 23, 2009).

6. John Pemberton, "Eshu-Elegba: The Yoruba Trickster God", African *Arts* ix, no. 1 (1977), 26.

7. Pemberton, 26.

8. Aiyejina.

9. Abimbola, 69.

10. 1Idowu, 81.

11. Samuel Johnson, *The History of the Yorubas*, (1921; repr., Lagos: C.S.S Bookshops, 1976), 28.

12. J. Olumide Lucas, *The Religion of the Yorubas*, (Lagos: C.M.S Bookshop, 1948), 67.

13. G.J. Afolabi Ojo, *Yoruba Culture: A Geographical Analysis,* (London: University of London Press, 1966), 179.

14. Ade Dopamu, *Esu the Invisible Foe of Man*, (1992 rev., ed. Ijebu-Ode: Shebotimo Publications, 2000), 185.

15. Geoffrey Parrinder, *West African Religion*, (1949; repr., London: Epworth Press, 1973), 56.

16. Toyin Falola, *A Mouth Sweeter than Salt*, (Ann Arbor: University of Michigan Press, 2005), 27.

17. Idowu, 80.

18. Abimbola, 75.

19. Parrinder, 56.

20. George E. Simpson, *Yoruba Religion & Medicine in Ibadan*, (Ibadan: Ibadan University Press, 1980), 17.

21. Falola, 27.

22. Louis Pojman, *Moral Values and the Meaning of Life*, (Swindon: The Waterleaf Press, 1980), 9.

23. See Louis Pojman, ed, (Boston: *Environmental Ethics: Readings in Theory and Application*, 1994). This work contains various positions of 72 scholars on the environmental crisis around the globe.

24. Eugene P. Odum, "Environmental Ethic and the Attitude Revolution" in William T. Blackstone, ed., *Philosophy & Environmental Crisis*, (Athens: University of Georgia Press, 1980), 12.

25. I owed the idea expressed here to my former teacher Robert P. Armstrong at University of Texas Dallas, 1982.

26. Robert P. Armstrong, *Wellspring: On the Myth and Source of Culture*, (Berkeley: University of California Press, 1975), 99-100.

27. Armstrong, 132.

* Segun Ogungbemi, (2013) "Esu: The Phenomenon of Existence" in *Esu: Yoruba God, Power, and The Imaginative Frontiers* (ed.) Toyin Falola, Durham: Carolina Academic Press, 77-86.

CHAPTER 16
A Philosophical Analysis Of Yemoja In A Cross Cultural Context

Introduction

If there is an encyclopedic metaphysical mythology that encapsulates almost all aspects of reality, Yemoja's is one. The versatility of this goddess is immediately measurable from the declension of the etymology of her name, "*Yeye omo eja*" that translates literally to "Mother of fish children." This in turn represents diverse epistemological standpoints as depicted in the number of different fishes in the sea. Her vastness and globalism can be seen in the fact that she is worshiped in Nigeria, Brazil, Cuba, America, Haiti, among other places, where she has been contextualized. Yemoja, as a giver and sustainer of life, has a symbolic representation of the maternal aspect of divinity depicted in fecundity. Her association with water, believed to be a source of life, places her in high ranking among the deities such that she can be viewed from a wide philosophical framework from cross cultural perspectives. This chapter is broadly divided into two sections, viz.: historical and philosophical dimensions of the nature of Yemoja. The first provides a mythical-historical conceptualization of Yemoja and also espouses how the goddess has assumed a global phenomenon as a result of her being worshiped in places beyond the geo-historical Yoruba. The second part raises some critical questions in relation to the goddess and contextualizes them within the ambit of salutary philosophical contemplation of the Yoruba and the Yoruba-influenced cultures.

The Myth of the Origin of Yemoja

Yemoja has been described as one of the primordial deities who descended from heaven. A myth has it that she was a very good friend of Sango in heaven and later they both got married at their arrival on earth. However, before Yemoja got married to Sango, Sango had married two other wives namely, Osun and Yemoji. Not too long after their marriage, Sango had a revelation, which made him to consult Orunmila for interpretation. The Orunmila told Sango that there were three fortunes in his house (representing his three wives), which he could only retain by sacrificing his most precious possession. The most valuable thing to Sango was his *Ikoode*, ornamental regalia, which he felt he could not sacrifice for any reason.[1]

It is only customary for the deities to have their annual festival. When the time for the festival – Odun-Ilero – came, all the divinities were present. The festival was celebrated with all sorts of drinks, in accordance with their preferred ones. On one of the periodic festivals, Sango drunk himself to stupor and abandoned his wives. The three wives could not continue to wait for their absentee husband. Therefore, they decided to celebrate in their home individually. In the course of the celebration, Osun and Yemoji observed that Yemoja's gathering attracted more guests than theirs. This called for their investigation, and of course, resulted in rivalry. The already upset Osun and Yemoji discovered to their chagrin that Yemoja was putting on the *ikoode*, a sign that she had become the favorite wife of Sango.[2] Since Osun and Yemoji could not stand it, they packed their belongings, especially the pots of herbs and left home. When the news got to Sango, and he came to himself, he ran after them and pleaded with them to come back. Unfortunately, they would not but rather broke their pots of herbs and turned into water. Sango made frantic efforts to retain the only remaining wife, Yemoja, but all to no avail. Yemoja also left with her pot of herbs, which as others broke hers and turned into a river.[3]

Another myth states in a nutshell that "Sango was the son of Oranyan, a son or grandson of Oduduwa, and of Yemoja, a Nupe princess and daughter of Elenpe, a powerful chieftain north of the Niger River bend."[4] This traces the origin of Yemoja to the northern part of Nigeria. Not many people subscribe to this myth because of the fact that there are not many rivers in the north and because the northerners hardly had any concept of water goddess. Oyeronke Olademo however notes that rivers play important function in identity construction as a result of the mythical connections between them and the people who subscribe to such myths. Such connections operate at three levels: human, nature and divine. And River Niger plays such a role in association with Oya, one of the Yoruba goddesses. According to her, River Niger used to have a shrine dedicated to Oya, which accounts for why the river is called *Odo Oya*, Oya's river.[5] It is instructive to state that Yemoja as the name of the goddess has to do with water or river. Another version has it that Aginju and Yemoja were married and had a son called Orungan. The latter committed incest with his mother who fled after the incidence; "she became exhausted and poured forth water from her body before she died."[6] It was from the water that she poured forth that several water deities emanated.

Olumide Lucas adds that Yemoja is the daughter of Obatala and Odudua, who as a female deity represents waters. From her emanated Olosa, Olokun, Dada, Sango, Ogun, Oya, Osun, Oba, Orisa, Oko, Osisi, Oke, Aje, Saluga, Osu, etc.[7] This suffusing belief of the primordiality of Yemoja is crisply put forth by Kola Abimbola where she is depicted as either the biological or patron mother of the deities.[8] It is this motherly role that has come to define a goddess, which thousands of people venerate, and worship as capable of making the barren mothers have children of their own.

Apart from being a source of fertility and reproduction, Yemoja is generically associated with water. No wonder then that *Yeye omo eja* (mother of fish children) is her name since it is only in water that fish can survive. In fact, J. Omosade Awolalu rightly observes that she is a spirit that resides in rivers, lagoon or sea and worshiped mainly by riverine dwellers.[9] This espouses much on geography of religion, a descriptive discipline that builds a correlation between landscape and religious beliefs, practices, and symbols. The relevant questions are: how do different landscapes affect religious belief? Why do different people of different ethno-geographical entities respond differently to the same religious and philosophical phenomenon? Why do different people of different cultural backgrounds with similar landscapes generate similar religious and philosophical stimulus? And why is Yemoja worshiped by riverine dwellers across the globe? What is the relevance of the body of water to the Yemoja phenomenon and how does it generate both religious and philosophical feelings? The connection between Yemoja and rivers explains why she is prominent and worshiped among various peoples who live on the coastal regions of big waters and rivers. This is important because, as observed above, those who live in the semi arid region do not think or conceive generally any water goddess. If this is so, why will those on dry land, e.g. Native Americans worship water goddess? Could this be as a consequence of lack of water? What are the connections between the Yemoja-water relation and such dry land more especially that she is popular among such people?

Yemoja in the Nigerian Landscape

Mei-Mei Sanford notes that water spirits are not only "ubiquitous" but also "vitally important in southern Nigeria."[10] Yemoja is one of such spirits. The Yoruba believe that Yemoja was originally known as *Omujelewu* that is, a "person whose breast is longer than her garment."[11] The idea of *Omujelewu* is best depicted in symbolism of fertility and of motherhood. John S. Mbiti explains:

> Breasts are the symbols of life, and the bigger they are, the more people appreciate them: they are signs that the woman has an ample supply of milk for the child…. These are the pride of motherhood, announcing the message that 'I am fertile.' And this is the ideal wish of every African woman.[12]

Let us reiterate once again that barrenness is generally considered among Africans as a curse and not a disease, which every family strives to remove. This is because "motherhood is defined in terms of having the ability to procreate and give birth to as many children as are available in the womb of any female parent."[13] It is for this reason that barren women flock Yemoja's shrines which contain "a pot filled with 'sacred' water from the River Ogun which is given to barren women begging for children from Yemoja and to the children that are born as a result"[14] wherever they are located. Naturally, grateful devotees whose prayers have been answered by the benevolent goddess, Yemoja, must perform sacrifices of thanksgiving in the shrine. At least, "festivals of gods belong to the god and sanctuaries."[15] During the festival, she is offered her favorite: mashed maize, pounded yam, yam porridge, goats, hens, ducks and fish.[16]

According to Mei-Mei Sanford, Mami Wata is one of such spirits which can "bestow good fortune …in return for some kind of relationship, usually framed as a sexual attraction."[17] Among the Niger Delta people of Nigeria, Yemoja is most widely called Mami Wata. This variation is based on cultural peculiarity of the people. But more importantly, it is to be noted that Mami Wata is never the traditional name of Yemoja or any of the goddesses. Rather, it is so called because of the influence of Christianity and colonialism. However, it is interesting to note that 'mammy' is a variant of 'mama', 'mom', 'mommy' or 'mummy', which means mother. The first Christian missionaries probably used mammy Water in the

16th century who arrived Warri, in the Niger Delta. It was also likely that those missionaries observed the worship of the mother goddess by the people and referred to her as Mammy Water, which has been tainted as Mami Wata. It is widely observed that many of the European words have been corrupted in an attempt to understand and contextualize them. That the mother goddess was called Mammy Water by the Europeans attests to the belief in the generic connotations of Yemoja with water, that is, the owner of water. Generally, the people believe that Mami Wata dwells at the bottom of the sea with heavy ornamental adoration in a ritzy palace. The devotees are blessed with children when appropriate sacrifices (such as mashed maize, pounded yam, yam porridge, goats, hens, fish, ducks) must have been offered.[18]

Among the Edo-Delta of South-South Nigeria, Yemoja is referred to as Olokun or Mami Wata. Generally, Olokun among the Yoruba of South-West Nigeria is a male deity while she is a goddess in Edo State, especially among the Bini. Among the Owan people of Edo State, Olokun is a female goddess. She possesses male and female but more females than males. Folake Onayemi explicates that when Yemoja assumes the feminine personality, she is known as Olokun. As she succinctly puts it, "Olokun is represented in the female form as Yemoja or Oluweri."[19] She further states:

> Olokun is identified with Yemoja or Oluweri who is the goddess of the sea. Yemoja is believed to be a very beautiful goddess who in form is half-fish, half-woman. From the waist down, she is a beautiful silvery, shinning fish. She is believed to be a queen living in a breathtaking palace under the sea where she has many attendants...[and] the ability and authority to grant children to barren women.[20]

As Osadalor observes, granting children to barren women makes the people to be attracted to the goddess. This is because in a society where barrenness is conceived as a curse, everything must be done to remove it. As a paragon of beauty, Courlander describes Olokun when identified with Yemoja as beautiful, morally excellent and extremely attractive to beautiful things. It is for this reason that beautiful girls are regarded as her daughters.[21] Onayemi compares her with the Greek goddess of beauty – Aphrodite, who is also "a fertility goddess whose domain embraced all nature, vegetable as well as human."[22]

Yemoja across the Globe

The myth that Yemoja is the goddess of waters is significant because the use and functions of water are universal.

In Haiti as well as in the New World as a whole, the definition of religion is intricately associated with ancestral spirituality. Although this belief has passed through "momentous transformation" no thanks to colonialism, slave trade and globalization, the events depicted in the spiritual deities constantly remind them of the traumatic changes occasioned by these forces. Terry Rey elucidates further:

> For Africans and their descendants in the New World, contact with Europeans resulted in a collective trauma that "not only changed older ways of thinking about self and the world by offering alternative meanings, it also encouraged different memories about the past...." Universal spirits managed greater success in traversing the Atlantic with enslaved Africans... because many of them were associated with natural phenomena that are "universal", like wind, metal, and water.... [which] are originally universal West African spirits. Major cults of these spirits thus readily emerged in the Americas because there was of course wind, metal, and water there just as in Africa.[23]

The above explains how Yemoja among other spirits got to the New World. Thus among the Ewe-Anlo[24] (the African-born and African-socialized people who trace their origin to West Africa and Central Africa, who in the Haitian Revolution of 1804 gained their freedom), Yemoja is called Mami Wata, a mermaidlike spirit that suffuses their religious life. Water is essential for life and Yemoja is the source of it. For them, the place of water in human life is irreducibly important. Rey explains:

> From the normative offer of water to visiting guests to the use of this substance in the many rituals surrounding birth, death, and religious worship, water is believed to have the power to cool the hearts of men and [the] gods, to mediate relations between humans and the spiritual world, and purify the physical body both literally and ritually.[25]

While Rey is right to say that water cools the hearts of men, it is equally true that water does the same for women, and all other living things. These uses of water are connected with Mami Wata in West and Central Africa as well as in the Caribbean Islands where the spirit is known as the *Iwa* Lasyrenn. According to Karen McCathy Brown,

> Lasyrenn is connected to Mammy Water, whose shrines are found throughout West Africa. Some suggest that the mermaid persona, also common for Mammy Water, was derived from the carved figures on the bows of the ships of European traders and slaves. Thus the Vodou *Iwa* Lasyrenn may have roots that connect like nerves, to the most painful parts of the loss of homeland and the trauma of slavery. It is therefore fitting that she also reconnects people to Africa and its wisdom.[26]

Rey argues that there is a strong feeling of nostalgia among communities in African Diasporas, and thus there are always attempts to reconnect to their roots. As such, African traditional belief systems are pervasive. Solimar Otero has argued recently that there are some modifications and creolization, and that these ways of innovating culture have deep roots in African creativity and fluidity. In essence, even during the slave trade African slaves carried with them their religious and cultural belief systems which formed the foundation of their religious praxis in the New World. The inspiration many of them got from further 'communication' with their ancestral roots through the arrival of new slaves rekindled their religious impetus as well.[27] In this connection, Rey points out that the composite nature of African cosmology is strong in *Iwa*, that is, the belief in the world of the living and the world of the dead. These two worlds are divided by water, which a person crosses at death to the world of the dead, and which an ancestor to be reborn also crosses to be born into the world of the living. The living and the dead are believed to live across a body of water just like the people of Haiti do from their African ancestors. This symbolism of water is instructive because Yemoja, which is believed to represent water, becomes the connecting rod between the Africans and the Africans in Diaspora.[28]

The sense of syncretism is underscored when we consider how Christian symbolism and ritual paraphernalia are adopted in abundance in relation to African spirituality. For instance in Brazil, Yemoja is conceptualized "as mistress of the sea" who is "the great purifier of earthly passion."[29] The paths of morality and righteousness are ascribed to her such that she is believed to "discharge all the impurities introduced into the building by man's sinful body."[30] As a consequence, "Yemanja protects sailors and helps anyone who wishes to improve himself to follow the path of righteousness."[31] The sycretizing flair here is that, as Bestride points out, Yemoja among other African deities, is made more moral by the modification of her mythical characteristics, particularly as she is identified with Immaculate Conception. Although the various myths of Yemoja do not in reality present her as immaculate, there is an enthusiastic effort by Afro-Brazilian devotes to make her equal with "the Virgin Mother of the Catholics."[32] Sanford clarifies such idea of syncretism as not "mechanistic, in which each religion is engaged not just strategically, but religiously"[33] in multiple religious practices.

Apart from the foregoing analysis, there is a widespread belief among the Bahians of Brazil that the powers that dwell in the waters do not discriminate against races. African deities stretch their contours to "persons from all ethnic roots and social levels."[34] African deities are pervasive in the Bahian culture so significantly that a newspaper once said that, "the blond Oxum and the brunette Iemanja."[35] This is being interpreted to mean that these goddesses have been assumed to have Brazilian origin rather than African. It denotes, however, the widespread acceptance, and influence that Yemoja among other deities has in that culture. Alternatively, it could be the case that the deities have been fully assimilated and adopted in the Brazilian culture. The pervasive influence of Yemoja in Bahia can be confirmed, when Manoel Bonfim, a Bahian artist made "a statue of Iemanja at Rio Vermelho beach that has become a symbol, of Salvador."[36]

From the mythical perspective of Afro-Cuban tradition, Osun is believed to be an aggressive personality who fought with Yemoja that led to the separation of their kingdom. They both share dominions over the waters such that Osun dominates the fresh water, which in Spanish is called *agua dulce*, which literally means sweet water, while Yemoja (Yamaya) rules over the sea. Ultimately, Osun empties its waters into the sea (Yemoja).[37] Water symbolizes life and as such fertility, reproduction and human sexuality, which form "the theme of life" and are associated intimately with Yemoja. As Isabel Castellanos puts it: "Yemaya nurtures life. She is depicted as a black woman or a black siren whose belly and breasts are swollen in pregnancy. Moreover, Yemaya is the womb from whom existence emerges."[38]

The Cubans believe that the excruciating experiences of the slaves were constant reminder of man's inhumanity to man and the ineffable love of their deities even though they at times are incapable of salvaging some situations, for instance the slave trade. This belief is recalled in the frank counsel Yemoja gave to Osun at the onset of the iniquitous trade in human beings that the gods would be unable to stop their 'children' from being carried away to far away land. Therefore, Osun decided to go with her children after asking Yemoja to "straighten her hair and lighten her skin to the color of copper" in order to stimulate worship from all Cubans irrespective of their races.[39]

In the United States, Yemoja's devotees speak about her in flowery adoration. She is regarded as simple, caring, humble and understanding deity who respects people's lives. She only comes in when invited and will not invade their privacy. An Afro-American devotee depicts Yemoja's energy thus:

> For me, Yemoja does not force herself, does not make demands. She steps back and doesn't ask until the need is there. Then she'll step in and say, "Baby, this is what you need to do." Then she'll step back unto her place of observation.[40]

This speaks volume about Yemoja in different cultural milieus. For instance, Americans are known to respect individual right and privacy unlike the communal culture of the Africans who respect their communal norms. While Yemoja in the United States does not invade people's privacy, she is always available to render help when invited whereas in Africa, she is believed to live in the communal setting with the people. This is a pointer to cultural adaptability, which is the hallmark of civilization.

Yemoja-Water Nexus with Ancient Egyptian-Greek Philosophy

The idea of fertility cults dates back to pristine time. For example, the "venus of Willendorf" in Austria is a figurine of "a woman with prominent breasts, belly and vulva." Even though it has been argued by some that during the Stone Age and the Bronze Age that the existence of the worship of goddess depicted lack of complex social, political, legal and religious institutions, others argued that there was a social structure even if the society had not advanced as it is today. Evidence abounds that these societies had and many still have goddess worship based on fertility cults just like Yemoja.[41]

So when Castellanos took a detour from Osun to interpret one of the myths describing Yemoja "as a universal mother,"[42] she would not have readily realized that he had struck a cord on the very essence of Yemoja. The description of universal motherhood of Yemoja is very significant for a goddess widely believed to generate rather than diminish life. Life in every conceptual plain is universal; not only of human beings but also other organisms irrespective of their kind and degree. The thrust of life in mythical conception largely relates to water, an important substance that has been universally acknowledged to generate and sustain life. The second aspect relates intensively with the fact that Yemoja is worshiped not only in Yoruba land, her popular provenance but also widely and profoundly beyond Africa e.g. Brazil, Bahia, Cuba, Haiti, America, etc.

The first point is water. Let us for the sake of understanding discuss water as a substance that has universal with conceptual and philosophical explanation. For instance among the early Greek philosophers, we have on records Thales of Miletus, who argued that water was the single substance from which all life sprang out, and that the process of change might have arisen from within water itself, in which case the principle of motion might be "inherent in the basic material of which the universe is made,"[43] at first thought there might not be any logical and historical linkage with Yemoja. But when we argue herein that Thales' philosophy, which is a major part of the early Ionian School, originates from Egypt, at least another bloated controversy is expected. But again, how does this connect with Yemoja?

First and foremost, we must accept, at least from Afrocentric philosophical perspective that "Thales, studied in Egypt and was equally conversant with the cosmogony of the Mystery System, Hermopolitan, Heliopotan and Memphite."[44] The historical-philosophical projection here is that, contained in the Egyptian hieroglyphic writings of the Mystery School are the creation stories in which the gods created with earth, water and air. Even though there is no record that Anaximander – who thought that the Boundless was the primitive matter that gave rise to the universe – and Anaximenes – who thought of air as the source of life – studied in Egypt, there are ample evidences that they were Thales' students. Thales influenced them greatly because of his study of the creation elements in the Mystery School in Egypt.[45] Thales, in fact, did not adduce any reasons for choosing water as the source of life. Thus Aristotle expressed some misgiving about Thales' philosophy by stating:

> Some think that even the ancients, who lived long before the present generation and first framed accounts of the gods, had a similar view of nature, for they made Ocean and Tethys the parents of creation and described the oath of the gods being by water.[46]

Granted that Thales studied in Egypt and philosophized that the universe came about through water, it is how the task of connecting this with Yemoja that calls our attention. Olumide Lucas built a historical connection. Although his argument might appear controversial for some, the implications for our study cannot be underestimated if at least for the sake of argument. Lucas etymological and linguistic declension of Yemoja is that she represents water.[47] He says that Yemoja is a contraction of *Yeye Omo-eja* that is, "the mother of fishes" wherein the word "*omo(n)*" is understood as *omo enia* (human beings), and used in "a generic sense."[48] He further argued that it is doubtless that Yemoja is one of the few survivals of "the Nile goddesses, probably of Mirit Qimait or Mirit Mihit, who together with their male associates were regarded as guardian deities or progenitor of fishes."[49] Lucas substantiated his argument by providing a salient connection with Egypt a list of gods and goddesses which have stark correlation with the Yoruba e.g. Olosa, Olokun, Dada, Ogun, Oya, Oshun, Oba, Ososi, Oke, Aja Saluga, Sopono, Orun and Osu.[50]

What therefore is the relevance of the fore going analysis to our study? It must be borne in mind that the association of Yemoja with River Nile is perspectival, for in history we are taught the slogan and reality: "No Nile, no Egypt." River Nile has been described as "the artery of Egypt" and Herodotus adds that Egypt is "a gift of the Nile."[51] Luc Croegaert asserts:

> It remains no less obvious that the river has played there, as everywhere else, an irreplaceable role of catalyst. It was the river that enabled this long historical continuity of Egypt over six millennia and that gave it the means of integrating the elements of an originally African culture into a coherent and dynamic whole.[52]

Similarly Herodotus writes:

> The first human king… was Min. In his time all Egypt save the Thebaic province was a marsh; all the country that we now see was then covered by water…. And I think their account of the country was true. It is clear that any judicious person, without prior information, could see at once that Egypt to which the Greeks sailed belonged to the Egyptians, given them by the river.[53]

From the foregoing the point being made is that if Thales' thought "broke the worldview of his day," that thought was got from Egypt's cosmos: the Nile. Thales might have wondered at the vast roles of the river to Egypt and Egyptians: that it was the source of life; sustenance of life that he concluded in agreement with the teaching of the Mystery School that water is the substance from which life generated. The implication of this is that Thales' philosophy had contributed to philosophical development of ideas in trying to explain the physical reality. Thales held that the cosmos is inhabited by an avalanche of forces such as gods, goddesses, godlets, demigods, demons, and ancestral ghosts etc. who literally willed everything that existed.[54] And Yemoja was one of the goddesses.

The link between Egypt and the Yoruba as Lucas tried to build is a mythical-historical assignment which is not the focus of this chapter. However, there is a strong point that the universality of the motherhood of Yemoja has passed a crucial test. In the meantime, it can be suggested that a transnational relations be developed on the basis of such mythical-historical basis to foster continental peace and fecundity of vital force which Yemoja represents.

An Appraisal

Generally, the Yoruba believe that white symbolizes purity, peace, spotlessness, corruption-free, joy, good luck, good health, and fertility. This explains why the devotees of Yemoja among other Yoruba deities are usually dressed in white. The *Iyaji* – priestess – is one who has passed menopause; a belief that she has attained the age of purity having been freed from the monthly menstrual cycle.[55] This symbolic depiction speaks eloquently of the nexus between socio-cultural and human life on the one hand, and religious or spiritual reality in concrete terms on the other. The symbols of Yemoja as in all other deities express abstract ideas, values and notions in concrete representation. This makes symbols to transcend the limits of "physical intrinsic property of the object" and discernible within the context of the people's culture.[56]

The symbolic or anthropomorphic characterization of white has to do with human fertility, which is one of the extant significance of Yemoja. Yemoja symbolism has a symbiotic connection with morality. Although there are divergent views on the moral personality of the goddess, it seems clear however that she largely represents critical moral virtues required for social engineering and transformation. For example, a critical examination of the mythical characteristics of Yemoja who married her brother and committed incest with her son, Aganju naturally enervates standard moralization ascribable to her.[57] However, myths, as we know are usually subjected to human intellectual scrutiny or rationalization. But they have didactic import. So we subject them to the crucibles of modern rationalization, we may miss the point. This is why Mendes argued that there is always a continuous evolution such that it is "only when we have overcome the imperfections of our physical and astral bodies can our spirit enter the mental body and prepare itself for the higher life."[58] Yemoja, having undergone this soul purificatory-transformative process qualifies to be regarded as "the great purifier of earthly passions" as Roger Bastide punctiliously noted about her.[59] Her experiences of earthly passions as a deity coupled with the transformation puts her in a position to guide her devotees who wish "to follow the path of righteousness."[60] This is why in Minas, "the phalanxes of Yemanja are invoked at the opening of the session in order to "discharge" all the impurities introduced into the building by man's "sinful body.""[61]

Here morality is linked with the people's worldview. It is also this that binds the people with their object of belief. Even though there are some controversies about the foundation of morality, there is however a wide acceptance in Africa that Yoruba morality has strong religious connection. Bolaji Idowu argues that "our own view is that morality is basically the fruit of religion and that, to begin with, it was dependent on it. Man's concept of the Deity has everything to do with what is taken to be the norm of morality."[62] Laurenti Magesa also subscribes to this notion, namely that morality is steeped in religion.[63] However, some scholars have questioned this supernatural foundation of morality; they speak of anthropocentric basis of morality. Kwasi Wiredu argues in this direction:

> What is morally good is what befits a human being; it is what is decent for man – what brings dignity, respect, contentment, prosperity, joy to man and his community. And what is morally bad is what brings misery, misfortune, and disgrace. Of course, immoral conduct is held to be hateful to God; the Supreme Being, and even to the lesser gods.[64]

But the point is made clearer by Benezet Bujo who argues that in spite of the first generation African religious theological perspective on the nature of things being grounded in theocentricity, their anthropocentric dimensions are also increasingly becoming realized. However, this does not make Yoruba society a godless one.[65] When we glean both sides of the moral arguments and weave them into our discourse, we can argue that the belief in Yemoja by her devotees and what she represents for them have stirred up moral consciousness. For instance, it is the case that after sacrifices are made on behalf of a supplicant and if she does not become healed or pregnant that she would be advised to do a self examination and confession of sin,[66] where there is; and there is usually some.

In the same token a few days ago there was flood in the city of Ibadan, South-West of Nigeria where about 100 people died. During a group discussion, it was said that some goddesses had earlier warned of the dire consequences if the people persisted in throwing refuse indiscriminately on them (goddesses). But the people would not heed the admonition of the goddesses on environmental ethics, which traditionally connects with religion. Oloruntoba, Coker, Olowookere and Sridhar, corroborate this in their observation of the waste situation in Ibadan:

> Waste management is poor and solid wastes are dumped along roadsides and into open spaces, attracting vermin causing inconvenience and environmental pollution, and being a risk for public health. Although government authorities apply all the waste clearing means at their disposal, the piles of wastes only seem to grow from day to day…. The problem is likely to intensify unless alternate approaches can be developed.[67]

One of the alternative approaches is metaphysical. It is widely believed that when a signboard is placed somewhere warning people against throwing of refuse, they do not generally adhere. Whereas when a signboard reads 'the native doctor' needs your refuse or waste, people fear and desist from either throwing refuse or defecating on that spot. Although some of the discussants explained the Ibadan incident naturalistically citing the Hurricane Irene in the US, the tsunami in Japan and other volcanic eruptions elsewhere as not having anything to do with any deity, the point was also stressed by others that to ignore the moral significance of the 'mythical deities' in the management of the environment may spell doom for a religio-sphere. Jacob Olupona argues:

> We are beginning to see a new understanding arising from various societal authorities – including scientists, politicians, and religious leaders – that there is a religious or spiritual dimension to these crises which include, but are not limited to, political or scientific explanations. Some argue, for example, that the looming collapse of the environment has great significance as a spiritual crisis. It is also absurd that we need an authority to tell us this. Perhaps it is the aloofness of global religions… which has made this oversight possible; it is hard to imagine a practitioner of traditional African religion failing to see the spiritual import of a destabilized biosphere.[68]

This explains why the devotees of Yemoja are adjoined to keep their environment clean. It is for the same reason that the importance of water is stressed. Apart from the literal and spiritual uses of water, the modern uses, including transportation, power generation, etc are crucial developmental projects that require that human beings must maintain the essence of water as enjoined by its goddess - Yemoja.

Conclusion

We have tried to demonstrate in this chapter that *Yeye omo eja*, the *Omujelewu* of humanity is indeed "a universal mother." Her universality has been shown to cut across different geographical and cultural climes whether in Nigeria, Africa or in the West and America. This global goddess remains true to all these contexts and also helped in their generation of spiritual energies to face the vicissitudes of life. The moral and ecological challenges posed for humanity though can be explained in existential terms remain crucial for a goddess who emphasizes orderliness, truth, righteousness, reticence, qualities that are grossly deficient in most human societies today. We must bear in mind that the mythologemic discourse of Yemoja with her variant names in the universe cannot be subjected to a deep cut of butcher's knife of "reason" because doing so will not give its cultural and religious imports that are very significant to the adherents and admirers of the deity. Be that as it may, we cannot lose sight of the pertinence of the philosophical dimension of what Yemoja represents as power of invocation and power of virtuosity both in the consciousness of people and in the practical dimension of character formation among the devotees of the goddess. It has contributed robustly to a web of relationship between Africans at home and Africans in Diaspora in the context of divine-human-nature interconnectedness. This symbiotic affiliation or bond between Africans in the continent and those in Diaspora who relate more closely on the basis of their common beliefs in Yemoja regardless of the names the goddess is called rekindles the common cultural affinity and philosophical orientation. As Fela Anikulapo Kuti rightly noted it in one of his songs that water has no enemy, which is a common saying among the Yoruba that *omi o lo ta*. So it could be argued by extension that since water has no enemy, Yemoja the source of waters could not have enemies because the source is a blessing to all humans and nature where we all derive our environmental support for sustenance. Thus proves the universality of Yemoja, a benevolent goddess of waters, fertility and sustainability.

Endnotes

1. C. L. Adeoye, *Igbagbo ati Esin Yoruba* (Ibadan: Evans Brothers 1985), 220-226.
2. Adeoye, 221.

3. Adeoye, 223.

4. Diedre L. Badejo, "Sango and the Elements: Gender and Cultural Discourse" in J. E. Tishken, T. Falola and A. Akinyemi, (eds.) *Sango in African and the African Diaspora* (Bloomington and Indianapolis: IUP, 2009), 116.

5. Oyeronke Olademo, "Water Heritage and the Sustainability of the Environment: The Nigerian Experience" in S. O. Oyewole, et al. (eds.) *Science in the Perspective of African Religion, Islam & Christianity* (Ilorin: LSI & NASTRENS, 2010), 540.

6. J. Olumide Lucas, *Religions in West Africa and Ancient Egypt* (Lagos: Nigerian National Press, 1970), 127.

7. J. Olumide Lucas, *The Religion of the Yorubas* (Lagos: CMS Bookshop, 1948), 98.

8. Lucas, *Religions in West Africa and Ancient Egypt*, 128.

9. J. Omosade Awolalu, *Yoruba Beliefs and Sacrificial Rites* (UK: Longman 1979), 46.

10. Mei-Mei Sanford, "Osun, Mami Wata and Olokun in the Lives of Four Contemporary Nigerian Christian Women in Murphy and Sanford (eds.) *Osun Across the Waters: A Yoruba Goddess in Africa and the Americas* (Indiana: IUP, 2001), 238.

11. Kola Abimbola, *Yoruba Culture: A Philosophical Account* (Birmingham: Iroko Academic Publishers, 2006), 128.

12. John S. Mbiti, *African Religions and Philosophy*, (London: Heinemann, 1969), 120.

13. David O. Ogungbile, "Yoruba Cultural Identity: A Phenomenological Approach to Osun Festival" in P. A. Dopamu & E. A. Odumuyiwa (eds.) *Religion, Science and Culture* (Ikenne-Remo: NASR, 2003), 182.

14. Awolalu, 46.

15. Folake Onayemi, *Parallels of Ancient Greek and African/Yoruba Gods* (Akropong-Akuapem: NeatPRINT, 2010), 85.

16. Awolalu, 46.

17. Sanford, 238.

18. Awolalu, 46.

19. Onayemi, 58.

20. Onayemi, 57-58.

21. Onayemi, 57-58.

22. Onayemi, 66.

23. Terry Rey, "Vodou, Water, and Exile: Symbolizing Spirit and Pain in Port-au-Prince" in O.B. Stier and J. S. Landres (eds.) *Religion, Violence, Memory and Place* (Bloomington and Indianapolis: IUP, 2006), 202-203.

24. The Ewe-Anlo people were hundreds of thousands of West and Central Africans enslaved and forced to labor across the Atlantic in the French colony of Saint-Domingue, which in 1804 became independent as Haiti. Of the Haitian population after the success of the Revolution, more than half originated from the West African Ewe-Anlo ethnic group and half from Central African Kongo. For further details, see for instance, Keren M. Brown, *Mama Lola: A Vodou Priestess in Brooklyn* (Berkeley: University of California Press, 1991); David Eltis, Stephen D. Behrendt, and David Richardson, "National Participation in the Atlantic Slave Trade: New Evidence" In *Africa and the Americas: Interconnections during the Slave Era*, ed. Jose Curto and Renee Soulodre-LaFrance, (Trenton and Asmara: Africa World Press, 2005), 13-42; David Eltis, Stephen D. Behrendt, David Richardson, and Herbert S. Klein, *The Transatlantic Slave Trade: A Database on CD-ROM*, Cambridge, 1999; Sandra E. Greene, *Sacred Sites and the Colonial Encounter: A History of Meaning and Memory in Ghana* (Bloomington: Indiana University Press, 2002); Paul Lovejoy, "The Volume of the Atlantic Slave Trade: A Synthesis" *Journal of African History*, 23 (1982): 473-501, and Paul Lovejoy, "The Impact of Atlantic Slave Trade on Africa: A Review of the Literature" *Journal of African History*, 30 (1989): 365-394.

25. Rey, 203.

26. Cited in Rey, 203.

27. For further details, see Solimar Otero, *Afro-Cuban Diasporas in the Atlantic World* (USA: University of Rochester Press, 2010), 23-50.

28. Rey, 204.

29. R. Bastide, *The African Religions of Brazil: Toward a Sociology of the Interpretation of Civilizations* trans. H. Sebba (Baltimore: The Johns Hopkins University Press, 1978), 325.

30. Bastide, 325.

31. Bastide, 325.

32. Bastide, 257.

33. Sanford, 238.

34. Ieda Santos, "In the City Everyone is Oxum's" in *Osun Across the Waters*, 68.

35. Santos, 68.

36. Santos, 77.

37. Isabel Castellanos, "A River of many Turns: The Polysemy of Ochun in Afro-Cuban Tradition" in *Osun Across the Waters*, 42-43.

38. Castellanos, 42.

39. Maguel A. Torre, "Dancing with Ochun: Imagining how a Black Goddess became White" in A. B. Pinn (ed.) *Black Religion and Aesthetics: Religious Thought and Life in Africa and the African Diaspora* (Palgrave: Macmillan, 2009), 114.

40. Rachel E. Harding, "What part of the River you're In: African American Women in Devotion to Osun" in *Osun Across the Waters*, 172.

41. Katherine Aaslestad, *Historica's Women: 1000 Years of Women in History*, (Elanora Heights: Millennium House, 2007), 24.

42. Castellanos, 42.

43. James L. Christian, *Philosophy: An Introduction to the Art of Wondering* (Australian: Wadsworth, 2009), 23.

44. Innocent C. Onyewuenyi, *The African Origin of Greek Philosophy: An Exercise in Afrocentrism* (Nsukka: University of Nsukka Press, 1993), 209.

45. Onyewuenyi, 209.

46. Onyewuenyi, 210.

47. Lucas, *The Religion of the Yorubas*, 97.

48. Lucas, *The Religion of the Yorubas*, 97.

49. Lucas, *Religions in West Africa and Ancient Egypt*, 127.

50. Lucas, *The Religion of the Yorubas*, 98-99.

51. Luc Coegaert, *The African Continent: An Insight into its Earliest History* (Nairobi: Paulines, 1999), 31.

52. Coegaert, 31.

53. Coegaert, 34.

54. Christian, 23.

55. The point is the Yoruba just as most other African people believe that

menstruation neutralizes the efficacy of powers and rituals. So they believe that women during their monthly cycle are ritually 'unclean' and cannot participate in religious worship. Women who have attained menopause are however viewed as 'permanently clean'. Cf Tekena N. Tamuno, "Traditional Police in Nigeria" in E. A. Ade Adegbola (ed.) *Traditional Religion in West Africa* (Ibadan: Daystar Press, 1983), 184, see also S. I. Fabarebo, "Diversity of Sexual Morality: The Yoruba Experience" in Ade P. Dopamu, et al eds. *Issues in the Practice of Religion in Nigeria* (Jos: NASR, 2006), 364-374.

56. Matthew Omijeh, "The Significance of Orhue in Bini Symbolism" in *Traditional Religion in West Africa*, 195.

57. Bastide, 257.

58. Bastide, 328.

59. Bastide, 328.

60. Bastide, 328.

61. Bastide, 328.

62. E. Bolaji Idowu, *Olodumare: God in Yoruba Belief* (London: Longman, 1996), 145.

63. Laurenti Magesa, *The Moral Traditions of Abundant Life*, (Nairobi: Paulines, 1997), 41-44.

64. Kwasi Wiredu, *Philosophy and an African Culture* (London: Cambride, 1980), 6.

65. Benezet Bujo, *The Ethical Dimension of Community: The African Model and the Dialogue between North and South* (Nairobi: Paulines, 1998), 70.

66. Bolaji Idowu debunks the notion that Yoruba Religion does not have the sense of sin. According to him, though it might not have had a systematic way of expressing it, or that there was seeming lack of a 'theology' of sin; the very sense of guilt and the fear of judgment bring the sense of sin. He states that the Yoruba word, Ese carries the dual meaning of sin and offence whereas the word Eewo is more encompassing as it connotes breach of ritual laws, breaking taboos and "all acts of breach of moral law." See his *Olodumare: God in Yoruba Belief*, revised and enlarged version (Ikeja: Longman, 1996), 154-156.

67. E. O. Oloruntoba, A. O. Coker, A. O. Olowookere and M. K. C. Sridhar, "Gender Dimension of Household Solid Waste Management: A Comparative

Study of Two Cities in Southwestern Nigeria" in T. Falola and S. U. Fwatshak (eds.) *Beyond Tradition: African Women and Cultural Spaces* (Trenton: Africa World Press, 2011), 283.

68. Jacob K. Olupona, "Sacred Ambiguity: Global African Spirituality, Religious Tradition, social Capital and Self-reliance" in T. Babawale and A. Alao (eds.) *Global African Spirituality, Social Capital and Self-reliance in Africa* (Lagos: CBAAC, 2008), xvii.

* Segun Ogungbemi and Benson Igboin (2014) "A Philosophical Analysis of Yemoja in Cross Cultural Context" in *Beyond the Boundaries: Toyin Falola and the Art of Genre-Bending* (ed.) Nana Akua Amponsah, Trenton: Africa World Press, 675-695

CHAPTER 17
The Yoruba Philosophical Narratives Of Curses And Misfortunes

Introduction

The prime mover of the concept of curses and misfortunes or *forigbepe* in Yoruba language is Professor Toyin Falola. His original intention was to generate provocative discourse amongst scholars and intellectuals from the perspective of traditional Yoruba thought of moral and spiritual consequences of human behavior. I have used the word "forigbepe" interchangeably with curses and misfortunes. It is generally believed in Yoruba culture that nothing happens to an individual or group of individuals in life without a cause. In other words, nothing comes as mere accident without tracing it to its primordial, metaphysical and empirical causes. In my contribution to this narrative of *forigbepe* in Yoruba social, moral, spiritual and cultural space, I have attempted to do an analysis of the word, *"forigbepe"* to give it a philosophical clarity. Beyond the analysis, it is my intention to trace the sources of *forigbepe* from the primordial existence of beings i.e., Ori, Ajala and the generative beings namely, *omoaaraiye, elenini* and *alaroka*. The question is: can a *forigbepe* victim be rescued using propitiation mechanism to ward off the curse on him or her? There is no preponderance of evidence that any theological or orthodox medicine has efficacious potency to remedy the curse. Be that as it may, there are certain morally and epistemologically driven evidences that the concept of *forigbepe* must justify to prove its acceptability in modern and digital millennium. The justification is necessary to warrant the assertions credible enough to believe. The chapter concludes that the moral paradigm that is inherent in the narratives of *forigbepe* in Yoruba culture ought to serve as an essential moral compass in a world riddled with contradictory values, if we are to grow and flourish. And finally, is the concept of *forigbepe* a negative and positive virtue that is worth living with?

What is *forigbep*e in Yoruba?

The word "*forigbepe*" is a short form made from a sentence phrase, *fi ori gba epe* or *fo'ri gbe epe*, meaning literally, to use one's head to incur a curse. The important thing to note here is the significance of *ori* in one's life. According to Yoruba narratives of human existence nobody becomes anything in life without the vital force called ori. J. Omosade Awolalu explains:

> …when the Yoruba speak of Ori they mean something more than the physical head. They are referring to the personality-soul, which is believed to be capable of ruling, controlling, and guiding the life and activities of man. The people believe that success or failure in life depends on Ori and its quality. Generally, a fortunate person is called Olori-ire (one who possesses good ori) while one who is unfortunate in life is described as olori-buruku (one who possesses a bad ori).[1]

Wande Abimbola further digs this concept a little deeper when he writes about the binary nature of Ori, that: "Whatever the name by which predestination is known, it is always associated with Ori (the inner head). It is believed that the symbol of free choice is Ori (the inner head), which everyone received in heaven. A man's destiny, that is to say his success or failure in life, depends to a large extent on the type of head he chose in heaven…."[2] Thus he further notes the saying that:

> Eni t'o gbon,
>
> Ori e l'o ni ogbon,
>
> Eeyan ti o gbon.
>
> Ori e l'o ni o go j'usu lo,
>
> (He who is wise
>
> Is made wise by his Ori
>
> He who is not wise
>
> Is made more foolish than a piece of yam by his Ori).[3]

From the foregoing it is the *Ori* that is responsible for someone's choice in life and not the vice versa. Therefore *fori'gba ire* meaning use your *ori* to receive *ire*, a fortune, has a positive meaning, which nobody will reject. When however, *fori'gba* ends with the word *epe* (curse) no Yoruba will take delight in it because it signifies a bad omen or misfortune. That is why the Yoruba will reject *forigbepe* as his or her lot in life. If you tell a friend, *eo ni forigbepe l' aiye*, meaning, you will not incur a curse in your life, he will not hesitate to say *aase* Edumare. No reasonable person takes offense when a prayer of success is made for him but a negative one can damage a good relationship.

Background and Sources of *forigbepe*

The Yoruba mythological pantheon of beings provides metaphysical narratives of causes of successes and failures in the universal *beings*. Two essential categories of beings that are germane to this discourse are *Ori*, the essence of rational beings and *Ajala,* a crafty semi-divine being whose roles in human affairs in the primordial existence constitute an apt explanation of *forigbepe* in Yoruba social, religious and cultural spaces. Let me begin with *Ori* because the concept of *forigbepe* will have no meaning without it. It is on it that the whole discourse derives its significances or imports.

1. *Ori* is the self-conscious being with rational capacity to decide for himself or herself the choice of existence to live after living the super-sensible world, which is the abode of Olodumare, the Supreme Being and his lieutenant deities. Some prominent Yoruba scholars in the field of religion and theology namely, J. Olumide Lucas, E. Bolaji Idowu, J. Omosade Awolalu among others have written extensively about Olodumare who is often given a superlative expression as Olorun Olodumare, the Supreme Being or simply the Deity from whom *Ori* derives his or her existence. In the pre-existent life, *Ori* is a co-tenant with other beings and he owes his allegiance only to the Olodumare, the foundation of everything that is. From the perspective of Idowu the *Ori* has the prerogative freedom of choice to live either in the pantheon of the gods or to live in the universe of humans where you find individuals or group of individuals with diabolic characters or evil machinations.[4] The identity of individuals is therefore pre-ordained that is, good and evil. For instance, the good finds its characterization and expression of identity with *Ori* as *forigbade, forigbare* and the evil as *forigbepe*. All these will be explained later but from the foregoing, I have shown that we cannot make any proposition of *forigbepe* without recourse to Olodumare, the Supreme Being and *Ori* the choice maker of human identity and behavior.

2. *Ajala* is a crafty and dubious *being* that plays a pivotal role in our understanding of human afflictions i.e., *forigbepe*. According to Yoruba oral traditions and Professor 'Wande Abimbola, Ajala was the maker of *ori*, human destiny. On coming to this world everyone has to go through him to get his or her allotted destiny.[5] In Yoruba oral traditions Ajala has a disposition to know the heads that contain good and bad destiny. As one gets to him to make his choice, if Ajala is given some gratifications he will lead one to choose a good destiny but if one fails to give him any gratifications for instance a bribe or a gift, and goes to make a choice, there is a probability for one to choose a bad destiny and once it is made it cannot be returned.[6] It is not like going to Wal-Mart or Apple Stores to buy their products and for some reasons you make a change of mind and have them returned. In other words, if one chooses a destiny of *forigbepe* and he wants to return it no matter how hard one tries Ajala will not collect it. And however hard working he is, there lays somewhere misfortunes to ambush him. Is the myth shifting the blame of human imperfection from Olodumare to *Ajala*, a lesser semi-divine being? This will be examined later as we discuss reversibility and irreversibility of *forigbepe* a frustrating misfortune that can lead to psychological depression.

3. The gods, ancestors and elders can also be the sources of *forigbepe*, an eternal misfortune that is irremediable. Considering the role the gods supposedly played in the Yoruba concept of forigbepe, J. Olubi Sodipo notes, "It is generally believed that the gods take over too soon in the explanations of most African societies. Where in the scientific mode of thought an attempt will be made to push the application of general laws as far it can go, the African traditional thinker, it is argued, has an easy and premature recourse to the gods."[7] For instance, Malokun is a goddess in Ode Irele in Irele Local Government Area of Ondo State, Southwestern Nigeria whose action of retributive justice is illustrative of a moral concept of *forigbepe* in Yoruba thought. Niyi Akinnaso reports that in April 2015 there was an outbreak of mysterious deaths in the community.[8] At first nobody really knew what caused it. There were speculations that it was probably Ebola, one of the most deadly diseases in West Africa even though its threat to life has been eradicated. But the symptoms of this mysterious disease were headache, blurred sight, loss of consciousness, loss of weight and death within 24 hours. It is more deadly than Ebola. Investigation however revealed that a group of motorcycle riders in Ode Irele, Irele Local Government Area of Ondo State, Nigeria went to the shrine of the Malokun, a deity to remove its costume for sale in April 2015. According to Yoruba oral and written traditions of metaphysics of morals, it is sacrilegious and reprehensible to steal any parts of the costumes of a divinity in Yorubaland. For those who committed the heinous crime against the Malokun the punishment was

death. Akinnaso writes, "The deaths began to occur on Monday, April 13, 2015, but they were locally interpreted in terms of the vengeful anger of the Malokun god [goddess] at the desecration of its shrine by vandals, who looted and stole artifacts from it and opened its sacred eye to public glare."[9] Within six days it was reported that not less than 18 victims were dead. Of course, government officials and World Health Organization were not satisfied with the local narrative of its cause hence they made several attempts to give the mysterious deaths of the Malokun's victims a medical and scientific explanation. They argued that the victims probably died of pesticides or ethanol poisoning. People in the area however believed otherwise because the scientific explanation was a mere theoretical assumption. The local people living around the place informed me that there were some of the victims who confessed that they actual participated in stealing the artifacts of the Malokun for sale and consequently the goddess asked for pardon. Normally, in a situation like this the Yoruba elders in the community and the priests of the deity would have made some propitiation to appease Malokun to stop the untimely death of the victims and spare the community from public embarrassments. From this episode the youths would have learnt that the deity takes an exception to pervasive moral decadence. And anyone among them or any person for that matter that attempts to tamper with its shrine and artifacts again will get instant retributive justice. The concept of *forigbepe* found in the oral and literary cannons of the Yoruba is corroborated in the 20th century existentialist philosophy and the Christian holy book, the Bible. For instance, in Albert Camus' book, *The Myth of Sisyphus* in which Sisyphus the protagonist is illustrative of a divine curse. Sisyphus, we are told stole the secrets of the gods and they got annoyed and cursed him. Camus explains, "A decree of the gods necessary. Mercury came and seized the impudent man [Sisyphus] by the collar and, snatching him from his joys, led him forcibly back to the underworld, where his rock was ready for him."[10] Sisyphus is to roll the stone from the bottom of the mountain to the peak of it. And as soon as he puts the stone on the top of the mountain it rolls down the mountain.[11] You can imagine the kind of absurdity, frustration and hopelessness going on in the mind of Sisyphus and his burden of *forigbepe* an eternal punishment in Yoruba metaphysics of retributive justice. It is not only the gods that can cast a spell on humans but also the ancestors for example, in the Old Testament, (1Samuel 28:7-24) the story of King Saul who went to the Witch of Endor to invoke the spirit of Samuel and to elicit a divine support for victory over their enemies, the Philistines at the impending warfare. Samuel felt that King Saul did not need to disturb him in his grave having got enough evidence that Yahweh was not on his side since he did not obey the divine command to destroy all the Amalekites.

Samuel sanctioned Saul with a deterministic divine curse that ended his reign. Saul would have no reason whatsoever to ask Samuel for help given the historical engagement of competition for power and authority of office between two of them particularly when Saul usurped the sacerdotal role of Samuel by not waiting enough for the priest's arrival to offer a sacrifice. The King probably assumed that he could perform the exclusive duty of the priesthood even though there was separation of powers, the administration of the state was the responsibility of the King and the sacerdotal functions were the exclusive reserve of the priest. That was one of King Saul's sacrilegious crimes that caused his rejection as King of Israel (1 Samuel 13:7-14). For Saul to ignore the deep-seated hatred Samuel had for him when he was alive it was preposterous to seek help from the ancestor no matter the imperatives of the demand. Therefore what has happened to Saul in this narrative amounts to forigbepe in Yoruba thought.

The power to cast spells on disrespectful persons by highly placed elders in Yoruba society is well known.[12] It appears as if there is an unwritten moral code in Yoruba society that stipulates that elders are to be accorded their due respects regardless of the position one holds. Any violation of this rule could lead to a disastrous consequence of *forigbepe*. Let me give an hypothetical scenario of a rookie politician in Nigeria who decided to run for the post of president against an elderly veteran politician in his zone and was advised not to compete with the veteran politician but he was not persuaded or convinced that there was nothing to dissuade him from the race. It was not the competition between the rookie and veteran politician that caused a conflict of interest but the defamatory comments and the show of disrespect for an elder made the veteran politician to tell the rookie politician that he would never get to rule the country as president. The spell on the rookie politician came to reality when the rookie later in a few years later went to re-contest for the post of president and he had the majority support of the electorate but when he was about to be announced the winner the election was cancelled and he never became the president of his country before his death. Did he *forigbepe* or not? Of course, in Yoruba traditional thought he did because there is a mantra, which says, *aje ke la'na omo ku loni tani ko mope aje to ke la'na lo po'mo je*, which literally means, a witch cried yesterday and a child dies today, who does not know that the witch that cried yesterday was responsible for the death of the child? Similarly, the Ajala myth may be relevant here. As Abimbola recorded in the minor Odu, Ogbegunda, of the three individuals that were to make a choice of their Ori at Ajala's place, only one actually received the favor of Ajala and was able to choose a good one. That was the only one of the trio paid homage to his own father before approaching Ajala; the other two did not; they ignored their fathers and consequently missed out on divination and divine counsel, to their own perils, rotten Ori (ill fate), which haunted them throughout their abode on the earth.[13]

4. Human beings of certain categories called *Omo araye* and *Elenini* are conceived as personification of evils or simply regarded, as agents of evil that individuals are advised to avoid in life because if offended they are capable of making some to *forigbepe*. Idowu explains:

> *Omo ar'-aiye* and *Elenini* draw their power from the evil principle which is described comprehensively as *Aiye-* 'The World'. Here resides the concentrated power of evil.... In *aiye*, however, we meet unmitigated evil in its essence, malignant, obstructing, spoiling, and out-and-out diabolic. It is not at all clear from the oral traditions what will account for this 'power'.[14]

From the foregoing, *Omo ar'-aiye* and *Elenini* have some mysterious power of making sure that the spell of *forigbepe* is a thing that once inflicted on anyone the victim will not succeed in any endeavor or enterprise in life. Therefore in Yoruba traditional society parents warn their children to avoid them. If, however, one unavoidably gets in their way, one's parents are always advised on what to do so to ward off the spell. In most cases the propitiations may be in form of offering kola nuts, a fowl,[15] etc.

5. *Alaroka* is another terrible individual with evil machinations that can cause his victim to *forigbepe* if indeed the accusation he has alleged his victim of is true. If on the other hand the accusation is false, the spell invariably falls on his head. Generally, *Alaroka* is someone who is never satisfied with any good thing done for him or her. He is an ingrate but he does not see himself as one. He is constantly unsatisfied with the help rendered to him and goes through life unfairly casting those who have supported him as being obstructive and speaks ill of them. The Yoruba will say, *Ta' ba seni lo're ope la'du*, when translated; it means when someone is helped, the person is expected to show gratitude. Furthermore, the Yoruba have this saying, *Won ki fi'bi san fun olo're eni*. This means when someone has been of help to you, it is offensive to return the favor with an act of malevolence.

According to oral tradition, *ebo Oso iye se ru, ebo Aje iye seru, ebo Alaroka ko se ru*, (*Oso*- Sorcerer and *Aje*- Witch, if offended they can be appeased with a sacrifice but that of *Alaroka* is not appeasable). There is however another category of being of evil machinations which Kola Abimbola has identified in Yoruba thought system. He is Ajogun and his agents: "death, diseases, loss, paralysis, big trouble, curse, imprisonment and afflictions."[16]

In retrospect there are people in our lives we have had cause to call them *Alaroka* because they are never satisfied with little help they received from their benefactors. To describe someone as *Alaroka* is a form of stigmatization. It is a stereotype or profiling that nobody is comfortable with because it devalues the dignity and pride of the individual in the society. More so, it makes such an individual to be seen as irresponsible and untrustworthy to be associated with. If an *Alaroka* becomes a victim of his whims and caprices he carries his burden of *forigbepe* alone. The Yoruba will say it serves him right.

Moral and epistemological implications of *forigbepe*

The concept of *forigbepe* brings back the memory of moral device by which the Yoruba in their social, religious and cultural interactions emphasize the importance of respect and deep appreciation that enhances social relationships. Does this form of moral compass have relevance in contemporary society? Today, if something bad happens to an individual we are quick to define this as bad karma, as punishment for the bad acts the individual might have done. The theory of Karma harps on the Yoruba concept of *forigbepe*, Karma refers to the principle of causality, every action we produce will create an equal consequence. Thus, the people say, *"Bi o ba nidii obinrin kii je Kumolu"* (Without a probable cause, a woman would never bear the name Kumolu). Therefore, intentions of the individual can play a role in influencing the future of the individual. Producing good acts translates into good Karma and bad acts translate into bad Karma. When a Yoruba person goes through a rough patch of misfortune, he tries to trace his ill luck back to its origin, which in his mind could come from angering supernatural forces. If I don't succeed in any venture, could it be attributable to a probable curse from some reified divine, ancestors, elders etc? Or must I believe that there is some evil genius lurking behind to thwart my effort? Could it not be the case that perhaps, I have not got it right and therefore need to go back and reassess my methodological approach? To believe the veracity of the proposition of *forigbepe* one needs to consider its impact on human psyche. Can it lead to a psychological resignation and depression?[17] The Yoruba will admit that it is possible to lead to a psychic problem, but before it gets to such a critical stage, a proper atonement could have been made by the parents or relations of the victim to ward off the evil machination that is capable of tormenting him and save him from the haven of misfortunes. There is another dimension to the incurability of the victim of *forigbepe* i.e., the case of Sisyphus and King Saul. The two cases are a spiritual violation of taboos that cannot be treated as empirical truth in the universe of the mortal. What can be done is to give the stories an existential interpretation. For instance, the myth of Sisyphus according to Albert Camus is meant to teach us the futility of human existence. There is however an underlying existential question that the story raises that is, the meaning and purpose of life.

Given the influence of Christian religion in Yorubaland, using example of King Saul in the Bible will resonate the significance of *forigbepe*. What the writer of the book of 1 Samuel 28:3-25 did in the story was to pontificate between the man of God, the prophet and a disobedient King and put an end to their rivalry. It was a story of the consequences of the Israelites had to pay for rejecting theocracy and embracing monarchy as a system of governance.

There is an epistemological issue that the speech-act demonstrates in the narratives of *forigbepe* that need to be addressed. How do we determine that the words spoken, which carry the message of ill will, have the potency of cause and effect that is responsible for the fate of the victim? Here we are dealing with an epistemological discourse that is verifiable and believable. In other words, how does the speech-act of *forigbepe* work? Is it by accident or a mere coincidence or chance? If it is by a coincidence or chance it may not be credible to claim its veracity because it can be attributed to one of the random occurrences that happens in the body chemistry of the patient. And in that case it will require a medical scientific explanation to determine the cause. I am not saying that all diseases in human body can be explained empirically. Rather in orthodox medicine the pathological study of an ailment or a disease like Ebola or cancer has taken several years of investigation to unravel and yet the pathological studies continue as an unfinished job whereas the traditional causes of curses and misfortunes in Yoruba are taken as a matter of fact that need not be investigated beyond its metaphysical assumption.

The epistemological debate of *forigbepe* as a concept of retributive justice may not appeal to an individual who is vehemently bent on believing its cause and effect. To him the people who are seen to be suffering from *forigbepe* syndrome are sufficient evidence to believe its veracity. And more importantly, the Yoruba do not take the concept of *forigbepe* lightly when dealing with matters of success and failure in life. That is why the Yoruba will say, *awa ko'ni forigbepe la'ye* meaning; we will not encounter misfortunes in life. The same message resonates in Adeshina

Afolayan's contribution to the debate of *forigbepe* and concludes, "In spite of all these philosophical musings, *ori mi ko ni gb'epe o*!"[18] To which the Yoruba will say *at'emi na o*, meaning, including myself. Aase Edumare.

Let me say categorically that it is not only an individual alone that can suffer a monumental defeat of *forigbepe*. Therefore, I would like to divert my *forigbepe* dart at the leadership of Nigeria that has left those poor Chibok schoolgirls "naked in the amphitheater of life." If a father of the house is on seat and a frivolous bandit would have the audacity to invade the home and take away his girls, leaving only the mothers to cry and beat their chests in abject helplessness, that father is suffering from the feat of, and is a candidate for serious *forigbepe*, just as much as the abductor of his prized girls. If the father in the house and members of the household continue to live as if a major evil has not bedeviled their home, partying, chatting, campaigning, and laughing around in the public square, that family has truly incurred the curse of *forigbepe* upon itself. In my mind, until the girls, the symbol of peace, normalcy, continuity, procreation and fertility are returned home, life or dead, the home is jinxed and the anathema is irrevocable because "I buried my child" is a better declaration than "I lost my child." The former is a painful closure, while the latter is permanent stain of unforgivable filial irresponsibility. For Nigeria as a nation and Nigerians as a people not to be partakers of the *forigbepe*, the black smoke that hovers over the land, they must join hands to proactively seek and find the schoolgirls, other people's daughters, future, and the 800 pound-guerrilla that would not let the nation sleep! In the last few months the present administration at the centre appears to have woken up from its slumber and it has taken a more proactive onslaught on the insurgents in the northeast of Nigeria. Ikenna Emewu reports, "Since securing a six-week extension of the 2015 general elections date in February, Nigerian troops have essentially flushed out Boko Haram terrorists from the 21 local government areas that they occupied in three states of Adamawa, Borno and Yobe."[19] The attempt to secure all the people in the custody of Boko Haram by the Federal Government is rather coming too late considering the number of months that most of them have been in captivity and more importantly the Chibok schoolgirls. The question then was: would the Jonathan administration be able to secure the release of the schoolgirls before its term ends on May 29, 2015? Time will tell as Nigerians await the fulfillment of the promise made by the outgoing leadership of the present administration.

Conclusion

And finally, is the concept of *forigbepe* a negative and positive virtue that is worth living with? In Yoruba culture that lays emphasis on respect for the divine, ancestors and elders the concept of *forigbepe* as retributive justice explains its dimensional values as signposts for any rational being to observe and respect if she/he wants to succeed in life. The Yoruba concept of *Ori* as a determinant factor for who we are, what we are, and what we shall be which some scholars consider as destiny[20] explains pungently the metaphysical ethics of the people. In this metaphysics of morals there is an inherent existential use of freedom. Thus, the narratives of *forigbepe* have exemplified the pragmatic misuse and abuse of freedom, choice and action. In this modern pervasive morality and paradigm shift, the traditional institutions of the Yoruba have zero tolerance for it.

The case of the mysterious death of some youths who went to steal the artifacts of the Malokun in Ode Irele in April 2015 is instructive. Does the existence of Malokun in Ode Irele frustrate the maximization of human freedom in the community? What if Malokun does not exist, does it mean everything is possible? The same question is applicable to the existence of Olodumare, the Supreme Being from where all human beings and everything in existence derive their origin. If Olodumare does not exist, does it necessarily mean everything is permissible? In that case human beings will enjoy freedom unlimited. The reality of the case is that when an individual chooses a way of life that leads to *forigbepe* in Yorubaland, the choice affects not only him but also his immediate family, the community and humanity in general.

The implication of Yoruba narratives of metaphysics of morals is that human beings cannot live in a society where Olodumare and his ministerial agents, the gods are absent. It is expedient for man in Yoruba thought system to have the Deity and his divinities control the propelling inner forces of his existential unlimited freedom. And thereby rescue him from the Hobbesian state of nature where, human life is described as "solitary, poor, nasty, brutish, and short."[21]

Are the gods to blame for the victims of *forigbepe*? It is absurd to blame the gods for whatever happened to those who egregiously violated the moral code of conduct of the divine beings in their religious abodes, the shrines. The Yoruba call it *eewo,* a taboo. From an existential point of view, Jean-Paul Sartre argues that even though "man is condemned to be free,"[22] he is nevertheless responsible for his behavior.[23] From the perspective of existentialism of Sartre, the captivity of the Chibok schoolgirls by the Boko Haram insurgents and the inability of Nigerian leadership to proactively marshal positive means to release them cannot be blamed on the gods but on the captors and Nigerian leadership. May the release of the Chibok schoolgirls by the Nigerian troops come soon and save us from being partakers of *forigbepe*.

Notes and References

1. J. Omosade Awolalu, *Yoruba Beliefs and Sacrificial Rites* (London: Longman, 1979), 9

2. 'Wande Abimbola, *Ifa: An Exposition of Ifa Literary Corpus* (Oxford: Oxford University Press, 1976), 113.

3. 'Wande Abimbola, *Ifa: An Exposition of Ifa Literary Corpus*, 114.

4. E. Bolaji Idowu, *Olodumare: God in Yoruba Belief* (London: Longman, 1962), 174.

5. 'Wande Abimbola, *Ifa: An Exposition of Ifa Literary Corpus*, 116.

6. Cf. 'Wande Abimbola, *Ifa: An Exposition of Ifa Literary Corpus*, 117.

7. J. Olubi Sodipo, "Notes on the Concept of Cause and Chance in Yoruba Traditional Thought" in *Philosophy and the African Prospect*, ed. Ayo Fadahunsi and Olusegun Oladipo, (Ibadan: Hope Publications, 2004), 86.

8. Niyi Akinnaso, "'Mystery' deaths: Ondo State is Safe," *The Punch*, April 21, 2015, 64.

9. Niyi Akinnaso, "'Mystery' deaths: Ondo State is Safe," 64.

10. Albert Camus, *The Myth of Sisyphus and Other Essays*, (New York: Vintage International, 1983), 120.

11. Albert Camus, *The Myth of Sisyphus and Other Essays*, 120-121.

12. See Deji Ayegboyin, "Epe (oath of cursing), Egun (generational curse), Ati (and Itusile (deliverance) Ni Oruko Re (in His Name)" in *Under the Shelter of Olodumare*, ed. S. Oyin Abogunrin and I. Deji Ayegboyin, (Ibadan: John Archers, 2014), 200.

13. See 'Wande Abimbola, *Ifa: An Exposition of Ifa Literary Corpus*, 117-118.

14. E. Bolaji Idowu, *Olodumare: God in Yoruba Belief*, 178.

15. See Deji Ayegboyin, "Epe (oath of cursing), Egun (generational curse), Ati (and Itusile (deliverance) Ni Oruko Re (in His Name)" in *Under the Shelter of Olodumare*, ed. S. Oyin Abogunrin and I. Deji Ayegboyin, 202.

16. Kola Abimbola, *Yoruba Culture*, (Birmingham: Iroko Academic Publishers, 2006), 70.

17. Kwasi Wiredu, *Philosophy in an African Culture*, (Cambridge: Cambridge University Press, 1980), 17.

18. See toyinfalola@austin.utexas.edu, Adeshina Afolayan, Re: *Forigbepe*, March 20, 2015.

19. Ikenna Emewu, "Shekau's Whereabouts Unknown, Says Military," *Daily Sun*, Friday, April 24, 2015, 10

20. cf. Jacob K. Olupona, *City of 201 Gods Ile-Ife in Time, Space and the Imagination*, (Berkeley: University of California Press, 2011), 71.

21. Thomas Hobbes, *Leviathan*, (London: Collier Books, 1978), 100.

22. Jean-Paul Sartre, *Existentialism is Humanism*, (New Haven: Yale University Press, 2007), 29.

23. See Jean-Paul Sartre, *Existentialism is Humanism*, 24-25.

CHAPTER 18

Death, Immortality **And Morality**

Introduction

Death has been something that human beings do not want to talk about but in reality there is nothing in human existence that is as real as death. To all human beings, death of relations and friends brings sadness but generally, death of enemies brings jubilation. The reality of this was what happened on September 11, 2001 when the terrorists attacked the World Trade Center in New York, the Pentagon in Washington and Pennsylvania in the United States of America. The death toll from the senseless and heinous attacks on innocent individuals was over 3000. Osama bin Laden, a fanatic Muslim and his Al Qaeda group claimed responsibility for the attack with jubilation while the rest of the world mourned. As I watched the tragic incident on the television on that day, I could not fathom any rational and moral justification for such a barbaric act. We remember and mourn the loved ones and even those we did not know because we value human life and regard it as sacred. Beyond this remembrance, there is this constant concern about death which brings an end to human existence but we don't feel comfortable discussing it. Is death such an evil that we don't want to talk about it or we are simply afraid of it? Or is it a moral good that we keep in our conscious and sub-conscious mind and we only talk about it at will? Does death serve any useful purpose in human life? Can human beings overcome death? Or is death part of human existence, which makes it inevitable? Is there any moral justification for death? There are many questions that the issue of death raises in our mind, which we cannot possibly answer because of the nature of our finitude.

Be that as it may, I have a compelling urge to consider a moral challenge that death poses. In pursuing this objective, it is necessary to consider the origin and nature of death, the attitude of man to death and its moral justification.

Origin and nature of death

Every human society has its own story of the origin of death. There is a saying that charity begins at home, so if there is any social environment that I am most conversant with, it is that of the Yoruba, South West of Nigeria. Writing on man's final destiny in Yoruba cultural and religious belief E. Bolaji Idowu explains:

> The common, orthodox is that *Iku* is a creation of Olodumare: he was made for the specific purpose of recalling any person whose time on earth is fulfilled. Hence he is known as *Ojise Orun* -"Heaven's Bailiff". When they think of death as "dying", then they describe it as a "debt"- the debt which everyone must pay. This is as much as to say that death is the inevitable and ultimate lot of every person who comes into the world.[1]

What Idowu is saying, it seems to me, is that Olodumare, the Supreme Being in his own creation of things made death as part of his creation. In other words, death is part of the Supreme Being's order of beings in terms of what constitutes creatureliness. Therefore, death cannot be isolated from the totality of the creation of things. It necessarily follows that all human beings metaphorically put on the garment of death. If that be the case, the Yoruba believe that death ought not to be seen or conceived as evil. Furthermore there is no need for humans to fear death because it is part of human nature.

The Yoruba also have another myth about the origin of death, which Idowu thinks it is not the orthodox belief of the people. He writes:

> *Iku's* mother was killed
>
> In Ejigbo-Mekun market:
>
> *Iku* heard it in the house,
>
> *Iku* screeched like the *agon* of Il'oye,
>
> *Iku* rang out like *arawo's* egg;
>
> He made cobra his spurs,
>
> He made boas his shoes,

He made scorpions his gardle;

Iku fell upon the Locus Bean Tree,

The Locus Bean Tree fell prone to the ground;

Iku fell upon the White Silk Cotton Tree,

The White Silk Cotton fell prone to the ground.[2]

While Idowu believes that in Yoruba traditional belief, the Supreme Being is responsible for the existence of death and its nature is to kill or recall anyone whose time has expired on earth whether the person is ready or not, like a diplomat serving in a foreign country. Olatunde B. Lawuyi and J. K. Olupona counter that position:

> An image of a nurturant death is raised in this myth, which Idowu has dismissed 'not the orthodox belief of the Yoruba about the origin of Death.' He could not understand the idea of Death as not responsible for death and consequently dismissed the significance of native metaphors and opted for the more seemingly Christian or Western influenced philosophy that construes Death as a lieutenant of the Supreme God, Olodumare.[3]

It seems to me that Lawuyi and Olupona misunderstood the hermeneutics of Yoruba traditional mythology of the origin about death which Idowu has brilliantly espoused. What could have informed Idowu in rejecting the second myth about the origin of death is because of the preponderant opinion among the Yoruba that Olodumare, the Supreme Deity is responsible for the creation of everything that is and without him nothing can have its independent existence. The idea of justice that Death has no recourse to before embarking on avenging the death of his mother goes contrary to the nature of the Supreme Being. In Yoruba society, before anyone is given capital punishment for an offence committed by an unknown person, there is generally a thorough investigation and nobody is expected to be punished until the culprit is found and guilt established. So what Death has done to avenge the death of his mother without investigation amounts to injustice. It is therefore more plausible to believe that the mythology of the origin about death which Idowu has explained is indeed the most orthodox than any scholar can postulate. As a matter of fact, the philosophy behind the position of Idowu, it seems to me, has nothing to do with Western or Christian influence as charged by Lawuyi and Olupona. One wonders why anyone would suggest that Yoruba traditional thought of the origin of death is not authentic in its own right simply because a scholar who espoused it is either a Christian or he has studied Western philosophy or both. It must be understood that the issue of death is a phenomenon that generally baffles the imagination of man. Therefore one should not be surprised to find some similarities in their philosophical assumptions of how it came to being. And when that happens one should not necessarily conclude that one tradition has borrowed or influenced by the other.

Let us find out from another tradition the explanation of the origin and nature of death. In the Christian tradition, the Bible is the most authoritative document that gives lucid information on how death came to be the portion of man. In the book of Genesis chapters 2 and 3, we have the dramatic account of man's predicament in the irresistible hand of his Creator, Yahweh. The Hebraic author of the Pentateuch presents a mythological Adam and Eve who were living a solitary life in the serene garden of confinement given to them by their Creator with a caveat, "You are free to eat from any tree in the garden; but you must not eat from the tree of knowledge of good and evil, for when you eat of it you will surely die." The death threat given to Adam made him to be religiously obedient to his Creator. But when Adam got married, his orientation changed. The woman that was given to him by God ate the forbidden fruit which they had been told not to eat. So when her husband came from where he went within the garden she gave him the forbidden fruit and he ate and both of them knew that they were naked. Since God could not tolerate the divided loyalty of Adam and his wife, they were both expelled from the garden. The attitude of God towards Adam and his wife is morally worrisome. God did not give them a warning since that was their first offence ,which ordinarily a natural father could have done. Worst still, God did not want the man to redeem himself by taking a second bite of the tree of life to escape the death penalty that was hanging on him and his wife. They were eternally banished from the eternal Garden of Eden. As from that time onward, death has become an inevitable lot of man. According to *The Woman's Bible,* Eve was not afraid of death, she preferred knowledge to death. "Then the woman fearless of death if she can gain wisdom takes of the fruit; and all this time Adam standing beside her interposes no word of objection."[4] To blame Adam for what happened in the Garden of Eden one must first note that, in fairness to the man, the author of the Pentateuch did not tell us that he needed a woman. And when the woman was made out of his body he was not notified of the intention of God before the surgical operation that produced the woman. Perhaps, Adam was aware of the consequences of rejecting a free gift from his Maker if not he could have turned down the offer. Having been in a solitary confinement for a long period of time, perhaps Adam was carried away by the excitement of the presence of a companion. Adam was probably not aware that the generous gift from his Maker would lead to his downfall and the consequent expulsion from his eternal blissful garden. The solace that emanates from this dramatic episode of the origin of death is the idea that Eve in Hebrew language means Life. "She was Life, the eternal mother, the first representative of the more valuable and important half of the human race."[5] In spite of the positive view expressed by some scholars of what has become a blessing in disguise of the Hebraic myth about the origin of death, one is quick to ask, can God be exonerated from the downfall of man? Or was it not the intention of God to make Adam and Eve to be free from the pangs of death. St. Augustine in his book, *The City of God* explains:

> For God did not create men in the same condition as the Angels, completely incapable of death, even if they sinned. The condition of human beings was such that if they continued in perfect obedience they would be granted the immortality of the angels and an eternity of bliss, without the interposition of death, whereas if disobedient they would be justly condemned to the punishment of death.[6]

If it were true that in the wisdom of God human beings were created in such a way that death is inevitable for them as explained by St. Augustine, then it necessary follows that Adam and Eve could not be morally blamed for what happened in the garden of Eden. From a moral perspective Bertrand Russell argues:

> If I were going to beget a child knowing that the child was going to be a homicidal maniac, I should be responsible for his crimes. If God knew in advance the sins of which man would be guilty, He was clearly responsible for all the consequences of those sins when He decided to create man.[7]

Considering God who is omniscient, omnipotent, benevolent etc; the haste he took to eject his tenants from their abode because of one offence casts doubt on his ability to have those attributes. It could be the case that man does not know for sure how death came to being. It is also probable that because man does not know for real who God is, it is therefore easy for him to attribute the source of his tragedy to a Being who is higher than himself. After all God cannot be invited to defend himself. The philosophical and moral stance of Russell and what I have said above may not be persuasive or convincing to those who hold tenaciously to the unquestionable nature of their religious traditions. But the truth of the matter is that the origin of death remains a mystery which is yet to be unraveled. Meanwhile let us consider some of the attitudes of man to death.

Traditional/Religious Attitude

Generally, Africans like any other race in the universe know that no matter how hard they try to prolong their longevity it will end in futility because death is not a respecter of any race, colour, age, status, etc. Death makes the decision to take anyone at will whether human beings like it or not. That is why the Yoruba say, all humans wear the garment of death. To traditional Africans however, death is not the end of man. J. Omosade Awolalu and P. Adelumo Dopamu write:

> That death is not the final end and does not write *finis* to the life of man, that death is only a transition from the physical world to the spirit world, and that the deceased is only making a journey from this earth to another place, is seen in the funeral arrangements and burial. The corpse is thoroughly washed; it is laid in state in very good costly cloths in preparation for the journey. It is believed that the deceased is being made ready and fit for the next world.[8]

Although in traditional Africa, death is not conceived as the end of man, it nevertheless brings sorrow to those that are left behind when it takes away their beloved ones. Some scholars in African traditional beliefs have argued that it is not the case that every death is mourned in most African societies. As a matter of fact there are two categories of death namely, good and bad death. In general terms they can be classified as natural and unnatural death.[9] Let us begin with the good death. Awolalu and Dopamu explain.

> The good death is that which comes when one lives to a ripe old age. Although death itself is always regarded as uncanny and disturbing, the death of an aged person is an occasion of much rejoicing, and the ritual elaboration is heaviest at their funeral, since people see nothing tragic about it. Also, there are occasions when the death of a young man or woman is not considered totally bad. Such a person must have lived an exemplary and good life and must have left behind children. People believe that he or she will have a good place in the abode of the spirits. And although they mourn the death, they still give it a befitting burial.[10]

If Africans recognize good death and give the victims all the necessary burial rites, one wonders what happens to the victims of bad death. The answer to this question is not far fetched. The answer is inherent in who are the victims of bad death. According to Awolalu, "Children and youths who die a premature death, barren women, and all who die a 'bad' death – e.g. killed by Ayelala or Sango or Soponno…"[11] cannot be accorded the kind of dignified burial rites as witnessed in the case of those who died a good death. What this means is that those who do not die a natural death are discriminated against instead of being given a dignified last respect. A moral and religious justification for such a practice is embedded in fear and ignorance. Fear and ignorance in the sense that if the deceased were not given a befitting burial, the divinities or the ancestral spirits concerned would punish the people while on earth. According to John S. Mbiti however, "…modern change tends to make such burial procedures more even or similar for everybody."[12] Since modern civilization has brought about that change from what Mbiti has said, have Africans experienced any negative reprisals? We may not be able to give adequate answer to this question because we do not live among most of the rural people. But it is fair to say that if such obnoxious practice still continues in any parts of Africa with the level of awareness and impact of communication the governments of those areas would have dealt with it.

Christianity offers another dimension of religious attitude to death. This dimension was introduced to Christendom by St. Paul. In 1 Corinthians 15: 54-56 Paul argues:

> …Death has been swallowed up in victory.
>
> Where, O death is your victory?
>
> Where, O death, is your sting?
>
> The sting of death is sin, and the power of sin is the law. But thanks be to God! He gives us the victory through our Lord Jesus Christ.

As a religious spectator who has witnessed the death of many Christians, one of the questions that come to mind is, must one take the above statement of Paul in its face value? In other words, have the followers or believers in Christ overcome death? Considering our daily experiences of the religious attitude of Christians to death and the above assurance given by Paul, hardly could you find any of them who are ready to die. As a matter of fact Jesus the Christ that Paul claimed to have given his followers the victory over death was actually a victim of death. No wonder therefore in the real sense of the matter, Christians like any other human beings if given the option to die or not to die, would invariably choose the latter. This reminds me of the story my former teacher, Louis Pojman told us in class at University of Texas at Dallas concerning the attitude of his former students at University of Notre Dame to death and the hereafter. The University of Notre Dame is a Catholic institution in the United States and so most of the students if not all are Christians. Given the kind of the promise that Jesus the Christ gave to his followers of his victory over death which Paul has reechoed above, Pojman asked, "How many of you are ready to die now? No hand was raised." I have another example that is germane to this discussion. We have all witnessed, I believe, occasions where Christian parents have a long battle with illnesses of their children and after they have done what was reasonable and humanly expected of them the children died. Let me give a personal experience that I have witnessed. Sometime in 1971, in Ilorin a devoted Christian couple had a miserable experience when their only child became critically ill and needed help to keep the child alive. Ministers and Church members came to show their concern for the child and as one of the ministers took her and began to pray for the recovery of the child, her eyes began to close gradually, the feet became colder and just before the benediction was given, she gave up. The weeping, crying and wailing of the parents, relations, and friends couldn't bring the child back. Has death not shown his victory? Was Jesus the Christ and even Paul not the victims of death? Of course Christians would say that what Paul has said should not be interpreted literally as I have done. What Paul has said is eschatological. At the initial stage when Jesus told his disciples that some of them would not see death before his second coming, it was taken literally but when they realized that it was not so, hence this futuristic interpretation. The eschatological hope that death is not the end of man has enabled Christians to cope psychologically with the loss of the loved ones. The moral choice to believe it as truth and to live according to its religious expectation becomes imperative for those who believe in Christ. We cannot undermine the moral and psychological import of this eschatological hope that is inherent in religious traditions but that does not obliterate the empirical fact that death still remains one of the greatest enemies of man. It seems to me that there is no substantial evidence of an apparent and lasting moral justification for the ravaging threat of death to man which can be found in any religion.

Philosophical Attitude

In *Phaedo* of Plato, we have a comprehensive view of Socrates about death. Socrates raised a rhetorical question to elucidate his own understanding of death. "Is death nothing more or less than this, the separate condition of the body by itself when it is released from the soul, and the separate condition by itself of the soul when released from the body?"[13] To Socrates, the body is the prison house of the soul and at death the soul gains its freedom. Socrates explains:

… the desire to free the soul is found chiefly, or rather only in the

> true philosopher. In fact the philosopher's occupation consists precisely in the freeing and separation of soul from body....if a man has trained himself through-out his life to live in a state as close as possible to death, would it not be ridiculous for him to be distressed when death comes to him?[14]

From the above quotation, is Socrates suggesting that a philosopher's responsibility is to willingly terminate his life? I don't think so because Socrates was of the view that it is the responsibility of God to call every individual at his own time and until that is done; it is not morally justified for anyone to put an end to his life. What Socrates was saying, it seems to me, is that we should not fear death as if it is the end of man. In other words, man must not see death as tragic but as a means of self-emancipation and a transition to the next life. Socrates actually demonstrated this stance when he was sentenced to death by the authority of Athens and his friends went to persuade him to jump bail like some Nigerian leaders had done in recent times but he remained resolute in his moral belief that it was morally wrong to do so. Furthermore, Socrates as a teacher of moral values, to escape from prison would contradict his philosophy of practicing what one teaches. To practice what one teaches is a quality of good leadership which Socrates was not ready to compromise even at death. When he was given the poison to drink, he told his friends not to feel sad and he offered a prayer to the gods. "But I suppose I am allowed, or bound, to pray the gods that my removal from this world to the other may be prosperous. This is my prayer, then, and I hope that it may be granted."[15] The courage to practice what one teaches as demonstrated by Socrates even at the point of death made him to be regarded as the father of Western moral philosophy. His view about the composite nature of man as body and soul and the latter has an independent existence after this life lacks concrete evidence to substantiate it. His last prayer as quoted above reveals uncertainty about his future existence. It is no surprise that other philosophers like Democritus and Epicurus conceived man as purely a material substance. Although Epicurus agreed that human beings and all other living beings have souls they are nevertheless regarded as soul atoms.[16] Avrum Stroll and Richard H. Popkin explain:

> When a person or an animal died, all that happened was that his soul atoms departed from the arrangement or collection that constituted the living being, leaving only the regular atoms. The soul atoms would then be gathered up into another collection, and hence another living creature would come into being. The soul atoms, like any others, could be neither created nor destroyed. But

combinations that contained them could be changed, giving rise to the apparent phenomenon of the life and death cycle among living things.[17]

If it were true that humans were nothing but a collection of atoms and death is the dissolution of the material atoms then what happens to their hope of reward and punishment in the hereafter? Is life nothing but a recycling commodity that is propelled by death without moral values? What then is the basis of moral responsibilities that bind human beings together? Are human beings not determined? And if that be the case, humans have no control over the way and manner they live. The credibility of the Epicurean materialistic view of human existence and the significance of death to that existence is to dissuade people from casting their hope on unrealizable objectives beyond this mortal life. That is why the Epicureans believe that we should be this-worldly and not other-worldly. Oruka Rang'inya a Kenyan natural philosopher has an insightful concept of death that is relevant to man's attitude to death. He explains:

> …death is not necessarily a bad phenomenon, for it is nature's way and means of easing congestion in the universe. So, if death did not remove some people, other people would not have enough, in the terms of food and land to live on. Upon death, we must accept that man's existence ceases therefore the only other possible life is a dream….the dead are in the wind; not in the sky or heaven or anywhere else for that matter. The dead and the living are therefore in the same one known world of the here and now.[18]

Rang'inya has given us a materialistic expression of not only what death is but also the final estate of man. His position embraces a rational and moral justification for death with a deep consideration for environmental conservation. To Rang'inya, death is a concomitant of being human. If that be the case, death is natural and nothing is wrong about it. Man must brace up to meet his death with courage because at death he has not lost everything, he remains part of this terrestrial world. In short, given the position of Rang'inya, man must not fear death. It is just and equitable to have consideration for others so that they too can have a share of the gift of the natural world. Given this rational and moral concern then death is not evil.

There are some philosophers who have argued that death is evil in the sense that it robs us our social and moral values that we have worked hard for. Russell argues, "All the labor of the ages, all devotions, all inspirations, all the noon day brightness of human genius, are destined to extinction in the vast death achievement must inevitably be buried beneath the debris of a universe in ruins."[19] Pojman also writes:

> But in death all our desires are frustrated. All that we value is separated from us. We are removed permanently from all we value: our loved ones, conscious experience, our work, beauty, creativity, pleasure and the like. Hence it seems that death must be seen as both natural and as that which will be feared so long as people have goals and recognize the Grand Frustrator that death is.[20]

The above quotations from Russell and Pojman if juxtaposed with Rang'inya will indict them and those who hold their views as social and moral egoists because nature was not designed for a perpetual and sit tight human beings who do not want to die. Death therefore emancipates the natural environment from being overstretched by all living things including humans.

Biomedical/Scientific Attitude

Let me say from the onset that I am not a specialist in this field. My study of science and biomedical technology grew out of interest and curiosity of mind because of its relationship to ethics. The works of Leon R. Kass, Tom L. Beauchamp, LeRoy Walters, Joseph Fletcher, Paul Ramsey among others have influenced my study. Contemporary science and biomedical researches consider the threat of death and how to deal with it in such a way that those who can afford the cost can have a prolonged longevity. To start with, we need to know what biomedical technology is all about. According to Kass:

> The biomedical technology can be usefully organized into three groups, according to their major purpose: (1) control of death and life, (2) control of human potentialities, and (3) control of human achievement. The corresponding technologies are (1) medicine, especially the arts of prolonging life and of controlling reproduction (2) genetic engineering, and (3) neurological and psychological manipulation.[21]

The general purpose and value of what Kass has said above is that man is developing the kind of scientific and biomedical means to enhance his quality of life and to prolong longevity. We are concerned about the effort of man to control and overcome death. In this regard Kass writes, "The real challenge to death will come from research into aging and senescence, a field just entering puberty. Recent studies suggest that aging is genetically controlled process, distinct from disease, but one that can be manipulated and altered by diet or drug."[22]

The question is, can man ever achieve his plan to overcome death? The answer is, let us wait and see the power of human knowledge to unravel the secret of death. We need all the necessary knowledge at man's disposal to wage unrelenting war against the ravaging power of death. But at what cost will it be? Will the answer be the end justifies the means? What will be the effect of the success of man over death on the ecology bearing in mind of the population growth that it will engender? Will all human beings benefit from it? Or will it be on a cash and carry basis? Which means only those who have the means will be the beneficiaries of the new biomedical technology of 'thou shalt not die'. The questions that I have raised are a reflection on the morality of this new medical technology that cannot be wished away. Experience has shown that the world as we know it today is divided between the rich and the poor, the developed and developing nations. The biomedical research that wants to ameliorate human suffering and to overcome death is undertaken primarily by the industrialized nations. Judging by what we know about human nature and the greed for power and the arrogance associated with its use, unless a holistic study of the genes is done so that all forms of human character that defy reason is modified, then there cannot be any assurance that such a knowledge will not be abused.

It will require a political and moral will on the part of the world leaders to assuage this fear. Before a permanent solution is found to the negative impact of death, man remains helpless.

Conclusion

I began the discourse on death with an event that shook the whole world, which took place in the United States of America that has been christened September 11. I remember the event as if it happened yesterday. The love for all humanity beckons on all men and women who have moral consciousness to have a reflection on the episode. As I conclude my view on death which touches my rational and moral nerves, I cannot but remember my departed loved ones namely, my parents, sister – Marion Titus, mentors and friends, Louis Pojman, Robert P. Armstrong and some of our contemporary African philosophers, Peter Bodunrin, H. Odera Oruka, J. Olubi Sodipo, C.S.Momoh, Samuel Ade Ali among others. Whenever I remember my loved ones, the moral issue of death becomes a philosophical obsession. Marcus Aurelius a Stoic philosopher has argued that we should not be disturbed by the threat of death because that is the cause of nature. As rich people die so also the poor, old and young, educated and uneducated, etc. So death is not a respecter of anyone, it strikes like a thunder bolt at wills whether the victim is ready or not. Above all death cannot be bribed and it does not take ransom. As birth is an entrance to life so is death its exit. We cannot have birth as entrance to life without death as its exit. Since we don't see any moral evil for being born to this world, it necessarily follows that we shouldn't raise the question of moral justification for leaving it. And nature has made death the means of exit of all living things including human beings. It is interesting to note that when a child is born it calls for celebration but when a child dies we mourn the loss.

We consider death, as evil because it does not satisfy our self desires hence, the moral question which man has been grappling with. It is that which has made modern man to seek solution to the menace of death through science and biomedical technology. Is man playing God? If man can remake himself and gain freedom from anything that will inhibit his desires which death is, it seems to me that there is nothing morally wrong about it. After all Adam and Eve were told in the mythical Garden of Eden that if they ate the forbidden fruit, they would know good and evil and they would be like gods. What that entails philosophically is that man has the rational capacity to improve himself positively whichever way he can. Although conscious effort is being made in the developed countries to remake man so as to free him from death, many African countries south of Sahara excluding South Africa for several decades have been busy waging senseless wars against themselves instead of saving lives and pursue the course of peace which is a necessary condition for development.

Unless African leadership takes a proactive role by funding biomedical research rather than stealing public funds that are meant for development and healthcare delivery, the war against death that is currently being undertaken by the developed countries if won, will in my mind, put African race at a disproportional advantage. If nothing is urgently done, Africans will be left with the mythical or metaphysical romance of belief in the spirit world of their ancestors. But the truth of the matter is that we have no empirical proof that it is self evident to substantiate the existence of after life including the spirit world of the ancestors; where nobody has gone and come back to tell us how the hereafter looks. And those who claim that there is immortality are not willing to go in spite of suffering and hardship in this world particularly in Africa. Meanwhile, why can't we take a philosophical counsel of Rang'inya that death is a necessity for man so that natural environment can be decongested of human population which on the whole it will be to the best interest of man? As humans die they are replaced by their offspring who have to depend on the environment for nurture and development. To take this course of looking at death it means man is determined and it is futile to take any course of action that will challenge it. This view as we have seen is totally unacceptable to a man of scientific and biomedical orientation. Man must strive to free himself from the shackle of death because he has moral justification to eternal existence on the planet earth that has been the best environment he is conversant with. If a man of science and biomedical mind is able to overcome death, I foresee in future he will say like Martin Luther King Jr. we are free at last. He is certainly free at last not from the bondage of racism that Martin Luther King Jr. was talking about but from the carnage of death that has been the enemy of human beings and all other living things.

Notes and References

1. E. Bolaji Idowu, *Olodumare God in Yoruba Belief* (London: Longman, 1975), p.187.

2. Ibid; p.187.

3. Olatunde B. Lawuyi and J.K. Olupona, "Metaphoric Associations and the Conception of Death: Analysis of Yoruba World View" *Journal of Religion in Africa*, Vol. Xviii/1 (1988), p.2.

4. Elizabeth Cady Stanton, *The Woman's Bible* (Seattle: Coalition Task Force, 1974), p. 26.

5. Ibid; p. 27.

6. St. Augustine, *City of God* (London: Cox & Wyman, 1976), p.510.

7. [7]Bertrand Russell, *Why I am not a Christian* (New York: Touchstone Book, 1957), p. 29.

8. J. Omosade Awolalu and P. Adelumo Dopamu, *West African Traditional Religion* (Ibadan: Onibonoje Press, 1979), p.256.

9. See Segun Ogungbemi, *A Critique of African Cultural Beliefs* (Ikeja: Pumark Educational Publishers, 1997).pp.70-76.

10. Awolalu and Dopamu, *op.cit*, pp.254-255.

11. J. Omosade Awolalu, *Yoruba Beliefs and Sacrificial Rites* (London: Longman, 1979), p.54.

12. John S. Mbiti, *African Religions and Philosophy* (Garden City: Anchor Books, 1970), p.208.

13. Edith Hamilton and Huntington Cairns (ed) *Plato* (Princeton: Princeton University Press, 1982), p. 47.

14. Ibid; p. 50.

15. Ibid; p. 97.

16. Avrum Stroll & Richard H. Popkin, *Introduction to Philosophy* (New York: Holt, Rinehart and Winston, 1979), p. 121.

17. Ibid; p.121-122.

18. H. Odera Oruka, *Sage Philosophy* (Nairobi: African Centre for Technology Studies, 1991), p. 244.

19. Encyclopedia of Philosophy 3&4 "Life Meaning and Value" ed. Paul Edward.

20. Louis Pojman, *Moral Values and the Meaning of Life* (Swindon: The Waterleaf Press,1978), p.9.

21. A. K. Bierman & James A. Gould, *Philosophy for a New Generation* (New York: Macmillan, 1977), p. 186.

22. Ibid; p.186.

CHAPTER 19

Towards The Perfectibility Of Man And Its Challenge To Africa

Introduction

The idea of perfectibility of man is as old as man himself. The issue is that since man is a finite being, is it feasible for him to be perfect? Perhaps, one needs to ask what perfectibility is and what are the necessary and sufficient conditions to meet in order to reach its goal and objective? There are those who hold tenaciously to the belief that man is perfectible and there are those who hold the opposing view. Those who believe that man is perfectible are called perfectibilists and those who deny it are called anti-perfectibilists. I want to argue in support of the perfectibilist position. My argument is based on the fact that philosophy, science and technology have clearly demonstrated that human perfection is possible. But in my view, to reach that level of perfection is a process since man has the capacity and capability to manipulate himself and his natural environment to enhance his well being. The means to achieve process-perfectibility is through education. The type of education that can make perfectibility possible in this century, it seems to me, is the one that embraces philosophy, science and technology. My argument will become more explicit as I analyse the nature and other dimensions of human perfectibility.

The Nature of Human Perfectibility

One of the functions of philosophy is to clarify terms or words for better understanding and communication. When a term is defined within an argument, one can follow the logic of the argument and see whether it is coherent or not.

But when a term is not defined within an argument, there is a general tendency to have unnecessary disagreement and confusion. And when that happens, one is not communicating. In order to avoid the ambiguous use of the term or word, it is necessary to know what perfectibility means within the context of our usage. The word, 'perfectibility' derives from the word 'perfect'. But the word, 'perfect' as currently being used in English language has its etymological background. John Passmore explains:

> Indeed, the Greek word teleos, commonly translated as perfect, is etymologically related to teleos (end) - the relationship between perfection and the achievement of an end is, as it were, written into it. The English word 'perfect', however ultimately derives, by way of Middle English, from the Latin word perficere, the roots of which, in turn, are facere, to make, and a prefix per suggesting 'thoroughly'. The perfect, that is, is etymologically definable as the 'thoroughly made' or the completed. Between the definition of perfection in terms of ends and the definition of it in terms of the 'thoroughly made' or the "complete" there are, of course, close links. If a thing is badly made or incomplete, it may, in consequence, be unable to fulfill its function.[1]

There is, however, another dimension to the definition of perfection which is worth considering. According to J.H Newman, something is perfect, if and only if, it has no flaw, or it is complete, consistent and sound.[2] From this definition, Passmore explains that perfection construed thus has nothing to do with an end. He writes: "...One can simply look at a person and describe him as perfect by seeing him to be free of flaws. 'Perfect,' in this sense, is an adjective applying to objects, to persons, to states, not (necessarily) to the performance of tasks or to the ends towards which those performances are directed."[3]

The above definitions of the word 'perfect' where perfectibility is derived, suggest that there is no definition that is not relative based on the particular background of its origin. How then is perfectibility defined? According to Dagobert D. Runes, the word, 'perfectibility' can be properly construed as having to do with morality. He defines perfectibility as, "The optimistic belief in the ability of man to attain an eventual complete realization of his moral possibilities." [4]

What Runes defines as perfectibility as man's ability to realize his 'moral possibilities' amounts to what is called "perfecting man" through moral progression. Is this what perfectibility is all about? Does man have the capacity to perfect himself absolutely? Even if man is morally perfectible, does that deal with the holistic or complete perfection? Is moral perfection not only a part and not the whole of man? If that be the case is human perfectibility absolute? There is, however, a notion of perfectibility that seems to capture the holistic nature of man. Passmore explains:

> The doctrine of the perfectibility of man can now be reformulated thus: all men are capable of being perfected, and to a degree that has no limit. Or, as Robert Owen spelled it out in more detail, to assert that man is perfectible is to assert the possibility of endless progress improvement, physical, intellectual and moral, and of happiness, without the possibility of retrogression or assignable limit'[5]

Both Passmore and Owen seem to see perfectibility of man within a broader context but they have left out the spiritual component of man. This ontological and metaphysical perfection of man is extremely important and it deserves mentioning. Perhaps, this ontological and metaphysical perfection of man is inclusive in the intellectual understanding of man's perfectibility. If that is not the case, then it necessarily follows that the concept is not broad enough or not all encompassing.

Broadly speaking, the concept of perfectibility touches all ramifications of man. I will only mention eight different components of perfectibility. These are:

i. Technical perfectibility which deals with an individual being perfect in his or her profession,

ii. Obedientiary perfection is obedience to God's command or rules,

iii. Teleological perfection focuses on achieving a natural end,

iv. Immaculate perfection - is to be free from any moral flaws.

v. Metaphysical perfection is also called 'theoretic perfection' which views man as not lacking in anything because he is no longer finite,

vi. Exemplary perfection is seen among leaders e.g., Socrates, Jesus, Ghandi, Awolowo, Mandela who have left some valuable and moral virtues for others to emulate.

vii. Aesthetic perfection is related to the way and manner in which an individual makes himself harmonious and orderly, and

viii. Deiform perfection is, to be godlike. This is also called authentic self-hood. When a person reaches this level, he does not need any God because he has become god himself. [6]

The nature of perfectibility of man from the above explanation is convoluted but very fascinating. The question is: Can man be perfectible in all ramifications? Taking a cue from the teaching of Jesus the Christ from his Sermon on the Mount, he instructed his disciples to be perfect. This kind of ethics seems to suggest a moral perfection in which an individual will be sinless. But this moral imperative demanded by Jesus from his disciples has been denied to have come from him. According to Albert Schweitzer, "It is now sometimes argued that the exhortation to be perfect is not a genuine saying of Jesus but a summing up by Matthew of what he took to be Jesus' demand upon men."[7]

Whether the command came from Jesus or Matthew it does not matter. What is significant from that command is that man is capable of being perfect? The moral warrant to be perfect as God suggests that since He is holistically perfect, man naturally can equally come to that realization from the Christian point of view. What is required to achieve that goal is an implicit faith and trust in God.

This moral-faith requirement by Jesus is to those who believe in God and obey his injunctions. But what of those who do not have that kind of belief-in which is based on simple and unquestionable faith in God but have a belief-that, that is characterized by rational approach to faith? And further still, those who are atheists or liberal humanists who also believe that man is perfectible and there is no need to have that kind of ontological and metaphysical approach since the basic premise on which one is to be perfect is not rationally and empirically verifiable. The nature of perfection therefore is devoid of religious persuasion with its psychological bait. It is believed that man is still perfectible without God because historically the idea of God is a by-product of human knowledge. In other words, it is not the case that God made man but rather it is man who made God in his imagination and philosophy.[8] Granted that this proposition about who made God is valid, it does not rule out the metaphysical and ontological presupposition of human perfectibility. Whichever way is it viewed it is man who believes intrinsically and extrinsically that he is perfectible. But does man take notice of his limitation as a finite being? Or does he think that his finitude has nothing do with his notion of perfectibility. Or does he believe that his finitude is the basis for aspiring to be infinite? Or is man the question and answer to his concept of perfectibility? These and many other relevant questions serve as paradigms through which a comprehensive understanding of perfectibility of man can be achieved.

The nature of human perfection is therefore a manifestation of man's ability to overcome any form of impediment or impairment in his existence. The power to achieve this goal lies with his intellectual capability and capacity to transcend beyond his finitude. How this can be done is basically through education, moral and political will.

Education

The cardinal function of education is self-discovery. The Greek philosophy from the story of the Allegory of the Cave gives a vivid picture of what education does to man. It is like the ray of light which penetrates into the cave and gives light to those in it. By his natural endowment, man has innate knowledge but it is through education that he rediscovers it. In Yoruba mythology of origin of man, in the primordial existence, an individual is conceived as a rational and moral agent who goes to the Supreme Being to choose freely to come to this world. He makes his choice and gets the Supreme Being to witness and seal it. After leaving the abode of the celestial beings, he comes to this world to be born by his choice of parents. All his moral and rational intellect in the primordial existence becomes a thing to be learnt after being born. In other words, like the Greeks, the Yoruba believe that man has innate knowledge but the instrument to discover himself and his environment is through education.

We need to tread gingerly when it comes to finding out the reality of innateness inherent in man. I am not unaware of John Locke's argument that denies human innate knowledge. But the reality on ground is that man is a self-conscious being and it couldn't have been hidden in the brain if the genes inherited from human ancestors did not contain innateness from which ideas and knowledge develop. It is a great chain of being but it requires education to uncover what has been concealed. But what is the form of this education? Is it any form of education or education that goes beyond the realm of accepted norms of society? And how does the education bring to fore the perfectibility of man? Generally, education is wide in scope and at some point, it is directed to some specific objectives. That is to say that, education is departmentalized because of its focus and goal. For the sake of my primary objective, I will limit the scope of education to philosophy, science and technology as a process by which human perfectibility is achievable.

I am not saying that psychology, theology, economics etc. are not relevant in this discourse of perfectibility of man but for the moment, I will not engage in how their contributions help to unravel the complex nature of human perfection.

Even though my focus limits its investigation to philosophy, science and technology in relation to human perfection, the truth remains that no amount of knowledge derived from those fields of education which does not have its psychological, social, and cultural implications. Robert K. Merton explains this further, "To be sure, the view that the science of any period is not divorced from its social and cultural context has become, properly enough, a common place, but there are few empirical studies of the relations which do obtain."[9]

The advancement that has been made in science and technology to discover man's ability to perfect himself is all encompassing although biomedical technology and more specifically, genetic engineering takes the lead.

Science and Technology/Genetic Engineering

In the last century, man had intensified his effort vigorously to know more about his environment and to control his destiny or shape his life as he deemed fit through science and its offspring, technology. The result of this effort has served to ameliorate human miseries and sufferings. It has encouraged man to forge ahead in his attempt to control any of obstacles that mystify his existence.

The praxis of modern science and technology has made transportation, communication, commerce, trade and infrastructural developments that made human habitation more conducive, coupled with a better understanding of the universe attest to the giant strides that man has made to perfect himself technically. In recent times, the effect of information technology has added to man's ability to facilitate and control dissemination of information that is essential to knowledge. With the new study in biomedical technology and genetic engineering to be precise, man has taken the centre stage to perfect himself. What we have witnessed in the field of science and technology today is summed up in Francis Bacon's vision. According to him, "the power over nature is for the relief of man's estate." On modern biomedical technologies as they relate to the relief of man's estate, Leon R. Kass explains:

> The biomedical technologies can be usefully organized into three groups according to their major purpose: (i) Control of death and life, (ii) Control of human potentials, and (iii) Control of human

achievements. The corresponding technologies are: (i) medicine, especially the arts of prolonging life and of controlling reproduction, (ii) genetic engineering, and (iii) neurological and psychological manipulation.[10]

Furthermore, Kass argues:

> Biomedical technology may make it possible to change the inherent capacity for choice itself. Indeed, both those who welcome and those who fear the advent of 'human engineering' ground their hopes and fears in the same prospect; that man can for the first time recreate himself.[11]

Man in his own estimation believes that to be an engineer of engines is not enough to perfect himself; he needs to become de facto the engineer of himself. Genetic engineering has been defined appropriately as the "the engineering of the engineer". In spite of criticisms, geneticists continue their research to improve human life. According to Joseph Fletcher:

> The expectable benefits of DNA research are considerable, but still finite. They include inserting new genetics information to correct genetic, faults in the treatment of human diseases such as hemophilia, diabetes, Tay-sachs, and the like, to design a new bacteria for quick dispersion of oil spills and other pollutants; to make drugs, to produce hormones and enzymes in greater quantity than nature allows, to improve and increase food crops by improving their nitrogen-fixing capabilities, to increase the supply of meat and dairy animals.[12]

The recent advancement in genetic research in which cloning is perceived as a solution to human defects when perfected; it will enhance the well being of man. For instance, if it is possible to identify the genes that are responsible for aging in human and they can manipulate them in such a way that aging becomes prolonged; it will be a welcome development. Similarly, if the geneticists are able to manipulate genes that are responsible for social misbehavior like, armed robbery, thuggery, racism, greed, hatred, rape, etc and human beings become better behaved, love, peace, harmony, respect for human dignity will foster unity and the money spent on security will be spent on something that will maximize human happiness. If this is achievable, man will be able to produce good leaders and that will eliminate social and political conflicts that lead to war and human displacement. There will be no asylum seekers in Europe, America, Nigeria, Canada, Germany, Japan etc. Generally, there will be justice and fairness and life will be abundant. It will be paradise on earth. And if this happens, perhaps, most people who have their hopes in paradise beyond will contend with what is on earth. Perhaps, there will be no need for churches, mosques, shrines etc because what they stand for and the miracles and doctrines of reward and punishment in the hereafter, plus the expected separation of husband and wife, parents and children who, while on earth, did not share the same religious beliefs. With the achievements of genetic engineering in making man to be self sustainable in agriculture and health, all the fears entertained by skeptics and adherents of religious beliefs will have no epistemological and ethical warrant. I agree with the view of William Godwin to some extent when according to Passmore says:

> A little more enlightenment and men will begin to liberate themselves from their irrational institutions; that degree of liberation will in turn make them more rational and so on indefinitely to an earthly paradise. For by such a process of gradual, rational improvement inspired by an enlightened few, men finally become godlike, not only fearless and courageous, truthful, honest and intellectually advanced but more than that: 'They will perhaps be immortal'.[13]

What Godwin believes about perfectibility of man is mainly for a few intellectuals, leaving behind majority of people who cannot attain godlike state or progression. But from what geneticists are able to achieve for now and perhaps in future, if properly channeled towards improving all mankind, it will be morally praise worthy. Perhaps, man will begin to create his own kind that will not suffer all the natural inhibitions that are currently being experienced and witnessed. In other words, there will be no agony in child birth, no disease, no gender superiority, perhaps the fear of death will have no place in the psychology of man. If the presupposition of what genetic engineering will achieve becomes a concrete reality, it necessarily follows that education as a tool to rediscover man's original ontological position as a free being in the godlike is not antithesis to beinghood. What geneticists are doing is congruent with man's natural and intellectual functions.

I am aware of the fear that genetic engineering has aroused in modern times. For instance, the World Council of Churches has expressed its doubts about biological engineering.

> We note the use of false biological theories to justify slavery in the United States, and the passing of eugenic laws in the US, Japan

and Germany permitting or encouraging the sterilization of certain underprivileged groups of people, who are labeled 'feeble-minded' or 'degenerate'. We must never forget that the massacres in the Nazi concentration camps evolved from an explicit eugenics policy of removing 'inferior genes' from the Aryan population. Furthermore development of human genetic analysis will not in itself prevent such misuses; the closest scrutiny of the social and economic conditions of its application will be continuously required to ensure that such technologies contribute to a just and participatory society.[14]

Similarly Kass writes:

> What will be the consequences of the perpetuation of our permissive and fatalistic attitude toward human engineering? How will the large decision be made? Technocratically and self-servingly, if our experience with previous technologies is any guide. Under conditions of laissez-faire, most technologists will pursue techniques, and most private industries will pursue profits.[15]

The fears being expressed above are valid if one takes a cursory look at human nature of self-centeredness espoused by Thomas Hobbes and religious doctrines of sinful nature of man. But the kind of education that is necessary to overcome the above expressed fears is embedded in genetic engineering since it is man that is recreating himself. Of course, the ethical imperative that takes into consideration the interests of all mankind is what is morally praise worthy which, it seems to me, a rational agent will pursue and maintain. But at the initial state, geneticists might make mistakes which is natural and that is why their goal to perfect human beings is a process. I do not see genetic engineering or the science of human manipulation to improve himself as dangerous as ignorance. In any case, there is an urgent need philosophically and politically to intensify a collaboratory effort to make genetic engineering broadly based and to allay the fears being expressed by critics until such a time that man is able to make his own kind of beings devoid of natural and social ills. There is yet another concern which says that man is playing God. There is no need for this position that man is playing God because naturally man has been endowed rationally and intellectually to exercise his capacity to be himself and if it were not so, Providence would have not given him that talent. And if it goes contrary to what Providence has given to man, assuming that the presupposition is true, it is plausible to argue that he can take it away from him. Meanwhile, the preponderant evidence of scientific and technological advancement that has improved human quality of life probably gives credit to Providence acceptance of human genius. Perhaps, we need to leave the issue of Providence out of man's effort to make himself since he is not remaking God. The perfectibility of man through genetic engineering becomes more imperative in the 21st century since it is natural to be evolutionary. The question that needs to be raised now is what contributions have African made in this ongoing evolution? Or are the Africans immune to evolutionary changes? Or are the Africans simply sitting on the limbo waiting to repeat from western science and technology? What have Africans done on their own toward the perfectibility of man?

Africans and the Perfectibility of Man

The progress being made so far in biomedical technologies and particularly in genetic engineering has been dominated by the white race. If the white race succeeds in producing their own kind of beings through genetic engineering, what will happen to the black race? What the white race has achieved scientifically and in recent times technologically ought to serve as a serious challenge to Africa scholars, intellectuals and political elite. What made the white race to achieve the enormous success in the last two centuries is their ability to exploit human and natural resources to their advantage, of which some of them trickled down to Africans, is based on sound or quality education. Their investments on education became the bedrock of their scientific and technological achievements.

The present classification of Africa as one of the third world continents has its root in her educational achievement plus lack of industrial and military sophistication if compared with the western world. That is, the level of education of Africans, and its achievement compared with the west is not on the same scale of balance. In Nigeria, for instance, where they have about forty Universities, their science and technology departments, faculties etc. lack essential materials for research. This demonstrates the kind of premium and values the government has placed on education.

It is not the case that Africans both at home and in the Diaspora lack human and natural resources to make investments on quality education achievable but the political class seems not to have the moral will to do it. If the current trend of lukewarm attitude toward quality education continues in Africa and the perennial social conflicts that endanger peace, unity and harmony among its people fail to subside, no matter how well the people are naturally and humanly endowed; to join the biological or eugenic race to perfect human race will be a tortuous journey.

I am not suggesting that genetic engineering is the only means by which human perfectibility is made feasible. There may be some other means yet to be discovered, but so far, that seems to be the only one known scientifically. If Africans can come up with their own hypotheses, theories and practical demonstrations of their capacity to make man perfectible, it will be another major breakthrough that will have its indelible marks on African history of scientific and philosophical achievements. But may Africans not assume that producing human beings by cloning the embryo is unrealistic. It is recently reported that, "Six couples trying to become the parents of first clones will be flown to unnamed developing country by a leading fertility expert before the end of the year."[16]

If the geneticists who want to carry out this scientific reproduction of humans go by the historical account of human origin, then one of the African countries ought to be the right place to begin. Africa being the origin of human race is acknowledged by one of the population geneticists, Neil Risch. "When modern humans spread out of Africa and across the globe, these early populations bred for many generations in substantial isolation from one another, allowing genetic differences to build up."[17]

Since some of the descendants of those who left Africa million of years ago are now saying that they want to improve or remake themselves, they need to come to Africa to have the moral and ancestral assent. But then, it has a direct intellectual challenge to Africans which should not be ignored. It should not be ignored because human development is evolutionary and probably this scientific manipulation of genes can lead to the authentic perfectibility of man

Conclusion

I have given an etymological meaning of perfectibility and have argued that human perfectibility is achievable through education. But it is not just any form of education but quality education. I, however, emphasized that since human perfectibility is a process, genetic research currently being undertaken in advanced countries gives the promise and hope of its attainability. If genetic engineering is perfected, it will probably enable man to correct not only defective genes but also recreate genes that can make man to be immortal. Furthermore, the genetic research can also correct aging and prolong life. It is expected that progressively man will be able to create his own type of beings who will be more intelligent, rational, and moral.

This is what I refer to as man attaining the level of beinghood. But the question that remains unanswered is what will happen to those who still remain unable to make their own kind of race? It has become more imperative for the black race and others to begin to work seriously on the quality of education that will be equal if not superior to what the white race has achieved so far in the field of biological research. The present progress being made by the white race in the engineering of man is a signal to what is yet to come. My position is that Africans should not be caught off guard when the white race begins to reap the fruit of their labour on biomedical technologies and genetic engineering. We can remember how they started their vigorous study of science that led to industrial revolution. The outcome of their superior products from science and technology made it possible for them to suppress the unrefined ones produced by Africans. This made them to colonize the whole Africa and beyond. It also made them to impose on Africans their own cultural values and religion. Also African countries became compulsorily their trade zone. But if Africans had developed their science and technology like the western world, they would have been operating from the point of strength and the principle of balancing of power. While the white race imposed their form of education, moral values, and cultural orientations on Africans, they also imposed their forms of government and when Africans resented such arrogance, force and divide and rule tactics were used to make Africans subdue.

Of course, African benefited from the white man's education, commerce, trade, health, religion, science and technology but would it not have been better if they had developed on their own? That is the more reason why Africans need to embark on quality education that will enhance their ability to make man perfectible. What Passmore says about education is instructive. "So 'education' includes not only the process by which a teacher develops in his pupils new capacities, habits, and tastes, but also the processes by which a state modifies the behaviour of its citizens, in order to make them conform to higher moral standards."[18]

Until Africans are able to develop their own biological research or join the western world in the race, we have to contend with man's persuasive method of injecting good habits, and proper behaviour and good governance. If, however, Africans are able to develop their own form of genetic engineering to perfect the genes that are responsible for human behaviour, there will be no need of moral persuasive method of living morally. In fact, there will be no need for security apparatus, police, army, lawyers and judges to dispense justice etc. The universe will become a paradise of new human beings. It may sound utopia but one should not undermine the ability of man to actualize his potentials.

Philosophy has an important role to play in this enterprise of man remaking himself. It is the duty of philosophy to raise fundamental questions, which scientists will probably not raise. The reason is that philosophy gives a critical look at what the impact of scientific achievements will have on man and his environment. It also raises the question of justification of scientific claims and assertions. But politicians who make policies have a role to play in this regard because they have to look at the financial implications as well as the overall interests of their people and the world at large.

Be that as it may, it is necessary to emphasis that the study of genetic engineering that will make man perfectible should not be hindered simply because some people don't believe in it. This form of education to make man reach his authentic selfhood is not antithesis to his well being. It is therefore an indubitable fact that the need for knowledge has no limit. The need for human perfectibility in the 21st century is imperative. But to realize the need is not enough, our scientists, philosophers and political stakeholders must act. I quite agree with Merton when he says:

> The fact is that need is not sufficient in itself to induce invention but acts as a precipitating and directive influence. Moreover it plays this role only if the cultural context is one which places a high value upon innovation, which has a tradition of successful invention and which customarily meets such needs through technological invention rather than through other expedients.[19]

Considering human miseries and the attendant threat of death that frustrates human happiness, if eugenic research is pursued vigorously as it is currently being done in the advanced countries, and there is a collective effort to make it beneficial to all mankind then, human perfectibility will not only be achieved but also perfect happiness. The biological research of the new millennium will be a decisive factor in realizing this noble expectation.

Endnotes

1. John Passmore, *The Perfectibility of Man* (London: Duckworth, 1972), p. 20.
2. Ibid., p. 20.
3. Ibid., p. 20.
4. Dagobert D. Runes, et al, *Dictionary of Philosophy* (Totowa: Littlefield, 1979), p. 228.
5. Passmore, Op; Cit, p. 158.

6. See Ibid; pp. 1 - 27.

7. Ibid; p. 68.

8. Passmore gave a good historical background of how the idea of God/gods developed (pp28-45). His historical analysis has given credence to the position and conclusion reached that man made God/gods.

9. Robert K. Merton, *Science, Technology and Society in Seventeenth Century England* (Sussex: Harvester Press, 1978), p. xxxi.

10. Leon R. Kass, "The New Biology; what Price Relieving Man's Estate?" in Charles L. Reid, *Choice and Action* (London: Collier Macmillan, 1981), p. 513.

11. Ibid; p. 512.

12. Joseph Fletcher, *Humanhood: Essays in Biomedical Ethics* (Buffalo: Prometheus Books, 1979),

13. p. 195.

14. Passmore, Op; cit, p.180.

15. Paul Albrecht, *Faith and Science in an Unjust World* (Philadelphia: Fortress Press, 1980), p. 49.

16. Kass, Op; cit, p. 528.

17. *Punch* (Lagos) 7th August, 2002.

18. *Punch* (Lagos) 6th August, 2002.

19. Passmore, Op; cit, p.172.

20. Merton, Op; cit, p.158.

* Segun Ogungbemi, *Philosophy and Development,* (Ibadan: Hope Publication, 2007), pp. 180-194.